PRODUCTION AND DISTRIBUTION THEORIES

Classics in Economics Series

American Capitalism: The Concept of Countervailing Power
John Kenneth Galbraith, with a new introduction by the author

Adam Smith and the Founding of Market Economics
Eli Ginzberg

The Chicago School of Political Economy
Warren J. Samuels, editor

The Economic Consequences of the Peace, John Maynard Keynes

Economic Semantics, Fritz Machlup

Economics and the Good Life, Bertrand de Jouvenel
edited and with a new introduction by Dennis Hale and Marc Landy

The Economics of Population: Key Classic Writing
Julian L. Simon

The Economics of Welfare, Arthur Cecil Pigou
with a new introduction by Nahid Aslanbeigui

Economists and the Economy: The Evolution of Economic Ideas
Roger F. Backhouse

Economists and the Public, Harold William Hutt

The Economy as a System of Power: Corporate Systems
Marc R. Tool and Warren J. Samuels, editors

Epistemics and Economics: A Critique of Economic Doctrines
G. L. S. Shackle

Essays: On Entrepreneurs, Innovations, Business Cycles, and the Evolution of Capitalism
Joseph A. Schumpeter

The Ethics of Competition, Frank Hyneman Knight
with a new introduction by Richard Boyd

The Future of Economics, Alexander J. Field, editor

The Future of Industrial Man, Peter F. Drucker

History and Historians of Political Economy
Werner Stark, edited by Charles M. A. Clark

The Illusion of Economic Stability, Eli Ginzberg

Institutional Economics volumes 1 & 2, John R. Commons

The State in Relation to Labour, W. Stanley Jevons

PRODUCTION AND DISTRIBUTION THEORIES

George J. Stigler

With a new introduction by
DOUGLAS IRWIN

Second printing 2013

This book is printed on acid-free paper that meets the American National Standard for Permanence of Paper for Printed Library Materials.

Library of Congress Catalog Number: 93-36977
ISBN: 978-1-56000-710-4
Printed in the United States of America

Library of Congress Cataloging-in-Publication Data

Stigler, George Joseph, 1911-
Production and distribution theories/George J. Stigler; with a new introduction by Douglas Irwin.
p. cm. — (Classics in economics)
Includes bibliographical references and index.
ISBN 1-56000-710-9
1. Economics—History—19th century. I. Title. II. Series.

HB85.S668 1994
330.1-dc20 93-36977
CIP

Table of Contents

INTRODUCTION TO THE TRANSACTION EDITION

George J. Stigler's doctoral dissertation, "Studies in the History of Production and Distribution Theories," was completed in 1937 (submitted in March 1938) under the supervision of Frank H. Knight at the University of Chicago. Macmillan published a revised version of the thesis, *Production and Distribution Theories: The Formative Period,* in 1941 for the price of $3.50. According to Mark Blaug, his former student, the book "represented the first serious attempt to trace the slow evolution of neoclassical production and distribution theory from 1870 onward and was hailed immediately as a major landmark in the history of economic thought."[1] The dissertation was also the beginning of a lifelong study and enjoyment of the history of economic thought, and much of Stigler's later work in the field remained devoted to the period (late nineteenth century) covered in the dissertation.

His introduction states the motivation for the dissertation. In 1870, according to Stigler, "the fundamental defect" in prevailing economic theory "was clearly the failure to develop a theory of the prices of productive services." Indeed, as he put it, "in 1870 there was no *theory* of distribution." Though the "marginalist revolution" of the 1870s led to a restructuring of value theory, the theory of distribution was left largely untouched. While precisely this area of economic theory urgently needed reformulation, it was here that theoretical improvements progressed slowly in the period 1870-95. Consequently, the purpose of the dissertation was to trace the development of the theory of distribution in the writings of major economists of the period–Jevons, Wicksteed, Marshall, Edgeworth, Walras, among others–that gradually culminated in the marginal productivity theory of distribution and the Euler equation.

Stigler's thesis reflects two aspects of his graduate studies in economics at the University of Chicago in the 1930s. The first was the stress placed on a thorough training in neoclassical price theory. In Economics 301, Price and Distribution Theory, Jacob Viner and Frank Knight drilled students in Marshallian price theory, which was then the centerpiece of the Chicago curriculum. While many studies in the history of economic thought construed economic "thought" broadly, *Production and Distribution Theories* was rare in being a history of economic *theory*. This firm theoretical foundation is consonant with the strong emphasis put on neoclassical theory in Economics 301.

A second element of his training at the University of Chicago was exposure to Frank Knight's course on the history of economic thought. Stigler's interest in the history of thought was clearly cultivated at the University of Chicago under the tutelage of Knight and, to a lesser extent, Jacob Viner. Stigler writes in the introduction and elsewhere that Knight suggested the topic of the dissertation to him. Knight also appears to have played a key role in the particular approach taken in the thesis. Certainly others read Knight's imprint on the dissertation: Joseph Dorfman stated quite simply that "the point of view is that of Professor Frank H. Knight, the author's teacher at the University of Chicago." [2]

What was Knight's view? Knight's approach to the history of economic thought was critical in nature, often severely so. Don Patinkin describes in this way: "Knight's approach to the history of economic thought was that of providing a purely logical criticism of the nature of the assumptions made by the various schools of thought, and the validity of the conclusions that they drew from them; he was concerned almost exclusively with the logical consistency of the theories he was examining."[3] In a famous article on Ricardo, for example, Knight worked with "the assumption that the primary interest in the 'ancients' in such a field as economics is to learn from their mistakes." He then proceeded to contrast the "classical" system with "correct" views by pointing out seven "aberrations" in classical thought.[4] This sharply critical focus on correcting mistakes could sometimes appear as ridicule, but there was seriousness behind the critiques. Stigler recalled that Knight certainly "got great relish out of emphasizing the perversities and blunders of Ricardo and other historic figures in economics. . . . [but] we were taught by example that Ricardo's errors and Marshall's foibles deserved more careful and thorough attention than the nonsense or froth of the day."[5]

Although Stigler states in his autobiography that he acquired his fascination with the history of economic thought at Chicago in the early 1930s, there is evidence that this interest predates his arrival on the Midway and was independent of Knight.[6] While doing work at Northwestern University for an M.B.A. degree, Stigler wrote papers on "The Theory of Distribution" and "The Theory of Value from Adam Smith to Stanley Jevons."[7] Thus, even before his exposure to Knight, Stigler had written on two themes–distribution and the history of thought—that later coalesced in his dissertation. In addition, the dissertation does not always reflect Knight's biases. Stigler expresses tremendous praise and admiration for Carl Menger, for example, while Knight's assessment in an introduction to the English translation of Menger's *Principles* was more critical.[8] Still, Stigler acknowledged Knight's deep influence on his thesis, later writing: "He was so strong-minded and so critical a student of the literature that it was a good many years before I could read economic classics through my eyes instead of his. I have never brought myself to read through my doctoral dissertation, *Production and Distribution Theories: The Formative Period*, because I knew I would be embarrassed by both its Knightian excesses and its immaturity."[9]

Several reviewers picked up on the strongly critical positions Stigler takes in the book. One observed that "the general tone is didactic and even dogmatic; but it does have the refreshing quality of definiteness."[10] Eric (later Lord) Roll praised the book, but noted examples of "naively patronizing tone" and commented that "the critical points, though they may be well taken, are put forward with a certain air of condescension which is not helpful to the reader."[11] While cheeky in parts, these passages are often humorous and give today's reader an early glimpse at Stigler's renowned wit, even though doctoral dissertations are rarely the forum for mirth.

To this day, Stigler's dissertation remains a classic work on the evolution of distribution theory during a critical juncture in its development. As Joseph Schumpeter noted in his monumental *History of Economic Analysis*, "This excellent work by a competent theorist is perhaps the best survey in existence of the theoretical work of that period's leaders and is strongly recommended."[12] Its republication more than fifty years after its original composition and publication stands as adequate testimony that Schumpeter's judgment continues to hold true.

Douglas Irwin

Notes

1. Mark Blaug, *Great Economists Since Keynes* (New York: Cambridge University Press, 1989), p. 240.
2. Dorfman's review of *Production and Distribution Theories* in *Political Science Quarterly* 57 (September 1942): 468. Dorfman chided Stigler for entertaining "the familiar misconception that Clark's *Distribution of Wealth* differs radically in point of view and procedure from the earlier *Philosophy of Wealth*. Such a position springs from unfamiliarity with the meaning of certain terms in the social sciences in the United States during the [eighteen] seventies and eighties."
3. Don Patinkin, "Frank Knight as Teacher" in *Essays On and In the Chicago Tradition* (Durham: Duke University Press, 1981), 35.
4. Frank H. Knight, "The Ricardian Theory of Production and Distribution," in *On the History and Method of Economics* (Chicago: University of Chicago Press, 1956).
5. George J. Stigler, *Lives of the Laureates: Ten Nobel Economists*, ed. William Breit and Roger W. Spencer, 2nd ed. (Cambridge: MIT Press, 1990), 95-6.
6. George J. Stigler, *Memoirs of an Unregulated Economist* (New York: Basic Books, 1988), 27.
7. I am indebted to Stephen Stigler for calling my attention to these papers and making them available to me.
8. Mark Blaug calls attention to this divergence of views in his *Economic Theory in Retrospect*, 4th ed. (New York: Cambridge University Press, 1985), 326.
9. Stigler in *Lives of the Laureates*, 97-98.

10. Review by S.H. Patterson in *Annals of the American Academy*, March 1942, 259.
11. Review by Eric Roll in *American Economic Review*, December 1941, 855-57. See the accompanying review by Wassily Leontief, 857-58.
12. "This recommendation does not imply agreement in every point of fact or evaluation." Joseph Schumpeter, *History of Economic Analysis* (New York: Oxford University Press, 1954), 849.

PRODUCTION AND DISTRIBUTION THEORIES

Chapter I

INTRODUCTION

THE present work is a critical study of the theories of distribution which rose out of the theory of subjective value, and which were finally systematized into the general marginal productivity theory. The period covered, therefore, lies between 1870 and 1895. It was in this quarter-century that economic theory was transformed from an art, in many respects literary, to a science of growing rigor. The support for this generalization will be suggested by the most general comparison between Mill's *Principles*, the apogee of theoretical English economics at the beginning of the period, and Marshall's *Principles*, near the end of the period.

Nor was the movement towards a more scientific economic theory restricted to England alone. Wicksell in Sweden, Walras at Lausanne, and Irving Fisher and J. B. Clark in the United States were prominent exponents of the advancing study of economics. Barone and Pareto testify to the corresponding progress in Italy. In Austria the movement was rapid but uneven, as subsequent studies of Menger, Wieser, and Böhm-Bawerk will indicate. Only in France and Germany is it difficult to find truly outstanding representatives of a renaissance of interest in theoretical studies—a state which has continued to the present day.

Although economic theory advanced rapidly in the 1870's, it is unfortunate that the advance was restricted largely to one branch of price theory. Jevons, Menger, and Walras, the "revolutionaries" of the period, concentrated their efforts primarily on the theory of subjective value, and their immediate followers continued along much the same path. The demand factor certainly deserved much fuller analysis than the classical economists had accorded it, but the new emphasis was not an unmixed blessing. All three discoverers were hedonists (although this viewpoint had relatively small incidence on Menger's theory), and their statements of value theory led to many pseudo-scientific applications of hedonist ethics to economic policy. Only in very recent years has there begun a real movement to abandon the utilitarian viewpoint for the more colorless but less vulnerable theory of substitution.

The branch of economics which was in most urgent need of reformulation was, in fact, distribution. In 1870 there was no *theory* of distribution. Most English economists after Smith devoted separate chapters to rent, wages, and profits, but without important exception such chapters were only descriptive of the returns to the three most important social classes of contemporary England.[1] Rent went to the landowners, wages to the

[1] This emphasis on the income of social classes goes back at least as far as Adam Smith, who said: "The whole annual produce of land and labour of every country . . . naturally divides itself . . . into three parts; the rent of land, the wages of labour, and the profits of stock; and constitutes a revenue to three different orders of people; to those who live by rent, to those who live by wages, and to those who live by profit. These are the three great, original and constituent orders of every civilized society, from

laboring masses, and capitalists secured the "profits of stock." This type of analysis may have had its uses in the England of Ricardo and Mill, but its analytical shortcomings are obvious. Extended criticism is unnecessary at this point;[1] the fundamental defect was clearly the failure to develop a theory of the prices of productive services.

One would probably expect the "revolutionaries" to concentrate on this major hiatus in the classical structure. Once the marginal utility theory was applied to determine the value of a consumption good, the next step was logically that of determining the value of the productive services which produced the good. Under perfect competition, the sum of the values of productive services clearly equals the value of the product, and the distributive share going to each service is easily ascertainable by use of the type of incremental analysis so prominent in the marginal utility theory.

But these rather obvious implications of the theory of subjective value were not followed. The subsequent chapters of this study will indicate in detail how slow the progress was. Jevons, so critical of the classical economists when he dealt with demand theory, was a close follower of the "wrong-headed" Ricardo in distribution theory. Walras' approach to the problem was excellent in many respects, but he waited until 1896 to abandon

whose revenue that of every other order is ultimately derived." *The Wealth of Nations* (Modern Library [Cannan] ed., New York, 1937), p. 248. Compare, for example, the equivalent statements of David Ricardo, *Principles of Political Economy and Taxation* (Gonner ed., London, 1932), Author's Preface; J. R. McCulloch, *Discourse on Political Economy* (Edinburgh, 1824), pp. 103–4; J. S. Mill, *Principles of Political Economy* (Ashley ed., New York, 1929), Bk. II, Chap. iii.

[1] Cf. F. H. Knight, "The Ricardian Theory of Production and Distribution," *Canadian Journal of Economics and Political Science*, I (1935), 3–25, 171–96.

the assumption that the coefficients of production are fixed, which until then completely vitiated his theory. Menger, however, is the true enigma. He differentiated consumption and production goods only by calling the former goods of the first order, the latter goods of higher order. Yet in his theory of price he disposed in a single, obscure footnote of the allocation of goods (including resources) among different uses. He went on to develop the essential notion of the marginal productivity theory, but the fundamental element of this theory, the variability of the proportions in which productive services combine, was completely lost to his followers.

In the nineties the marginal productivity theory finally appeared.[1] As with the subjective value theory of twenty years before, the marginal productivity theory seems to have been "in the air," for it emerged independently in several countries. Walras at Lausanne, Marshall and Wicksteed and others in England, Wicksell in Sweden, Clark in the United States, and Barone in Italy—all appeared in the nineties with theories which incorporated the substance of the marginal productivity approach to the problem of distribution. However, the simultaneity with which the marginal productivity theory was finally formulated by so many economists is less astonishing than is the fact that it had not been clearly formulated at the same time as the theory of subjective value and

[1] The inevitable (but incomplete) anticipations of the doctrine are not treated explicitly in the present study. The marginal productivity theory implicit in Ricardo's rent theory is considered in Chap. XII, *infra.* Compare also H. von Thünen, *Der Isolierte Staat* (3d ed., Jena, 1930), esp. pp. 495 ff.; M. Longfield, *Lectures on Political Economy,* London School Reprints No. 8 (London, 1931), esp. Lecture IX; H. von Mangoldt, *Grundriss der Volkswirtschaftslehre* (1st ed., Stuttgart, 1863), pp. 117, 131, cited by M. Bowley, *Nassau Senior* (London, 1937), p. 114. On Longfield's successor, Isaac Butt, whose work has not been accessible, compare E. R. A. Seligman, "On Some Neglected British Economists," *Economic Journal,* XIII (1903), 532–33.

become at once an integral part of the general body of doctrine.

The period from 1870 to 1895 is, of course, still recent—in part because its leading economists enjoyed extraordinary longevity. Of the ten great economists who fall within the scope of the present work (to be defined in a somewhat arbitrary manner), all but Jevons lived into the twentieth century; six died only in the second decade of this century; and one lived until 1938.[1] Their works are as recent as their lives; only an extremely audacious or sagacious economist dare answer an important question in contemporary theory without having consulted their works.

The writer feels, accordingly, no necessity for defending the importance of his subject matter. Rather his early reaction was one of astonishment that it had not already been studied in detail. The standard histories of economic thought do indeed cover some of this territory, but most of their writers suffer from either ignorance of the literature or inadequate theoretical equipment for critical analysis, or from both handicaps. Even the authors of several excellent recent histories of economics have, necessarily, surveyed this difficult terrain through a telescope rather than a microscope. In addition, several European, particularly German, students have written monographs on *Zurechnungsgeschichte*, but some have been grossly incompetent, and none has been at all satisfactory.[2]

[1] Compare Table 1, *infra*, p. 11, for a few biographical details.

[2] The following is a complete list, as far as I can ascertain:

W. Mohrmann, *Dogmengeschichte der Zurechnungslehre* (Jena, 1914).
H. Hefendehl, *Das Problem der ökonomischen Zurechnung* (Essen, 1922).
C. Landauer, *Grundprobleme der functionellen Verteilung des wirtschaftlichen Wertes* (Jena, 1923).
K. Stephans, *Das Problem der ökonomischen Zurechnung* (Vienna, 1928).

(*Continued on next page.*)

Turning now to the branches of economic theory which are to be covered, it is obvious that some arbitrariness is essential. Distribution theory, the primary concern, is closely related to every branch of economic theory, as the general equilibrium theory has so properly emphasized. The actual phases which are covered here are essentially two: production and distribution theory. The two are so closely interwoven that it would be absurd to attempt to separate them. All other fields have been excluded as far as possible, not only to reduce the subject to manageable proportions, but also for an additional reason. Almost every economist included in this study treated production and distribution theory in this way. It has been and is possible to treat production and distribution rather fully without devoting much attention to general value theory, to say nothing of foreign trade, public finance, and the like.

The second restriction of scope is essentially a recognition of the contemporary practice. The discussion will relate only to stationary, competitive economies. In excluding monopoly, we are but following the writers themselves. In excluding historical change, again the dominant trend is followed. This exclusion is buttressed by the fact that all historical economics of the period were fundamentally descriptive and not analytical. Only in

W. L. Valk, *The Principles of Wages* (London, 1928).
E. Haydt, *Die ökonomische Zurechnung* (Vienna, 1931).

I have not been able to examine Stephans' dissertation. Morhmann and Hefendehl deny the possibility of any theory of distribution. Landauer accepts Böhm-Bawerk's theory with only minor qualification. Haydt's dissertation is an elaboration and defense of Hans Mayer's theory of distribution (cf. Mayer, "Zurechnung," *Handwörterbuch der Staatswissenschaften* [4th ed., 1928], VIII, 1206–28). Valk's study is the only one of the five that attempts to cover other than the Austrian literature. His book is a useful introduction to the literature, but the divergence of his interpretation from that in the text will become apparent in the subsequent chapters.

the case of Marshall, as we shall see, does this criterion lead to difficulties.

The present study is critical in attitude. It is critical, first, in the obvious and indispensable sense of being selective. To analyze or even to describe is to select—the theme is too trite to be elaborated. As a corollary, it must be mentioned, not all of the discussion of production and distribution made by any one economist has been included. The central structure, the theoretical skeleton, has been treated fully; detailed theories are noted only if novel or erroneous.

This study is critical in a second sense. It attempts to discover and to evaluate all important errors in formal reasoning. No economist has been able to avoid all logical fallacies; on the other hand, the economists here studied have been, with rare exception, good logicians. The role of formal reasoning in economic theory is so important that a short digression may be in order.

Economic theories are conclusions drawn from assumptions according to the rules of logic. "Pure" economic theory is therefore a field of logic, essentially mathematical in nature. It follows that an economic theory is "correct" if its assumptions are not inconsistent and its reasoning is not fallacious. It is no contradiction, however, to add immediately that economics loses its interest and importance if the assumptions do not correspond to the "facts."

This feature of economic analysis introduces the final critical aspect of this study. The writer has gone beyond mere selection and attention to logical consistency; he passes also on the empirical validity of the theories under discussion. Have the "right" assumptions been chosen? Historians of economic thought have often asked this, and on the whole the results have not been very satisfactory. The failures have been many, but Böhm-Bawerk's history of interest theories may be selected as typifying the important pitfall. Starting, the writer is convinced, with the purpose of rejecting all previous doctrines of interest so that his own theory might reign unchallenged as to either validity or originality, he was led to distortions and unfair interpretations. The great difficulty is obvious: What is the standard of reference as to correctness?

The basis of evaluation in this work is that body of contemporary theory which is given the nebulous description, neo-classical economics. This theoretical corpus stems directly from Marshall, but it has gained much in rigor at the hands of Walras, Wicksteed, and Edgeworth, and more recently the theory has been advanced by a host of economists too numerous even to mention. There is no unanimity regarding "neo-classical" theory, but on the other hand, the divergences of opinion between competent students are certainly less than at any time since Mill. This statement is somewhat circular, it must be confessed, since a fundamental test of competence is the comprehension and acceptance of this theoretical system. Yet some theoretical system must be used for evaluating specific doctrines, if history is to be truly critical.

And to be useful, that is to say, instructive, a history must be critical. History which contents itself with the discovery of logical missteps is only an exercise in formal reasoning. Although such exercises are interesting and perhaps useful to the writer, the reader does better to toil through a treatise on logic. Economics is, after all, political economy, and social policy is, as it has always been, its central problem.

Since the specific details of the frame of reference will

become apparent in the subsequent analyses, we may pass on to the final problem, the difficulty in applying the standard to any economist. Every economist—and non-economist—necessarily knows a great deal about economics from observation. As a result almost every economist would answer correctly point-blank questions on general economic theory. Thomas Mun must have been aware of the marginal productivity doctrine in his conduct of the East India Company, yet the doctrine was not formulated satisfactorily before 1890. Marshall remarks that "the law of diminishing return must have occupied thoughtful men in every densely peopled country," [1] but he states the law in several analytically distinct forms! [2]

This problem is most serious in the history of economic theories before 1850; it is less significant in the later period. The explanation lies in the professionalization of economists and the consequent systematization of their theories. But correct "insights" still complicate interpretation. In such cases the test to be applied, the writer submits, is: Does the observation fit into the economist's general theoretical system, or is it an *obiter dictum*, either inconsistent with or irrelevant to his structure as a whole?

The question of impartiality in applying the critical approach deserves a final word. The writer has naturally been vexed by "a certain evasiveness in Marshall's scientific character"; [3] it has taxed his endurance to read and re-read Wicksteed's prolix *Commonsense of Political Economy;* he has been outraged by Böhm-Bawerk's pedantry and dialectical *tours de force;* and so forth. Such

[1] *Principles of Economics* (8th ed., London, 1920), p. 172.

[2] Cf., *infra*, p. 66.

[3] Talcott Parsons, "Economics and Sociology: Marshall in Relation to the Thought of His Time," *Quarterly Journal of Economics*, XLVI (1931–32), 335–36.

reactions are doubtless experienced in some degree by all readers, and it is difficult, even though essential, to disregard personal characteristics in judging an economist's contributions to theoretical analysis. It is hoped, however, that the evidence here marshaled substantiates the writer's conclusions, and in any case the reader is not apt to misinterpret personal opinions as established conclusions.

With regard to the extensive and intensive scope, it will be obvious that this work consists of a set of independent studies. Ten outstanding economists are covered; their names and a few biographical details are given in Table 1. The list includes, as will be seen, primarily European economists, the one exception being J. B. Clark. In addition to these ten men, certain important views of Pareto, Barone, and others are brought together in the final chapter.

On the side of intensivity, all known and available works of each economist have been consulted, with two exceptions. The first exception is Walras, and is due to Professor Jaffé's impending though as yet unavailable variorum translation of the *Eléments*. Here chief reliance has been placed on the 1926 edition, although earlier editions were consulted on certain issues. The second is Marshall. In the time available it has been impossible to collate eight editions of the *Principles* and numerous other writings. In neither case, however, is it believed that present interpretations would be modified significantly by collation of editions.

Lastly, the order of presentation deserves a word of explanation. The fundamental alternatives in arrangement are treatment by topic and treatment by men. The former approach greatly reduces duplication and emphasizes the continuity (but often the discontinuity) of

TABLE 1

Biographical Details of Economists Included in the Present Study

NAME	BORN	DIED	SCHOOLS ATTENDED	OCCUPATION	APPEARANCE OF FIRST IMPORTANT WORK
Jevons	1835	1882	University College, London	Teaching (Manchester)	1871
Wicksteed	1844	1927	University College, London	Ministry Lecturing Teaching	1888
Marshall	1842	1924	Cambridge	Teaching (Cambridge)	1890
Edgeworth	1845	1926	Trinity College, Dublin; Oxford	Teaching (Oxford)	1881
Menger	1840	1921	Vienna Prague	Teaching (Vienna)	1871
Wieser	1851	1926	Vienna Heidelberg Jena Leipzig	Teaching (Vienna Prague)	1884
Böhm-Bawerk	1851	1914	Vienna	Teaching (Innsbruck Vienna) Finance Ministry	1884
Walras	1834	1910	Ecole des Mines	Teaching (Lausanne)	1874
Wicksell	1851	1926	Uppsala	Teaching (Lund)	1893
J. B. Clark	1847	1938	Brown Amherst	Teaching (Carleton Amherst Columbia)	1886

development. Nevertheless, the arrangement by men, under national groups, has been chosen as preferable. The great advantage of such a scheme is that it makes possible the interrelating of various parts of an individual's unified theoretical system. As a result it is much easier to appraise a man's total contribution, and this is a not unimportant objective in histories of doctrine. The discussion of each economist is carried on under certain mildly standardized subtopics, however, so that comparisons on points of theory are facilitated.

With one topic it has been expedient to depart from the above described order and assemble all writings on one subject. This is the famous controversy over the Euler theorem problem in distribution. Except for certain anticipations by Walras, J. B. Clark, Edgeworth, and Wicksell, all of this material is brought together in Chapter XII.

Chapter II

WILLIAM STANLEY JEVONS

WILLIAM STANLEY JEVONS is the forerunner of neo-classical economics.[1] He did not so much depart from as supplement the classical theory, although the hasty *lecteur* can easily secure a contrary impression. Jevons, indeed, considered his theory to be revolutionary; he gave an impetus to and enthusiastic statement of the utility theory of value; "his belief that all evil economic influences were incarnate in John Stuart Mill" is well known; [2] and his mathematical mode of exposition was calculated to emphasize his apparent opposition to classical theory. But his theory of production and distribution, with which the present chapter deals, is fundamentally classical. An indication of the orthodox nature of his approach is suggested by the fact that both Marshall and Edgeworth accepted his wage theory *in toto*.

Jevons developed his major contribution to the theory of capital almost completely at the same time that he formulated his theory of subjective value. In a letter dated June 1, 1860, he wrote: "Most of the conclusions

[1] For biographical details consult H. W. Jevons and H. S. Jevons, "William Stanley Jevons," *Econometrica*, II (1934), 225–37. Compare also *Letters and Journals of W. S. Jevons* (London, 1886); L. Robbins, "The Place of Jevons in the History of Economic Thought," *The Manchester School*, VII (1935), 1–17; P. H. Wicksteed, "Stanley Jevons," reprinted in *Commonsense of Political Economy*, II (London, 1933), 801–13; and J. M. Keynes, "William Stanley Jevons," *Journal of the Royal Statistical Society*, XCIX (1936), 516–48.

[2] Wicksteed, *op. cit.*, p. 813.

[of the 'true theory of economy'] are, of course, the old ones stated in a consistent form; but my definition of capital and law of the interest of capital, are, so far as I have seen, quite new." [1] In later correspondence with his brother Jevons occasionally referred to his theory of capital and interest, which he conceived to be second in importance only to his theory of value. Already in 1860 the doctrine that the interest rate is determined by the marginal productivity of the extension of the period of production had been formulated in a manner essentially similar to that presented in the *Theory of Political Economy* eleven years later.[2] His suggestive paper, "Brief Account of a General Mathematical Theory of Political Economy," which he delivered before the British Association in 1862, outlined the principles of this doctrine, as well as those of his theory of value.[3]

The appearance of his distribution theory in more extended form in the *Theory of Political Economy* attracted little attention, even less, of course, than his theory of subjective value. Several factors contributed to this relative neglect. The treatment of distribution (with the possible exception of capital) was distinctly inferior in originality and organization of content to his sections on value. The distribution theories were presented (along with Chapter IV on Exchange), moreover, in semi-mathematical form, although Jevons' awkward use of symbolic statement obscured rather than clarified the development.[4] Finally, in the delightful prefaces to the *Theory*,

[1] *Letters and Journals*, p. 152.

[2] Thus, "But I shall show that the whole capital employed can only be paid for at the same rate as the *last portion added;* hence it is the increase of produce or advantage, which this last portion gives, that determines the interest of the whole" (*Letters and Journals*, pp. 155–56).

[3] Reprinted as Appendix III of the *Theory of Political Economy* (4th ed., London, 1911).

[4] Marshall, in speaking of Jevons' use of mathematics, said, ". . . he

he placed little emphasis upon distribution; indeed, he emphasized his acceptance of most of the classical theory in this field.[1]

General Considerations

Certain advances essential to the formulation of a correct theory of distribution are made by Jevons. He emphasizes the fact that no productive agent—he speaks specifically of labor—is a cause of value (cf. "The Origin of Value," pp. 161–66).[2] He sees with increasing insight in the second edition that all productive factors bear the same relationship—that of scarcity—to value; "We must regard labor, land, knowledge, and capital as conjoint conditions of the whole produce, not as causes each of a certain portion of the product" (p. xlvi). In the preface to this latter edition, Jevons arrives at a substantive statement of the alternative cost doctrine. He points out that Mill's exceptional case of value, in which it was asserted that the rent which manufacturing uses must yield to attract land from agriculture entered into the cost of production of manufactures, is in fact the typical case. It follows at once that one type of agricultural

seemed like David in Saul's armour" (*Memorials of Alfred Marshall* [London, 1925], p. 100). Jevons frequently confessed his difficulties in the study of mathematics, and his training never extended beyond the rudiments of the differential calculus. (*Letters and Journals*, pp. 29, 32, 36, 48, 88, 118, 158.) It is unquestionably true that Jevons' "abstruse mathematical symbols"—so they appeared to Cairnes—served to obscure important sections of his work from contemporary economists. Cf. J. E. Cairnes, *Some Leading Principles of Political Economy* (London, 1874), p. 21 and note.

[1] Jevons conceded the validity of the classical doctrines of rent and population, while denouncing the wages-fund theory as a truism.

[2] References are to the *Theory of Political Economy*. The second edition was the last to appear during his lifetime; subsequent editions are reprints without alteration of text. All references will be to the fourth edition unless otherwise indicated. I am indebted to The Macmillan Company for permission to quote from this work.

product must bid land away from alternative agricultural uses of land. And this is not peculiar to land:

> It will be seen that exactly the same principle applies to wages. A man who can earn six shillings a day in one employment will not turn to another kind of work unless he expects to get six shillings a day or more from it. *There is no such thing as absolute cost of labour; it is all a matter of comparison* (pp. xlix–l, Preface).[1]

The relationship of wages to value is thus identical with that of rent to value. The shares, rent, wages, and interest are completely symmetrical; "the parallelism between the theories of rent and wages is seen to be perfect in theory. . . . Precisely the same view may be applied, *mutatis mutandis*, to the rent yielded by fixed capital, and to the interest of free capital" (p. l, Preface).[2] The income and value of fixed (sunk) capital, as contrasted with free (transferable) capital, are determined by the law of rent, as this passage indicates.

Labor Theory and Production

Despite these very suggestive prefatory observations, Jevons makes no essential change, in the text, in the exposition of the relation of cost of production to value. The chief discussion of this problem is found in the chapter on labor.[3] Its place here, rather than in Chapter IV (Theory of Exchange), where it more appropriately fits, is due to the fact that Jevons retains much of the

[1] My italics. Marshall objected to this type of argument on unconvincing grounds. *Principles of Economics* (8th ed., London, 1920), p. 437 n. Cf., also, *infra*, pp. 92 ff.

[2] Also, ". . . rates of wages are governed by the same formal laws as rents" (p. xlvii).

[3] Five sections (pp. 183–203) deal with the relationship of cost to value. "Relations of Economic Quantities" (pp. 189–93) and "Joint Production" (pp. 197–202) were added in the second edition, but they contribute nothing new to the discussion.

classical emphasis on labor cost.[1] He begins the chapter on labor with a famous quotation from Smith: "The real price of everything, what everything really costs to the man who wants to acquire it, is the toil and trouble of acquiring it. . . . Labour was the first price, the original purchase-money, that was paid for all things." Jevons believes that this is "substantially true." [2]

The organization of production is not consciously considered. In the section on "Distribution of Labour" (pp. 183–86), Jevons attempts to ascertain how an individual would allocate his labor between two kinds of commodities. The allocation is determined in such a manner that marginal utility of the product has the same ratio to the marginal disutility of labor in the two (or other number of) occupations.[3] He grants the probable unrealism of the example, but defends the illustration because the principles which guide an individual are "identical in general character with those which apply to a whole nation" (p. 183).

That such a principle does not guide "whole nations" is apparent.[4] Jevons is usually careful to deny the comparability of the subjective magnitudes of different persons: "Accordingly, it will be found that not one of my equations represents a comparison between one man's

[1] "The main element of production and the chief source of wealth is undoubtedly labour." (*Principles of Economics* [London, 1905], p. 71).

[2] He adds the following qualification immediately after the quotation, in the second edition: "If subjected to a very searching analysis, this celebrated passage might not prove to be so entirely true as it would at first sight seem to most readers to be" (p. 167).

[3] Mathematically, the distribution of labor between occupations will be such that $\frac{du_1}{dx}\frac{dx}{dp_1} = \frac{du_2}{dy}\frac{dy}{dp_2}$, where p_1 and p_2 are painfulness of labor in producing commodities x and y with utilities u_1 and u_2, respectively.

[4] Jevons commits the same error here as in his famous theory of "trading bodies" (pp. 88–90), *i.e.*, he attempts to apply individualistic analysis directly to competitive groups.

labour and another's" (p. 166). It therefore follows that (with the division of labor) utilities or disutilities bear no simple relationship to the allocation of labor or other resources as between different uses in an enterprise economy. If money costs and income are substituted for disutility and utility, this line of analysis leads to an allocation of resources between industries according to the alternative cost doctrine, but nowhere does Jevons take this step. Nor is the theory easily applied to the individual in an economy in which division of labor is important.

The reconciliation of cost and utility theories of value is made at some length. The concept of mutual determination is hinted at: "The ratio of exchange governs the production as much as the production governs the ratio of exchange. . . . They [the ratios of exchange] depend upon a general balancing of producing power and of demand as measured by the final degree of utility" (p. 188). And, in the conclusion, the problem of general equilibrium is briefly sketched: "Given, a certain population, with various needs and powers of production, in possession of certain lands and other sources of material: required, the mode of employing their labour which will maximize the utility of the produce" (p. 267; italicized by Jevons). But such observations—and they constitute virtually the whole of Jevons' production theory—never get beyond a general statement of the problem involved.

Similarly, in the section on "Joint Production" (pp. 193–202), the entire analysis is rendered superficial and worthless by the assumption that the jointly produced commodities can be produced only in a fixed ratio. It is very unfortunate that the restatement necessary to bring his cost theory into a position consistent with the prefatory suggestions is never attempted by Jevons.

The presentation of the Jevonian theories of distribution which follows will deviate from the order in which he presents them (*i.e.*, Chap. V, Theory of Labour; Chap. VI, Theory of Rent; Chap. VII, Theory of Capital). Consistency requires that rent be first eliminated, according to his theory, to determine the net product. Interest is then determined by a variant of the marginal productivity theory, and wages form a residual.

The Theory of Rent

Jevons contributes virtually nothing to the development of rent theory except fairly concise symbolic and geometrical methods of restating the classical theory.[1] His acceptance of the Ricardian rent doctrine is complete: "by far the best statement of the theory" was that of McCulloch.

Rent is due to the two conditions of variations in fertility and diminishing returns in the cultivation of land. Since the price to be paid to secure a stock of goods must be equal to the cost of that portion of the stock produced under the most expensive conditions, the excess secured by more fertile lands and by "infra-marginal" (in modern terminology) applications of labor and capital is rent, the landlord's share.

Jevons also follows the classical tradition of confusing proportionate and incremental diminishing returns. In the same paragraph both definitions are implicit: ". . . if more or less labour and capital be applied to the same portion of land, the produce will not increase proportionally to the amount of labour. . . . The last increment

[1] There is a possible suggestion that Jevons is shifting his views. In the second preface he expresses dissatisfaction with the discussion of rent in his *Primer of Political Economy* (New York, 1881), p. 94, which is similar to that in the *Theory*. Cf. *Theory*, p. li. The *Primer* does not contain a discussion of diminishing returns, however.

of produce will come to bear a smaller and smaller ratio to the labour required to produce it" (p. 212; also p. 217). Jevons, moreover, asserts that the product of a piece of land always increases with an increase in the labor applied to it, although the rate of increase "diminishes without limit towards zero" (p. 217). This is substantially true but formally incorrect:[1] A less than infinite amount of labor applied to a finite quantity of land must yield a zero product.

In the symbolic development, for the sake of convenience and because certain of the classical writers considered capital to be reducible to labor,[2] Jevons considers

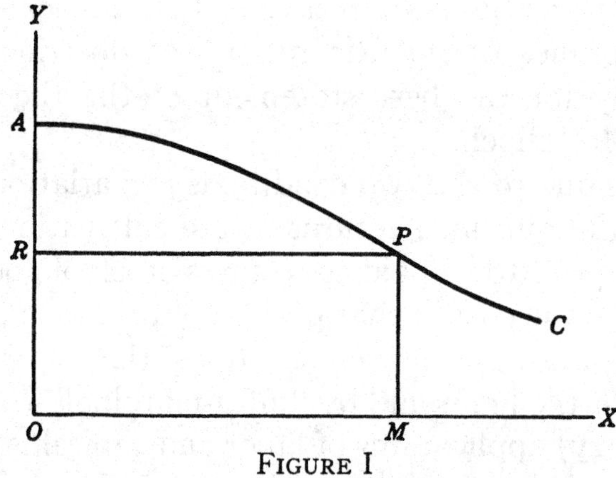

FIGURE I

only variations in the amount of labor expended on a given piece of land. The mathematical exposition is given in a note to this chapter. The geometrical statement is reproduced above, since it was the first graphic

[1] Cf. F. H. Knight, *Risk, Uncertainty and Profit* (Cambridge, 1921), pp. 99 ff.

[2] In the second edition there is added the statement that this doctrine is "altogether erroneous," but Jevons does not alter the exposition, because he believes it permissible to simplify the problem by assuming that the increments (a word he prefers to "doses") of labor are equally assisted by capital (p. 216). This point does not affect his treatment of rent; it will be returned to presently.

presentation in the form still predominant in textbooks on economics. Letting *OX* represent quantity of labor expended, and *OY* the marginal product of labor, then *APC* represents the marginal productivity of "labor" on a given piece of land. The line *RP* is determined by drawing a horizontal line through the point where the supply of labor *OM*, which is determined by equalizing the marginal productivity of "labor" on all land, intersects the curve *APC*. In the present case the wage bill is *OMPR*, and rent is the excess product, or *RAP*.

Only in superficial form does this analysis resemble a true marginal productivity theory of wages.[1] The resemblance is due to terminology; if "capital-and-labor" is substituted for "labor,"[2] the separate elements of wages and interest become indeterminate. Later, indeed, a special variant of the marginal productivity theory is advanced to explain interest, so that wages form a residual.

What his sort of analysis suggests, but Jevons fails to see, is that by a reversal of approach, rent can be shown to be fixed according to the marginal productivity of land (and fixed capital).[3] Had he actually analyzed the

[1] Luigi Amorosa, "W. S. Jevons e la economia pura," *Annali di Economia*, II (1925–26), 98–99; Walras, *Elêments d'économie politique pure* (Lausanne, 1926), p. 375; and B. H. Higgins, "W. S. Jevons—A Centenary Estimate," *The Manchester School*, VI (1935), 109, attribute (too freely, I believe) a marginal productivity theory of wages to Jevons. Indeed, in a very confused argument in one of his last works, Jevons seems to deny the possibility of isolating the product of labor from that of other productive resources combined with it. Cf. *The State in Relation to Labour* (London, 1882), pp. 99 ff.

[2] It must be remembered that Jevons is concerned here with the theory of rent, and other factors of production are of incidental importance. It is interesting to note that the same assumption of fixed proportions between labor and capital is strongly criticized when used by Mill. Cf. *Principles of Economics*, Chap. xxiv.

[3] This was first done by Wieser (*infra*, p. 172), later by J. B. Clark and J. A. Hobson (cf., *infra*, Chap. XI). Wicksteed's analysis is presented in Chap. XII.

application of rent theory to fixed capital, a thing he merely suggests, he might have been led to broaden his concept of capital so as to permit variations in capital, and in the marginal productivity thereof, in other ways than the varying of the period of production. This last restriction was the major defect in his theory of capital, which is now to be considered.

The Theory of Capital

THE CAPITAL CONCEPT

Jevons' concept of capital is essentially that of the later "period of production" school, of whom the leaders were Böhm-Bawerk and Wicksell. Jevons is correct in his assertion that his theory is in fundamental agreement with Ricardian analysis, but his approach differs in several respects from that of the classicists.[1] In the first place, Jevons both restricts and expands the term capital, relative to its use by Ricardo. In the former respect, Jevons eliminates all but currently "free and uninvested" means of sustenance: [2] "Capital consists merely in the aggregate of those commodities which are required for sustaining labourers of any kind or class engaged in work" (p. 223). Capital includes "articles in common daily use," such as food and clothing, but not lodging (p. 262). On the other hand, Jevons enlarges the capital

[1] The entire Chapter xxiv, "Mill on Capital," in Jevons' *Principles of Economics*, is a polemic against Mill's four fundamental propositions of capital. The refutation of two: that industry is limited by capital, and that a demand for commodities is not a demand for labour, is complete. The refutation of the other two propositions falls into the same error of which Jevons accuses Mill, sophistry, or at least logomachy. V. Edelberg, "The Ricardian Theory of Profits," *Economica*, XIII (1933), 51–74, attempts, unsuccessfully it appears to me, to find in Ricardo's writings a marginal productivity theory of profits. Edelberg's formula for the Ricardian theory of profits (*op. cit.*, p. 64) is identical with that offered by Jevons.

[2] This definition is not always adhered to. Cf. *Principles*, Chap. xxiv; *Theory*, pp. 260 ff.

category to include all consumable commodities in the hands of consumers (cf. "Are Articles in Consumers' Hands Capital?" pp. 259–65). His argument is essentially that the accident of ownership should not be decisive in determining whether an article is capital. "Whenever one person provides the articles and another uses them and pays rent, there is capital. Surely, then, if the same person uses and owns them, the nature of the things is not fundamentally different" (p. 263). The second change, it should be observed, partially contradicts the first, for fixed capital comprises most of the capital goods excluded by the ownership criterion (pp. 260 ff.).

Both changes from the classical position are typical Jevonian half-truths. Regarding the first change, which is essentially one of terminology, it is of course true that only the return on uninvested capital is explained by interest theory (and the classicists would admit this); the return on fixed capital goods and "land" must be described in terms of rent theory. In the second case Jevons arrives at a correct conclusion on incorrect grounds. Capital properly consists of all goods which yield a flow of income or services over a period of time. From this viewpoint, however, capital ceases to be different from things which yield consumable services only when the value of the services capitalized over time differs by only a negligible amount from the value of the services as they accrue, *i.e.*, when the period itself is negligible.

Jevons lays great emphasis on the time element in capital. It is because there is a gap between the beginning of a project and the time when it yields services that the fund of goods of which capital consists is necessary to support the laborers. This may be called the construction period. "Capital simply allows us to expend labour in advance" (p. 226). The total produce will increase with the increase of the amount of capital used in constructing a project (cf. esp. pp. 224, 225, 226).

It is implicitly assumed that every increase in capital involves an increase in the durability of the capital equipment constructed (cf. pp. 226, 228–29, and esp. p. 245). This "period of utilization" is not even closely related to the "period of construction," but Jevons confuses the two completely (pp. 227–29). His theory of interest is applied only to the "construction period" problem, and indeed it is hardly applicable to the "utilization period" case. His formal discussion, however, applies to a general production period, including both the period of construction and the period of utilization (if the good is durable). Jevons states explicitly that every lengthening of this general production period involves an increased use of capital,[1] and his development postulates the converse, that every increase in the use of capital is equivalent to a lengthening of the production period.

As a final aspect of his capital concept, Jevons distinguishes sharply between the amount of capital invested and the amount of investment (capital and capitalization, respectively, in his terminology), in definition although not in his usage. The former is composed of only one "dimension," capital—*i.e.*, means of subsistence invested in the purchase of labor; the latter has the two dimensions of time and capital.[2] This is illustrated graphically:

[1] ". . . whatever improvements in the supply of commodities lengthen the average interval between the moment when labour is exerted and its ultimate result or purpose accomplished, such improvements depend upon the use of capital" (pp. 228–29; italicized by Jevons).

[2] "The amount of investment of capital will evidently be determined by multiplying each portion of capital invested at any moment by the length of time for which it remains invested" (pp. 229–30).

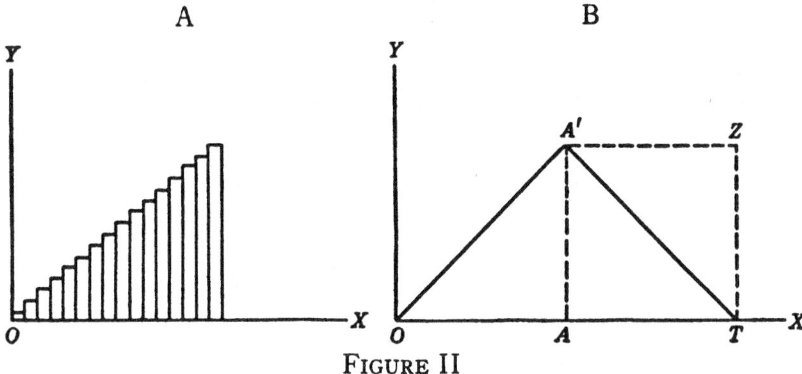

FIGURE II

Time is measured along OX, capital (or labor purchased) along OY. Figure IIA represents a rate of investment which is a linear function of time, as, for example, the hiring of one laborer for a year. Since increments of capital may be made infinitesimal, this becomes a continuous curve of investment (Figure IIB). A similar procedure is followed "uninvesting" (to use Jevons' term) capital, graphically represented by the downward sloping line from A' to T in Figure IIB. The height of any perpendicular from OX between O and A represents the amount of capital invested up to that moment; the area enclosed up to any such line represents the amount of investment of capital, ignoring, as Jevons does, interest on earlier outlays.[1] The amount of "uninvestment" (or consumption of the capital good) may be represented in Figure IIB by the area included within the triangle $A'ZT$ up to any point of time.[2] Jevons does not discuss the relations between investment and "uninvestment"; only a simple symmetrical case is presented for illustrative purposes (p. 231).

[1] Interest on investments is considered elsewhere, however (pp. 239–41).

[2] Mathematically stated, the *net* amount of investment of capital will be $\Sigma t \cdot \Delta p - \Sigma t \cdot \Delta q$, where t is time, Δp the amount of capital invested in time Δt, and Δq the amount of capital "uninvested" in time Δt.

The major error in Jevons' capital concept, the assumption that increases of capital are equivalent to increases in the length of time consumed by the production period, will be discussed later in connection with Böhm-Bawerk's theory. Two other errors seem noteworthy. First, he implicitly assumes that every capital good is completely liquidated, once it is completed, when in fact once created it does not begin to yield net income, by the very definition of net income, until it has provided for maintenance and replacement. In this respect one of Jevons' examples suggests that he is influenced by the classical assumption of an annual cycle of production (in agriculture). The other error lies in the assumption, likewise classical, that free capital contributes to the creation of new capital equipment only through the maintenance of labor.

THE RATE OF INTEREST

It is in the determination of the rate of interest on (free) capital that Jevons' distribution theory makes its only significant contribution to the development of the marginal productivity theory.[1] Here is evolved a theory of the marginal productivity of the *length* of the period of construction, which, while necessarily an inadequate explanation of interest, is within limits correct.

Jevons assumes that the productivity of a given amount of capital (invested labor) is a function only of the time elapsing between the expenditure of the labor and the sale of the final product. The aging of wine, for example, may be cited.[2] A slight increase in the period

[1] The important section is, "General Expression for the Rate of Interest" (pp. 245–47).

[2] Since the wine is assumed to be consumed at once, there is no period of utilization.

will increase the produce by a given amount.[1] It follows that "the ratio which this increment [of produce] bears to the increment of investment of capital will determine the rate of interest" (p. 245). This is equivalent to saying that the (instantaneous) rate of interest is equal to the rate of increase of the produce (as a function of time) divided by the whole of the produce. The determination of the interest rate is presented mathematically (see below) and graphically, in the latter case by a curve equivalent to the marginal productivity of capital.[2]

A summary of Jevons' mathematical statement will show the heroic nature of his assumptions and the limited scope of his conclusions:

i. Let p be the product and t time, so $p = F(t)$. Then to extend the period of construction by Δt will increase the product to $F(t + \Delta t)$. The increment of product is therefore $F(t + \Delta t) - F(t)$.

ii. The increase in the amount of investment, capital multiplied by time, is $\Delta t F(t)$. Dividing the increment of produce by the increment of investment, one secures the rate of return on the increment of investment, or

$$\frac{F(t + \Delta t) - F(t)}{\Delta t} \cdot \frac{1}{F(t)}.$$

iii. At the limit this becomes the instantaneous rate of interest, or

$$\frac{d[F(t)]}{dt} \cdot \frac{1}{F(t)} = \frac{F'(t)}{F(t)}.$$

But it must be emphasized that this is not the annual rate of interest; it is the instantaneous rate or "force of

[1] The assumption is implicit that all of the other productive factors will be held constant or that none is used.

[2] The graph (p. 258) contains an error; the ordinates do not represent, as Jevons asserts, the marginal productivity of the extension of the period of production $[F'(t)]$, but rather the marginal productivity, or instantaneous interest rate, of capital $[F'(t)/F(t)]$, where $F(t)$ is produce and t is time.

interest." Böhm-Bawerk failed to perceive the distinction between these two rates (as did also Jevons),[1] and therefore imputed to Jevons' theory an error which it does not contain.[2] The difference between the actual annual rate and the instantaneous rate (sometimes called the force of interest) can best be shown mathematically.[3]

i. Assume, as with Jevons, that $p = F(t)$, except that now p is the value of the product at the time of realization or sale. If V is the present value, and r the annual rate of interest, then

$$V = p(1 + r)^{-t} = F(t)(1 + r)^{-t}.$$

ii. Given a constant annual interest rate, r, maximize the present value, $V[= g(r,t)]$. Then

$$\frac{\partial V}{\partial t} = F'(t)(1 + r)^{-t} - F(t)(1 + r)^{-t} \log_e (1 + r) = 0.$$

iii. Since $(1 + r)^{-t}$ cannot be zero, it may be divided out, leaving

$$F'(t) - F(t) \log_e (1 + r) = 0$$

or

$$\log_e (1 + r) = \frac{F'(t)}{F(t)}.$$

This is the relationship between the instantaneous interest rate and the annual interest rate.

Presumably—but Jevons does not so state—the period of construction should be extended by any entrepreneur until the instantaneous rate of return equals the market rate of interest.

[1] Witness the error in the graph (p. 258).

[2] Cf. *Positive Theory of Capital* (Eng. trans., London, 1891), p. 399 n. Wicksell defended Jevons, "Kapitalzins und Arbeitslohn," *Jahrbücher für Nationalökonomie und Statistik*, LIX (1892), 867–68; and *Über Wert, Kapital und Rente* (Jena, 1893), pp. 116–19. Böhm-Bawerk failed to understand the refutation however, and retained his criticism; cf. *Positive Theorie des Kapitals* (4th ed., Jena, 1921), I, 461 n.

[3] Cf. Wicksell, *Über Wert, Kapital und Rente, op. cit.*, p. 117 n.; also R. van Genechten, "Über das Verhältnis zwischen der Produktivität des Kapitals, den Lohnen und Zinsen," *Zeitschrift für Nationalökonomie*, II (1930–31), 219–20. Wicksell (*op. cit.*) expands the formula to include wages.

Although Jevons has a marginal productivity theory of interest, it is a very incomplete theory. It is developed only for the special case of a commodity which increases in value through time without any additional expenditures. Accordingly, Jevons' interest rate bears no relationship to wages or rent,[1] nor, for that matter, does he consider its relationship to the market rate of interest. And more generally, he does not give the conditions for a maximum rate of return.

It is apparent that Jevons does not depart far from the classical theory. His conception of capital and its rate is basically the same as that incorporated in the wages-fund doctrine. The fundamental difference, in fact, is that the classical theory assumes a fixed period of production (one year), and therefore resorts to the notion of a subsistence wage in order to divide the produce-less-rent between labor and capital. Jevons merely adds one further element, the variability of the production period, to provide a determinant of the rate of interest.

The Theory of Labor

In the analysis of labor, Jevons concentrates attention exclusively on the problem of pain or disutility costs. The discussion is entirely in terms of the individual and, primarily, his labor in one occupation. The analysis is suggestive, therefore, of the factors determining the supply of labor in an economy, but in the absence of a general investigation of the interrelations of costs and value no light is shed on the problem of the laborer's reward in an enterprise economy.

Labor is defined as the painful exertion undergone to ward off pains of greater amount, or to produce pleasures

[1] He asserts in fact that wages are independent of the amount of capital (pp. 254–55).

of greater amount. This definition is supposedly a corollary of his hedonistic premises of value theory; Jevons considers the utility scale to possess a definite zero point and believes sensations to be measurable (and capable of algebraic treatment) in both positive (utility) and negative (pain or disutility) directions.[1] As a further restriction, labor to be of economic significance—that is, to exclude play, recreation, and the like—must be undergone partly or wholly with a view to future good (p. 168). The cases in which immediate pleasures offset labor are conceived to be identical with those generally considered to be "non-economic" from the common-sense viewpoint. Both stages in the definition reveal the strong influence which classical economics exerts on Jevons. His general definition of labor reflects a typically classical interpretation of psychological magnitudes as absolutes. The unrealism of an algebraic scale of human motivation is not the chief defect of this concept; the fact that it obscures the principle of competition between leisure and productive alternatives of the laborers (or resources, more generally) is much more to be deplored. The entire discussion of psychological absolutes, such as "consumer's surplus" and "minimum sacrifice," has been an unfortunate heritage of this propensity to treat economic motivation in algebraic and even arithmetic terms, or through the device of definite geometrical areas.

The attempt to differentiate labor from play on the basis of futurity of remuneration is unsound.[2] It is a matter primarily of social convention, whether based on

[1] Labor is "by far the most important instance of negative value" (*Principles*, p. 135).

[2] Jevons recognizes the "great difficulty" in applications of this concept, but his suggestion that labor be distinguished by the negative sign of its utilities is even more unfortunate (p. 168 n.; *Principles*, Chap. xiv). He does not, of course, share the classical view of unproductive labor, but, on the contrary, completely refutes it (cf. *Principles*, Chap. xviii).

accident or convenience, that in perhaps a majority of cases productive agents are compensated after rendering services, rather than before. The only thoroughgoing definition of labor, in contradistinction to play, is that labor consists of all forms of human activity which exist in small enough quantities relative to the demand for them to require remuneration for their economic allocation between competing uses.

Quantity of Labor

Jevons treats time as the primary dimension of the quantity of labor. Intensity of effort is the second dimension, and quantity of labor is equal to intensity times duration when the former is uniform. In those cases in which intensity is not uniform, the amount of labor is that represented by "the area of a curve" (p. 170). Intensity of labor may refer to either painfulness or productiveness; productiveness, in turn, may be subdivided into physical product and utility added.[1] If the application of labor is not subject to diminishing returns, productiveness should be proportional to intensity and duration for a given person. Jevons seems to realize this, for he restricts his discussion to variations in painfulness, and leaves variations in productiveness to be discussed in the chapter on rent.

The labor supply of the individual is determined by equating painfulness of labor to utility of produce, at the margin. Irksomeness of labor is an increasing function of amount of labor, that is, of both its intensity and its

[1] In other words, quantity of labor of any one laborer is composed of:
(a) Duration of labor, and
(b) Intensity of labor, which depends on
  1) Painfulness, or
  1′) Productiveness, in the senses of
    a) Physical product, or
    a′) Utility value product.

duration. Marginal utility, on the other hand, is a decreasing function of the quantity of a commodity possessed. To render utility of product and disutility of labor comparable, Jevons seems to waver between two different approaches.

One consists of assuming that painfulness is a linear function of productiveness of work, despite the distinction he has drawn between them.[1] This method may underly his graphic approach, which he introduces by saying, "We may imagine the painfulness of labour in proportion to produce to be represented by some such curve. . . ." (p. 172). It is apparent that one set of postulates justifying this treatment could consist of the assumptions (i) that units of painful effort remain uniform in efficiency; [2] and (ii) that labor (in the sense of productive power) is not subject to diminishing returns when applied to other resources.[3]

The second approach, which is more general in application and less violent in assumption, is probably the one Jevons relies upon. It is given explicit mathematical statement in a parallel case (pp. 174–76). Painfulness and productiveness are considered as functions of time, and by eliminating this parameter between them, he secures the derived curve of painfulness in terms of product, as shown in Figure III below.[4]

Using either set of assumptions, then, Jevons is able

[1] Of productiveness and painfulness, he says, "The two things must be carefully distinguished, and both are of great importance for the theory [of value of labor]" (p. 170).

[2] If P is product, A the amount of work, and E the efficiency of the work, then $P = AE$; and $\frac{P}{A} = E$, which is assumed to be constant.

[3] Amusingly enough, all these qualifications would not have been necessary if Jevons had followed a labor theory of value.

[4] Analytically this procedure is as follows: p (painfulness) $= f(t)$, P (productiveness) $= g(t)$; then $P = h(p)$.

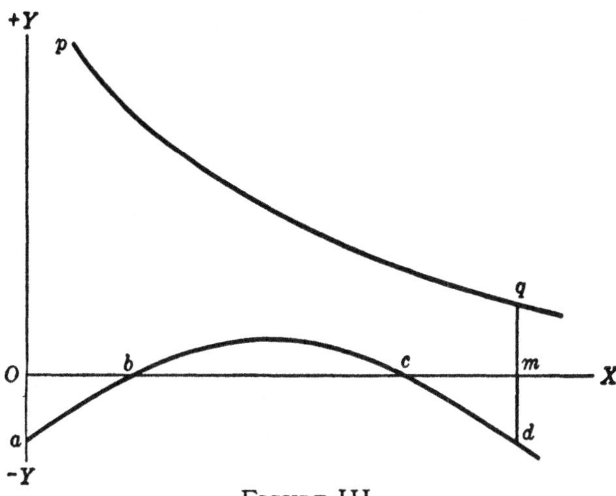

FIGURE III

to equate utility and disutility to determine the individual's labor supply and its price in terms of utility of product and disutility of labor.[1] The method is geometrical. The *OX* axis is ostensibly "amount of produce"; the *OY* axis measures utility of product (positively) and disutility of effort of production (negatively). Actually the *OX* axis is described completely in terms of duration of labor (as fractions of a working day) when the supply curve (*abcd*) of "degree of painfulness of labour" is presented (cf. pp. 172–73).[2] This involves the further assumption, under either of the above approaches, that intensity is also uniform.[3] The conventional curve

[1] Gossen used virtually the same graph to illustrate the identical theory. Cf. Edgeworth, "Gossen," *Palgrave's Dictionary of Political Economy* (London, 1923), II, 231–33.

[2] Cf. *Principles*, pp. 74–75. In the symbolic statement, the degree of painfulness of labor is defined as $\frac{dw}{dt}$, where "t is time, or duration of labour," and w "is amount of labour, as meaning the aggregate balance of pain accompanying it [time], irrespective of the produce" (*Theory*, p. 174).

[3] Thus, if $P = AE$ (see note 2, p. 32, *supra*), and $A = TI$ (T for time, I for intensity), then $\frac{P}{T} = IE =$ constant, is assumed. The section, "Limits to the Intensity of Labour" (pp. 203–9), contains no theoretical analysis of

of decreasing final utility of product is represented by *pq*.[1] The equilibrium of utility and irksomeness is reached when increments of utility and pain are equal (when $dm = mq$).[2]

This explanation is accepted by both Marshall and Edgeworth.[3] Yet major changes would have to be made in this analysis before it would be suggestive of the determination of the labor supply of an individual in an enterprise economy. It would be more appropriate, to this end, to speak of the marginal utility of income, rather than the marginal utility of the commodity actually produced. All discussion of disutility would be dropped, of course, and for it the concept of the competition of non-monetary uses of time should be substituted. Proper graphical presentation of Jevons' labor theory, moreover, would require at least three dimensions, which would make it a very clumsy method of solving his problem.[4]

Jevons devotes a section of his chapter on labor to variations in efficiency.[5] He considers only historical

the problem, but merely describes some elements contributing to variability of intensity (cf. p. 175).

[1] It is secured, however, by the second approach (if we are to render the graph consistent): The amount of commodity produced in each unit of time is first ascertained; then the utility of this amount of commodity is found, from a graph of diminishing final utility for the individual, and this last quantity—utility per unit of time—is then graphed directly against disutility of labor per unit of time.

[2] Compare the mathematical statement (pp. 174–77).

[3] Marshall, *Principles of Economics, op. cit.*, pp. 141–42; Edgeworth, *Collected Papers Relating to Political Economy* (London, 1925), I, 35–36; II, 298 ff.

[4] The essential dimensions would be efficiency of labor, duration of labor (per working day), and intensity of labor (or product could be substituted for any one of these), if indifference surfaces were used.

[5] "Balance Between Need and Labour" (pp. 179–83). Jevons touches here upon an acute problem of recent theory which, as usual, he does not pursue: "It is not always possible to graduate work to the worker's liking; in some businesses a man who insisted on working only a few hours a day would soon have no work to do" (p. 181). This is an important cause of asymmetry between consumption and production.

changes, arising say from technical advances. Such advances would cause both a shift in the *abcd* curve and a change in its shape. Here Jevons has forgotten the assumption that the efficiency of labor (per fraction of the working day) is constant under given technical conditions. He is obviously correct in his not too helpful conclusion, however, that whether such historical changes increase or decrease the amount (presumably time) of work depends upon the nature of the utility and disutility functions.[1]

Conclusion

Jevons' theories of distribution contribute little to the solution of the problem of distribution, although they contain the germs of some important later developments.[2] Rent theory is improved by the implicit inclusion of "fixed" capital; interest theory receives a partial explanation in terms of marginal productivity; wages remain a residual. The failure to pursue the competition of different uses for given resources; the failure to develop the relationship of different resources in the production of a given product; the omission of the relation of capital and interest to resources and to rent—all these were fatal to the creation of a comprehensive and internally consistent theory. Although the "adding-up" or "exhaustion-of-product" problem could not arise until all distributive shares were determinate (*i.e.*, none was residual), Jevons relates the various shares. Eliminating

[1] On this problem, compare A. C. Pigou, *The Economics of Stationary States* (London, 1935), Chap. ix.

[2] Marshall's review of the *Theory*, reprinted in *Memorials of Alfred Marshall*, *op. cit.*, pp. 93–99, is disappointingly vague with respect to this portion of Jevons' theory. Allyn Young's review, reprinted in *Economic Problems New and Old* (Cambridge, 1927), pp. 213–32, is brief but balanced and fair.

rent by Ricardian analysis, and taxes (as being negligible!), he gives the formula:

$$\text{Product} = \text{Profits} + \text{Wages.}$$

The classical dictum, that wages and profits bear a reciprocal relationship, is denied on the ground that two unknowns cannot be solved by one equation. He further repudiates any subsistence theory of wages. This repudiation is based upon two unconvincing arguments: wages vary widely between occupations and districts; and the concept of "necessaries of life" is indefinite. Although he grants the validity of the wages-fund theory as a short-run explanation (cf. pp. 268–71), Jevons inconsistently emphasizes the mutual independence of the returns of capital and labor (cf. pp. 255–56).

Mathematical Note on Jevons' Rent Theory

i. Labor will be allocated between two pieces of land so that the increments of product from equal units of labor will be equal. Where x_1 and x_2 are the products of two pieces of land, and w is the labor (here in the sense of productive effort),

$$\frac{dx_1}{dw} = \frac{dx_2}{dw}.$$

ii. The presence of diminishing returns is established by assuming $\frac{dx}{dw}$ to diminish "without limit" toward zero, after a certain possible early period of increasing returns. Jevons adds that x will never decrease when w increases. This is erroneous: it would deny the possibility of securing a maximum product from a given piece of land.

iii. The theorem is then recalled from Chapter V, that labor will be expended only until the utility is equal to the pain, at the margin. Forgetting the subjectiveness of these magnitudes (which would render impossible the previous assumptions that production functions are continuous as between individuals, and that final degrees of utility of similar wages are necessarily equal for different individuals), he defines the wage rate as the marginal productivity of labor, *i.e.*,

$$\frac{dx}{dw}, \qquad \text{or} \qquad P'(w).$$

iv. The total wage bill, amount of labor times marginal return, is

$$w\frac{dx}{dw} = wP'(w).$$

v. Rent is then the difference between the total product and the wage bill, and is defined as

$$P(w) - wP'(w).$$

Chapter III

PHILIP H. WICKSTEED

PHILIP H. WICKSTEED is probably the least known of the leading English economists of the last generation, and this was equally true in his own time.[1] Although his reputation was high among his outstanding contemporaries, such as Marshall, Edgeworth, and Pareto, he was scarcely known by most of his fellow economists. Yet two of his three books on economics, *The Alphabet of Economic Science* (1888) and the *Commonsense of Political Economy* (1910), were expressly designed to popularize economic theory. The paradox, however, is only superficial. The *Alphabet* is a rigorous introduction to marginal analysis, and contains a difficult although excellent development of margins and rates of change, limits, and other mathematical concepts. The *Commonsense* is not so technical, but it is painfully verbose and excessively elaborate, at times even pedantic, in its thoroughness and its attention to "detailed and even minute precautions." [2]

Wicksteed constitutes, in a certain sense, the Jevonian "school." He and William Smart, the translator of Böhm-Bawerk and Wieser, were the only important

[1] For Wicksteed's life, consult C. H. Herford, *Philip Henry Wicksteed, His Life and Work* (London, 1931); also L. Robbins, Introduction to the reprint of the *Commonsense of Political Economy* (London, 1933), pp. v–xxiii.

[2] *Commonsense*, p. 385. All subsequent references are to this work, unless otherwise noted. I am indebted to George Routledge and Sons for permission to quote from this work.

English economists of the period between 1870 and the World War who explicitly abandoned the classical tradition. This is an additional reason for Wicksteed's comparative obscurity. He was, however, much more thorough and consistent than Jevons. He extended marginal analysis to all parts of man's rational life; [1] he developed a cost theory which was consistent with the general application of the utility theory; he gave the first detailed and reasonably satisfactory statement of the general marginal productivity theory. This last topic, dealt with chiefly in his famous *Co-ordination of the Laws of Distribution* (1894), will be considered in Chapter XII. Before Wicksteed's general theory of production and distribution is presented, some of his earlier writings will be noted.

Early Writings

Two of Wicksteed's early works on economics relate to production and distribution. The first of these is his *Alphabet of Economic Science* (London, 1888),[2] which

[1] Book I of the *Commonsense* contains many colorful examples, of which one group may be quoted:

"Thus the same law holds in intellectual, moral, or spiritual as in material matters. Caesar tells how when surprised by the Nervii he had barely time to harangue his soldiers, obviously implying that the harangue was shorter than usual. He felt that a few moments, even at such a crisis, were well devoted to words of exhortation to his troops; but their value declined at the margin, and the price in delaying the onslaught rapidly rose: so the moment was soon reached when the time could be better spent than in prolonging a moving discourse. In a story of South America, after the war, we are told of a planter who, when warned by his wife in the middle of his prayers that the enemy was at the gate, concluded his devotions with a few brief and earnest petitions, and then set about defending himself. Had he been a formalist those final petitions would never have been uttered at all; but under the circumstances the impulse to prayer, though sincere and urgent, became rapidly less imperative and exacting relatively to the urgency of taking steps for defense, as the successive moments passed" (pp. 79–80).

[2] At the time Wicksteed wrote the *Alphabet*, he expected to supplement

deals primarily with demand theory but sheds incidental light on resource allocation. In this early manual the alternative cost theory is sketched:

> There will always be a tendency to turn all freely disposable productive forces towards those branches of production in which the smallest sum of labor and other necessaries will produce a given utility; that is to say, to the production of those commodities which have the highest marginal utility in proportion to the labour, etc., required to produce them; and this rush of productive forces into these particular channels will increase the amount of the respective commodities, and so reduce their marginal usefulness till units of them are no longer of more value at the margin than units of other things that can be made by the same expenditure of productive forces. There will then no longer be any special reason for further increasing the supply of them.
>
> The productive forces of the community, then, like the labour of a self-sufficing industrial unit, will tend to distribute themselves in such a way that a given sum of productive force will produce equal utilities at the margin (measured externally by equivalents in "gold") wherever applied.[1]

In the case of constant costs,[2] the theory of price follows simply: "If *a* contains *x* times as much work as *b*, then there will not be equilibrium until *a* and *b* are produced in such amounts as to make the exchange value of *a* just *x* times the exchange value of *b*." [3]

it by volumes on other phases of economic thought and life. The *Alphabet's* reception, however, while warm, was restricted to a small group, and this discouraged him for his purpose was to popularize.

[1] *Alphabet*, p. 111.

[2] It is interesting to note that Wicksteed had not yet reached the central idea of the *Co-ordination*, for he says: "And here we must make a simplification which would be violent if we were studying the theory of production, but which is perfectly legitimate for our present purpose. We must suppose, namely, that however much or little of the new product is secured it is always got under the same conditions, so that the yield per unit effort-and-sacrifice is the same at every stage of production" (*Alphabet*, p. 113).

[3] *Ibid.*, p. 116.

In the following year there appeared Wicksteed's acute essay, "On Certain Passages in Jevons's *Theory of Political Economy*." [1] This article is notable for its discussion of the theory of interest. Jevons' fundamental thesis, that the produce of given labor increases continuously with the time between the expenditure of the labor and the securing of the product, is properly rejected because it "is not based upon a typical case of the use of capital" (p. 753). The typical case is one in which capital yields a product continuously, and the capital is continuously worn out and replaced, and co-operates in its own replacement. The interest rate is established by this typical case, which is characteristic of "the great staple industries."

> If, by way of exception, an investment of capital is proposed which will, after an interval, yield not a revenue, but an absolute utility; or if, as is extremely common, a gradual investment of capital is proposed, with the expectation that when the investment is complete the whole invested capital (in the shape of a ship or a machine, for instance) will be purchased by some one . . .; or, lastly, if an immediate investment of capital is proposed in order that after an interval a periodic yield may be enjoyed by the investor—in all these cases the investor has to consider what quantity of commodity he would command at the expiration of the given time, had he invested at first in one of the staple industries, and then continuously reinvested his continuously accruing return in the same industry again (p. 753).

Formally this statement is incorrect, since all methods of employing capital will affect the interest rate. Substantively the statement is sound, however, for peculiar

[1] Reprinted in the *Commonsense*, pp. 734–54. The article appeared originally in the *Quarterly Journal of Economics*, III (1889), 293–314. I am indebted to the President and Fellows of Harvard College for permission to quote from this and other articles which appeared in the *Quarterly Journal of Economics*.

modes of investment—as well as consumption loans—affect the interest rate only to a negligible extent.

How is the interest rate determined in the staple industries? The answer is extremely compact (pp. 748–52). Consider an entrepreneur who possesses a given amount of labor and employs a variable amount of capital, c. Capital goods will be worn out and completely replaced in some period of time, t, which is assumed for simplicity's sake to be constant.[1] The maintenance and replacement charge is then $\frac{c}{t}$ per unit of time. If t is constant, the replacement charge may be represented by the straight line OW in Figure IV. In this graph OX is amount of capital, OY is product per unit of time. The total return

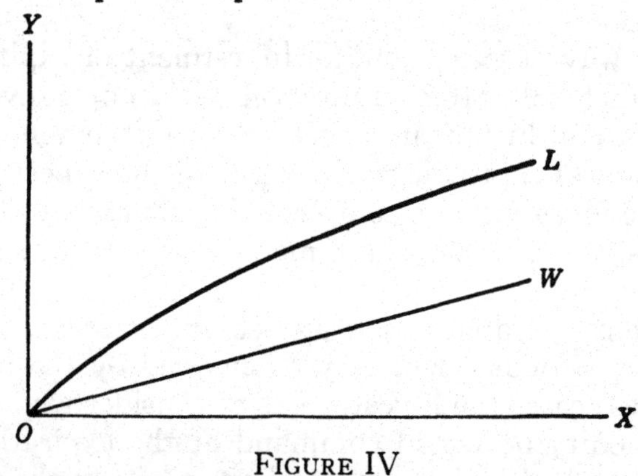

FIGURE IV

(after deduction of non-labor operating costs of the capital, such as materials) from a capital good in t years is q, so the return per unit of time is $\frac{q}{t}$, represented by OL in the graph. The difference between $\frac{q}{t}$ and $\frac{c}{t}$ (or between

[1] Wicksteed believes that t is really a function of c; the more capital is used, the less adequately it can be maintained by a given labor force (p. 748). In this case, the replacement charge will be represented by a curve OW (see Figure IV), which is convex to the X axis.

OL and *OW*) is total net return to c units of capital; it is total hire or interest. If $\frac{q - c}{t}$ is differentiated with respect to c, *i.e.*, if the "rate at which increments of capital are increasing the annual return made by the capital" is ascertained (p. 751; italicized by Wicksteed), then the interest rate is secured. The rate of interest, in other words, is equal to the annual (perpetual) income produced by an increment of capital.

This skeleton of a theory of interest deserves high praise. Wicksteed had grasped the fundamental perpetuity of the income source; his method of dealing with the time dimension of investment leaves very little more to be said. It is greatly to be regretted that Wicksteed, instead of elaborating this approach in the later *Commonsense*, devotes primary attention to the relatively unimportant and uninteresting problem of consumption loans.

The Nature of Costs

The *Commonsense* is the first English work in which the alternative cost theory is explicitly applied to the ascertainment of the quantity as well as the allocation of resources.[1] As a preliminary to the discussion of this problem, a few words concerning Wicksteed's theory of economic behavior are in order. His fundamental thesis may be summarized in two propositions: (i) where resources are limited (relative to ends), more of one good (A) can be secured only at the cost of less of some other good (B); and (ii) satisfaction is maximized when the utility of the increment of A foregone equals the utility of the increment of B received.[2] It is this general process

[1] Walras, as we shall see, anticipated the doctrine; cf., *infra*, Chap. IX.

[2] The term "satisfaction" is used here with qualification. While Wicksteed expressly disassociates himself from hedonism (pp. 434–35), his discussion (pp. 146 ff., 189 f.) of "vital significance" contains a good deal of this system.

of relative valuation which reduces "fresh eggs and friendship" to comparability for the prospective suburbanite, for instance (p. 776). Such an "all-permeating law" of economic behavior is clearly equivalent to rationality. To act economically is to act sensibly.[1]

Whether one accepts or rejects this generalization of economics, its applicability to the resources problem is very apparent. Indeed Wicksteed offers the solution of the resources problem in the early chapter (II) on diminishing psychic returns:

> It is not only such things as bread, water, plums, and potatoes that change their marginal value according to the breadth of the supply. I value an extra hour's leisure in the day, or an extra half or quarter day to my week-end, more or less according to the amount of daily leisure or the amplitude of the week-end I already enjoy. If I am considering whether I will take a piece of work for which I shall be paid at the rate of 10s. an hour, then (if we neglect the consideration of any irksomeness or any pleasure the work itself may give me, . . .) it is easy to see that if I have abundant leisure and am severely straitened for cash, I shall be likely to accept the offer, and if repeated offers come to me I shall go on accepting them. But each successive half-sovereign a week becomes less important, as I am better provided with cash, and each successive hour withdrawn from other occupations involves a greater sacrifice as my reserve of leisure contracts. At last I shall reach the point at which the sacrifice of another hour, at the raised margin, will just compensate the acquisition of another half-sovereign at the lowered margin (pp. 76–77).[2]

As consistency requires, the same theory is also applied to other resources: "It should be noted, too, that land

[1] Cf. p. 404: "I have maintained from first to last that the laws of Economics are the laws of life."

[2] Also pp. 327–28. Cf. pp. 522–25, where the Jevonian curve of labor supply is utilized, but Wicksteed generalizes the construction by substituting the desire for leisure for the irksomeness of labor.

itself may yield a direct revenue of enjoyment when used as a garden, park, or hunting-ground, and that the desire for this direct revenue of pleasure will enter the market for land, and compete there with the desire for its service as a tool, or increaser of the industrial efficiency of effort" (p. 290).

This theory is not elaborated to any considerable extent, and Wicksteed fails to notice the great limitations to which it is subject. He is careful to point out that an increase in the price of commercial uses of a resource may lead to increases or decreases in the supply of the productive service from the given stock of resources, depending on the relative marginal utilities of money and leisure. It is "more likely," however, that wage increases will lead to shorter working hours (p. 77).

But the implicit assumptions of the alternative cost theory are not examined at all critically. Wicksteed recognizes very explicitly that in an economy which practices division of labor, men cannot move freely from one occupation to another (pp. 332–37). Nevertheless he finds, as with Marshall, an escape from this problem: ". . . it must always remain true that, in an age of specializing and of division of labour, manual and intellectual, development of any particular capacity constitutes a demand upon the general store of undifferentiated human power that is perpetually poured into the world in the form of fresh human lives, and limits the amount available in other directions" (pp. 332–33).

Even this tendency, however, is subject to many limitations. Parents may be financially unable to train their children for the most remunerative callings (p. 334); and, most important, "It is only under very exceptional circumstances that we can suppose free-born children to be bred with a view to the market, that is to say, produced in order that economic advantages may accrue to their producers" (p. 336). Wicksteed makes one further admission, the significance of which he is apparently unaware: the attractiveness, not the monetary returns, of different occupations will be equalized in a perfectly competitive state (p. 335). This must refer, of course, to the individual as a unit (not portions of an individual's time spent in various occupations), or the admission is as untrue as the doctrine of equal monetary returns.

Occupational specialization and the failure to equalize monetary returns even in the case of occupational mobility lead to basic limitations on the alternative cost theory. If total monetary returns to the same or identical laborers in two occupations are not equalized, for instance, it is not possible to say that the cost of a laborer to industry *A* is the amount that laborer could produce in industry *B*. The inability of an individual to practice two occupations at once leaves the ultimate explanation of costs in a very nebulous state. In this connection one may mention Wicksteed's suggestion that enough individuals of a given group will be on the margin between occupations to insure equality of attractiveness (p. 206). But this is not sufficient; the alternative cost theory requires that all of the units of a resource be qualitatively and psychologically identical, so that if some of the units are on the margin of transference, all of them must be.

The allocation of non-human services, in contrast with the determination of their quantity, is based on the equalization of the marginal significance of all the uses of each such resource.[1] In this respect resources are identical with directly consumable goods: "The law of the market never changes" (p. 262; also pp. 517–18, 540,

[1] Bk. I, Chap. vi, esp. pp. 258–65; also pp. 380 ff., 517–22; Bk. II, Chap. v, *passim;* pp. 776 ff., 820–21.

543), nor does it exclude any goods which enter into economic calculation (pp. 261–62).[1] The general theory is given a pithy statement:

> The guiding principle of all administration . . . is so to select between open alternatives as to direct our resources toward the fulfilment of that purpose which, given the terms on which it is open to us, takes the highest place on our scale of preferences. And seeing that the securing of that alternative perpetually lowers its marginal significance, and the neglect of other alternatives raises theirs, we shall always be able to bring our marginal increments of satisfaction into balance with the respective terms on which they are open to us (p. 373; also pp. 360–61).

From this statement of resource allocation it is of course only a very short step to the interpretation of cost of production as "simply and solely 'the marginal significance of something else' " (p. 382). Or, in more conventional terminology, "By cost of production, or cost price, when the phrase is used without qualification, I mean the estimated value, measured in gold, of all the alternatives that have been sacrificed in order to place a unit of the commodity in question upon the market" (p. 385). Wicksteed's presentation of the alternative cost theory must command admiration from all, but only the most fanatic rhetorician could condone the endless criticism levied at the concept of historical cost (pp. 373–80 *et seq.;* also pp. 89–93). His conclusion, however, is clear and correct: "Cost of production, then, in the sense of the historical and irrevocable fact that resources have been devoted to this or that special purpose, has no influence on the value of the thing produced, and therefore does not affect its price" (p. 380). One picturesque illustration of this principle, however, deserves quota-

[1] Even entrepreneurial ability is so allocated (p. 271).

tion: "The misdirection of energy which makes me regret that I devoted myself to the study of Greek and took my University diploma in Arts, instead of in Brewing, is irreparable so far as I am concerned . . ." (p. 383).

Substitution; The Law of Costs

No part of the theory of production is more admirably developed than the principle of substitution. This part of his doctrine will be presented at some length in the later chapter on the Euler theorem, so here it will be sufficient merely to indicate the nature and breadth of Wicksteed's views. He assumes the possibility of substituting any productive factor for any other productive factor, within fairly wide limits (pp. 361 ff., 778 ff., 798). Thus, the manufacture of bricks requires both intelligence and straw, but at the margin one may be substituted freely for the other without affecting the quantity of the output. One aspect of this theory deserves special mention: managerial ability and land are treated as quantified factors which are exactly comparable with other resources (pp. 362–72 *passim;* p. 545). Wicksteed accepts, as we shall see, the logical implication of this treatment for his theory of distribution: no distributive share, not even "profits," can be a residual since there is complete substitutionality.

The Laws of Return

The laws of return applicable to variations in the quantity of one resource are clearly separated from those applicable to variations in the scale of plant, and this practice will be followed here.[1] With regard to the variation of product when the quantity of one resource is varied (the others being held constant), Wicksteed is as explicit

[1] He implicitly assumes, therefore, that one firm possesses only one plant.

as possible. Under such conditions the law of diminishing returns "is really no more than an axiomatic statement of a universal principle that applies equally to all forms of industry, and to a great range of non-industrial experiences and phenomena as well" (p. 529).[1] No rigorous proof is offered; it is held to be obvious that if only one factor in a combination is doubled, the product cannot double (p. 529). Wicksteed's development is open to criticism on three counts.

The law of diminishing returns is rarely defined, and then apparently accidentally, in its economically relevant, incremental form (pp. 527, 550, 560); on many pages it is used in the less appropriate, proportional form (pp. 530, 531, 532, 534; also pp. 556, 563). More important, Wicksteed does not emphasize that the "axiomatic" nature of the law is true only with complete divisibility of the resources. The heaviest indictment, however, is his failure to understand the nature of the *a priori* proof of diminishing returns. The proof holds only if it is assumed that the production function is homogeneous and of the first degree.[2] But Wicksteed, in

[1] Also p. 530: ". . . an axiomatic and sterile proposition."

[2] The proof of diminishing returns in Wicksteed's argument involves the assumption of a homogeneous, first degree production function. Let the product $(P) = C^k L^{1-k}$, where C and L are capital and labor respectively; then the marginal product of capital is $\frac{kP}{C}$, and of labor, $\frac{(1-k)P}{L}$. It follows that both marginal products decrease, *i.e.*, $\frac{\partial\left[\frac{kP}{C}\right]}{\partial C} < 0$ and $\frac{\partial\left[(1-k)\frac{P}{L}\right]}{\partial L} < 0$. But this conclusion no longer follows necessarily if the production function is not linear. Thus, if $P = C^k L^{a-k}$, where $a > 1$, then one and perhaps both marginal products might be increasing. On the whole subject of *a priori* proofs of diminishing returns, consult the excellent papers of Karl Menger, "Bemerkungen zu den Ertragsgesetzen," "Weitere Bemerkungen zu den Ertragsgesetzen," *Zeitschrift für Nationalökonomie*, VII (1936), 25–56, 388–96.

discussing economies dependent on scale of plant, expressly denies that a doubling of all factors is necessary to a doubling of output. This latter proposition is inconsistent not only with the *a priori* proof of diminishing returns, but also with his entire theory of rent—and accordingly with the general marginal productivity theory.[1] The grounds for denial of the Euler theorem assumption in production theory, by the man who initially introduced it into economic analysis, demand our attention.

After asserting the ubiquity of diminishing returns, Wicksteed proceeds to the importance of increasing returns to scale of output: "If you increase *all* the factors in a suitable proportion you will in many cases be able to secure double the product without more than doubling any of the factors and without as much as doubling some of them" (p. 529). This condition "will generally be found" in manufacturing (p. 528); agriculture, particularly wheat, is also an example (p. 534). And as if intent on astonishing the reader, he states that virtually *all* industries are subject to decreasing costs (pp. 531, 534)! This novel theory requires proof. What has Wicksteed to offer?

The explanation of decreasing costs from plant expansion is not adequate. There is only a suggestion that certain economies appear with large scale production (p. 529). A man may require one wagon for a 50-acre tract, and only two wagons for a 200-acre tract. This is a clear case of indivisibility of a resource (wagons),[2] and lack of substitutionality of other resources, and it offers absolutely no support for the sweeping generalization to which Wicksteed immediately proceeds:

[1] Cf., *infra*, Chap. XII.

[2] Which undermines the axiomatic nature of the law of diminishing returns, it may be noted in passing.

> No limit seems yet to have been reached to the possibility of economising in one direction or another as the bulk of any industry increases. It is always possible, at every stage, to introduce some new process of specializing or division of labour, and so to effect some new economy for which the industry was not ripe until it had reached its present dimensions (p. 529).

This analysis obviously rests on indivisibilities of certain of the productive resources. While such indivisibilities do exist and in certain cases may be of great importance (*e.g.*, public utilities), there is little empirical evidence for ascribing wide scope to them. Indivisibilities, moreover, will sink in importance with the increase of the size of the firm; they are not "without limit."

Wicksteed's remaining observations on economies of scale are of variable merit. His sharp criticism of historical curves of the cost of production deserves commendation (pp. 536–37). We may accept also his strictures on the use of the "particular expenses" curve of costs (pp. 538 ff.). Contrariwise, he fails to note the importance for the theory of competition of whether decreasing costs accrue to the firm or to the industry—and he says this is in fact a matter of indifference (pp. 529–30)! Finally, Wicksteed emphasizes the limitations of partial equilibrium analysis (pp. 518, 545), and yet inconsistently applies his theory of economies of large scale production to major world crops (pp. 533–34).

The Theory of Distribution

Wicksteed secures an important position in the history of economic thought primarily through his contributions to the theory of distribution. He gave the first impetus to the study—and to much of the correct solution—of the basic problem, the general marginal productivity theory. His chief work on this subject is the *Co-ordination of the Laws of Distribution* (1894), which gave rise to a controversy so extensive and important as to deserve a separate chapter in the present study.[1]

In the present chapter, therefore, only such portions of the general marginal productivity theory will be anticipated as are necessary for the coherent treatment of the analyses of more detailed distribution problems. The chief topics to be discussed here are Wicksteed's criticism of the classification of factors of production by the classical economists, and his theory of capital and interest.

The Classification of Productive Factors

The tripartite division of productive factors into land, labor, and capital is categorically rejected. In the light of his general theory of cost and substitution this attitude is almost necessary, certainly not astonishing. If innumerable varieties of land are substituted for producible resources, and if "land" can be used for numerous purposes, all analytical distinctions between it and other resources disappear. This is the gist of Wicksteed's argument (pp. 365–67; also pp. 290, 535, 540, 687).

The general argument, which is of course valid as he applies it, is supplemented by several less important considerations. The ill-guided attempt to differentiate land on historical grounds is refuted: "What we mean by land in practical life is something which admittedly consists very largely of the accumulated result of human effort . . ." (p. 365).[2] A second basis for criticism of the received theory is that it is "in flagrant and irreconcilable contradiction with the usages of language" (p. 366; also

[1] *Infra*, Chap. XII. Most of the argument of the *Co-ordination* was later restated in non-mathematical terms as the chapter on rent in the *Commonsense* (Bk. II, Chap. vi).

[2] In the case of urban land, the capital has been expended "not upon the site itself but upon the surrounding areas." Cf. also pp. 573–74.

pp. 573–74). This point is too familiar to detain us. The third ground, the uselessness of the distinction even if it is true, is of more interest. Wicksteed's stand is that even an empirically valid classification would be of no advantage, since "it would throw no light on the laws of the market" (p. 366). This is a half-truth. It must be admitted that the Ricardian theory cast more shadow than light on theoretical price relationships, but if land were (relatively) fixed in supply,[1] as was assumed, the social implications of this fixity would be more than important enough to justify the classification. In Ricardo's England this was probably a legitimate assumption, and its implication for social policy was so strong, the writer submits, that its formal weakness (in a science then full of formal errors) was not important enough to justify its abandonment.

Two further aspects of Wicksteed's discussion of land remain to be noted. He attempts a mistaken refutation of the notion that because rent is not paid on marginal land, therefore it does not enter into the cost of production.[2] Wicksteed says:

> The argument, such as it is, would of course apply just as much to labour, raw material, or capital, as to land. For some wheat less has been paid in wages than for other wheat of the same quality; it would follow that if cost of production determines exchange value, wages are not part of the cost of production (p. 541).

This argument carries no conviction that rent is a cost, because it ignores the central thesis of the Ricardian theory, the fixity of the supply of land.

[1] Wicksteed denies the truth of this assumption (p. 533).

[2] The identical argument was previously raised by Herbert M. Thompson in his very able but neglected work, *The Theory of Wages* (London, 1892), but Thompson properly restricted the argument to a proof that rent enters the price, not the cost, of the commodity produced.

The final excellence in Wicksteed's treatment is his penetrating criticism of the "residual" concept of rent. The practice of labeling as "rent" any economic quantity which is left under a curve once a rectangle has been inscribed, has been truly unfortunate (pp. 568–70). And if one residual is formally correct, there is no justification for the practice of defining two or more distributive shares as each in turn a residual (pp. 571–72).

Labor

The chapter on earnings of labor is of little theoretical interest, although it contains many judicious observations of fact (Bk. I, Chap. viii). Labor services are in general rewarded according to their marginal significance, exactly as with other productive resources (thus, p. 323). The limitations on this theory due to the restricted mobility of laborers under a system of division of labor have already been discussed above.

Certain miscellaneous topics nevertheless deserve at least passing mention. There is considerable emphasis upon the perishability of labor in contrast with other resources: "the power of rendering services flows to waste as fast as it accrues unless it is directly applied, or embodied in material commodities" (p. 320; also pp. 320–22). This is largely true, but Wicksteed errs in holding that this peculiarity of labor renders it similar only to "the most swiftly and irrevocably perishable commodities." Any resource is to some extent wasted if it is not employed, and all durable resources are really identical with labor in this respect. The land that yields no crop this year is not fundamentally different from the laborer who does not work this month. It is suggested that the qualities of managerial ability are so diverse and so difficult to measure that there is an unusually large speculative element in their reward (pp. 328–29). No attempt is made to introduce profits into the analysis, however; the manager's reward is fixed by the same "underlying principles."

The Theory of Capital

Wicksteed's theory of capital is of very uneven quality. It, more than any other section in his theoretical structure, has lost rigor without gaining comprehensiveness or lucidity in the process of popularization. There is a noticeable failure to appraise the importance of the elements of his theory: fundamental aspects are skimmed over, and minor points are belabored until the reader cries for deliverance. These are criticisms of presentation rather than content, but their weight is none the less great.

A general feature in Wicksteed's exposition may, in contrast, be strongly commended. He presents one of the earliest and clearest proofs that all contracts of hire are fundamentally identical with loan contracts. The lender who secures $5.00 each year for the use of $100 may renew the loan at the end of each year. In that case it is irrelevant whether the transaction is called a loan at interest or the hire per year of the commodity in which the money is invested. Since goods are exactly comparable with money, and as a rule the loan is expended on goods, it is clear that any contract of hire can be translated into terms of a contract of loan (pp. 275–76, 310–14).[1] Since all hire or lending is in essence the fractional sale of the commodity in question, it can be only a matter of convenience which form the contract

[1] The argument is, however, inaccurate in two respects: indestructibility is the fundamental characteristic of the loan good; and, as a corollary of this, the rental rates in hire contracts must always be greater than the rate of interest in otherwise identical loan contracts.

takes. And since rent is only a particular form of hire, it is also basically identical with interest (pp. 311–12).

We may turn now to the theory of capital and interest. The important topics are the accumulation of capital, consumption loans, and production loans.

Savings and the rate of interest.—The theory of saving is essentially unoriginal. The term "saving" is extended to include investment, as the following summary statement indicates: ". . . saving seems to consist in (1) increasing our stock of relatively permanent or slowly maturing commodities by the application of resources and efforts which might have been applied to the increase of our stock of relatively perishable or quickly maturing ones, and (2) deflecting energies and resources to relatively indirect means of securing our ends (by embodying them in tools and apparatus) from relatively direct means of securing them (by employing the tools and apparatus we already have)" (p. 283). As the quotation indicates, Wicksteed does not distinguish a *flow* of services from the *source* of services; he speaks of capital goods as both durable sources of services and the services themselves in any given period of time. The rate of accumulation of capital is determined chiefly by "the providence or improvidence of the members of a community, together with the amount and the distribution [ownership] of its resources" (p. 307).

Wicksteed is also conventional in his concept of saving, the exchange of present for future *wealth*, *i.e.*, the deferring of consumption. His entire analysis runs in terms of saving now and consuming later; he speaks of the postponement, not of the abstinence, involved in saving (pp. 279–80, 283, 293–99, etc.).[1] This misconception of

[1] Thus he speaks (p. 279) of "the market between wealth in the present and wealth in the future."

the saving process is probably due to Jevons, whose influence on Wicksteed was great.

A final element in this part of Wicksteed's theory may be criticized briefly. The supply of capital—or advances—is set up as a coordinate factor in the determination of the interest rate (p. 292), and, indeed, at times it is difficult to avoid the implication that the supply conditions exercise the dominant influence on the interest rate.[1] Wicksteed is too vague to be successfully convicted of ignoring the difference between the flow of savings and the stock of capital, but he is certainly open to criticism for his failure to recognize that the elasticity of demand is relatively high for capital under a given technology and the elasticity of the real supply is very low, and that technological advances are very influential in shifting the demand curve for capital. It may also be noted that there is an inconsistency in asserting both the importance of accumulation and the fact that it is an act of postponement. Single acts of postponement will have only a minor effect on the supply of capital; if saving is to influence greatly the long-run interest rate by creating a substantial stock of capital, it must involve true "abstinence."

Consumption loans.—One of the best discussions in economic literature of the origin and rationale of consumption loans is that presented by Wicksteed (pp. 268–80). The general situation in which consumption loans appear is succinctly stated: "It may be a matter of vital importance [to a person] to bring the rate at which his command of commodities accrues into some kind of correspondence with the irregular way in which the neces-

[1] Cf. esp. pp. 309–10. Thus (p. 310), "it is well to observe that with increasing intelligence, integrity, and providence [all supply factors] we have no means of fixing on any definite limit above zero to the fall of interest."

sity for providing for his wants asserts itself" (p. 268). The problem of equalizing income and expenditure streams may be illustrated by the case of expensive, durable articles of consumption. Clothing, furniture, and houses are cited as typical expenditure items which require unusually large expenditures at the time of acquisition (pp. 268 ff.). Sometimes the discrepancy between income and expenditure streams may be removed by the use of hire (pp. 108–9), but where ownership is desired (or often, as with personal clothing, is imperative), consumption loans must be used.

If the demand schedule for consumption loans is more readily visualized,[1] nevertheless the supply schedule of such loans is "equally conceivable" (p. 269). The individual who possesses $1000 but has no prospect of earnings in the future will be glad to exchange his capital sum for an income of some given duration. If necessary, indeed, he might accept less than an equivalent income in exchange (*i.e.*, a negative rate of interest), since it would be expensive to store many of the things required in the future, and many articles (*e.g.*, perishable foods) would be completely excluded.

There are, then, at any given time, some people who value present goods relatively highly and others who value future services more highly, the future being some fairly definite date or period—a sufficient condition for exchange to take place. It would be better to restate this exchange of goods in terms of service streams: some people prefer shorter (and larger) service streams; others desire longer (and smaller) service streams. Wicksteed is very ambiguous concerning the probable rate of interest. In the section on interest, he consistently implies that a small premium (*i.e.*, a positive interest rate) will

[1] The presence of the prodigal is also noted (p. 286).

emerge (pp. 270–76, 280).[1] Yet no explicit reason is given for this conclusion, other than the intimation that almost all people prefer present goods to future goods. This assumption, which is Böhm-Bawerk's "second" ground, is hardly in keeping with Wicksteed's earlier and very convincing assertion:

> Ordinary prudence estimates the significance of a unit [of a commodity] in the future just as high as that of a unit in the present. . . . In a word, the fact of remoteness or proximity should not, and within limits does not, in itself affect our estimate of the significance of things that are really of even and continuous importance to us (p. 113; also pp. 295–99).

Applied to a stationary economy,[2] this argument could hardly lead to other than a zero interest rate on consumption loans, or a rate fluctuating on both sides of zero.

Production loans and the rate of interest.—The analysis in the *Commonsense* of production loans is definitely inferior to the theory in Wicksteed's earlier essay, "Jevons's *Theory of Political Economy*." The discussion is so greatly simplified that there is little possibility of either originality or error. The productiveness of capital, for example, is described briefly and illustrated by such painfully familiar and completely misleading cases as the fisherman's net (pp. 281–85). The productiveness of capital goods is subject to the usual limitation: "Successive increments of tools and appliances, after a certain point, while they still increase the efficiency and economy of efforts and resources, will do so at a decreasing rate" (p. 284). In measuring the net productivity of a capital

[1] " . . . under existing conditions there is a premium on present as against future wealth." This observation, based on the market, is a *non sequitur*. Cf., *infra*, p. 102, n. 2.

[2] Of which Wicksteed is certainly speaking; cf. pp. 280, 281.

instrument it is necessary to deduct the charges necessary for maintenance and replacement of the instrument (p. 289). If adequate allowance is made, the machine becomes truly "immortal" in an economic sense. Its perpetual future income, whose gross total is of course infinite, will nevertheless be a definite sum, due to the element of discount.[1]

The industrial demand for capital is then easily deduced. The business man will borrow until the return on the last increment of capital is just enough to pay the current interest charge on that increment of capital.[2] If this industrial demand is added to that for consumption loans, the total demand schedule of the economy for capital is secured (pp. 285–87). There is no discussion of the relative importance of these components of the total demand or of their relative elasticities. Competition will serve to bring the marginal significance of capital (*i.e.*, the interest rate) to equality in all possible fields of use (p. 288).

[1] Wicksteed places another limit on the value of perpetual future incomes: the inability of individuals to forecast, and, indeed to appreciate, the remote future (pp. 284–85, 298–99).

[2] The discussion is very loose; Wicksteed illustrates this marginal productivity theory with increments of £10,000.

Chapter IV

ALFRED MARSHALL

ALFRED MARSHALL ranks so high among the greatest figures in Anglo-Saxon economics that it is still almost presumptuous to praise his accomplishments, and indeed there is little need for doing so.[1] Perhaps, however, there is now some danger that his contributions may be underrated, for in the full half-century which has elapsed since the *Principles* first appeared (and it was never revised on fundamentals), economic theory has gained much in rigor, in structural consolidation, and in symmetry. A true appreciation is best secured by comparing the *Principles* with the standard works on political economy current in 1890. Marshall was almost incomparably superior to his immediate predecessors and his early contemporaries in the profundity and originality of his thought, in his consistency, and in the breadth of his vision.

The present chapter assumes Marshall's pre-eminence to be unquestioned. Here the chief purpose will be that of criticism, and only secondarily will the general theory of production and distribution be summarized. This treatment seems justified by the wide familiarity with his work. No attempt will be made to discuss the numerous commentaries. On the other hand, there is no need to reproduce Parsons' path-breaking analysis of

[1] Cf. J. M. Keynes' classic memoir, "Alfred Marshall," reprinted in *Essays in Biography* (New York, 1933), pp. 150–266, as well as in *Memorials of Alfred Marshall* (London, 1925), pp. 1–65.

Marshall's philosophical preconceptions and their influence on his doctrines;[1] nor to do more than refer to Robbins' acute criticisms of the concept of the representative firm.[2]

Before turning to an examination of Marshall's theory of production and distribution, however, something of an explanation is in order. In his case it is not simple to apply the frame of reference which is appropriate to every other economist treated in the present survey. It may be well to discuss briefly two important characteristics of Marshall's work which, from the present viewpoint, serve to diminish his contribution to theoretical economics.

A first generalization is that Marshall was so concerned with historical economic developments that he had relatively small patience with the theoretical economics of a stationary state. Almost every important subject in the *Principles* receives its exposition in terms of evolutionary change. Diminishing return is considered primarily in connection with the growth of population relative to land; and the theory of productive organization is well-nigh exclusively historical. External economies and his theory of long-run distribution equilibrium may be cited as further examples. No one can question the importance of historical studies, nor is it easy to deny that Marshall's treatment of difficult historical problems is masterful—vastly superior to the "analysis" of the typical economic historian. But the question of expediency is basic. Was it expedient to attempt to achieve (as Marshall did) a high degree of realism, without first establishing the very

[1] Talcott Parsons, "Wants and Activities in Marshall," *Quarterly Journal of Economics*, XLVI (1931–32), 101–40; "Economics and Sociology: Marshall in Relation to the Thought of His Time," *ibid.*, 316–47.

[2] L. Robbins, "The Representative Firm," *Economic Journal*, XXXVIII (1928), 387–404.

much simpler theory of stationary economics? And was it expedient to mix inextricably historical and stationary analysis in a work which was path-breaking, especially in the latter field? The writer is convinced that both questions should be answered in the negative.

The other important characteristic, from our viewpoint, is Marshall's veneration for the classical economists. He was probably the most loyal of all the great economists. One side of this attitude is shown in his extremely generous interpretations of the statements of his predecessors. It is not necessary to debate here the desirability of such an attitude, but in his case there appeared a corollary which is certainly questionable: he had a pronounced tendency so to phrase his own doctrines as to minimize the change from the classical tradition. This placed a heavy burden on his treatise; his unsatisfactory treatment of diminishing returns, the writer submits, is due largely to this desire for continuity of tradition. And in terminology,[1] capital theory, and the marginal productivity theory, the effects are again noticeable and regrettable.[2]

The Theory of Production

THE NATURE OF COSTS

Two general types of costs, it is well known, are recognized in the *Principles*. The first and more fundamental type is "real" costs—the psychological costs which must

[1] Only Marshall would say, "All the distinctions in which the word Productive is used are very thin and have a certain air of unreality. It would hardly be worth while to introduce them now: but they have a long history; and it is probably better that they should dwindle gradually out of use, rather than be suddenly discarded" (*Principles of Economics*, p. 67 n.).

[2] The present discussion is based primarily on the eighth edition of the *Principles* (London, 1920), to which all references are made unless otherwise

be compensated if a given productive service is to be available:[1]

> While demand is based on the desire to obtain commodities, supply depends mainly on the overcoming of the unwillingness to undergo "discommodities." These fall generally under two heads:—labour, and the sacrifice involved in putting off consumption . . . (p. 140).[2]
>
> . . . the price required to call forth the exertion necessary for producing any given amount of a commodity, may be called the *supply price* for that amount . . . (p. 142).

The detailed analysis of these psychological costs may better be deferred to the section on Marshall's distribution theory, since "real" costs receive only verbal attention in his theory of production.

The relationship between real and money costs may be indicated briefly. Marshall defines money costs as the payments necessary to secure the painful exertions of laboring and waiting (pp. 142, 339, 362). The correspondence between the two costs "is never to be assumed lightly"; however, "If the purchasing power of money, in terms of effort has remained about constant, and if the rate of remuneration for waiting has remained about constant, then the money measure of costs corresponds to the real costs . . ." (p. 350).

The proof that real costs and money costs are propor-

noted. It was impossible to attempt even a rough collation of editions, although certain significant changes from the first edition were traced through subsequent revisions. I am indebted to The Macmillan Company for permission to quote from this work.

[1] The most frequently quoted sentence is doubtless the following: "The exertions of all the different kinds of labour that are directly or indirectly involved in making it; together with the abstinences or rather the waitings required for saving the capital used in making it: all these efforts and sacrifices together will be called the *real cost of production* of the commodity" (pp. 338–39).

[2] Land is excluded, except in certain special cases, since its supply of services available for production is assumed to be fixed. Cf., *infra*, p. 89.

tional requires much more than the constancy of money income in terms of effort. It requires that the money costs (and prices) of all commodities be proportional to their marginal disutilities of labor, and also the condition of equal earnings in alternative occupations at the margin. This necessarily implies that each laborer is on the margin of transference between all occupations at the same wage or that, among other things, all laborers have identical disutility functions. Otherwise it is impossible to infer, from the equality of wage costs (to take only one element of cost) of two commodities, that each represents the same amount of disutility of labor.

Marshall does not consider this problem, which arises primarily out of division of labor; rather he considers at some length the difficulties in securing a correspondence between "net advantages" and earnings of the various occupations.[1] One could find little to criticize in his classic presentation of the difficulties in securing such a correspondence; it manifests his usual sound judgment, interpretive power, and great factual knowledge. His conclusion on this point is also acceptable: "Since human beings grow up slowly and are slowly worn out, and parents in choosing an occupation for their children must as a rule look forward a whole generation, changes in demand take a longer time to work out their full effects on supply in the case of human agents than of most kinds of material appliances for production; and a specially long period is required in the case of labour to give full play to the economic forces which tend to bring about a normal adjustment between demand and supply" (p. 661). But surely the next sentence is a *non sequitur:*

[1] Bk. VI, Chaps. iii, iv, v. Net advantages are defined as "the true reward which an occupation offers to labour," calculated by "deducting the money value of all its disadvantages from that of all its advantages" (p. 73).

"Thus on the whole the *money* cost of any kind of labour to the employer corresponds in the long run fairly well to the *real* cost of producing that labour" (p. 661). Marshall has stated a necessary, but by no means a sufficient, condition for the validity of a real cost theory.

The doctrine of alternative or opportunity cost is not explicitly mentioned by Marshall. The idea of competition of various uses for given resources is, of course, fundamental to his treatise and it may well be described as the underlying theme of the entire discussion in Book V.[1]

SUBSTITUTION AND DIMINISHING RETURN

The general theory of substitution had best be deferred to Chapter XII on the marginal productivity theory. Marshall's statement of the theory of substitution is well known: Under the pressure of competition and the desire to maximize profits, the entrepreneur will substitute cheaper for more expensive resources (where cheapness and expensiveness are measured in terms of product divided by cost).

The treatment of the theory of diminishing return is, on the other hand, one of the most disappointing parts of the *Principles*. Marshall's discussion portrays, first of all, the usual careless confusion of incremental and proportional diminishing returns. The doctrine is mentioned most often in Book IV, Chapter III, on the return to land. The law of diminishing return, in its "final statement," reads: "the application of increased capital and labour to land will add a less than proportionate amount to the produce raised" (p. 153). This inappropriate definition is repeated many times.[2] On the other hand,

[1] The theorem of equalization of returns is applied specifically to labor (pp. 511–14, 547 ff.), to land (p. 418), and to capital (p. 591).

[2] Thus, pp. 150, 151 (twice), 153 (thrice), 440, 651, etc. The grounds for preferring the incremental form are discussed in the next chapter.

the law is frequently defined in its appropriate, incremental form, as in the sentence immediately following the last quoted sentence (p. 153).[1]

The second defect in the exposition is his failure to grasp the relationship between the law of substitution and that of diminishing return. The former, it is seen, is "linked up" with the latter (p. 356), but in fact diminishing return is only an aspect of substitution. Diminishing return arises out of the fact that resource *A* is not a perfect substitute for *B*, and that *A* becomes an increasingly less efficient substitute as the ratio of *A* to *B* increases.

Closely related to the second criticism, the third point is Marshall's tendency to restrict the law of diminishing return to agriculture, and there to view it primarily as an historical law.[2] In speaking of the law in other branches of industry, he speaks of the "excessive application of resources or of energies in any given direction" (p. 356; also pp. 169, 170, 407–9, 537). Scarcely ever does he refer to diminishing return to a factor, except when applied to land, without using some modifier—"inappropriately," "too much," or the like. Marshall doubtless knew of the generality of the law of diminishing return, witness his comment regarding the hypothetical meteoric stones in his discussion of rent: "But the more intensively they were applied, the less net return would be reaped from each additional service forced from them; thus illustrating the law that the intensive working, not only of land, but of every other appliance of production is likely to yield a diminishing return if pressed far enough" (p. 416; also pp. 168–69). As is too often the case, Marshall perceives the correct answer, but states

[1] Also pp. 149, 157, 166 (twice), 168, 170, 680, etc. Both definitions will also be found in the earlier *Economics of Industry* (2d ed., London, 1881), pp. 22 and note, 83 n.

[2] Cf. also, *infra*, p. 87.

it in a form and place calculated to conceal it from all but the already informed reader.

With regard to the "law of increasing return," Marshall deserves even more severe criticism. The "law" is stated as follows: "An increase of labour and capital leads generally to improved organization, which increases the efficiency of the work of labour and capital" (p. 318). It is obvious that this "law" is not at all parallel with that of diminishing return, for in the former case *all* factors of production are increased, and in the latter case all resources but one are held constant. It is thoroughly misleading, then, to speak, as Marshall does, of "the straining of the tendencies towards increasing and diminishing return against one another" (p. 319, margin); the two are distinct generalizations. The one is an empirical fact (if and when true), while the other is a logical prerequisite for the very existence of the problem of production.

EXTERNAL ECONOMIES

Of the many concepts which Marshall has contributed to economic analysis, none is in more urgent need of reexamination than the celebrated distinction between external and internal economies. For it is the existence of external economies, and not, as Robertson has suggested,[1] that of the representative firm, which permits reconciliation of competition and decreasing long-run average costs. As the subsequent discussion will show, external economies receive very inadequate analysis from Marshall, despite the obvious importance of their role in his theory of production.

[1] "Increasing Returns and the Representative Firm," *Economic Journal*, XL (1930), 86. There is reason to believe, however, that Marshall would agree with Robertson. Compare Marshall's theory of entrepreneurship, *infra*, p. 78.

External economies are defined as those economies which are "dependent on the general development of the industry," in contrast with internal economies, which are "dependent on the resources of the individual houses of business engaged in it [the industry], on their organization and the efficiency of their management" (p. 266). Internal economies are therefore those secured within the firm (which Marshall fails to distinguish from the plant); all other "economies arising from an increase in the scale of production of any kind of goods" are clearly implied to be external economies. The latter category is therefore residual, and, as a consequence, the two groups must exhaust economies of large scale production as a whole.

The precise nature of external economies is most difficult to ascertain. Two general types are discussed in the *Principles:* [1]

> (i) Economies in the use of specialized skill and machinery . . . which depend on the aggregate volume of production of the kind in the neighborhood (p. 265).
>
> (ii) Others again, especially those connected with the growth of knowledge and the progress of the arts, depend chiefly on the aggregate volume of production in the whole civilized world (p. 266).[2]

The first group, that arising from localization of industry, seems to form the chief part of external economies of an industry, at least for relatively short periods.

[1] The discussions in Marshall's other work add nothing new. Cf. *Elements of the Economics of Industry* (3d ed., London, 1899), pp. 150, 179; *Industry and Trade* (2d ed., London, 1921), pp. 167, 187.

[2] These two categories are inconsistent: the former depends on geographic specialization; the latter depends on "world" production. Neither of these categories is defined satisfactorily. Marshall does not consider the difference between increased localization, the industry remaining constant in size, and increased localization, the industry growing. Again, it is not clear whether the increase in world production refers to the industry alone, the industry relative to all other industries, or all industries as a whole.

Indeed, in re-defining external economies, Marshall places exclusive emphasis on localization: external economies of division of labor are "obtained by the concentration of large numbers of small businesses of a similar kind in the same locality . . ." (p. 277; also p. 166). The advantages of localization are summarized as follows:

> When an industry has thus chosen a locality for itself, it is likely to stay there long: so great are the advantages which people following the same skilled trade get from near neighbourhood to one another. The mysteries of the trade become no mysteries; but are as it were in the air, and children learn many of them unconsciously. Good work is rightly appreciated, inventions and improvements in machinery, in processes and the general organization of the business have their merits promptly discussed; if one man starts a new idea, it is taken up by others and combined with suggestions of their own; and thus it becomes the source of further new ideas. And presently subsidiary trades grow up in the neighborhood, supplying it with implements and materials, organizing its traffic, and in many ways conducing to the economy of its material (p. 271).

In short, the major external economies of localization are cross-fertilization of ideas, the development of auxiliary and subsidiary industries, and the availability of skilled labor.

But external economies may rise from other sources as well. The growth of knowledge and invention has already been cited. This general factor of "progress" is re-emphasized in Marshall's third definition: external economies are "those dependent on the general development of the industry" (p. 314).[1] The central notion, it seems, is "the growth of correlated branches of industry which mutually assist one another, perhaps being con-

[1] The broadest definition of all, however, says that external economies "result from the general progress of the industrial environment" (p. 441).

centrated in the same localities, but anyhow availing themselves of the modern facilities for communication offered by steam transport, by the telegraph and by the printing press" (p. 317; also p. 441).

Marshall's treatment of external economies has been widely accepted, and only in recent years has the concept begun to be examined critically.[1] No exhaustive analysis can be made here of the many complicated problems involved in rendering precise the concept of external economies, but certain leading issues demand consideration.

At the outset it should be emphasized that Marshall's external economies form an essentially historical category. The development of knowledge and invention, cross-fertilization,[2] the emergence of subsidiary firms to exploit by-products and to supply equipment, the accumulation of skilled labor, all are characterized by *growth*.[3] Indeed the notion of external economies may

[1] Perhaps the first reference of importance is D. H. MacGregor, *Industrial Combination* (1906), reprinted in London School Series of Scarce Works, No. 1 (1935), pp. 20 ff. MacGregor's discussion is elaborative rather than critical.

Professor F. H. Knight was apparently the first to question the importance of external economies. Cf. "Fallacies in the Interpretation of Social Cost" (1924), reprinted in *The Ethics of Competition* (New York, 1935), p. 229. L. Robbins raises the same criticism in "The Representative Firm," *op. cit.*, p. 398.

Piero Sraffa opened a new series of criticisms in his article, "The Laws of Return Under Competitive Conditions," *Economic Journal*, XXXVI (1926), 537 ff. From this source has stemmed an extensive English discussion, primarily in the *Economic Journal* between 1927 and 1933. This recent discussion is too detailed and wide-ranging to permit consideration in the present study.

[2] This factor is due primarily to imperfection of knowledge, and will not be considered in the present discussion, which is restricted to perfect competition, in the rigorous theoretical sense.

[3] Marshall's dictum that external and internal economies both increase with the expansion of the industry (pp. 318, 393) is suggestive of his own historical outlook on this question. Compare, also, the remark, "An industry which yields an increasing return, is nearly sure to be growing, and

be a useful interpretive tool in economic history. For the purpose of modern theoretical analysis, however, the question must be raised: Do external economies have any importance in a stationary economy?

The central issue is: what external economies are compatible with partial equilibrium (*i.e.*, Marshall's) analysis? The analysis of one industry by this method presupposes that the cost and demand conditions of other industries remain fixed or are only negligibly influenced by changes in the industry under consideration. This assumption throws out a portion of Marshall's external economies, for it is clearly illegitimate to assume the cost or demand conditions of other industries to remain unaffected by "the modern facilities for communication offered by steam transport, by the telegraph and by the printing press." [1] As Sraffa has pointed out,[2] partial equilibrium analysis is completely applicable only to those economies external to the firm but internal to the industry.[3] Here, he says, "nothing or virtually nothing," is to be found.[4]

Two possible escapes from this apparent impasse suggest themselves. The first lies in the rejection, at this point, of partial equilibrium analysis, resorting instead

therefore to be acquiring new economies of production on a large scale" (p. 469 n). Marshall does not indicate whether the industry in question is growing absolutely, or in relation to other industries.

[1] The definition of an industry is, of course, crucial. If an industry be defined as the group of firms producing a single homogeneous commodity, industries producing related commodities certainly will be affected. If industries producing related commodities are lumped together, the difficulty is only postponed, for where do commodities cease to be related? And if economies could be secured by joint production, why does this not come about?

[2] *Op. cit.*, pp. 537 ff.

[3] There is, of course, the exceptional case where external economies are shared by other industries which are not closely related (through substitution of products) with the industry in question. It seems impossible to ascertain the importance of this exception.

[4] *Ibid.*, p. 540

to general equilibrium analysis.[1] This expedient is certainly appropriate to the treatment of many broad economic problems, although the notorious difficulties of application of the general equilibrium theory should undermine overly sanguine hopes of thus securing useful conclusions quickly or easily. This alternative may be passed over without further comment, since it involves essentially the abandonment of Marshall's technique of analysis.

The second escape lies in restricting partial equilibrium analysis to those economies which are external to the firm and internal to the industry, recognizing the restricted scope of economies of this type. While such economies, as Sraffa says, do not appear to be important, some cases can be found if partial equilibrium is not too strictly defined. Professor Viner, who has offered a partial defense of Marshall's theory,[2] offers the case of laborers (and this might be true also of capitalists) who have a preference, rational or otherwise, for working in a large industry.[3]

Granting the existence of such external economies, it is important to note that several rather diverse types may be isolated and illustrated. Without attempting an exhaustive classification or analysis, three types will be considered.

One of the most important of the external economies comes from the purchase of materials or the sale of products and by-products to subsidiary firms which are oper-

[1] Where, incidentally, external economies have never made an appearance, probably because they need not be introduced *explicitly* into the formal system of equations of general equilibrium. That is not to say, of course, that such economies cannot be introduced.

[2] Cf. "Cost Curves and Supply Curves," *Zeitschrift für Nationalökonomie*, III (1932), 38–39; "The Doctrine of Comparative Costs," *Weltwirtschaftliches Archiv*, XXXVI (1932), 396–98. Haberler follows Viner in his *Theory of International Trade* (*English ed.*, London, 1936), pp. 206–8.

[3] "Cost Curves," *op. cit.*, p. 39.

ating subject to decreasing costs.[1] It is probably this type that gave rise to Professor Knight's stricture:

> . . . the doctrine of "external economies" . . . surely rests upon a misconception. Economies may be "external" to a particular establishment or technical production unit, but they are not external to the industry if they affect its efficiency. The portion of the productive process carried on in a particular unit is an accidental consideration. External economies in one business unit are internal economies in some other, within the industry. Any branch or stage in the creation of a product which offers continuously a chance for technical economies with increase in the scale of operations must eventuate either in a monopoly or in leaving the tendency behind and establishing the normal relation of increasing cost with increasing size.[2]

The cogency of this argument is not to be denied: firms in a subsidiary "industry" [3] operating under decreasing costs will tend to be monopolized unless they expand to a region of increasing costs. It is still possible that the monopolistic subsidiary firms will have decreasing supply prices, although decreasing costs are not sufficient to insure this.[4] There is a strong inducement, as perhaps the quotation from Professor Knight suggests, for firms to take over such monopolized subsidiary industries and appropriate any monopoly profits, leading to "vertical integration." [5] This category, to conclude, really does

[1] Cf. Viner, "The Doctrine of Comparative Costs," *op. cit.;* also his *Studies in the Theory of International Trade* (New York, 1937), esp. pp. 481–82.

[2] *The Ethics of Competition, op. cit.*, p. 229.

[3] This raises again the difficulty, discussed by Sraffa, of what an industry may properly include in partial equilibrium analysis. If the subsidiary firms supply only the industry in question, however, it should be permissible to consider them as internal to the industry.

[4] The elasticity of the demand curve may be such that prices are increased by increases in demand, even if marginal costs are falling.

[5] Marshall may have had this in mind when he said, "In spite of the aid which subsidiary industries can give to small manufactures, where many in the same branch of trade are collected in one neighborhood, they are still

not require an analytical concept such as "external economies," since it turns on economies which are necessarily internal to some production unit.

A second type of external economy consists of those situations where the production functions of various firms in an industry are technically related. Thus, a coal mine may find that the amount of water to be pumped from its shafts decreases as the number of mines operated in the neighborhood increases.[1] In such a case economies external to one firm are not internal to any other firm. Nevertheless, this type of economy will usually be converted into an internal economy if the industry is monopolized, and may (or may not, depending in part on questions of technique) lead to combinations, mergers, etc.

We will note finally a third, rather amorphous, type of external economy which may be characterized as "institutional." Professor Viner's example of laborers' preference for a large industry illustrates this case very well. Such economies are in a certain sense inappropriable: the amount of them secured by one firm cannot be increased by vertical or horizontal integration, and accordingly they presumably have only a remote influence on the size of the bargaining unit, other than through their effect on the relative prices of productive services.

Although Marshall places considerable emphasis on the first type of external economy, he seems to reason pri-

placed under a great disadvantage by the growing variety and expensiveness of machinery" (p. 279). His subsequent argument does not follow the analysis in the text, but there does not seem to be any important reason (aside from cases where it is not feasible from a technological viewpoint) why subsidiary firms could not usually take over "bottle-neck" processes which require machinery beyond the reach of small firms. Cf. *Economics of Industry* (2d ed.), p. 53.

[1] The corresponding diseconomy is illustrated by the familiar situation where a common oil pool is being exploited by competing firms.

marily from the third type. It is difficult to understand otherwise why he virtually ignored the question of the relation of external economies to the size and nature of the bargaining unit. Marshall's concept of the "representative firm," which assumed rather than analyzed the equilibrium of the firm, may well provide the explanation for his neglect of this fundamental problem.

It is difficult to pass final judgment on the theory of external economies. Marshall's chief purpose in creating the category, the writer submits, was to explain the great historical reduction in production costs, which were associated with increases of output, size of plant, and size of firm, and which to a large extent were *not* accompanied by monopolization. As a tool in the explanation of economic history, the doctrine of external economies (but in a different form than proposed) seems to have considerable serviceability. As a device for the elucidation of relative prices, it seems to have a very restricted scope.

INTERNAL ECONOMIES

If Marshall's treatment of external economies be judged ambiguous, certainly the same criticism is appropriate to his treatment of internal economies. In the latter case the difficulty is of another sort, however. Internal economies are emphasized so strongly that one finds difficulty in explaining the very existence of competition.[1] It will be well to consider first the nature of internal economies.

Internal economies are "those dependent on the resources of the individual houses of business engaged in it

[1] Marshall clearly sees the incompatibility between decreasing costs and competition (pp. 395, 549 n., 805, 808 n.). He erroneously accuses Cournot of overlooking this incompatibility (p. 450 n.). Cf. A. Cournot, *The Mathematical Principles of the Theory of Wealth* (Bacon trans., New York, 1929), p. 91.

[the industry], on their organization and the efficiency of their management" (p. 266; also pp. 277, 314). All of Book IV, Chapter XI ("Production on a Large Scale") is devoted to the discussion of internal economies. We may distinguish several important types of such economies:[1]

i. Economy of materials, or the utilization of by-products, which is "rapidly losing importance" (p. 278).[2]

ii. Economy of machinery:
   a. "In a large establishment there are often many expensive machines each made specially for one small use," which a small manufacturer cannot afford to use (pp. 279–80).
   b. Larger machines are more efficient (p. 282 n.).
   c. Small manufacturers are sometimes ignorant of the best types of machinery to use in their businesses (p. 280).[3]
   d. Small manufacturers cannot undertake expensive experiments (pp. 280–81).

   In certain stable industries, *e.g.*, textiles, the economy of machinery has virtually disappeared, however (p. 281).

iii. Economy in the purchase and sale of materials:
   a. In addition to securing discounts for quantity purchases, the large firm "pays low freights and saves on carriage in many ways, particularly if it has a railway siding" (p. 282).
   b. It is cheaper to sell in large quantities. It is implied that there is better advertising coverage and fuller information regarding the market (p. 282).[4]

[1] Cf. also the summary, p. 315, and the more empirical and descriptive account in *Industry and Trade*, Bk. II.

[2] The utilization of by-products may be an external economy to a localized industry (p. 279). This is one of the two points at which Marshall mentions any explicit relationship between external and internal economies. See the next note. In *Industry and Trade*, pp. 238 ff., more weight is placed on this economy.

[3] Trade journals are turning information on markets and methods into an external economy (pp. 284–85).

[4] See previous note. One may mention also the economies of this type due to the variety of output of a large firm (*Industry and Trade*, p. 216).

The economies of highly organized buying and selling are among the chief causes of the present tendency towards the fusion of many businesses in the same industry or trade into single huge aggregates (p. 282).

iv. Economy of skill:

a. Each man can be assigned to the task for which he is best fitted, and there acquire additional proficiency by repetition (p. 283).[1]

b. High grade managerial ability can be concerned exclusively with problems of policy, leaving routine details to subordinates (p. 284).

v. Economy of finances. It is frequently urged that the larger (and older) firm secures credit on easier terms (pp. 285, 315).

The question naturally comes to mind, and indeed Marshall explicitly raises it (p. 291): If the economies of large scale production are so important as this formidable list and his discussion imply, how do small concerns manage to exist at all? The primary answer seems to be the mortality of able business men and the likelihood that their descendants will be of inferior caliber. This doctrine, buttressed by biological analogies (pp. 305, 316), is advanced at several points (pp. 285–87, 299 ff., 316–17):[2]

[1] This point is applicable only if the work is so specialized that a small firm could employ one man only part time at his most effective task.

[2] In *Industry and Trade* this point is stated more circumspectly: "It is obvious that, under this tendency (of Increasing Return) a firm, which had once obtained the start of its rivals, would be in a position to undersell them progressively, provided its own vigour remained unimpaired, and it could obtain all the capital it needed. . . . It seems, therefore, that, if there were no other difficulty in the way of the unlimited expansion of a strong manufacturing business, each step that the firm took forwards in supplanting its rivals, would enable it to produce profitably to itself at prices below those which they could reach. That is, each step would make the next step surer, longer and quicker: so that ere long it would have no rivals left, at all events in its own neighborhood. That condition must, of course, not be omitted; because the expense of marketing heavy goods at a distance might overbear the economies of large scale production. But for goods, of which the cost of transport is low, and which are under the law of Increasing

After a while, the guidance of the business falls into the hands of people with less energy and less creative genius, if not with less active interest in its prosperity. If it is turned into a joint-stock company, it may retain the advantages of division of labour, of specialized skill and machinery. . . . But it is likely to have lost so much of its elasticity and progressive force, that the advantages are no longer exclusively on its side in its competition with younger and smaller rivals (p. 316; also p. 457).

Incidental and alternative to the limitation of the size of firms due to entrepreneurial problems, Marshall offers an explanation in terms of economies. Internal diseconomies play no explicit role in his thinking,[1] but a related notion is advanced:

The continued very rapid growth of [a] firm requires the presence of two conditions which are seldom combined in the same industry. There are many trades in which an individual producer could secure much increased "internal" economies by a great increase of his output; and there are many in which he could market that output easily; yet there are few in which he could do both. And this is not an accidental, but almost a necessary result (p. 286).

Where marketing is easy, the commodity is standardized and well known. But most of the commodities of this

Return, there might have seemed to be nothing to prevent the concentration in the hands of a single firm of the whole production of the world, except in so far as it was closed by tariff barriers. The reason why this result did not follow was simply that no firm ever had a sufficiently long life of unabated energy and power of initiative for the purpose. It is not possible to say how far this position is now changed by the expansion of joint stock companies with a potentially perpetual life: but every recent decade has contained some episodes which suggest that it may probably be greatly changed, either in substance, or in the methods by which new life is brought into old bodies" (*ibid.*, pp. 315–16). Compare the less qualified statement in the *Economics of Industry* (2d ed.), pp. 141–42. I am indebted to The Macmillan Company for permission to quote from *Industry and Trade*.

[1] It is significant that when Marshall devotes passing attention to the role of management in small and large firms, he speaks of the advantages of small firms, not the limitations of large firms (p. 284). In *Industry and Trade* (pp. 323 ff.) the question of the "plasticity" of large firms is examined in detail.

type are "raw produce, and nearly all the rest are plain and common," and their production can easily be reduced to a routine, so large and small firms are almost equally efficient. Where marketing difficulties are great, on the contrary, the firm may be operating in a region of sharply falling costs but output cannot be expanded rapidly (pp. 286–87; also pp. 453–58, 501).[1]

The second limitation on the size of a firm is almost too vague to permit criticism. The argument consists essentially of two parts. It is held, first, that in many industries the economies of large scale production become unimportant after a certain stage is reached. The other element of the argument is that marketing difficulties will inhibit firms from securing possible economies of large scale production. This must mean one of three things:

i. The market is small.
ii. The commodity is unknown and it requires time to familiarize consumers with it, or
iii. Related to the preceding, the new and superior commodity must supplant older rivals.[2]

The first possibility clearly implies monopoly.[3] The second and third cases are difficult to reconcile with competition, for consumer ignorance, which is surely ruled out by perfect competition, is obviously present. These latter cases, in fact, are leading types of what Chamberlin has called monopolistic competition.[4]

[1] The implication is that marketing costs are not included in costs of production.

[2] All three cases are suggested but not analyzed (p. 286).

[3] The second case is also a monopoly of the actual market and *a priori* it should have a lead in monopolizing the potential market. The same is true of the third case, to the extent that the new commodity is really superior.

[4] *The Theory of Monopolistic Competition* (Cambridge, 1936), Chap. i *et seq.* Marshall speaks, indeed, of the demand curve of the firm in its own market (p. 456 n.).

Marshall finds that the major limitation to growth of the individual firms seems to be, however, the essential mortality of great entrepreneurial ability. It must be emphasized that such a limitation must be inoperative in a rigorously stationary economy, where by definition resources do not change. Here, as usual, Marshall's realistic, historical attitude finds no place for methodological refinements.

As a loose description of historical process the theory of entrepreneurial mortality is unquestionably significant. But the role such considerations play in limitations of firms is of very uncertain importance. If Marshall's discussion of economies is correct and approximately complete, it would not require an extraordinarily high caliber of entrepreneurship to secure a monopoly, or at least a position of dominance, in almost any industry. In competitive, stationary economies, the concern of the present study, Marshall clearly fails to provide the conditions of stable equilibrium.

Marshall's discussion of specific economies of large scale production, which was outlined above, suffers in three fundamental respects. In the first place, Marshall is perpetuating the confusion of the firm, an economic bargaining unit, with the plant, a technical production unit.[1] The economies of machinery, for instance, are in part technical (*e.g.*, ii, a) and in part organizational (*e.g.*, ii, c, d). The second defect is the high evaluation (in the absence of pertinent empirical data) of the importance and scope of economies. The tenor of the discussion clearly implies that additional economies are without limit, albeit perhaps at a decreasing rate, as the scale of plant or firm is increased (cf. esp. p. 318).[2] It is

[1] There is one faint suggestion of such a distinction (p. 289).

[2] Marshall's earliest conclusion was extreme in this regard. In *The Pure*

not self-evident either *a priori* or empirically that this should be so. The last objection is closely related; *diseconomies* are almost completely neglected.

The various internal economies can be separated into three classes, each depending on one fundamental circumstance. The first class arises out of the indivisibility of productive resources or processes. This group includes: i; ii, a, b, d; iii, a, b (in part, especially advertising); iv; and perhaps v.[1] Information on their quantitative importance is almost totally lacking. The second class of economies arises out of the (unexplained) absence of competition in other parts of the economy. The assumption that smaller entrepreneurs are ignorant of processes and markets (ii, c; iii, b) is surely a gratuitous one, and one that would clearly be irrelevant in a competitive economy. The important instance in this second class is, however, quantity discounts. Why any firm in a competitive industry should offer quantity discounts when it can sell an unlimited quantity at the ruling price is not clear.

The last class of economies arises out of the factor of change.[2] The important case is that of the advantage of

Theory of Domestic Values (1879; London School Reprint, No. 1, 1930), he asserted: "It may then be concluded that an increase in the total amount of a commodity manufactured can scarcely fail to occasion increased economies in production, whether the task of production is distributed among a large number of small capitalists, or is concentrated in the hands of a comparatively small number of large firms" (p. 10). The views expressed much later in *Industry and Trade* are more temperate: " . . . the influence of technical economies on the expansion of the business unit tends to weaken after a certain size has been reached; partly because the specialization of plant, and the substitution of mechanical forces for that of the human hand, increase the standardization of products; especially in those engineering and other industries, which are ever changing most rapidly under the impulse of technical progress" (p. 509).

[1] Cf., *supra*, pp. 77 f.

[2] These economies may in general be subsumed under the preceding two classes, but there is some advantage in emphasizing the aspect of change.

large firms in the field of research and invention (ii, d). The case of the possible improvement of the credit of a growing firm, due perhaps to decrease in risks, is of a related character (v). The managerial problem (iv, b), which might also disappear in a rigorously defined stationary economy, may also be mentioned in this connection.

The Theory of Distribution

The theory of distribution is accorded three different treatments in the *Principles*. The first approach is based on the assumption of fixed coefficients of production; the second is a marginal productivity theory. The two are obviously alternative, and it seems clear that the fixed coefficients approach is intended only as a first approximation. Consideration of the second theory, based on marginal productivity, is deferred to Chapter XII. There remains an extensive discussion in Books V and VI along the classical lines, where land, labor, and capital are the chief topics. This third and final approach is supplementary, and not alternative, to Marshall's marginal productivity theory, but it is not difficult to treat it separately at this point.[1]

JOINT DEMAND: FIRST APPROXIMATION TO THE THEORY OF DISTRIBUTION

The theory of joint demand is, as has been pointed out, essentially a theory of distribution. The problem of distribution theory is in fact clearly present in Marshall's definition of joint demand:

[1] In addition to the classical trichotomy of productive factors, Marshall makes many references to the "ultimate factors," labor and waiting (*e.g.*, pp. 139, 171 n., 339, 523 and n., 541). Since ultimate factors do not play any important part in Marshall's theories, it is sufficient to refer to the subsequent discussion of Böhm-Bawerk's use of the "ultimate factor" analysis. Cf., *infra*, Chap. VIII.

> The demand for each of several complementary things is derived from the services which they *jointly* render in the production of some ultimate product, as for instance a loaf of bread, a cask of ale. In other words there is a *joint demand* for the services which any of these things render in helping to produce a thing which satisfies wants directly and for which there is therefore a direct demand: the direct demand for the finished product is in effect split up into many derived demands for the things used in producing it (p. 381; his italics).

The solution of this problem in Book V, Chapter VI, is the subject of the present section (cf. also pp. 652–56).

Marshall makes several explicit assumptions in presenting the first approximation to a theory of production. It is assumed first that "the general conditions of demand" for the final commodity remain unchanged, and, secondly, that "there is no change in the general conditions of the other factors" (p. 382). The final and basic assumption is that the proportion in which the productive factors combine is *fixed*, *i.e.*, the technical coefficients of production are constants.[1] The "Law of Derived Demand" then follows: "The demand schedule for any factor of production of a commodity can be *derived* from that for the commodity by subtracting from the demand price of each separate amount of the commodity the sum of the supply prices for corresponding amounts of the other factors" (p. 383).

The theory of derived demand is illustrated by the famous example of knives, made up of handles and blades. The geometrical presentation is based on Figure V (pp. 383–84 n.). The quantities of knives, handles, and blades (all in a one-to-one relationship to each other)

[1] Cf. "Then a temporary check to the supply of plasterers' labour will cause a proportionate check to the amount of building" (pp. 382–83); also, ". . . the unit of each of the factors remains unchanged whatever be the amount of the commodity produced" (p. 384 n.).

are measured along OX; prices along OY. Three fundamental curves are given by Marshall:

DD'—the demand curve for knives;
SS'—the supply curve of knives;
ss'—the supply curve of handles.

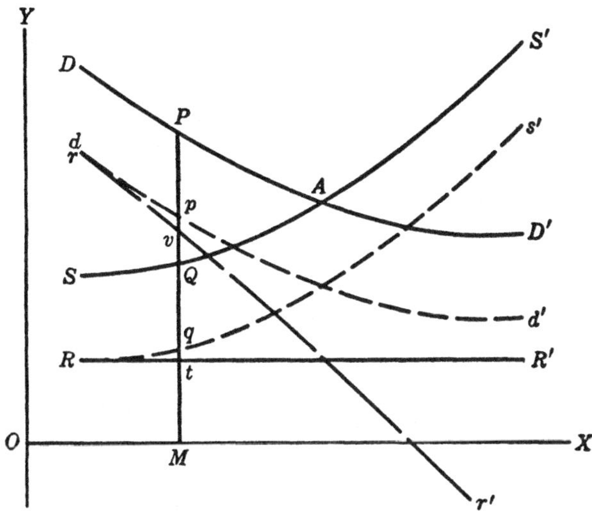

FIGURE V

The demand curve for handles is derived as follows: At any point M on OX, erect a perpendicular cutting ss' at q, SS' at Q, and DD' at P. Then the distance between SS' and ss' ($= qQ = pP$) is the supply price of blades. If qQ is not affected by ss', then at output OM, MP minus qQ ($=Mp$) is the maximum price that will be paid for handles. The locus of such points is given by dd', the derived demand curve for handles.

The absurdity to which this approach leads as a general solution may best be brought out by deriving the demand for blades, following Marshall's method. The supply curve of blades is already given by subtracting the supply curve of handles (ss') from that of knives (SS'). The difference, qQ ($=Mt$), is represented by RR', the supply curve of blades. The derived demand for blades at output *OM* is secured by subtracting from *MP* the supply price of handles, or *Mq*. The difference, *qP* (=*Mv*) is the maximum amount that will be paid for *OM* blades. The locus of such points produces the derived demand curve for blades, *rr'*. This curve necessarily has *negative* values for all points beyond the intersection of the supply curve of handles (*ss'*) and the demand curve for knives (*DD'*).

The proposition that beyond a certain point one resource of a combination will be hired only at a negative price is surely misleading. But the region to the left of *A* is equally difficult to interpret. At output *OM*, for instance, *Mv* would be paid for a blade, *or Mp* for a handle, depending upon whether the price of handles or of blades is assumed to be fixed. Marshall cautions that "the ordinary demand and supply curves have no practical value except in the immediate neighborhood of the point of equilibrium," and "the same remark applies with even greater force to the equation of derived demand" (p. 384 n.). The writer would submit that the equation of derived demand holds *only* at the point of equilibrium.

The real question is, why does Marshall bother to introduce the theory of derived demand? He clearly recognizes (in the same chapter) the possibility of varying the proportions in which factors of production combine (pp. 386, 395). Similarly, in his discussion of joint supply, Marshall assumes at one stage that two or more commodities are produced in fixed proportions (pp. 388 ff.), although "there are very few cases" where the proportion is strictly fixed (p. 389).[1] The device of fixed

[1] When the proportions are variable, as Marshall says, "we can ascertain what part of the whole expense of the process of production would be saved,

coefficients of production may be explicable on the ground of its simplicity. Marshall wrote with an eye to the general reader, and three-dimensional graphs or arguments are not adapted to such a public.[1] Simplicity, however, is sometimes an expensive luxury. The *Principles* would have been definitely improved by eliminating the chapter on joint demand.

We turn now to the specific distributive shares. The theory of rent, which receives its last thoroughgoing defense from Marshall, will be considered first. Certain aspects of the theory of labor will then be noted briefly, and the theory of capital will conclude this section.

The Rent of Land

The classical theory of rent receives considerable revision in Marshall's hands.[2] The external continuity of the doctrine is great, particularly in terminology, but so many qualifications are introduced that Marshall's doctrine is on the whole more classical in spirit than in content.

A few remarks may be directed, at the outset, to the problem of diminishing returns. As was pointed out previously, the definition of the law is very careless and is usually couched in terms of proportionate changes, which is clearly inappropriate. But it is of more interest

by so modifying these proportions as slightly to diminish the amount of one of the joint products without affecting the amounts of the others" (p. 390). Cf. also *Industry and Trade*, pp. 192 ff.

[1] We may note Marshall's approval of Edgeworth's criticisms of Wieser's theory of imputation, which is substantially identical with Marshall's above theory (p. 393 n.).

[2] Reference may be made to F. W. Ogilvie, "Marshall on Rent," *Economic Journal*, XL (1930), 1–24, who makes some suggestive criticisms but who seems more intent on criticizing than on understanding Marshall. On the other hand, the reply to Ogilvie by M. Tappan Hollond, "Marshall on Rent," *ibid.*, XL (1930), 369–83, contains a useful, sympathetic statement of Marshall's position but errs somewhat on the side of loyalty to Marshall —and to the rent theory.

to note that Marshall defines diminishing returns primarily with respect to the growth of population relative to land ("Note on the Law of Diminishing Return," pp. 169–72). Diminishing returns in manufacturing, indeed, seems frequently to be attributable to the expenditure by the entrepreneur of "an inappropriately large amount of his resources on machinery" (p. 169). The case of land differs:

> When the older economists spoke of the Law of Diminishing Return they were looking at the problems of agriculture not only from the point of view of the individual cultivator but also from that of the nation as a whole. Now if the nation *as a whole* finds its stock of planing machines or ploughs inappropriately large or inappropriately small, it can redistribute its resources. It can obtain more of that in which it is deficient, while gradually lessening its stock of such things as are superabundant: *but it cannot do that in regard to land:* it can cultivate its land more intensively, but it cannot get any more. And for that reason the older economists rightly insisted that, from the social point of view, land is not on exactly the same footing as those implements of production which man can increase without limit (p. 170).

To Marshall the law of diminishing return in its primary sense is still an historical law of the relative growth of different factors of production.[1]

Land is but a form of capital to the individual; this is an emphatic element of Marshall's theory (pp. 170, 430). The theorem, which is necessarily explicit or implicit in every classical economist's writings, is so obviously true

[1] Ogilvie, *op. cit.*, pp. 5 ff., accuses Marshall of introducing historical elements into his graphs, and indeed there is some support for this charge (*Principles*, p. 158). Yet it should probably be attributed to somewhat careless terminology, for Marshall states elsewhere that "the return due to a dose of labour and capital is not here taken to include the value of the capital itself" (p. 172), which fairly meets Ogilvie's charge.

as to require no attention.[1] The problem relates to land and its return from the social viewpoint.

Land does not, from the social viewpoint, differ significantly from other capital goods in a "new country." The argument is simply that, in new countries, land has a definite supply price:

> People are generally unwilling to face the hardships and isolation of pioneer agriculture, unless they can look forward with some confidence to much higher earnings, measured in terms of the necessaries of life, than they could get at home. . . . The land is peopled up to that margin at which it just yields gains adequate for this purpose, without leaving any surplus for rent, when no charge is made for the land (p. 430; also pp. 411–12).

In this circumstance, rent (as the return to land) is a cost of production even from the social viewpoint.[2]

In an "old country," to use a favorite phrase, the land is all settled, so costs of bringing it into use (construction costs) have disappeared from economic life.[3] The conditions which make for an "old country" are not defined, but contemporary England seems to have been an example (*e.g.*, pp. 425, 663 n.). The essential differences of land from capital are summarized: [4]

> . . . the fundamental attribute of land is its extension. The right to use a piece of land gives command over a certain space—a certain part of the earth's surface. The area of the earth is fixed: the geometric relations in which any particular part of it stands to the other parts are fixed. Man has no control over them; they are wholly unaffected by

[1] It is suggested rather timidly at one point that land has a rising supply price to an individual (p. 169), but this must clearly be due to imperfections of competition, and it plays no part in Marshall's theory.

[2] The same theory applies to certain types of urban land (pp. 443–44).

[3] Marshall ignores depreciation and maintenance costs in this connection.

[4] Compare especially Bk. IV, Chap. iii; Bk. V, Chaps. ix, x. Natural fertility is no longer one of the differences (pp. 146–47, 630).

demand; they have no cost of production, there is no supply price at which they can be produced (p. 145; also p. 629).

It is from these "space-relations" and the "annuity of nature" that the theory of rent derives its special character (p. 147).

Marshall's restatement of the Ricardian theory of rent is too well known to require detailed exposition here. Capital and labor will be applied to any piece of land out to a margin of cultivation,[1] both intensive and extensive, at which the last dose of capital-and-labor produces an additional product just sufficient to cover the cost of the dose. The marginal application measures the return to capital-and-labor; rent is a residual. Marshall's discussion is very detailed and exact,[2] but it is of little interest here.

[1] All that follows is, of course, equally applicable to any other physical matter used in production.

[2] One exception perhaps deserves attention, since it illustrates so well the chief pitfall in partial equilibrium analysis. Marshall presents a graphic restatement of Ricardo's theory of the effect of an improvement on rent (Appendix L, esp. p. 835), and repeats a rather obvious fallacy in Ricardo's analysis. In the accompanying graph, *OX* measures units of capital-and-

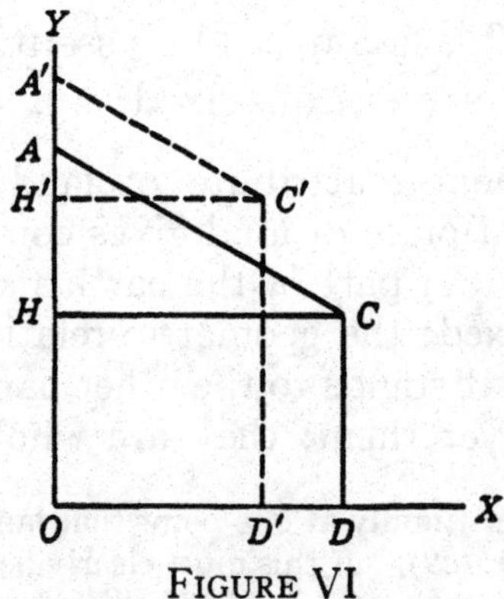

FIGURE VI

labor, *OY*, product. *AC* is the curve of marginal productivity of capital-and-labor before some improvement in technique, *A'C'* is the same curve after the improvement has taken place. If the demand is absolutely inelastic, and if the new marginal productivity curve is parallel to the old

Two critical aspects of this theory deserve analysis. The first is the assumption that land is fixed in quantity in an old country. This fixity of supply is not necessarily absolute; the famous analogy to a meteoric shower of exceptionally hard stones is designed to emphasize that fixity could be associated with any productive agent, and is essentially relative to that of other resources (pp. 415 ff.).[1] Land is, therefore, in an even more famous analogy, "but the leading species of a large genus" (p. 421). Continuity is the essential aspect of economic life, and it is to be expected that commercial rent contains only an element of true rent and, contrariwise, that other returns (*e.g.*, wages) contain rent.[2] Marshall's theory reduces to this: In an old country (which is defined as a country in which virtually all land is settled), the supply is relatively fixed and hence the return to land

curve, rents will decline. That is, the same total product will be produced if "demand" is fixed, so only OD' of capital-and-labor will be used, where $ODCA$ is equal to $OD'C'A'$. The new rent, $H'C'A'$, is obviously less than the old rent, HCA. If the new productivity curve is not parallel to the old curve, rents may increase, decrease, or remain the same.

All this is true, but Marshall continues, "the only change in the interpretation of this diagram which is required by our making it refer to the whole country instead of a single farm" is to allow for varying transportation costs (p. 835). He must be assuming that "all other things remain equal," but this they cannot possibly do. Before the improvement a unit of capital-and-labor received a return of DC, whether in agriculture or elsewhere (if there previously was equilibrium); Ricardo never tired of saying there cannot be two rates of "profit." But after the improvement, capital-and-labor receive, according to Marshall, $D'C'$ per unit, while $D'D$ of capital-and-labor seeks employment elsewhere (presumably subject to diminishing returns). The return elsewhere will, therefore, fall below DC. This is then clearly a situation in disequilibrium, and there are two rates of "profit."

[1] Cournot's mineral springs were the vehicle for illustrating this point in the first edition (pp. 484 ff.), although the meteoric stones were also present (pp. 664 n. *et seq.*). The continuity of form between rent and interest, as limiting concepts, is increasingly emphasized in the subsequent editions of the *Principles*.

[2] The extension of the theory to quasi-rents will be discussed in the next section.

is determined primarily by its fixed supply and the supplies of the other factors of production (cf. p. 156 n.). If this conclusion is restricted to a closed economy, it is open to only one, but that a fundamental, qualification: it is possible to add to the yield and value of given land by appropriate investments in the land, and this is all that can be done with any other productive resources. This qualification does not, of course, mean that "rents" will disappear.

Marshall is indeed forced ultimately to virtually this conclusion. Having conceded that fertility may be augmented or diminished, he includes the cost of "improvements" in the expenses of production.[1] The rent theory applies only to the allegedly fixed space relationships and annuities of nature, which are in point of fact, of course, also alterable by investment.[2]

The final problem concerns the relation of rent to price when the supply of all factors is given, *i.e.*, in a stationary economy. Marshall does not discuss this problem explicitly, but he does consider the alternative uses of land, which is essentially the same thing. The general similarity is recognized: "Each crop strives against others for the possession of the land; and if any one crop shows signs of being more remunerative than before relatively

[1] "On the other hand those chemical or mechanical properties of the soil, on which its fertility largely depends, can be modified, and in extreme cases entirely changed by man's action. But a tax on the income derived from improvements which, though capable of general application are yet slowly made and slowly exhausted, would not appreciably affect the supply of them during a short period, nor therefore the supply of produce due to them. It would consequently fall in the main on the owner; a leaseholder being regarded for the time as owner, subject to a mortgage. In a long period, however, it would diminish the supply of them, would raise the normal supply price of produce and fall on the consumer" (p. 630).

[2] Marshall does not always restrict the rent theory to the limiting case to which it is appropriate, however. Thus, "The amount of that rent is not a governing cause [of prices]; but is itself governed by the fertility of the land, the price of the produce, and the position of the margin . . ." (p. 427).

to others, the cultivators will devote more of their land and resources to it" (p. 435). The law of substitution is completely applicable; it is in fact quoted in the very same paragraph.

It would appear, then, that, to use Marshall's example, the price of hops must be sufficient to cover the rent of the land that would be secured from cultivating oats. Rent would then be, even socially considered, a cost of production. This conclusion is denied on a very peculiar ground: "There would be no simple numerical relation between the surplus, or rent, which the land would yield under oats, and the marginal costs which the price of the hops must cover" (p. 436; also pp. 437 n., 438, 500, 579).[1] The argument is that the land in question may raise hops "of exceptionally high quality," so perhaps £30 could be secured in rent from hops, and only £20 from any other crop (p. 436 and note). In the case of unspecialized

[1] There is an interesting history of the development of this point. In the first edition Marshall says of the doctrine that rent does not enter into the expenses of production that if it is applied to one agricultural product, "in order to make it true we must add conditions, the effect of which is almost to explain it away" (p. 487). He concludes, after a somewhat discursive analysis, that "the rent of that land on which oats could be grown, can be made to pay for other purposes, does indirectly affect the expenses of production and the normal value of oats" (p. 488). But no outright charging of the foregone rent as a cost is permitted; the footnote criticizing Jevons is already present in substantially its final form (p. 490 n.). A year later, in the second edition, Marshall is more restrained and says that if the doctrine that rent does not enter the expenses of production is applied to one commodity, "the doctrine is liable to be understood in a sense in which it is not true" (p. 459). His conclusion is also altered: "the rent that land on which oats could be grown, can be made to pay for other purposes, though it does not 'enter into' the expenses of production and the normal value of oats, yet does affect them indirectly" (p. 460). It would require undue space to trace the subsequent changes in detail, but we may note that by the fifth (1907) edition, Marshall's definitive position is virtually reached. It may seem that concentrating attention on one crop will lead to a new principle, but "that is however not the case" (p. 435). His argument is now much more extensive but still unconvincing; in the end, the absence of a "simple numerical relation" between alternative rents is denied (p. 436).

lands (*i.e.*, equally suited to several uses), there is, however, a simple numerical relationship: the "rent" secured from any one use must *equal* that from any other possible use, otherwise there is obvious failure to maximize returns and the situation is in disequilibrium. In the case of specialized land (like any other specialized resource), the return beyond the amount the resources could produce elsewhere is, of course, a pure rent, a price-determined quantity. But here the ground has shifted; it is not the fixity of supply but the varying qualities of land (which Marshall himself has held to be subject to human control; cf. Bk. IV, Chap. ii) that govern the causal relationship to price. It follows in this latter case that it is permissible to say that rent is not a cost of production, but then we must refrain from saying rent is the return for the use of land, for the two rents are not at all directly related.[1]

THE EXTENSION OF THE RENT CONCEPT: QUASI-RENTS

The doctrine of quasi-rents is an extension of the classical theory of rent to the return from all "fixed" investments.[2] The chief income sources to which quasi-rent analysis is applied are the durable capital goods (p. 74). Quasi-rents are twice defined as follows:

> That which is rightly regarded as interest on "free" or "floating" capital, or on new investments of capital, is more properly treated as a sort of rent—a Quasi-rent—on old investments of capital. And there is no sharp line of division

[1] They are directly related in one possible case: if the specialization of land is permanent where that of other productive services may be only temporary (through recovery and reinvestment of capital).

[2] No attempt is made here to cover the extensive ground opened up by R. Opie's excellent analyses of Marshall's position, in "Die Quasirente in Marshalls Lehrgebäude," *Archiv für Sozialwissenschaft und Sozialpolitik*, LX (1928), 251–79, and "Marshall's Time Analysis," *Economic Journal*, XLI (1931), 199–215.

between floating capital and that which has been "sunk" for a special branch of production, nor between new and old investments of capital; each group shades into the other gradually (pp. viii, 412).

The theory of quasi-rents is essentially the explanation of the return on what is called fixed (overhead) investment (pp. 359 ff.). Once capital has been invested, it will remain invested until it can be depreciated through use and salvage value, and throughout its service life it will continue in that use regardless of its return.[1] This is merely another way of saying that only prime or variable costs are price-determining in the short run (pp. 374–77).[2] The earnings of the fixed investment are price-determined in the short run,[3] and thus partake of the nature of rent (pp. 424 n., 426). In the long run, however, they must be covered or capital will leave the industry (pp. 420–21, 424 n.).[4]

The quasi-rent of any fixed equipment is its net return, after full allowance for replacement (pp. 418–19, 426 n.), so quasi-rents may clearly fall to below zero.[5] The re-

[1] Unless, of course, the capital good is unspecialized, which is not typically the case. The greater adaptability of labor is a difficulty in the application (but not in the principle) of quasi-rent analysis to wages.

[2] Marshall does not state this in so many words. He makes a qualification for the fear of "spoiling the market" (pp. 374–75), but the qualification certainly rests on imperfect competition.

[3] The relationship between fixed investment and price is not necessarily symmetrical for price rises and declines, however. In a period too short to depreciate existing plants it may be possible for new plants to be constructed, and then quasi-rents cannot long exceed the earnings of new capital equipment.

[4] "The Supplementary costs, which the owner of a factory expects to be able to add to the prime costs of its products, are the source of the quasi-rents which it will yield to him. If they come up to his expectation, then his business so far yields good profits; if they fall much short of it, his business tends to go to the bad" (p. 362 n.).

[5] That is to say, quasi-rents may be negative (pp. 622, 664). Opie, who cites these pages, nevertheless asserts that Marshall "would not have admitted the concept of a negative quasi-rent" ("Die Quasirente in Marshalls Lehrgebäude," *op. cit.*, p. 265). But the definition of quasi-rents, as the net

muneration to fixed investment is presumably determined by the marginal productivity of the equipment.[1] The capital value of the equipment, once constructed, is the discounted value of its future quasi-rents (p. 424 n.).

Certain aspects of Marshall's theory of quasi-rents deserve more detailed attention.[2] There is some question regarding the legitimacy of calling the return on fixed investments a quasi-rent, for, strictly speaking, such returns are not at all parallel to the return on land (as treated by Marshall). Quasi-rents are price-determined for both the entrepreneur and society (unless there are alternative uses of the machinery, etc.); land rent is price-determined only for the economy as a whole.

There is, moreover, some difficulty in properly measuring the gross product of an element of fixed plant. The proportions of the productive factors (sunk and free) can be varied within relatively short periods of time, but this is not a satisfactory test. The law of diminishing return postulates complete freedom to readapt all of the other factors to changes in the variable factor. A complete rearrangement, however, is clearly ruled out by the very presence of capital investment. The short-run marginal product of a fixed resource will, in general, be smaller than the long-run marginal product (especially if the fixed plant is operated at much less than "capacity"), when full rearrangement is possible. This line of

return in excess of replacement and maintenance, surely involves the possibility of negative excesses, and, in fact, the certainty of such excesses whenever an investment turns out badly. Quasi-rents are zero when no return is secured on the investment; they are negative when the investment is not maintained.

[1] This point is implied rather than expressed (pp. 418, 430–31, 630). Remuneration is used in the text in the sense of the actual earnings; the money return to fixed investment may be fixed contractually, as when bonds are issued.

[2] Compare the interesting remarks of R. S. Merian, "Quasi-Rents," *Explorations in Economics* (New York, 1936), pp. 317–25.

reasoning suggests that the quasi-rent analysis must be based on an approach which utilizes the assumption of temporary (and decreasing) fixity of certain of the coefficients of production.[1]

An element akin to quasi-rent is also found in wages. The doctrine is cautiously extended to all wages of specialized laborers in the short run (pp. 570 ff.),[2] and, whether considered socially or from the laborer's viewpoint, this conclusion is certainly consistent with the general theory. The failure to emphasize the importance of quasi-rents in wages may be attributable to Marshall's desire to rest value ultimately on real costs and satisfactions.[3]

Labor and Its Supply

Marshall follows Jevons closely in the definition of labor. "We may define *labour* as any exertion of mind or body undergone partly or wholly with a view to some good other than the pleasure derived directly from the work" (p. 65; also pp. 138 n.). This definition differs from Jevons' only in that exertion need not be "painful," since, as Marshall says, on the one hand idleness is painful, and on the other, all labor confers some pleasure on the laborer. The definition is, as he inevitably qualifies,

[1] The extent of the fixity of production coefficients depends upon the divisibility of the fixed plant and its adaptability to changing amounts of variable factors employed. Compare my "Production and Distribution in the Short Run," *Journal of Political Economy*, XLVII (1939), 305–27.

[2] It is asserted, however, that "a large part of the whole" of wages is "true earnings of effort," only a minor part being quasi-rent (p. 622). It is difficult to imagine either a defense or a criticism of this view that would convince anyone not very willing to be convinced.

[3] Special emphasis is placed on the applicability of the doctrine of quasi-rent to the earnings of "extraordinary natural abilities" (pp. 577–79). Here, however, Marshall deserts the viewpoint of the individual for that of the occupation, and points out that some large gains may be required to offset the failures, if the occupation is to secure sufficient recruits. The argument is not very relevant when applied to the entire occupational group. It is appropriate only to "the true or 'long-period' normal" case, and in such a period, of course, there are no quasi-rents of *any* sort.

"elastic" (p. 65 n.). But it appears to be too elastic, for it includes perhaps most of the deliberate recreational activities of adults. Labor, to repeat, cannot be defined except in terms of its demand—and this is equally true of all other productive services.

All labor, "if we had to make a fresh start," would be productive if it produced utilities, but "an almost unbroken tradition compels us to regard the central notion of the word [productive] as relating to the provision for the wants of the future rather than those of the present" (pp. 65–66). Although Marshall sees the tenuous basis for the distinction (p. 65; also p. 138 n.), it also coincides roughly with the element of Puritanism in his philosophy.[1] But though the verbal allegiance to classical theory is great, Marshall makes no use of this concept.

The supply of labor is determined exactly along the lines of Jevons' analysis. The marginal disutility of labor is an increasing function of the time that is worked per day, and eventually it equals and then exceeds the marginal utility of the product secured.

> As Jevons remarks, there is often some resistance to be overcome before setting to work. Some little painful effort is often involved at starting; but this gradually diminishes to zero, and is succeeded by pleasure; which increases for a while until it attains a certain low maximum; after which it diminishes to zero, and is succeeded by increasing weariness and craving for relaxation and change (pp. 141–42; cf. also pp. 330, 527–28, 844).

The amounts of product sufficient to call forth various quantities of labor are the supply prices of labor (p. 142).[2]

[1] Thus, " . . . the true interest of a country is generally advanced by the subordination of the desire for transient luxuries to the attainment of those more solid and lasting resources which will assist industry in its future work, and will in various ways tend to make life larger" (p. 66).

[2] Marshall does not tell us how to measure the supply of labor; presumably he would use a measure in terms of product.

The problems raised for this type of analysis by division of labor and socially organized production receive little attention.[1]

With regard to the long-run supply curve of labor, Marshall's theory is even less realistic. Although Book VI of the *Principles*, we are told, is necessary chiefly because "human beings are not brought up to their work on the same principles as a machine, a horse, or a slave" (p. 504), yet a significant functional relationship between the amount of labor (*i.e.*, the number and quality of laborers) and their wage rate is asserted (pp. 529–32). The nexus between these two variables is found in the (admirable) avoidance of unproductive expenditures by the working classes, so additional income leads to productive consumption or to an increase of population.

Brief mention may be made of the excellent discussion of the peculiarities of labor as a productive service (Book VI, Chaps. IV, V). The absence of a capital market for the production of labor, the long period required to alter the supply of specialized labor, and the inseparability of the laborer from his services are all more or less true, although the points fall rapidly in significance. Perishability is not a peculiarity of labor, as Marshall virtually admits,[2] and the laborer's relative disadvantage in bargaining is a narrow generalization, restricted primarily to the "lowest grades" of labor.

The entrepreneur.—Brief attention had best be devoted in this connection to the entrepreneur, whose return is "profit." Marshall adheres to the classical tradition of

[1] Compare, however, Marshall's reply to Böhm-Bawerk's criticisms of the disutility theory, *infra*, p. 185n.

[2] "It must however be remembered that much of the working power of material agents of production is perishable in the same sense; for a great part of the income, which they also are prevented from earning by being thrown out of work, is completely lost" (p. 567).

treating as profits the sum of interest on the entrepreneur's investment, the wages of superintendence, and an ambiguous residual profit. To the last two items he applies the name of "earnings of management" (pp. 74, 313).

The first of these, the wages of superintendence, is determined just like any other wage (and this is especially true in the case of managers of joint-stock companies [p. 604]): "On the whole then we may conclude that the rarity of the natural abilities and the expensiveness of the special training required for the work affect normal earnings of management in much the same way as they do the normal wages of skilled labour" (p. 608).[1] This element of profits is a cost of production, as is also the second element (pp. 605–6, 618–19).

The final element of earnings of management rests on what Marshall attempts, albeit rather feebly, to raise to the status of a fourth factor of production: organization. Organization "has many forms, *e.g.*, that of a single business, that of various businesses in the same trade, that of various trades relatively to one another, and that of the State providing security for all and help for many" (p. 139). This all-inclusive definition is supplemented in several ways. Organization provides the method by which "the appropriate business ability and the requisite capital are brought together" (pp. 313, 606); it involves, also, risk-bearing (pp. 612–13, 620) and a "business connection" (p. 618), as well as good will (p. 625); and, finally, organization appears to be equiv-

[1] Cf. also the *Economics of Industry* (2d ed.), p. 142: "Thus the Earnings of Management of a manufacturer represent the value of the addition which his work makes to the total produce of capital and industry: they correspond to the effective demand that there is for the aid of his labour in production, just as the wages of a hired labourer correspond to the effective demand for his labour."

alent to the "exceptional abilities or good fortune" of the entrepreneur (p. 624 n.). None of these characteristics is easily subjected to quantitative measurement, but Marshall speaks frequently of the supply price of organization.

The Theory of Capital

The concept of capital.—Marshall's analysis of the nature of capital is peculiarly illustrative of the characteristics of his approach which were discussed at the beginning of this chapter. He states with all possible clearness the fundamental identity of wealth and capital, and it is probable that he would concede that a capital good is really any good yielding services through time or requiring time to produce.[1] But houses are included in capital, and furniture is not, "for the former are and the latter are not commonly regarded as yielding income by the world at large, as is shown by the practice of the income tax commissioners" (p. 78). The additional reasons for retaining the word "wealth" are that "clear tradition" favors it (p. 81), and that the refined concept is one of which "no account is taken in customary discourse, and which cannot even be described without offending against popular conventions" (p. 78). This is indeed a heavy burden for the terminology of any science to bear.

Prospectiveness and the supply of savings.—In distributing his income through time, the individual makes allowances for two factors, assuming his income and

[1] *E.g.*, "It has already been indicated that the only strictly logical position is that which has been adopted by most writers on mathematical versions of economics, and which regards 'social capital' and 'social wealth' as coextensive . . . " (p. 786; also pp. 77–78, 81, 787–89). Marshall's concession to this view was much smaller in the earlier editions of the *Principles*.

tastes to remain unchanged (p. 122).[1] The first element of discount is due to the objective uncertainty of receiving the future pleasure, and this risk is appraised on an actuarial basis (pp. 119, 120 n., 841). The second element of discount is subjective; it is the familiar irrational preference for present pleasures. "Human nature is so constituted that in estimating the 'present value' of a future benefit most people generally make a second deduction from its future value, in the form of what we may call a 'discount,' that increases with the period for which the benefit is deferred" (p. 120; also pp. 225, 231, 581, 587, 841).[2] These two forces affect not only the tendency of people to save, but also "their tendency to buy things which will be a lasting source of pleasure" (p. 120).[3] Under a correct definition of capital, it may be noted, the purchase of durable goods out of income is a form of saving.

Lasting future pleasures will be discounted in similar fashion.[4] Marshall notes that *a priori* the subjective discount need not be uniform through time (pp. 132 n., 841). The individual may not discount pleasures two years

[1] The latter in particular will vary for some goods, as Marshall indicates: ". . . a young man discounts at a very high rate the pleasure of the Alpine tours. . . . He would much rather have them now, partly because they would give him much greater pleasure now" (p. 121 n.).

[2] In the first edition of the *Principles* the following passage occurs: "The great body of sensible people in a civilized country estimate a future pleasure at a lower, though not a much lower, value than if it were present: they *discount the future* at a moderate rate" (p. 153). Edgeworth objected to this argument, presumably without success, claiming that "the objective fact of interest" was the proper explanation. Cf. *Memorials of Alfred Marshall*, *op. cit.*, p. 69.

[3] The argument is also stated mathematically (p. 841). If r is the person's preference for present over future goods, h the future pleasure, p its objective probability, and time is t, then the present value of h will be $ph(1 + r)^{-t}$.

[4] In the notation of the previous footnote, the present value of Δh pleasure in unit of time Δt from now to T will be $\int_0^T p(1 + r)^{-t} \frac{dh}{dt}\, dt$.

hence, while thereafter the rate may become great. To assume a uniform time preference rate, in other words, is to assume that people are rationally irrational.

The influences which determine this subjective discount of future pleasures receive little attention. "Social and religious sanctions" are suggested as an important explanation (for either rapid or slow accumulation), but this argument is not pursued (p. 225). Most of the discussion of saving is concerned with objective factors, such as the increase of security and the development of a suitable investment mechanism (pp. 226–27). These factors seem, however, to serve only as an institutional background, "for, after all, family affection is the main motive of saving" (p. 227; also pp. 228 ff., 533). Although exceptions are duly noted (pp. 120, 241), the subjective preference for present goods outweighs family affections and social sanctions, and there is a net preference for present goods even in modern times (pp. 140, 224, 232). Interest is a necessary supply price for savings.[1]

It is held that in general an increase in the interest rate will lead to an increase in savings. "It is a nearly universal rule that a rise in the [interest] rate increases the *desire* to save; and it often increases the *power* to save, or rather it is often an indication of an increased efficiency of our productive resources . . ." (p. 236).[2] Marshall implies here, and elsewhere (p. 229), that in-

[1] "We are justified in speaking of the interest on capital as the reward of the sacrifice involved in the waiting for the enjoyment of material resources, because few people would save much without reward" (p. 232).

[2] Marshall repeats the well-known exception, among others, to this rule, that if a fixed income is sought, the higher the rate of interest, the less will be saved (p. 235). But a less frequently observed factor mitigates this exception: the less that need be saved to secure a given income, the more persons will embark on such a program, and the higher the sought-after income will be. In the earlier *Economics of Industry* (2d ed.), p. 41 n., Marshall attributes this point to Sargant's *Recent Political Economy* (London, 1867).

terest is one of the leading *sources* of savings, and this is indeed the only obvious important direct relationship between savings and the interest rate. His contention with regard to the effect of the rate on the desire to save is conventional, but probably exaggerated.

But even if the amount of new *savings* is a function of the interest rate, it is not possible to talk of the supply of *capital* in this way. For, as Marshall carefully notes, "It must however be recollected that the annual investment of wealth is a small part of the already existing stock, and that therefore the stock would not be increased perceptibly in any one year by even a considerable increase in the annual rate of saving" (p. 236; also p. 534).

Productiveness and the demand for capital.—As prospectiveness is the determinant of the supply of savings, so productiveness is the determinant of demand for capital. "Thus the chief *demand* for capital arises from its productiveness, from the services which it renders, for instance, in enabling wool to be spun and woven more easily than by the unaided hand, or in causing water to flow freely wherever it is wanted instead of being carried laboriously in pails . . ." (p. 81; also pp. 82 n., 233, 519–21, 580–81). To this general demand for production loans one must add the demand of "spendthrifts and governments" for consumption loans (p. 521)—or, preferably, it may be argued, deduct such loans from the supply.

The demand for capital by any enterprise is determined by the amount which an additional unit of capital will add to the total product of that firm. "The earnings of a machine can sometimes be estimated by the addition to the output of a factory which it might effect in certain cases without involving any incidental extra expense"

(p. 519).[1] The net product of new investment is in general subject to diminishing return, although this point is established more by illustration than by any explicit application of the law of return to capital (pp. 411, 474 ff., 519–21).

The nature of the investment process receives only brief attention. It is made clear that the productiveness of capital is measured only by the excess of its product over necessary maintenance and replacement costs (pp. 79, 61, 172, 354 n., 519, 523). The general principle is then stated succinctly and correctly:

> Each element of outlay has to be accumulated for the time which will elapse between its being incurred and its bearing fruit; and the aggregate of these accumulated elements is the total outlay involved in the enterprise. The balance between efforts and the satisfactions resulting from them may be made up to any day that is found convenient. But whatever day is chosen, one simple rule must be followed:—Every element whether an effort or a satisfaction, which dates from a time anterior to that day, must have compound interest for the interval accumulated upon it; and every element, which dates from a time posterior to that day, must have compound interest for the interval discounted from it. If the day be anterior to the beginning of the enterprise, then every element must be discounted (p. 353).[2]

[1] The presence of the qualifiers, "sometimes" and "in certain cases," arises out of Marshall's views on the difficulties in measuring net products of individual factors, which in the last analysis rests on his limited concept of substitution. Cf., *infra*, Chap. XII.

[2] The argument is lucidly expressed in Mathematical Note XIII (pp. 845–46). Using the notation of note 4, page 102, above, the discounted income of a project will be

$$H = \int_{T'}^{T} p(1 + r)^{-t} \cdot \frac{dh}{dt} \cdot dt,$$

where T' is the date of completion and T the date when the project is worn out. If Δv is the element of effort (or cost) in construction of time Δt, then

This is, of course, the proper form of capital account for the entrepreneur. In such calculations the interest rate is known and constant for the individual, and if at this rate accumulated costs equal discounted income, then "the business would be just remunerative" (p. 354).

Marshall does not apply this form of analysis to society as a whole, or he might not have said that it "cannot be made into a theory of interest, any more than [a similar application of the marginal productivity analysis can be made] into a theory of wages, without reasoning in a circle" (p. 519). For the individual, the marginal productivity theory does involve circularity, if the interest during the construction period is ignored. For then r, interest rate, is defined as the ratio of a perpetual net income, A, to capital value, C, *i.e.*, $r = \frac{A}{C}$. But C involves interest during construction, and there are thus really two unknowns and only one equation. However, if cost and return are stated in terms of income flows, and r is taken as the unknown, this difficulty of course disappears, and with it all circularity of reasoning.

It may be noted that the discussion of interest refers only to fluid capital funds.

> The rate of interest is a ratio: and the two things which it connects are both sums of money. So long as capital is "free," and the sum of money or general purchasing power over which it gives command is known, the net money income, expected to be derived from it, can be represented at once as bearing a given ratio (four or five or ten per cent) to that sum. But when the free capital has been invested

the sum of the construction cost is

$$V = \int_0^{T'} (1 + r)^t \cdot \frac{dv}{dt} \cdot dt,$$

which will equal H at equilibrium. An interesting application is made in estimating the capital value of an immigrant (p. 564 n.).

in a particular thing, its money value cannot as a rule be ascertained except by capitalizing the net income which it will yield; and therefore the causes which govern it are likely to be akin in a greater or less degree to those which govern rents (p. 412).

A final word may be added concerning Marshall's theory of the long-run interest rate. As in the case of labor and wages, savings are found—with many qualifications already mentioned above—to be functionally related to the interest rate. Since annual saving is a small proportion of the capital existing at any moment, "an extensive increase in the demand for capital in general will therefore be met for a time not so much by an increase of supply, as by a rise in the rate of interest . . ." (p. 534). But in the end, "interest . . . tends towards an equilibrium level such that the aggregate demand for capital in that market, at that rate of interest, is equal to the aggregate stock forthcoming there at that rate" (p. 534).

This doctrine is open to two fundamental criticisms. The functional relationship between the interest rate and saving [1] has a nebulous empirical existence. But even granting this relationship, his theory is somewhat too simple. He ignores, to name only two aspects of the problem, the cumulative nature of savings (*i.e.*, the fact that each increment of savings makes it easier to save another increment) and the effects of saving on invention.[2]

[1] Which, indeed, Marshall would not consider to be reversible; *i.e.*, a fall in the interest rate decreases the rate of increase of capital, not the amount of capital. Cf. pp. 235–36; also *Economics of Industry* (2d ed.), p. 125.

[2] Cf. F. H. Knight, *The Ethics of Competition*, *op. cit.*, p. 183.

Chapter V

FRANCIS Y. EDGEWORTH

NO economist in the period under consideration was more subtle or colorful than Francis Y. Edgeworth.[1] His was a strange mixture of talents: he was a classicist (in the literary sense) by training; a mathematician by inclination; an economist and statistician by—shall we say—exposure. His mind and his pen passed swiftly, yet smoothly, from Marshall to Aristotle, from Sidgwick to Todhunter to obscure Minutes of Evidence—and usually back again to Marshall. Edgeworth's elegant and unorthodox style, studded with cleverly appropriate quotations from the *belles lettres*, has a charm (and difficulties!) rare in economic discussion. Nor did he tarry long at one point; his keen, highly analytical mind touched upon most of the important problems of economic theory. Rarely did he fail to leave an original and pregnant suggestion; almost as often, alas, he was content to pass on immediately to a new problem, one still cloaked in the glamour of novelty or neglect. ". . . as I pass in the course of a rapid survey, I may sometimes root up a weed which has proved noxious, or drop a seed which may germinate." [2]

[1] Cf. J. M. Keynes, "Francis Ysidro Edgeworth," *Essays in Biography* (New York, 1933), pp. 267–93; A. C. Pigou, "Professor Edgeworth's Collected Papers," *Economic Journal*, XXXV (1925), 177–85.

[2] *Collected Papers Relating to Political Economy* (London, 1925), II, 370; cf. also II, 300. All subsequent references are to the *Collected Papers*, unless otherwise noted. Virtually all of these papers fall between 1889 and 1917; the chronology will be noted where relevant. I am indebted to The Macmillan Company for permission to quote from this work.

Edgeworth was, moreover, unquestionably the truly cosmopolitan economist of his generation. He possessed an extraordinary knowledge of contemporary American, German, French, Dutch, and Italian economics, as well as a close and sympathetic grasp of classical English theory. But in spite of all his erudition and originality, we must consider Edgeworth—as he considered himself—a disciple of Marshall. Where the former is silent, the latter must be assumed to speak. An excessive veneration for Marshall, and, for that matter, for all the "high authorities," had a heavy incidence on Edgeworth's own theories. Nor did he learn, as Keynes tells us, that footnotes, like most useful commodities, are not free goods.

In part as a result of this respect for authority, Edgeworth did not write exhaustively on general theoretical problems. His notable article, "The Theory of Distribution," is thoroughly typical; in it he presents not so much a theory of distribution as a commentary on the views of a large number of contemporaries and predecessors. The task of synthesizing such fragmentary observations is both difficult and treacherous. Nor is the task simplified by the fact that he directed his writings toward professional economists, not toward that Marshallian target, the "intelligent layman." One must accordingly interpret and supplement Edgeworth's writings, otherwise they are frequently incomprehensible.

Most of Edgeworth's important work falls outside the scope of the present study. His brilliant and more comprehensive writings on monopoly theory, taxation, and international trade are virtually excluded. We must be content with fragments on resource allocation, an exhaustive analysis of the laws of return, and notes on borderline aspects of distribution theory.

The Nature of Costs; Resource Allocation

Edgeworth follows classical tradition in his emphasis upon real costs. With regard to labor, he accepts almost completely the Jevonian analysis of the supply curve of labor for the individual laborer, *i.e.*, at equilibrium the marginal disutility of labor equals the marginal utility of product (I, 32 ff.; II, 278–79, 297 ff., 338; III, 32, 59 ff.).[1] Yet Edgeworth clearly recognizes several limitations to which this doctrine is subject.

The first limitation arises out of the impossibility for the typical modern laborer of varying freely the amount of his labor (I, 36–37; III, 60 ff.).[2] In mechanized production every man must ordinarily work as long as the plant is running. This offers a certain limitation to the validity of the Jevonian theory, but on several grounds Edgeworth holds that the theory is only slightly impaired. The laborer may change his occupation; piece-work wages offer greater flexibility; the supply of labor of a given sort is affected by the cost of education and training; and, finally, even under fixed hours the amount of labor performed by the laborer may vary.

Edgeworth's arguments for the Jevonian theory are pertinent but not wholly convincing. The transfer between occupations is permissible under the pain (or the alternative) cost theory only if the transfer can be made without varying wages per unit of productive effort. It must also be assumed, and this is generally untrue, that other things, especially the consumption of the laborer, remain unchanged in his new occupation. The piece rate system is only a partial escape, for with mechanized production the output of the laborer per unit of time must still be essentially standardized. The last two points, cost

[1] Also *Mathematical Psychics* (London, 1881), pp. 65–66, 140.

[2] Cf. also, *infra*, pp. 185 f.

of education and real variations in effort, are questions of fact—unfortunately the sort of economic facts that are never secured. Neither would seem important.

A second type of indeterminacy in the Jevonian theory arises out of what Edgeworth, following Cairnes, calls industrial competition, or competition between occupations (I, 18 ff.). Edgeworth's pain cost theory requires that the laborer equate the marginal attractiveness of all occupations, just as he equates the weighted marginal utilities of all commodities. Yet it is proverbial that no man can serve two masters—let alone the *n* masters required by mathematical economics! But if, as is almost universally the case under division of labor, the laborer works at only one occupation, it is difficult to see how the marginal advantageousness (or, reciprocally, the marginal disutility) of various occupations can be equated. The pain cost and the alternative cost theories collapse. No real solution is offered; it is merely hinted that the problem may be overcome by comparing the disutilities of various laborers.[1] But it is now well established that comparison of the subjective magnitudes of different people is even conceptually impossible. As a result little is left of Edgeworth's pain cost theory.

The disutility theory is also applied to savings, where (following Marshall) it is suggested that the equilibrium condition requires equality of the marginal disutility of abstinence and the marginal utility of savings, *i.e.*, interest (I, 44 n.). This point will receive further attention in connection with distribution theory.

The alternative cost theory as applied to the allocation of productive resources, in contrast with its application

[1] ". . . the theory of value and distribution, involving the equation of net advantages in different occupations, suggests at least, if it does not require the comparison between, the welfare of different persons" (II, 475).

to determine *supplies* of productive resources, is strongly implicit in Edgeworth's writings, as with Marshall. But very little is explicitly stated. In his disutility theory, sketched above, Edgeworth implies that marginal disutilities will be equated, presumably because similar laborers will have similar utility schedules. Similarly with land, the "margin of cultivation" will be the same for land in all possible uses (II, 78, 80, 219). He attributes a much wider scope than does Mill to competing uses of land: it is an unusual condition to find "land for which there is no other use at all comparable in profitableness" (II, 219). The tendency toward "industrial" competition is, in fact, accepted, and this amounts to the assertion that resources move between various uses until the same return is secured in every use (I, 18 ff.; II, 5, 78 ff.).

The Laws of Return

Edgeworth's analysis of the laws of return is one of his most important contributions to economic theory. Confusion regarding these "laws" was virtually universal in economic discussion previous to his analysis in 1911 (I, 61 ff., also 151–57). Proportionate and ratio increases of product from the variable factor were used as synonymous with incremental increases by even such careful technical economists as Marshall and Wicksell, and less able theorists almost seemed intent on exhausting the possible number of methods of misusing the general relations.

Two fundamental definitions of decreasing return are recognized by Edgeworth. The primary concept is that of marginal return, "preferred as more directly related to the theory of *maxima*"; the secondary concept is that of average return. These definitions had been used as synonymous since the very "discovery" of the law of diminishing return,[1] although the slightest consideration should have revealed the difference between them.

The preliminary definition of the law of return in the primary sense is as follows: "When on the application of two successive equal doses of productive power, the increment of product due to the first dose is less than the additional increment due to the second, the law of increasing returns is said to act; and conversely it is a case of diminishing returns when the increment due to the first dose is greater than the increment due to the second" (I, 63).[2]

TABLE 2[3]

RETURNS FROM VARYING AMOUNTS OF LABOR AND EQUIPMENT APPLIED TO A GIVEN PLOT OF LAND

DAYS' LABOR OF MAN WITH TEAM AND TOOLS	TOTAL CROPS IN BUSHELS	INCREMENTS DUE TO SUCCESSIVE DOSES
2	0	0
5	50	50
10	150	100
15	270	<u>120</u>
20	380	110
25	450	70
30	510	60

The point where diminishing return begins to operate is indicated by the underlined figure in Table 2 (taken from Edgeworth), *i.e.*, after the third dose of five units.[4]

[1] Sir Edward West's belief in the equivalence of the two definitions is cited (I, 70 n.). Before writing his articles, Edgeworth himself had confused the two definitions. Cf. "Mathematical Method in Political Economy," *Palgrave's Dictionary of Political Economy* (London, 1923), II, 711; *Collected Papers*, II, 65.

[2] Edgeworth should have stipulated that the units of the variable productive power be homogeneous.

[3] *Collected Papers*, I, 63.

[4] Analytically, where y is product and x the variable amount of productive power, diminishing return is defined by the conditions, $\frac{dy}{dx} > 0$ and

The secondary or average form of the law is more general: ". . . the law of increasing return acts when the *average* product per unit of productive power applied increases, with the increase of productive power . . .; and the law of diminishing return, in the converse case" (I, 67). That this definition does not coincide with the primary concept can readily be shown from Table 3 (again taken from Edgeworth), where the large doses of Table 2 are divided into unit increments. Using the incremental concept, diminishing return sets in with the 16th dose of capital-and-labor; under the average concept it sets in with the 21st dose. In Table 2 diminishing return by either definition sets in at the same point, an accident due to the large size of the doses.

TABLE 3[1]

RETURNS FROM VARYING AMOUNTS OF LABOR AND EQUIPMENT APPLIED (IN SMALL DOSES) TO A GIVEN PLOT OF LAND

DAYS' LABOR OF MAN WITH TEAM AND TOOLS	TOTAL CROP IN BUSHELS	INCREMENTS DUE TO SUCCESSIVE DOSES	BUSHELS PER DAY'S LABOR
..	...	..	.....
12	195	23	16.25
13	219	24	16.85
14	244	25	17.43
15	270	26	18.00
16	295	25	18.44
17	319	24	18.74
18	341	22	18.94
19	361	20	19.00
20	380	19	19.00
21	398	18	18.95
..	...	..	.....

$\frac{d^2y}{dx^2} < 0$. Geometrically the interpretation is that the total product curve is concave toward the X axis,—the region beyond B in Figure VII, below.

[1] The figures are here altered slightly from those of Edgeworth to secure greater consistency (I, 68).

The statement of the law in the first or primary sense may be generalized for the case in which successive doses are of different sizes (I, 66–67). In general, ". . . the law of increasing cost or diminishing returns holds good when the ratio of the last increment of cost to the last increment of produce is greater than the ratio of the penultimate increment of cost to the penultimate increment of produce . . ." (I, 66 n.).[1] An algebraic statement may be added to emphasize this definition. Let x_0, x_1, and x_2 be different amounts of the variable factor, such that $x_0 < x_1 < x_2$. If $f(x)$ is total produce, then diminishing return operates at x_1 when

$$\frac{x_2 - x_1}{f(x_2) - f(x_1)} > \frac{x_1 - x_0}{f(x_1) - f(x_0)}.$$

If x_0 and $f(x_0)$ are set equal to zero, the primary definition is made to include the secondary case, but "the difference of degree almost amounts to a difference of kind." We may defer slightly Edgeworth's demonstration of the

[1] An almost equivalent definition is offered: ". . . when on the application of two (not in general equal) doses of productive power the increment of produce due to the two doses has to the increment of product due to the first dose alone a ratio greater than the ratio which the sum of the two doses has to the first dose, Increasing Return acts; and conversely if the former ratio is *less* than the latter, Diminishing Return" (I, 66). That the two definitions are not identical may be shown by restating this latter form in the notation used in the text. Then decreasing return holds at x_1 when

$$\frac{x_2 - x_0}{f(x_2) - f(x_0)} > \frac{x_1 - x_0}{f(x_1) - f(x_0)}.$$

The left members of the two inequalities differ, but will give the same qualitative conclusions. This follows from the fact that $x_0 = x_1 - \Delta x$, so that the left member of the latter inequality may be written

$$\frac{x_2 - x_1 + \Delta x}{f(x_2) - f(x_1) + \Delta f(x)}. \text{ Relative to } \frac{x_2 - x_1}{f(x_2) - f(x_1)},$$

the former term will be greater when decreasing return operates, since $\frac{\Delta x}{\Delta f(x)}$ is greater, and conversely for increasing return; they will coincide for constant return.

superiority of the primary definition,[1] to note an incidental point.

It is noted that Tables 2 and 3 may readily be translated from physical units to pecuniary units (I, 68–69). If the prices of the product and the productive resources are constant, this involves only the multiplying of the two variables, produce and capital-and-labor, by these constant prices. Figure VII illustrates equilibrium in such a case. *OBCD* now portrays cost in money terms;[2] *OA* represents receipts. Under competition, capital-and-labor will be employed up to the output where the tangent to total cost is parallel with the line of revenue (*OA*), or in more recent terminology, where marginal cost equals marginal revenue.

Edgeworth's argument for the priority of the primary concept rests essentially on one ground, that this concept "is the criterion of a maximum." The secondary definition of diminishing returns is not always misleading; it is suggested that in certain important cases the secondary criterion does not diverge from the primary. Several such cases are noted:

i. Diminishing return in the primary sense may hold at all points on the produce curve; then diminishing return in the average sense will be operative at all points also (I, 70).[3] But this is not universally true (see below).

ii. Under perfect competition, such an amount of the variable resource will be used that both forms of the law of decreasing return hold, even when there is initially increasing return. In Figure VII, point *B* marks the

[1] Although almost all contemporary American economists favored the average concept, *e.g.*, Walker, Bullock, Carver, and Seligman.

[2] That is, the vertical axis has been multiplied by the price of the variable factor. Fixed costs are neglected, but their inclusion would not affect output.

[3] This case requires that the total produce curve begin at the origin.

place where increasing costs sets in according to the primary definition, and point *C* marks the point where it sets in under the secondary definition. With a certain price (*i.e.*, the slope of *OA*), it may appear conceivable that a point between *B* and *C* may have a tangent parallel to the slope of total revenue, or price. "But the

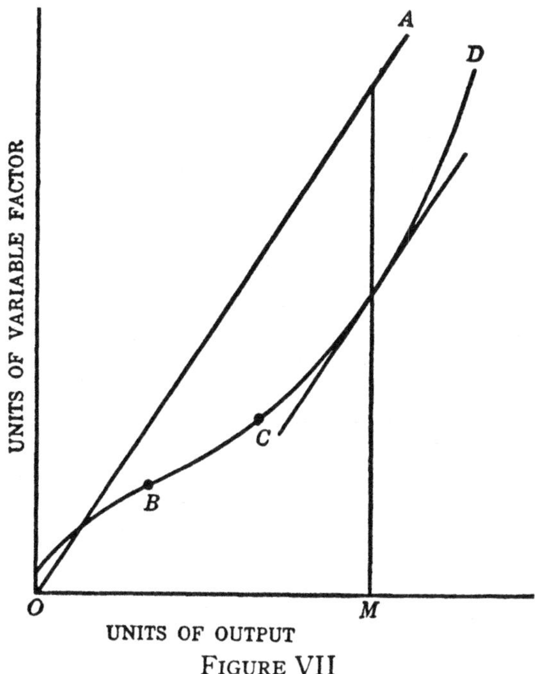

FIGURE VII

condition will be found to imply that the total gain obtained from the production is less than the total loss incurred; which is, normally and in the long run, absurd" (I, 71).[1]

iii. Under monopoly it may be possible to operate at a point between *B* and *C*, and the secondary definition

[1] The explicit proof is not given, but may be stated simply. Between *B* and *C* of Figure VII (corresponding to, but not identical with, doses 15 and 20 in Table 2), average cost is greater than incremental cost, hence a price equal to the tangent to *OBCD* along this region (which is equal to incremental cost) will not cover average costs; the firm will operate at a loss.

"becomes more significant." A government may subsidize a canal company to the extent of its "general expenses," or desperately competing railways may be "obliged in the struggle for survival to leave out of account past expenses of construction" (I, 72 ff.). Edgeworth is not clear at this point. In the short run, overhead or fixed costs do not affect marginal costs. But in the long run all costs are certainly variable. A general discussion of this problem will be taken up subsequently.

Nevertheless the priority of the incremental definition is defended on several grounds. Even in case iii, that of seller's monopoly, where the secondary definition will not diverge qualitatively from the primary definition, it is "fallacious" to speak of average return as the monopolist's criterion of output (I, 72).[1] And in the important instance of plural factors of production, the two definitions may give qualitatively different answers, even though the product shows diminishing return (in the primary sense) relative to each factor separately.[2]

Edgeworth's treatment of the two definitions is fundamentally correct, but his exposition is too subtle. Nowhere does he make the flat assertion, though it is

[1] Edgeworth also attributes precedence to the primary definition where a State Monopoly seeks to maximize "collective consumers' surplus."

[2] The argument is illustrated by the production function,

$$z = 9x - 5y - 3x^2 + 4xy - y^2. \text{ Here}$$

$$\frac{\partial^2 z}{\partial x^2} = -6 < 0, \quad \text{and} \quad \frac{\partial^2 z}{\partial y^2} = -2 < 0,$$

so diminishing return holds for each factor separately in the primary sense. By the analogy to one variable factor it is apparent that the secondary definition holds for both factors. Yet in this example increasing return would appear at certain outputs if both factors were increased at certain points, but in different amounts. This is true because the secondary condition for a maximum, *i.e.*,

$$\left(\frac{\partial^2 z}{\partial x^2}\right)\left(\frac{\partial^2 z}{\partial y^2}\right) > \left(\frac{\partial^2 z}{\partial x \partial y}\right)^2,$$

is not fulfilled, since $(-6) \cdot (-2) < (4)^2$. For the full argument, cf. I, 76 n.

strongly implied, that average return should not be used in short-run analyses. For nowhere does he offer a simple proof that such a use of average return will always lead to a misallocation of resources. His equivocation, which is verbal but not analytical, was probably that of a mediator, for the average concept was used by a preponderance of economists at the time he wrote.

The applicability of the laws of increasing and diminishing return furnishes the second theme in Edgeworth's discussion. He properly asserts the applicability of the law of diminishing return, with certain restrictions, to all industries, and not merely to agriculture—a restriction still prevalent at that time (I, 79–80). But on the other hand Edgeworth questions the universality of this doctrine. Wicksteed's assertion that the principle is axiomatic is not admitted; one must make the further restriction "that we take sufficiently large doses" (I, 80–81). Indivisibility of the factors is therefore implied to be the fundamental explanation for the presence of increasing return. This thought is not pursued, however; rather, Edgeworth turns to an enumeration of cases of increasing return (I, 81–84):

i. ". . . some things in order to be produced at all must be produced on a large scale—a railway, for instance. Here the outlay up to the large minimum requisite to produce any return at all may be considered as producing no return. . . ."
ii. ". . . size is favorable to multiplication of parts, and so to 'co-operation' . . . [or] 'organization.' . . ."
iii. Where the several factors vary discontinuously as compared with each other.[1]
iv. The three advantages of division of labor advanced by Adam Smith.

[1] This matter of discontinuous variation is treated at greater length at another point (I, 77–78), and will be treated below.

v. Certain miscellaneous cases, cognate to the above, such as:
   a. The water resistance to a ship does not increase proportionally with the ship's capacity.
   b. The stimulus arising out of the presence of numerous co-workers.

vi. The principle of self-insurance, when the firm is of sufficient size.

This list is not intended as a "full enumeration," but it is sufficient to raise an important question, enumeration of what? The law of return describes return from a variable amount of one productive factor, the other factors being held *constant.* Yet in the above list only cases (i) and (iii) are applicable to the problem of scale of output with a given plant, and (i) is really a special case of (iii). The remainder apply only to the variation in the *size of plant.* Classes (ii), (iv), and perhaps (vi) are relevant only to the theory of economies of large scale production, not to the theory of return.[1]

Both of the relevant cases, (i) and (iii), are clearly based on indivisibility of the factors of production. The argument for increasing return is clear and valid under this assumption. Edgeworth cites in illustration not only the familiar example of an additional box-car,[2] but also the case of the $(r + 1)$th foreman, who has not yet taken on his full complement of men. In general, whenever a finite quantity of an indivisible variable resource is essential before any return is secured, there will be a region of increasing return (I, 78). When Edgeworth says that a region of increasing return "is typical of many modern industries in which an initial outlay is required" (I, 71), he clearly suggests this point.

[1] Case (v,a) belongs in the former group; case (v,b) is in the latter group.

[2] But he is careful to note that the conditions must be specified, for an additional box-car may require an additional train, etc. (I, 93–94).

But he is not clear regarding the role of fixed or overhead expenditures. Increasing return (in the incremental sense) arises from the necessity for a finite initial amount of the variable factor, before any return is secured, not from the presence of fixed expenditures.[1] In cases previously cited he strongly implies that "general expense" and "past expenses of construction" are generally to be considered in determining incremental cost, which is clearly false. Yet, at the very end of his essay, he says:

> Not even Jupiter, as the ancients would have said, plans about the past. As the general in a campaign or battle acts *pro re natâ*, not strictly adhering to a preconceived plan, so Directors who would not have counselled investing in a railway that, as it has turned out, yields little profit over and above operating expenses, may still be well advised now in operating that unprofitable railway, since a little is better than nothing (I, 94).

The confusion must be ascribed to his failure to differentiate sufficiently the changes in scale of output with given plant, from the changes in the size of the plant and the industry. On the latter problem, variations in size of plant, Edgeworth does not differ enough from Marshall to merit special consideration.

The final topic in Edgeworth's discussion of the laws of return is joint cost (I, 84–91, also 178). The term "joint cost" is used to describe the case in which increasing the output of one commodity decreases the incremental cost of producing another commodity. "Rival production" is a name suggested for the converse condition. The discussion centers about the possibility of divergence between joint cost and increasing return, a divergence which Taussig had maintained as possible and Seligman had denied.

[1] Cf., *e.g.*, J. Viner, "Cost Curves and Supply Curves," *Zeitschrift für Nationalökonomie*, III (1931–32), 23–46.

Edgeworth presents a subtle geometrical argument which indicates that while joint cost and decreasing cost are not identical, they are generally associated. This elaborate analysis may be summarized very briefly in analytical form. Let x and y be the two products, and $z = f(x,y)$ the cost of producing both. Then incremental returns are increasing or decreasing, according as

$$\frac{\partial^2 z}{\partial x^2} \lesseqgtr 0, \qquad \text{and} \qquad \frac{\partial^2 z}{\partial y^2} \lesseqgtr 0.$$

Joint cost or rival production holds, however, according as

$$\frac{\partial^2 z}{\partial x \partial y} \lesseqgtr 0.$^{[1]}$$

The two sets of conditions are not directly dependent, and therefore joint cost may operate even when both products, separately, are subject to increasing cost, within certain limits.[2]

Joint cost and decreasing cost usually occur together. The more strongly joint cost operates, in the first place, the more probable it becomes that each product is sub-

[1] A more general condition is also suggested (I, 86 n.):

$$f(x + \Delta x,\ y + \Delta y) + f(x,y) \lesseqgtr f(x + \Delta x, y) + f(x, y + \Delta y).$$

This definition of joint cost, it should be noted, does not involve the condition that the cost of producing x and y together be less than the sum of costs of producing them separately, nor is either condition necessary to joint production.

[2] The full conditions for increasing cost in the primary sense include

$$\frac{\partial^2 f}{\partial x^2} > 0; \qquad \frac{\partial^2 f}{\partial y^2} > 0;$$

and

$$\left(\frac{\partial^2 f}{\partial x^2}\right)\left(\frac{\partial^2 f}{\partial y^2}\right) > \left(\frac{\partial^2 f}{\partial x \partial y}\right)^2.$$

Therefore $\frac{\partial^2 f}{\partial x \partial y}$ may be negative, but smaller than the product of the two second derivatives.

ject to diminishing cost;[1] although the converse reasoning does not hold. The important illustrative case, however, rests on the assumption of indivisibilities of the factors of production, *i.e.*, discontinuous variations take place in the amounts of the factors. The important illustration here is also in the railroad industry, where the facilities necessary to carry more freight of one kind decrease the cost of handling additional freight of another kind. Edgeworth may be accused of reasoning too generally on joint costs from "freak" mathematical cases,[2] and he exaggerates greatly the importance of joint costs in railroading. Carrying an increased amount of one kind of freight may reduce the cost of carrying a certain amount of another kind, but in general it would probably be cheaper to concentrate on just *one* kind of traffic.

Edgeworth emphasizes the incompatibility of decreasing marginal costs with competition, in either the short or the long run. ". . . if any producer can continually increase his supply at a constant or diminished cost, there appears no general reason why he should not, cutting out his competitors, supply the entire market" (II, 87, also 88–89, 436 ff.; III, 13).[3] He develops a virtually complete set of the cost curves used in present day analysis, but since most of these curves pertain to short-run problems and since he does not relate the curves to resource allocation or distribution theory, only a passing reference is necessary.[4] It should be noted that Edgeworth accepts Marshall's theory of external economics

[1] The reasoning is reinforced by the previous note, for if $\frac{\partial^2 f}{\partial x \partial y}$ becomes numerically great relative to the other second derivatives, the secondary condition for increasing cost in the primary sense will be violated.

[2] Cf., *supra*, page 118, note 2.

[3] The case of constant returns is discussed in Chap. XII, *infra*.

[4] Cf. the summary, "On Some Theories Due to Professor Pigou" (II, 429–49).

(I, 88 n., 273), and follows Pigou's theory—and accepts the criticisms thereof—that industries operating under decreasing costs should be subsidized (II, 428, 429; III, 187).[1]

The Theory of Distribution

Edgeworth's able paper, "The Theory of Distribution" (I, 13–60), which appeared in 1904, is his only important work in distribution theory proper. In it he pursues his usual practice of treating only with controversial problems in the neo-classical theory of distribution rather than attempting a consideration of the whole problem. Elsewhere in his writings, particularly in his essays on mathematical economics, very pregnant suggestions are also (and unfortunately, quite literally) dropped. These will be considered after discussing his orthodox treatment of the entrepreneur, land, labor, and capital.

An outstanding merit of Edgeworth's discussion must, however, be noted at the outset. The true relation of distribution to exchange is beautifully presented. He begins with the assertion, "Distribution is the species of Exchange by which produce is divided between the parties who have contributed to its production" (I, 13).[2] The mechanism of distribution, illustrated in the market of the "whites" and the "blacks," is nowhere more clearly and convincingly, and yet so briefly, portrayed. But these general features were well known by the time the essay appeared, and require no elaboration.

[1] The controversy over Pigou's theory is too involved to treat adequately here; and Edgeworth's position is too closely interwoven with Pigou's to permit separate treatment. Cf. esp. Edgeworth, "The Revised Doctrine of Marginal Social Product," *Economic Journal*, XXXV (1925), 30–39.

[2] Edgeworth frequently applies international trade theory to groups of resources or resource owners, but it would take us too far afield to trace these applications. Cf. II, 19, 376–78, etc.

THE ENTREPRENEUR

As an expository device in the analysis of the entrepreneur, Edgeworth resorts to the search for a definition. Four received conceptions of the entrepreneurial role are considered: the classical notion, the capitalist; Walker's view, the proprietor who borrows his capital; the risk-taker; and the no-profit entrepreneur presented by Walras. These will be considered in turn.

The capitalist in classical theory is, to repeat Edgeworth's quotation from Mill, one "who from funds in his possession pays the wages of the labourers, or supports them during the work; who supplies the requisite buildings, materials, and tools, or machinery; and to whom by the usual terms of the contract, the produce belongs to be disposed of at his pleasure." His reward was generally believed to be equal to the number of doses of capital multiplied by the rate of profit. But this theory does not accord well with the Ricardian rent theory, for, "as Sidgwick argues, there is no adequate reason for expecting that 'remuneration for management' as well as interest should tend to be at the same rate for capitals of different sizes" (I, 17).[1] The marginal productivity theory is, in fact, inapplicable to entrepreneurial activities (under the classical definition), since such activities are not bought and sold in the market in a variable number of units, as the theory requires (I, 17). Although the classical doctrine is accurate enough to support the "practical consequences" drawn from it, the explanation is inadequate from a theoretical viewpoint.

Nor is the second concept, that of Walker, completely satisfactory (I, 17–22). For after interest is paid on the capital, all of which is borrowed, there remains a surplus

[1] Compare his former opinion to the contrary, *Mathematical Psychics*, p. 33.

composed of both rent and the net income of the entrepreneur. The portion of the surplus accruing to the entrepreneur depends on two types of competition:

i. Commercial competition, or the pursuit of arrangements which will maximize profits within a given occupation.
ii. Industrial competition, or the selection of the most profitable occupation.

The first form of competition leads to the employment of each factor up to the point where the marginal product of a unit equals its cost. At this point Edgeworth borders on a general marginal productivity theory. In a footnote he sets up the equation which easily leads to the general solution (I, 20 n.). Letting P be net product; $f(a,b,c)$ the gross product; π the price of the product; p_a, p_b, and p_c the respective prices of factors, a, b, and c; then the entrepreneur seeks to maximize

$$P = \pi f(a,b,c) - ap_a - bp_b - cp_c,$$

subject to the condition that each factor of production be subject to diminishing returns.[1] The obviously implied solution yields the equation:

$$\pi = \frac{p_a}{f_a} = \frac{p_b}{f_b} = \frac{p_c}{f_c}.$$

But the context makes it clear that this theory is useful only in explaining how the entrepreneur maximizes his gain, and how it is separated from the total product; profits are still a residual. The next step in the argument, indeed, is to point out that the entrepreneur's effort is variable, and will be increased to the point where the increment of utility of product equals the increment of disutility of effort.

[1] *I.e.*, $f_{aa} < 0$; $f_{bb} < 0$; and $f_{cc} < 0$, and the usual secondary conditions, where the subscripts denote the variables with respect to which $f(a,b,c)$ is differentiated.

Once the second form, industrial competition, is introduced, the attractiveness of different occupations will be equalized. The return to the entrepreneur then takes on a similarity to the earnings of labor, "from a certain point of view, which is doubtless proper to the publicist and philosopher" (I, 20). But Edgeworth quotes with approval Taussig's view that the mechanism of distribution for the entrepreneur is too different, for practical purposes, to treat profits like other shares. And thus the second approach is most unsatisfactorily dismissed.

Certain minor topics are also considered (I, 21–22). When the competition between industries is imperfect, the entrepreneurs in the more favored industries will secure additional returns partaking of the nature of rent. And if the capitalist's efforts do not increase proportionally with the size of the concern, nevertheless at the margin the disutility of his effort will equal the utility of his return, due to commercial competition. This last line of thought would remove most of the justification for the "representative firm," if it were rigorously followed.

The third view of the entrepreneur, as the risk-taker, receives summary treatment (I, 22–24). Here the shareholder is the leading and most suggestive example of the entrepreneurial type. His investment secures a rate of return equal to its marginal productivity, plus compensation for risk. Whether risk-taking is an independent factor of production is left an unanswered question, but the implication of his latest views (1925) is strong that such a view, as in Pigou's earlier *Wealth and Welfare*, is proper (I, 59–60).

The last definition, that of Walras (and of Barone, Pareto, Clark, and Schumpeter, among others) is the no-profit entrepreneur (I, 24 ff.; also II, 311, 378–81, 469). Edgeworth refuses to accept the concept. The apparent reason, which is most paradoxical in Edgeworth of all contemporary economists, is that the idea of self-directed (or rather consumer-directed) production is too heroic a construction to possess any realism. He must be thinking of "captains of industry" when he cites approvingly Mangoldt's assertion, "We must suppose the existence of entrepreneur's gain,—otherwise what object has the entrepreneur to increase his business?"—and Edgeworth declares it "a strange use of language to describe a man who is making a large income, and striving to make it larger, as 'making neither gain nor loss' " (I, 25). He simply cannot visualize the entrepreneurial role—more properly its absence—in a stationary and perfectly competitive economy. He always associates, as the classical economists and Marshall did, the activities of contemporary English captains of industry with the concept. Yet Edgeworth sees that the argument is based largely on differences in assumptions, and goes on to say, "However, I am quite prepared to find that there is no material disagreement between us, that we are looking at different sides of the same shield—I at the gold side, he [Pareto] at the side which is devoid of all precious metal" (II, 381). The metaphor is not very fair, but if we accept it, the retort is obvious: gold is no longer the only important currency in either business or economic circulation. Edgeworth's view of the entrepreneur has been shown to be definitely inferior to that of Walras for the purposes of theoretical analysis.

Yet Edgeworth virtually accepts, after lengthy consideration (I, 26–30; cf. also II, 336–39), Barone's theory that the entrepreneur receives his marginal product, *i.e.*, that the earnings of managerial ability are essentially a wage.[1] The theory does not hold with complete

[1] Cf. Barone, *infra*, Chap. XII.

generality, for there is no reason "for regarding the remuneration of the entrepreneur as the product of the number of doses (*e.g.*, hours worked) and the marginal productivity of a dose (multiplied by a coefficient depending on the length of the productive process)" (I, 28). The reasoning is similar to that underlying wage indeterminacies (see below), arising out of indivisibility of the unit. But in the important special case of managers hired by stockholders (the third definition), the marginal productivity explanation may be said to hold. Managers will compete for positions so that no manager will secure more than the amount he adds to the product of a concern. Edgeworth thus arrives at what is, for all practical purposes, the "proof of the new law" of distribution, the general marginal productivity theory. The subsequent discussion of other factors of production should be understood as supplementary, not contrary, to this law.

LAND

In the discussion of rent of land, Marshall is closely followed: ". . . the most salient feature in the transactions respecting *land* is the circumstance that the quantity of ground, or at least space, is limited, not capable of being increased by human effort" (I, 32; cf. also II, 85, 133, 141, 143 n., 192 ff.).[1] The brief elaboration is also thoroughly Marshallian. Land is a form of capital to the entrepreneur although not to society; a tax on rent will not disturb production—subject to subtle qualifications (cf. II, 187 ff.); but tax reforms designed to secure unearned increments of value should be careful to observe existing equities (I, 32–34; II, 126–226, *passim*). Edgeworth differs from Marshall only in placing consid-

[1] However, it is intimated that in a static state it is permissible to group land with capital goods; cf. III, 100, and *Memorials of Alfred Marshall* (London, 1925), p. 68.

erably more emphasis upon the capital invested in present "land" (II, 200 n., 204 ff.).

LABOR

The discussion of wages is equally brief. A considerable portion of this section is devoted to a powerful criticism of Böhm-Bawerk's concept of the "marginal pairs" (I, 37–39). Of general wage theory very little is said. The Jevonian concept of equality of marginal utility of wages and marginal disutility of labor is accepted (I, 35), and this rate is determined simultaneously with the condition that the incremental product of the laborer must equal his wage (I, 36; II, 384).

Exceptional attention is devoted to the problem of the determinateness of wage contracts.[1] In the paper on distribution it is pointed out that if each employer hires but one man, there is no necessary relationship between wage rates and disutility of labor. This form of indeterminacy, which is "the exception in the general labour market," may be overcome, however, by selling labor in smaller doses, say hours instead of days. In the earlier *Mathematical Psychics* the problem is also alluded to, primarily in connection with contracts between combinations of laborers and combinations of employers.[2] Edgeworth's discussion is concerned chiefly with *curiosa;* it need not detain us.[3]

CAPITAL

Edgeworth's fragmentary observations on capital theory do not permit of a completely unequivocal interpretation. The discussion is strongly influenced by Böhm-

[1] Compare, on this point, J. R. Hicks, "Edgeworth, Marshall, and the Indeterminateness of Wages," *Economic Journal*, XL (1930), 215–31.

[2] *Op. cit.*, Part II, *passim.*

[3] The differentiation between land and labor should be mentioned, however (I, 47–48).

Bawerk,[1] and there is considerable emphasis upon stages of production (I, 42–45). The implication is strong that productivity of capital is synonymous with lengthening the period of production, as when Edgeworth says, ". . . a larger share will be conveyed to each producer (other things being equal), the greater his distance from the final stage [of production]" (I, 43). But the acceptance of Böhm-Bawerk's theory is not complete. Edgeworth accepts, for instance, the fundamental symmetry between Marshall's "prospectiveness" and "productiveness." The growth of value of capital goods through time is due therefore to two facts: "that future pleasures are discounted and that production is increased by 'roundabout' methods" (I, 44 n.).[2] With the Austrian, it will be seen, the discount of future pleasures plays no part in the productivity explanation of interest. Edgeworth does not believe that increases of capital necessarily result in lengthening the period of production, for he concludes, "It may be doubted whether any great lengthening of the trains [of production] is possible without a concomitant improvement in the arts of production; yet, as Sidgwick observes, invention is not necessarily followed by increase of capitalization" (I, 50). Perhaps the more accurate summary would be to say that Edgeworth fundamentally accepts Marshall's discussion, but makes more room in it for the concept of a period of production.

Early Statements of the Marginal Productivity Theory

With his usual acumen, Edgeworth states in some of his earliest writings the kernel of the general marginal productivity theory. He first suggested in 1889 the out-

[1] *E.g.*, "To represent the continual expansion of value as the present ripens into the future, a series of concentric circles has been happily employed by Professor Böhm-Bawerk" (I, 43).

[2] On the former point, cf. also II, 101; III, 23.

line of the doctrine in question (II, 298).[1] If $f(c,h)$ is total product, where c is capital and h is land, and z is the interest rate and r the rent per acre, the individual seeks to maximize $f(c, h) - zc - rh$, "whence $\frac{\partial f}{\partial c} = z$ and $\frac{\partial f}{\partial h} = r$." Nor is this in contradiction to the Ricardian theory of rent, which may be written, $rh = f(c,h) - zc$. Edgeworth has only to substitute for z and r to secure a simplified statement of the marginal productivity theory. In a highly condensed footnote, the general equilibrium theory is adumbrated in 1894 (III, 54).[2] Assume two products, u and v, and two factors, x and y, where x_1 and y_1 enter into u, and x_2 and y_2 into v. Let p_1 and p_2 be the prices of u and v respectively, and π_1 and π_2 of x and y respectively. There are then 10 unknowns, u, v, x_1, x_2, y_1, y_2, p_1, p_2, π_1, and π_2, which are determined by the 10 equations:

(1) $x_1 + x_2 = \phi(\pi_1)$, the supply function for factor x.
(2) $y_1 + y_2 = \psi(\pi_2)$, the supply function for factor y.
(3) $u = f_1(x_1,y_1)$, the production function for u.
(4) $v = f_2(x_2,y_2)$, the production function for v.
(5) $u = F_1(p_1)$, the demand function for u.
(6) $v = F_2(p_2)$, the demand function for v.
(7) $\frac{\partial f_1}{\partial x_1} \cdot p_1 = \pi_1$, "since the application of x will be pushed up to the point where the additional gain is just balanced by the additional cost," and similarly in the following:

[1] The notation has been modified slightly. Marshall cites this development with approval; cf. *Principles of Economics* (8th ed., London, 1920), p. 848.

[2] Again the notation has been modified, and misprints in equations (8) and (9) have been corrected.

$$(8)\quad \frac{\partial f_1}{\partial y_1} \cdot p_1 = \pi_2.$$

$$(9)\quad \frac{\partial f_2}{\partial x_2} \cdot p_2 = \pi_1.$$

$$(10)\quad \frac{\partial f_2}{\partial y_2} \cdot p_2 = \pi_2.$$

This able summary of the general equilibrium theory clearly includes the marginal productivity theory, for equations (7) to (10) state the equality of marginal products and prices of the factors of production. But again the theory is not amplified.

Chapter VI

CARL MENGER[1]

FOR a long generation Carl Menger has been in Anglo-Saxon countries a famous but seldom-read economist.[2] Historians of economic thought always give to him at least honorable mention as the man who, with Jevons and Walras, rediscovered and popularized the theory of subjective value. But the barriers of inaccessibility and language have served effectively to hide all but the barest outlines of his work from the bulk of English-speaking students of economics. None of Menger's writings has been translated, and his *magnum opus*, *Grundsätze der Volkswirtschaftslehre*,[3] was for long out of print. Menger's fame, in fact, has been largely a reflection of the achievements of his foremost disciples, Wieser and Böhm-Bawerk. This is a serious injustice; in important respects his theoretical structure was superior to that of his followers.

It will be interesting to begin by comparing Menger with Jevons, who published his *Theory of Political Econ-*

[1] This chapter appeared in substantially the present form as "The Economics of Carl Menger," *Journal of Political Economy*, XLV (1937), 229–50. The writer is indebted to the editors of the *Journal of Political Economy* for permission to utilize this material.

[2] Consult F. A. von Hayek's Introduction to the reprint of the *Grundsätze*, in the London School Series of Reprints of Scarce Tracts (1934), for a general outline of Menger's life and work; his intellectual environment is finely treated by J. Schumpeter, "Carl Menger," *Zeitschrift für Volkswirtschaft und Politik* (N.F.), I (1921), 197–206.

[3] Vienna, 1871. All subsequent references will be to the *Grundsätze*, unless otherwise noted.

omy in the same year (1871) in which the *Grundsätze* appeared. Several parallels can be drawn between the two men. Each was, in contrast with Walras, essentially non-mathematical in method; each wrote on certain parts of economic theory but intended eventually to write a comprehensive treatise which never appeared;[1] each was in sharp revolt against the classical political economy. But Menger's theory was greatly superior to that of Jevons. It was systematic and profound; it avoided the clumsy and unnecessary use of mathematics; and in particular it generalized value theory to include the groundwork of a sound theory of distribution, although this was left in a rather embryonic state.

The two men differed greatly in their influence on contemporary economic thought. Jevons had virtually no direct followers. A strongly intrenched classical school, his repellent mathematical formulation, and the lacunae in his theoretical structure explain in part the fact that no "Jevonian" school emerged.

Menger was more fortunate. In his steps followed a group of able economists who, adhering closely to his general approach and frequently accepting even details and terminology of the *Grundsätze*, developed into the so-called "Austrian" school. Wieser and Böhm-Bawerk were outstanding among the nineteenth-century follow-

[1] Jevons' fragmentary *Principles of Economics*, which was published posthumously (London, 1905), is well known; Menger added *erster, allgemeiner Teil* to the title-page of his first edition, very much as Marshall did nineteen years later.. Menger projected three additional parts to deal, respectively, with: distribution, money, and credit; production and commerce; and general economic policy. Cf. Introduction to second edition (1923), p. vi. This second, posthumous edition was edited by Karl Menger, his son. It contains more extensions than revisions, particularly in utility analysis, and no important changes are made in distribution theory. It will not be considered here; cf. F. X. Weisz, "Zur zweiten Auflage von Carl Mengers 'Grundsätzen,'" *Zeitschrift für Volkswirtschaft und Politik* (N.F.), IV (1924), 134–54.

ers, but there were many others—among them Sax, Komorzynski, Mataja, Gross, and Meyer. Menger's success is clear in the light of Jevons' failure. The former faced no established theoretical tradition—what little theoretical German economics there was at the time possessed a strong anticlassical bias; Menger's treatment was lucid, systematic, and comprehensive; and, to mention a factor of ambiguous importance, his was good economic theory.

It will be necessary to consider first Menger's theory of subjective value, since he applies this theory directly to the evaluation of productive services. Thereafter, his discussions of the theories of productive organization, imputation, and the specific distributive shares will be analyzed.

The Theory of Subjective Value

A thing secures *Güterqualität* (the quality of being a good), begins Menger, from the simultaneous fulfillment of four conditions (p. 3): (1) There must be a human want. (2) The thing must possess such properties as will satisfy this want. (3) Man must recognize this want-satisfying power of the thing. (4) Man must have such disposal over the thing that it can be used to satisfy the want. Things which fulfill the first two conditions are "useful things" (*Nützlichkeiten*); those fulfilling all four requirements are "goods" (*Güter*). The absence or loss of any one of these four conditions is sufficient to entail loss of a thing's *Güterqualität*. The last two of Menger's conditions are merely formal; the economic significance of the others deserves elaboration.

Human wants need not be rational; cosmetics, just as much as food, possess *Güterqualität* (pp. 4–5)—although Menger is optimistic enough to believe that irrational wants become less important as civilization progresses. Similarly, if the belief that a thing possesses want-satisfying power is mistaken (*e.g.*, quack medicines), that again does not affect its *Güterqualität*. And, finally, the word "thing" is purposely vague; Menger argues strenuously that useful human activities, as well as useful material goods, belong in the category of goods (pp. 5–7).

This emphasis upon non-material goods—which is properly extended to include such things as monopolies, goodwill, and patents (pp. 6–7)—is a genuine though neglected contribution to economic thought. Classical theory restricted economic analysis primarily to material goods (*e.g.*, "productive" vs. "unproductive" labor), and this practice served—and still serves—to obscure some of the most fundamental concepts of economics, such as income, production, and capital. Menger follows the classicists, however, in failing to distinguish between *goods* and *services from goods* on the basis of the time dimensions involved, as we shall presently see.

Menger immediately forestalls an obvious question: Do productive resources, which cannot be consumed directly, lack *Güterqualität?* Clearly not, for, although they cannot satisfy wants directly, they can be transformed into want-satisfying goods, and indeed most of man's economic activity is concerned with this transformation (pp. 8 ff.). Such productive resources are indeed goods; they are distinguished from directly consumable goods, "goods of first order," by the appellative "goods of higher order." If bread is a first-order good, flour, salt, fuel, and the baker's services are second-order goods, wheat is a third-order good, etc.

Menger's differentiation of productive resources from consumption goods solely on the basis of proximity to consumption led to a result important to economic theory. Why should not the same theory that is used to explain the value of consumption goods be applied to "unripened" consumption goods? Quite obviously it should be, and Menger's application of his value theory to production goods led to a correct if not wholly adequate statement of the marginal productivity theory of distribution.

The classification of goods into ranks was in itself, however, of dubious value. The same good, say coal, might be used both as a good of first order (in domestic heating) and perhaps as a good of ninth order (in smelting ore) in even a simple economy. And to attempt to trace in detail the stages in the production of even a simple commodity—a common pin, for instance—in the highly complex modern economy would amount to nothing less than a detailed description of economic life and its history. The concept of ranks is too precise, in other words, either for our analytical powers or for our analytical requirements. Menger himself makes no use of the concept of ranks other than to distinguish consumption goods from production goods; he says that the chief use of the concept is in providing an "insight into the causal relationship" between goods and want-satisfactions (p. 10). What Menger should have emphasized in connection with the rank of goods, however, is that only services are consumed (*i.e.*, are of the first order), and all durable goods are properly of higher order.

One peculiarity of goods of higher order, Menger notes, is that they cannot usually produce goods of lower order without the cooperation of other, "complementary" goods of the same order (pp. 11 ff.).[1] It follows that, if

[1] Menger saw what on occasion some of our modern theorists have failed to see: that where there is only one productive factor and one product that

the complementary goods of higher order are lacking,[1] the "good" in question cannot satisfy wants even indirectly, and is useless; it is no longer a good.

A second peculiarity of higher-order goods is the dependence of their own want-satisfying power on the want-satisfying power of their final, first-order products (pp. 17–21). This is the germ of the theory of distribution through "imputation"—*i.e.*, the derivation of the value of productive agents from the value of their products.

> It is now clear that the existence of unsatisfied human needs is the condition of each and every *Güterqualität*, and this substantiates the principle that goods lose their *Güterqualität* as soon as the needs whose satisfaction they previously served have disappeared. This is equally true whether the goods in question can be used directly in primary relationship to want-satisfaction or whether they secure their *Güterqualität* through a more or less mediate causal nexus leading to the satisfaction of human wants (p. 18).
>
> The requirements for goods of higher order are conditioned by our requirements for goods of first order . . . (p. 35).

Unsatisfied human wants are thus the ultimate basis of *Güterqualität*. Were people to lose their taste for tobacco, then cigars, cigarettes, and pipes, tobacco stocks, importers' services, factories, and even tobacco plantations—all these would lose their *Güterqualität*. It should be noted that the criterion of unsatisfied wants excludes

factor is almost always economically identical with its product, for no change could have taken place in the factor in the absence of another factor. Where this heroic construction is assumed, it is usually nonsense to speak of costs, returns, or distribution.

[1] The definition of complementary goods is extended (p. 14) beyond its original meaning to include all goods of higher orders needed to transform the higher good in question into a final product. This is done to avoid the situation where, for instance, all the necessary complementary goods of third order might produce a good of second order which, however, lacked the complementary goods of second order necessary to transform it into a final product.

free "goods" from the category of "goods," but Menger is not consistent in this terminology (cf. pp. 57 ff.).

The final peculiarity of goods of higher order to be noted at this point is the fact that their utilization always requires time (pp. 21–26). Since, in the absence of complete knowledge and of complete control over nature, the future is not certain, the *anticipated* want which will be satisfied by a good of higher order at the end of its production process determines its *Güterqualität.* We may defer further consideration of higher-order goods to the section on Menger's theory of distribution.

So far Menger's theory has been presented only in its broad lines of qualitative causality; the quantitative aspects must now be sketched. Two preliminary concepts are of importance: (1) *Bedarf* (requirements), or the amount of each kind of good which an individual requires to satisfy all his wants within a given period of time (p. 34); and (2) supply, or the quantities of the various goods which are available to meet these needs during the same period of time (pp. 45 ff.). Menger's concept of *Bedarf* has no exact English equivalent. His definition and treatment suggest that the *Bedarf* of an individual is the quantity of goods necessary to bring about a complete satisfaction of that individual's needs (cf. pp. 34 and note, 38, 41).[1] He admits that human needs are indeed capable of indefinite development (*ins Unendliche entwicklungsfähig*), but this is an historical phenomenon; for sufficiently limited periods of time *Bedarf* is a fixed datum for each good (p. 38). There is no recognition by Menger of the dependence of the *Bedarf* for one commodity on the available quantities of other commodities.

[1] *Bedarf* is therefore closely related to Walras' *utilité d'extension;* cf. *Eléments d'économie politique pure* (Lausanne, 1926), pp. 72 ff.

An elaborate argument is presented (pp. 35–50) to prove that these two types of information, on *Bedarf* and on supplies, can legitimately be treated as known data in the analysis rather than analytical results (such as prices). This demonstration was highly essential, for the classical economists, whose analytical methods were more advanced than those used in contemporary German economics, did not assume productive resources to be given in amount.[1] Menger, on the other hand, clearly includes goods of higher order, or resources, among his fixed stocks (pp. 45–51). He must be considered one of the first economists to introduce the indispensable methodological tool of "static" assumptions into economic analysis. His treatment is, to be sure, primitive and oversimplified in the light of present day accomplishments, but at the time it was a distinct innovation. In this respect, moreover, he was more influential, although less rigorous, than Walras, and distinctly superior to Jevons.[2]

With these two sets of data, supplies and requirements (each per unit of time), it is now possible to face the basic economic question: How should the given quantities be distributed to secure the greatest possible satisfaction of needs (pp. 51 ff.)? [3] Requirements (*Bedarf*) and available stocks stand in one of three possible relationships to each other: either may be greater than the other, or they may be equal.

[1] As Professor F. H. Knight has pointed out: "The stationary state of these classical writers was the *naturally* static or economic condition, which is the goal of progress . . . not a state made static by arbitrary abstraction as a methodological device" (*Risk, Uncertainty and Profit* [Cambridge, 1921], p. 143 n.). Cf. also the penetrating analysis of L. Robbins, "On a Certain Ambiguity in the Conception of Stationary Equilibrium," *Economic Journal*, XL (1930), 194–214.

[2] Jevons had but a suggestion (*Theory of Political Economy* [4th ed., London, 1911], p. 267); Walras' genuine advance was obscured from the view of most economists by its mathematical garb (*op. cit.*, esp. pp. 175 ff.).

[3] The present discussion will be limited to goods of first order.

Requirements, first, may exceed available quantities—the relationship which is to be observed "with the vast majority of goods." In this case the loss of a significant part of the stock will cause some known need to remain unsatisfied. Accordingly: "People will endeavor . . . to secure the greatest possible result by the intelligent application (*zweckmässige Verwendung*) of every given unit (*Teilquantität*) of the goods which stand in this quantitative relationship, and, similarly, to secure a given result with the least possible quantity of such goods . . . (pp. 52–53).[1] The individual will therefore devote such goods only to his "more important wants." Goods in this relation—*i.e.*, smaller in quantity than the requirements for them—are "economic goods"; they will be kept, conserved, and used only according to the principle of economic behavior just quoted. Costs of any sort are *per se* irrelevant to the question of whether a good is economic or non-economic (p. 61 n.).

The second possible relationship holds when available stocks exceed requirements (pp. 57 ff.). Under this circumstance there is no inducement to husband the goods in question, to conserve their useful properties, to consider the relative importance of the wants they can satisfy, or, in general, to treat such goods in an economic manner. They are, in short, "non-economic" goods.

Changing times or circumstances may turn "non-economic" goods into "economic" goods, or vice versa (pp. 60 ff.). Factors contributing to a change in the relationship of supplies to requirements include changes in population, changes in human wants, discovery of new want-satisfying powers of goods, and, of course, depletion of resources. But this is historical change, external to Menger's theoretical corpus, and need not be pursued.

[1] For the translation of *Teilquantität* as "unit" see *infra*, pp. 146 f.

The third possible relationship between requirements and supplies, that of equality, is even less significant and will be passed over.

We are now on the threshold of the quantitative determination of subjective value. One further preliminary step is necessary, the classification of wants according to their importance. "If we have indicated correctly the nature of the value of goods, so that it is established that in the last resort only the satisfaction of our wants has significance for us and that all goods clearly secure their value by a transfer to them of this significance, then the *differences* in value of various goods, which we can observe in actual life, can be based only on the differences in the significance of those want-satisfactions which depend on disposal over these goods" (p. 87). Obviously our different classes of wants are of widely differing importance to us: food, clothing, and shelter are indispensable; other goods, such as tobacco and chessboards, serve only to add comfort or pleasure (pp. 88 ff.). And not only do our specific kinds of wants, and accordingly their satisfactions, differ in importance, but our satisfaction of a particular want will be more or less complete as the quantity of goods available to meet it is greater or smaller (p. 90). A little food preserves life, more food insures health,[1] and additional quantities bring amenities, but to a decreasing extent,[2] until a point of satiation is reached (p. 91).

Menger illustrates by an arithmetical example the differences in the importance of the satisfaction of various kinds of wants and the decrease in the importance

[1] But this additional food will be of a different type. Menger is speaking of broad classes of wants, not of the wants for specific goods. This ambiguity is never cleared up, unfortunately.

[2] ". . . die darüber hinausgehende Befriedigung aber eine immer geringere Bedeutung hat" (p. 92).

of the satisfaction of each kind of want as the quantity of the good satisfying that want is increased (p. 93). This table is reproduced here in a slightly condensed form:

I	II	III	IV	...	X
10	9	8	7	...	1
9	8	7	...	...	0
8	7	...	1		
7	...	1	0		
...	1	0			
1	0				
0					

The columns I–X represent different kinds of wants, in the order of their importance; the numbers in any column represent successive want-satisfactions from unit increases of the stock of goods satisfying that want—in modern terms, the "marginal" utilities. Column I may represent food; Column IV, tobacco. Ten units of "food" represent the individual's *Bedarf* for food.

Menger probably does not mean to say that the first unit of tobacco yields a satisfaction equal to that of the fourth unit of food, but only to indicate orders of importance; but unfortunately he is not precise as to the meaning of his magnitudes. He states that the "economizing" individual seeks to equalize all these margins in order to maximize his want-satisfaction: ". . . The individual will endeavor . . . to bring the satisfaction of his needs for tobacco and for means of sustenance into equilibrium" (p. 94). Indeed it is this ". . . weighing of the different importances of wants, the choice between those which remain unsatisfied and those which, *according to the available means*, get satisfied, and the determination of the degree to which these latter wants get satisfied" that supplies the most consistent and influential motive in man's economic behavior (pp. 94–95, my italics).

Today it is a commonplace that this endeavor to maximize want-satisfaction by equating the "marginal" satisfactions of all wants can take place only through the allocation of income, and indeed Menger's theory of the distribution of "available means" seems to approach this.[1] Yet it is not clear that Menger sees the role of completely general purchasing power, for in the subsequent discussion he speaks of quantities of specific goods in relation to their limited possible uses—*e.g.*, the farmer's corn may be used for food, seed, feeding cattle, etc. (pp. 95 ff.).

Elsewhere he notes that the ability to satisfy more than one want (or column) is a power possessed by "most goods" (p. 112 n.). He does not distinguish satisfactorily between goods which satisfy the one want and those which can satisfy qualitatively different wants.[2] But Menger's solution is, for the latter case, clear and correct:

> If a good is able to satisfy different types of wants, each of which has decreasing significance with the degree of completeness with which it has already been satisfied, the economic man will direct the quantity at his disposal first to the satisfaction of the most important wants regardless of what type they may be, and the remainder will be devoted to those concrete want-satisfactions which are next in importance, and so on with the filling of less important wants. This practice has the result that the most important of all those concrete wants which are not satisfied are of the same significance for all types of wants, and accordingly all con-

[1] If the allocation of income is intended, then not marginal utilities but marginal utilities divided by prices, or in terms of units of equal value, are equated, of course.

[2] Menger does not seem to realize the fundamental difficulties involved in making this distinction—difficulties which have manifested themselves so successfully in preventing the development of a satisfactory definition of a commodity. But although the basic problem is still unsolved (and probably will remain so), Menger's development is crude in comparison with modern statements.

crete wants are satisfied to an equal level of importance [p. 98 n.].

Yet this is not a complete solution, since there are an infinite number of needs which any particular good cannot satisfy, and it is strange that one of the most important steps in the entire argument is found only in a footnote. Menger's failure to develop generally the method by which the individual maximizes his want-satisfaction is an outstanding weakness in his theory of value.

The valuation of a stock of goods follows directly from the principles of economic behavior and of variation in the quantitative importance of wants. Assume that the individual has five units of the good capable of satisfying wants I and II. He will apply this stock to the three most important stages of I, with satisfactions 10, 9, and 8, respectively, and to the two most important stages of want II, with satisfactions 9 and 8, respectively. The last unit, the "marginal" application in later terminology, will satisfy a want which has an importance of 8, and since by definition all units are identical, all will be valued at 8. We have then the principle of value: "The value of a unit of the available stock of a good is for every individual equal to the significance of the least important want-satisfaction which is brought about by a unit of the total quantity of the good" (p. 99 [italicized by Menger]; also pp. 107–8, etc.). Wants—equivalent to utility in Jevons—and supply are of correlative importance, so that although our need for air is great (represented by, say, Col. I), the supply is even greater and air is worthless. Diamonds are less needed (here perhaps Col. VIII), but the supply is so small that their value is high. The "paradox" of utility and value of the classicists is solved.

The interesting question of the right to attribute a

"marginal" or "incremental" utility theory of value to Menger may be considered briefly. His analysis is always in terms of the *Teilquantität*—literally the fraction or portion. Yet at numerous points the word is qualified: "practically significant portion"; "portion which is just observable." [1] It seems clear that Menger is thinking in terms of small, finite quantitative changes, and not of infinitesimals. He, unlike his co-discoverers of the utility principle, Walras and Jevons, probably had no mathematical training, and would therefore use such a common-sense approach rather than the convenient analytical concepts of continuity and derivatives. The concept of a small finite change is, of course, more realistic. In a mathematical treatment it yields a slightly indeterminate solution: the value found by withdrawal of a unit is larger than the value found by addition of a unit. But the realistic mathematician has the same problem if he postulates a limited power of discrimination on the part of the consumer, as with Edgeworth's "minimum sensible." [2] Accordingly, Menger seems clearly to have formulated a "marginal" utility theory (although, as with Jevons, Menger devotes little attention to total utility).

Productive Organization: the Allocation of Resources

Menger lays the groundwork for a correct theory of productive organization—*i.e.*, for the determination of the allocation of resources. The final development, however, the theory of alternative cost, is left for Wieser to formulate.[3] This great hiatus in Menger's theoretical

[1] Thus, pp. 52, 77 (twice), 83, 102, 103, etc.

[2] Cf. the remarks in *Mathematical Psychics* (London, 1881), pp. 7, 60, 99–100.

[3] Wieser's first publication, *Über den Ursprung und die Hauptgesetze des wirtschaflichen Wertes* (Vienna, 1884), pp. 146–70, gives the essentials of the alternative cost theory. Wieser himself, however, never applied the theory correctly to the problem of distribution. Compare the next chapter.

system is very hard to explain, especially since the correct allocation of resources is suggested in the footnote which has already been quoted in connection with his value theory.[1] There, it will be recalled, Menger suggests that the most economic utilization of a good which satisfies several wants is to equalize its "marginal" significance for all wants. This pregnant suggestion, which contains the heart at once of the alternative cost theory of value and of distribution theory, is never elaborated, nor is it applied directly to the problem of allocating productive services.

Menger's preoccupation with directly consumable goods probably plays a part in the fundamental defect in his theory—the complete neglect of costs—but a more important explanation lies in his failure to realize the continuity of production, *i.e.*, to realize that the price of a good must be sufficient to repay its costs (which are the products its resources could produce elsewhere) if the industry is to hold the productive resources used in it. This failure appears most clearly in his criticism of the cost theories of value (esp. pp. 119–22). As Menger says, historical costs are irrelevant to value; a diamond is equally valuable whether it has been found by chance or is the product "of a thousand days of labor." And it is true that "experience also teaches that the value of the productive factors necessary to the reproduction of many goods [*e.g.*, clothing which is no longer in fashion, obsolete machines, etc.] is much greater than the value of their product, and in many other cases their value is less than that of their product" (p. 121). But it is a *non sequitur* to argue from this, as Menger unfortunately does, that costs cannot influence value (pp. 119 ff.). He fails to consider the fact that although costs never have a

[1] Cf. p. 98 n.; *supra*, p. 145.

direct effect on value, yet they are—"in the long run"—of at least coordinate importance in its determination, and in the limiting case of constant costs they are completely dominant. Only for very short periods of time is the supply curve of a commodity, assuming it to be perishable, so inelastic in comparison with its demand curve that the former may be ignored in price determination. And supply curves become more elastic as the time available for readjustments of scale of output increases, because resources become more mobile as between industries, and the influence of supply on price first becomes equal to and then typically far exceeds that of demand. Under certain assumptions such as atomistic competition, non-specialization of resources, and unlimited time for full adjustment of the productive organization, constant costs tend to prevail and, in so far as that condition is approximated, demand determines only the quantity of a commodity sold, not its price. Menger's theory is therefore applicable only to very short-run "market" prices, and his failure to recognize the increasing mobility of resources through time vitiates, accordingly, his refutation of cost theories of value. This is also true of his criticism of classical theories of rent, wages, and interest (pp. 143–52), but this aspect may be deferred to a later point.

Menger does, however, make one specific contribution to production theory, a contribution the importance of which literally cannot be exaggerated. That contribution consists in the realization that the proportions in which productive agents may be combined to secure the same product are variable—later known as the law of "proportionality" or "substitution":

> Now it is quite true that we have disposal over quantities of goods of lower order only by means of complementary

> quantities of goods of higher order, but it is equally certain that not only fixed quantities of the individual goods of higher order can be brought together in production, somewhat in the manner in which this is observed in chemical compounds. . . . Rather we are taught by the most general experience that a definite quantity of any good of lower order can be secured from goods of higher order which stand in very different quantitative relationships to each other . . . [p. 139; also p. 140].

This formulation of the principle of variation of proportions as a *general* rule governing *all* resources is one of Menger's greatest achievements, one which he is not required to share with either Jevons or Walras.[1] Classical theory recognized, of course, the possibility of varying the amount of capital-and-labor which could be applied to a given piece of land, and this was basic to the Ricardian theory of rent. But the proportion between labor and capital was generally assumed to be fixed; certainly variations in this proportion played no part in accepted classical theory.

The significance of the principle of variation of proportions is apparent. It leads directly to the marginal productivity theory of distribution (see next section). Until the principle of proportionality was fully developed, furthermore, no satisfactory solution of the problem of resource allocation was possible. Finally, as long as discussion ran in terms of fixed proportions between productive agents (or as long as the question was ignored), the individual firm could not be used for purposes of analysis. A firm would require all factors in fixed relation to output; only socially—*i.e.*, by general equilibrium analysis—would it be possible to fix the values of indi-

[1] Walras recognized the principle as early as 1876 (*Théorie mathématique de la richesse sociale* [1883], pp. 65–66), but he did not add the marginal productivity theory to his original fixed-coefficients approach until the third edition of the *Eléments* (1896). Compare, *infra*, Chap. IX.

vidual agents. It was a genuine retardation of economic advance that Wieser and Böhm-Bawerk (the latter in an extremely crude manner) returned to the assumption of fixed-coefficients.

Quite surprisingly, Menger fails even to mention explicitly the technical principle of diminishing returns from an increasing proportion of any agent in a combination, and, accordingly, to realize its importance for his theory of distribution. The theory of marginal productivity leads to absurd results if any factor is assumed to be subject to increasing or even constant returns. But such an assumption is itself much more absurd, for no problem of resource allocation would arise. Nevertheless, opponents of the marginal productivity theory (*e.g.*, Hobson) have occasionally used examples of increasing returns in "refutation."

One final point of excellence in Menger's brief treatment of production deserves notice: the absence of the classicists' "holy trinity" of land, labor, and capital. Productive factors are simply goods of higher order; the services of labor, land, and capital goods are on the same footing (p. 139). In Menger's treatment, in fact, specific productive agents are not grouped into arbitrary categories which lack economic significance. As a result, his theory of imputation, now to be considered, gains a symmetry difficult to secure so long as the classical trichotomy ruled economic discussion.

The Theory of Imputation

The greatest contribution of the theory of subjective value to theoretical economic analysis lies in the development of a sound theory of distribution. This means the view of distribution as the allocation of the total product among the resources which combine to produce it, through valuation by imputation. Prior to Menger no satisfactory theory of distribution had emerged. The classical view was one of the division of income between social classes: Smith and his followers never confronted the problem of how a given product may be imputed to the resources which cooperate in its production nor did they consider distribution as a value problem or discuss the pricing of productive services. Menger was the first economist to raise this question, and, moreover, to suggest the proper manner of answering it.

The outlines of the theory of imputation (*Zurechnung*) [1] —*i.e.*, the valuation of productive goods on the basis of their contribution to the value of their products—have already been indicated. Productive goods—goods of higher order—secure value only because they can satisfy wants indirectly, by producing consumption goods (pp. 67–70, 123–26, etc.). This leads to the general theorem of imputation: "The value of goods of higher order is always and without exception determined by the anticipated value of the goods of lower order in whose production they serve" (p. 124). The element of anticipation arises from the fact, previously noted, that production requires time.

The theory of the valuation of individual goods of higher order then follows from the theory of imputation and the theory of variation of proportions: "The value [of a quantity of a good of higher order] is equal to the difference between the significance of that want-satisfaction which would result if we had disposal over the quantity of the good of higher order whose value is in question and the significance, in the contrary case, of that satisfaction which would follow from the most economic ap-

[1] The word *Zurechnung*, as well as the word "margin" (*Grenze*), is due to Wieser.

plication of the totality of goods of higher order in our possession [*i.e.*, the remaining resources of this and other kinds]" (p. 142). The context (esp. pp. 139–40) makes it fairly clear—though not as clear as could be desired—that Menger is here, as elsewhere, speaking of the effect on the total product of the withdrawal of a *Teilquantität* (a unit) of a resource. This marginal product fixes the value of the resource.

Two cases are distinguished. When the withdrawal of one unit forces cooperating agents to seek employment in less profitable lines—the case of fixed proportions—the value of the variable factor equals the total loss of product minus the product secured in other industries by the complementary factors. But more commonly the proportions in which the factors may be combined are variable, and then the withdrawal of one unit of one agent is accompanied by a rearrangement of the remaining factors,[1] and the diminution of quantity or quality of the product determines the value of the unit which has been withdrawn.

As far as this theory goes—and it is unquestionably superior to any preceding explanation of the determination of the value of productive agents, with the possible exception of that of von Thünen [2]—it is essentially correct. The only real criticism is to be leveled at its inadequacy: Menger has failed to develop the indispensable postulate of diminishing returns; it is not clearly brought out that the units withdrawn must be small; and the question whether this method of valuation of agents exactly exhausts the total product is not raised.

[1] This necessary element of rearrangement is strongly implied (esp. p. 140) but not separately considered.

[2] Menger appears not to have known of von Thünen. Gossen and Cournot are the other two important economists who appear to have been unknown to Menger.

One general weakness in Menger's exposition which clouds his value theory is the failure, previously mentioned, to differentiate between durable goods of any order and their services: the distinction is essential to a sound theory of interest and rent. The value of a good, whether used in production or in consumption, is less than the aggregate value of its services during its "lifetime" if this is of appreciable duration. Nowhere does Menger clearly recognize this fact; its incidence on his theory of capital will be seen to be particularly heavy.

The Distributive Shares: Menger on Classical Theory

In a noteworthy section, entitled, "On the Value of Land and Capital Uses and of Land Services in Particular" (pp. 142–52), Menger offers a trenchant criticism of the classical division of the "factors" of production. Ricardo had recognized (however rightly) that the value of land was not due to the labor expended upon it, and to reconcile this fact with his labor theory of value he established land as a separate category of goods. Menger's comment is penetrating but inconclusive:

> The methodological misconception which lies in this procedure is easily perceived. That a large and important group of phenomena cannot be reconciled with the general laws of a science which concerns itself with these phenomena, is clear proof of the need for reform of that science. It is not, however, a ground for the separation of one group of phenomena from the remaining objects of observation which are completely similar in their general nature—which would justify the most dubious methodological expedients—, and for erecting special highest principles for each of the two groups (pp. 144–45).

Menger's criticism is valid, but he fails to establish the fundamental economic identity of land and other forms of capital on which the criticism must rest. The recognition of this dualism in the classical theory of value had led some economists (Canard, Carey, Bastiat, Wirth, and Rösler are cited) to attempt to trace land values back to labor expenditures. Menger tries to refute this argument with the correct but inconclusive statement that historical costs are irrelevant to present value (p. 145).

Ricardian rent theory is explicitly but inadequately contested as a special case of classical distribution theory. Menger fails to see that "the different qualities and locations of ground-plots" are not an essential feature of the classical doctrine; rent may equally well be measured from the intensive margin. As a consequence it is wrong to say that, "if all plots of ground were of equal quality and of equally favorable location, according to Ricardo they could not yield any rent . . ." (p. 146). One must regret his too ready concessions that land is usually available only in a definite quantity, "not easily increased," and that immobility of land has the economic significance generally imputed to it. Under Menger's implicit static assumptions, capital and labor are also fixed in quantity; historically all three "factors" have experienced enormous increases. Immobility, again, is a technical attribute; the mobility of land as between different uses is much more important from the viewpoint of price theory (which, indeed, usually abstracts from transportation costs) than is spatial immobility.

Menger considers observable divergences of actual wages from those necessary to maintain a laborer to be a sufficient basis for a categorical denial of the subsistence theory of wages, and he asserts that wages depend, in fact, only on the value of the product of labor (pp. 150–51). This criticism of classical doctrine is also inconclusive, for, to the extent that wages govern population, the supply of labor may conceptually be so regulated that wages remain at a subsistence level. But again, as in the case of rent, he properly believes wages to be explicable by general value theory.

The Theory of Capital

The greatest hiatus in Menger's system of distribution is unquestionably the virtual absence of any theory of capital.[1] Here the failure to distinguish between goods and services from goods is a fundamental weakness. Some beginning is made: it is asserted both that increases in capital can take place only through extensions of the (undefined) period of production (p. 127), and that all such extensions increase the productivity of a given amount of capital (p. 136 n.). Menger thus sketches out what Böhm-Bawerk later developed.

Menger finds two limitations to increasing produce by extending the period of production: (1) the necessity of maintaining life (in a broad sense) in the immediate future, and (2) an irrational preference for present over future satisfactions (pp. 126–28). This second factor, it may be noted, was deleted by Menger from the second edition, lest it be construed as supporting Böhm-Bawerk's theory of interest.[2]

Finally a vague and unsatisfactory definition of capital is presented: "The possibility of participating in the economic advantages which are bound up with production by goods of higher order . . . is dependent for every individual on his disposal in the present over quantities of goods of higher order for the coming period of time, or, in other words, on possessing *capital*" (p. 130; also pp. 127–33). Capital, then, is defined as goods of higher

[1] Menger denies the validity of the abstinence theory of interest on his usual grounds for dismissing subjective costs—*i.e.*, capital value frequently appears without any self-denial on the part of the capitalist, as in the preemption of natural resources (p. 133 n.).

[2] Cf. Introduction to 2d ed. (Vienna, 1923), p. xiv.

order kept in possession through a production period. This is clearly an inadequate definition, and it provides no basis for a theory of interest, although such capital services (*Capitalnutzungen*) must, as Menger says, be compensated (pp. 133–36).

Other than the *Grundsätze*, Menger's only work in economic theory proper is the article already mentioned, "A Contribution to the Theory of Capital," which appeared in *Conrad's Jahrbücher* in 1888.[1] Here again no positive theory is presented, but the essay does contain two important principles. There is, first, an acute criticism of the classical emphasis on the technical, in contrast with the economic, character of capital. His comments on the validity of the practice of considering land and labor as "original" factors, capital as a secondary or derivative factor, really leave very little to be said on this subject.

The second theme of the article, which is in some respects even more important, is the necessity for conducting capital analysis in the monetary terms in which entrepreneurs deal with capital problems: "The real concept of capital includes the productive property, whatever technical nature it may have, so far as its money value [*Geldwert*] is the subject of our economic calculation, that is, if it appears in our accounting as a productive sum of money." [2] These are profound truths; we can only lament that Menger does not build on them. There is no discussion of the investment process, whereby productive services are employed to produce goods, and not satisfactions, which in turn yield a net, perpetual stream of services (income).

[1] Reprinted in Vol. III of the *Collected Works* (London School Reprint No. 19, 1935), pp. 133–83.

[2] *Ibid.*, p. 174.

Chapter VII

FRIEDERICH VON WIESER

FRIEDERICH VON WIESER'S place in the history of distribution theory is ambiguous.[1] The general practice of grouping all theorists prominent in the emergence of the theory of subjective value as the "Austrian School" is particularly misleading in this connection. Wieser's theory of the "productive contribution" is much more closely allied to the earlier writings of Walras than to those of Menger and Böhm-Bawerk. It is noteworthy, furthermore, that at the very points in Wieser's distribution theory where he strikes out from Menger's path, Wieser's own doctrines are weakest.[2]

But Wieser occupies a position of indisputable importance in the history of economics. He was the first of the Austrian economists to devote attention to the problem of the allocation of resources and the organization of a free enterprise economy. In essentials this analysis was sound and, except for Wieser's confused concepts of variation of proportions of productive factors and of marginal productivity, reasonably complete. His statement, perhaps the first satisfactory non-mathematical

[1] For biographical details, consult F. A. von Hayek's Introduction to Wieser's *Gesammelte Abhandlungen* (Tübingen, 1929).

[2] This was true also in value theory; Wieser's incomprehensible theory of "natural value," for instance, was designed to overcome purely imaginary difficulties in Menger's treatment due to the failure to consider differences in the marginal utility of money to various individuals. Wieser insisted on treating utility as "absolute" and comparing it from one individual to another—a practice condemned by Jevons.

solution of the organization of an enterprise economy, carried the analysis of Menger several steps farther, and gave a comprehensiveness and unity to the "Austrian" theoretical system, which in itself justifies Wieser's high place in the history of this period.

Early Views

In 1876 Wieser presented a paper, "On the Relation of Cost to Value," before Knies' seminar.[1] This early paper anticipated many essential points of his major works, but nevertheless it was an immature product, patterned closely after Menger's *Grundsätze.* The independent discovery of the general theory of alternative cost, *i.e.*, the doctrine that costs are actually the foregone utilities of other goods that might have been produced by the same resources, may be attributed to Wieser on the basis of the paper.[2] Two quotations will indicate the nature of his early views on the subject:

> To the extent that an individual follows the principle which the desire to improve his welfare dictates, he is—once we assume his desires to be given—bound to a completely determinate arrangement of production, from which he may not deviate without disadvantage: no good should be produced if it is able to satisfy only a less important desire, so long as it is possible to produce another good the consumption of which is able to yield greater pleasure to him.
>
> The value of a productive factor is determined by the value of the last unit of any particular commodity which is to be produced by it, and this value is then reflected in all other sorts of commodities.[3]

Great significance cannot be attached to this early work. The principle of valuation of individual productive

[1] "Über das Verhältnis der Kosten zum Wert," reprinted in *Gesammelte Abhandlungen*, pp. 377–404.

[2] Walras had already advanced substantially the same theory; cf., *infra*, Chap. IX.

[3] *Gesammelte Abhandlungen*, pp. 380, 394.

services was merely a restatement of Menger's loss-principle.[1] The crude arithmetical example upon which Wieser relied to illustrate the allocation of resources was completely misleading, because he failed to consider utilities relative to costs.[2] Furthermore, the work was not published until 1929, and presumably it had no influence on contemporary thought.

Productive Organization under Competition

The essential aspects of the alternative cost doctrine were analyzed, and their implications for the allocation of resources and the relation of cost to value adumbrated, in Wieser's first book, *Ursprung des wirtschaftlichen Wertes* (1884). The system there presented was refined and elaborated in *Der natürliche Wert* (1889),[3] but the latter work marked no great change in viewpoint. Finally, the *Theorie der gesellschaftlichen Wirtschaft* (1913),[4] attempted a synthesis of all phases of economic theory, but in the field of distribution theory it introduced no important changes from the treatment in *Natural Value.* The latter work will be the chief basis of the present analysis of Wieser's theory.

The general outline of Wieser's theory of the organization of a competitive economy may be briefly summarized. Starting with the implicit assumption of an economy with a fixed quantity of resources, a given set of desires, and a given technology, he shows that an economic distribution of that economy's resources would be

[1] *Ibid.*, p. 397 and esp. p. 381: "The value of a unit of a productive factor is determined by the size of that desire which would have to remain unsatisfied if the quantity of the productive factor were reduced by one unit."

[2] *Ibid.*, pp. 378–80. As a consequence his allocation of resources did not maximize returns. At another point the necessity of weighting utilities by costs was recognized, however (p. 388).

[3] The 1893 translation by A. Malloch, *Natural Value*, is used here.

[4] Translated into English in 1927.

one which would equalize the return from a unit of any given resource in all employments. The total return from a given set of resources will be maximized, in other words, by equating their marginal products in all industries.[1]

The larger a given stock of homogeneous resources, the less important are the needs which it may be used to satisfy. Diminishing returns is ignored by Wieser; only in agriculture—"and this is the general rule in old countries"—does it operate (pp. 100–101, 103 ff.).[2] The decreasing effectiveness is therefore usually due to the diminishing marginal utility of the goods which could be produced by a larger stock.[3] The resource's productive contribution (which is not, in Wieser's opinion, equivalent to the marginal product of modern theory) determines the value of a unit of a stock of resources, and the value of this marginal unit is decisive in the allocation of resources. All uses of the stock of resources must then yield this marginal product.[4]

The law of cost follows from these considerations: Units of cognate products, that is, products which have at least one productive factor in common, will exchange for each other (with respect to this factor) as the quantities of it requisite for the production of one unit of each product (p. 172). This is most easily shown when a single agent can produce two commodities, *A* and *B*, with one and

[1] The reader must be warned that Wieser's "marginal product" had an unusual meaning.

[2] References are to *Natural Value* (New York, 1930), unless otherwise indicated. I am indebted to *G. E. Stechert & Co.* for permission to quote from this work.

[3] Cf. *Ursprung des wirtschaftlichen Wertes* (Vienna, 1884), pp. 64–66, 100, 166–70.

[4] This analysis resolved the conflict between cost and utility. Utility determined the value of a unit of a stock of resources; this value was a cost in the production of any commodity in foregone utility. Cf. Bk. V, Chap. vi; *Ursprung*, pp. 146, 161.

two units of the agent, respectively. Then it involves a sacrifice of two units of *A* to produce one unit of *B*, and this choice is economic only if the unit of *B* is worth at least two units of *A*. In other words, "All economic demands are fulfilled when care is taken that goods of less marginal utility are never produced from production goods which, if employed in producing other things, might have brought a higher marginal utility" (p. 98).[1]

This principle does not operate in the case of resources which are used in only one product. Here the possibility of competition between products is absent, and the value of the product determines the value of the resources, *i.e.*, the return is a true rent (p. 175).[2]

While in general outline Wieser's statement of the alternative cost theory is satisfactory, in certain respects it contained important weaknesses. Wieser spoke of the "direct" effect of costs on value in exceptional cases, an illogical treatment which was plausible only because of his assumption that demand curves were not continuous (pp. 177–78).[3] His analysis of the nature of particular types of costs, too, is virtually worthless. The following quotation, which is characteristic of his views, stands in sharp contrast to the usual clarity of his thought on the subject of costs: "It is only 'socially necessary' costs, the smallest amount of costs required, that determines

[1] "The sacrifice [to the producer] consists in the exclusion or limitation of possibilities by which other products might have been turned out, had the material not been devoted to one particular product" (*Social Economics* [New York, 1927], p. 99).

[2] In *Social Economics* these one-purpose productive goods were called specific productive means, in contrast to transferable resources, or cost-means (p. 81).

[3] "A good having a use value of 10 [for one unit; a second unit worth only one], and a cost value equal to 6, must be estimated at 6, so long as its reproduction is possible" (p. 177). The same treatment was very prominent in Böhm-Bawerk's theorizing.

value . . ." (p. 182).[1] Finally, his concept of marginal product, a peculiar hybrid of truly marginal analysis and of fixed coefficients of production, inhibits a clear view of the nature of the margins to be equated.

General Theory of Distribution

Wieser follows closely Menger's theory of the valuation of combinations of productive goods. The anticipated value of the commodities produced by the productive agent determines its value. He emphasizes economic, in contrast with physical, imputation, for only scarce goods are considered in production. This point is clarified by a now famous analogy to legal imputation:

> The judge . . ., who, in his narrowly-defined task, is only concerned about the *legal imputation*, confines himself to the discovery of the legally responsible factor,—that person, in fact, who is threatened with the legal punishment. . . . In the division of the return from production we have to deal similarly not with a complete causal explanation, but with an adequately limiting imputation,—save that it is from the economic, not the judicial point of view (p. 76).

This view is not wholly correct; unless the (marginal) physical products of individual productive services can be separated analytically, it is impossible to separate their shares of the value product. The economist, therefore, must know the physical production function as well as relative prices, and Wieser himself postulates such functions.

Wieser argues that the general theorem of imputation is of no value in the determination of the prices of the individual productive agents which cooperate to make the consumable commodity. His solution of this problem will be considered presently.

[1] The most that can be read into this statement is that the best available technology must be used.

Before introducing his theory of distribution, Wieser points out certain alleged deficiencies in Menger's treatment which prevented the latter's explanation from giving "the entire solution quite perfectly" (Bk. III, Chap. iv). The crux of the argument is that the application of Menger's loss-principle (*i.e.*, the measurement of the share attributable to any productive agent by the effect on the total product of the withdrawal of a unit of that agent) will result in the distribution of a sum greater than the total product. Wieser uses the following example: Three productive agents yield a product of ten units in their most efficient combination. Each will yield a product of three units if employed in some other use.[1] The withdrawal of any one agent from the most efficient combination, therefore, would involve a total loss of four units of product, making the total remuneration of the three agents twelve units by the application of the "loss-principle." Since the total product is only ten, this absurd conclusion proves the error of Menger's theory. Wieser attributes this error to a failure to recognize that the withdrawal of an agent reduces the productivity of remaining agents. Implicit in Wieser's criticism of Menger is also the proposition that the proportion between the factors is not continuously variable (see below).

This refutation of Menger's theory does not deserve an elaborate analysis. The crude arithmetic example upon which it is based begs the entire question. If, instead of such discrete changes in total product and in the marginal productivity of the factors, homogeneous, first degree production functions are postulated, no problem of over-distribution of product can arise. Moreover, even

[1] The diversion of these resources would raise "the return of each of these three groups . . . by 3 units" (p. 83), which presumably assumes the proportions to be variable in the industries not under consideration.

if the principle of the example is accepted, it represents, obviously, a position of disequilibrium; resources would be diverted to this most profitable alternative until it was no more profitable than other industries.

Before turning to Wieser's solution of the problem of distribution, it is necessary to examine the different concepts of variation in the proportional factors which are found in his work. Numerous places can be found where he seems clearly to recognize the possibility of varying the proportions of agents in the production of any product (pp. 72–73, 77–78, 82, 117, 160, 200).[1] It is also not difficult, however, to find points at which he seems to believe that the proportions of the agents used in producing a commodity are fixed (pp. 86–88, 90 n., 103, 108, 200),[2] and this concept is basic to his theory of distribution. This ambiguity is to be ascribed, the writer believes, to a confused concept of variation of proportions of productive factors. Wieser sees, almost necessarily, that it is generally possible to vary the amount of one factor used in cooperation with given amounts of others, but he apparently believes that when the proportions are altered, a new and different product results. The following quotation is the only explicit support for this interpretation, but it receives additional verification from the general tenor of his thought:

> But however far exchange may be specialized, the classes of productive combinations are undoubtedly more numerous than the classes of production goods. The classes of combinations into which a good like iron or coal (even of one distinct origin or quality) may be introduced, are incalculable, and the same may be said of unskilled or day's

[1] *Ursprung*, pp. 45, 175, 176.

[2] *Ibid.*, esp. p. 175: "Während die grossen Gruppen der Productionsfaktoren allerdings in dem strengen Sinne complementär sind, dass keine ausfallen kann, ohne das sich die übrigen ihre Nutzkraft völlig einbussen . . ."

labour. One and the same field is planted in rotation with the most various crops. And thus it comes that a mere change in the quantity of the same kind of goods in a group is sufficient to produce a new equation [*i.e.*, a new product] (p. 90 n.; cf. also p. 176).

An "improved" theory of imputation is advanced by Wieser to remedy the alleged defects in Menger's treatment. Wieser's doctrine rests on the concept of the "productive contribution," *i.e.*, "that portion of return in which is contained the work of the individual productive element in the total return of production" (p. 88). The distinction between the "productive contribution" and the loss-principle share is a dialectical difference between "contribution" and "co-operation," a difference which Wieser acknowledges to appear "contradictory and artificial," as, in fact, it is (Bk. III, Chap. vi, *passim*). The nature of the productive contribution can best be shown by a detailed analysis of Wieser's theory.

Wieser postulates two conditions for his theory of imputation: (i) that the value of the productive agents is equal to the value of their products (pp. 88, 91, etc.); and (ii) that the productive agents combine in fixed proportions, which vary between industries (Bk. III, Chap. v).

These conditions are expressed algebraically by the following equations, in which x, y, and z represent the value of single units of productive agents X, Y, Z, and the values on the right sides of the equations are prices of single units of three products:

$$x + y = 100 \qquad (1)$$

$$2x + 3z = 290 \qquad (2)$$

$$4y + 5z = 590 \qquad (3)$$

By solving these equations simultaneously, the values of

the units of productive agents are discovered. That of x is 40; of y, 60; of z, 70. These are the "productive contributions" of these agents.[1]

It is interesting to carry out a suggestion from Professor Knight [2] and prove by Wieser's own equations that the "loss-principle" share and the "productive contribution" are identical. From his equations it is apparent that for these three industries to utilize the available resources so that one unit of each of the three commodities will be produced, the productive factors X, Y, and Z must exist in the quantities 3, 5, and 8 respectively. Let us withdraw one unit of X (leaving two units), and discover the effect on production of the new allocation of resources as between the commodities—which we may label a, b, and c, for equations (1), (2), and (3). The equations become:

$$A(x + y) = 100A \qquad (1.1)$$

$$B(2x + 3z) = 290B \qquad (2.1)$$

$$C(4y + 5z) = 590C \qquad (3.1)$$

where A, B, and C are the coefficients representing the new distribution of resources (they were of course all equal to unity before the withdrawal of a unit of X). The equations can be rewritten to discover the reallocation of resources resulting from the withdrawal of a unit of X:

$$Ax + B2x = 2x \qquad (4)$$

$$Ay + C4y = 5y \qquad (5)$$

$$B3z + C5z = 8z \qquad (6)$$

[1] In *Social Economics*, "specific factors" (see note 2, p. 162) are considered as residual claimants, even though there might be several in the production of a single good. When more than one specific factor is used in a product, their shares are indistinguishable.

[2] "A Note on Professor Clark's Illustration of Marginal Productivity," *Journal of Political Economy*, XXXIII (1925), 550–53.

The *x's*, *y's*, and *z's* can be cancelled out, and the system of equations solved for *A*, *B*, and *C*. The values found are $A = .45456$, $B = .77272$, and $C = 1.13636$. The total product can now be computed from the right-side members of equations (1.1), (2.1), and (3.1). It is 939.998, which is 40.002 units less than the product (980) secured before the withdrawal of one unit of *X*, and is almost exactly equal (the slight discrepancy is due to the rounding off of the figures) to the productive contribution as measured by the original equations!

It can also be shown that the same conclusion holds in general, no matter what the initial quantities or the withdrawals of the various factors are.[1] With a given set of prices of final products and a given set of fixed technical coefficients, the values of the productive agents are not affected by their absolute or relative supplies. The uselessness of such analysis in economic problems is self-evident; Wicksell's well-known criticism of Wieser that such equations prove only that the price of the productive agent is uniform throughout industry seems quite justified.[2]

It deserves notice that Wieser's doctrine has been adopted in the twentieth century by several economists. F. M. Taylor superimposes an almost identical structure on his marginal productivity theory because existing fixities of proportions in many industries are believed to be such a limitation on the principle of variation as to make the supplementary (and uncoordinated) fixed-coefficients

[1] See mathematical note at end of this chapter.

[2] *Über Wert, Kapital und Rente* (Jena, 1893), p. xii: "Allein es ist klar, dasz man durch ein solches Verfahren, und mag man die Zahl der Gleichungen noch so sehr vergröszern, überhaupt nichts mehr erfahren wird, als man schon im voraus wuszte, nämlich dasz bei freier Konkurrenz das Entgelt oder der Ertragsanteil eines und desselben 'Produktionsmittels' in allen Geschäften annäherungsweise derselbe sein musz. Das und nichts anderes besagen, wie man leicht sieht, die obigen Gleichungen."

system of "great importance." [1] J. R. Hicks has also outlined a system essentially similar to that of Wieser.[2] Hicks' theory is stated very briefly, however, and is used merely to suggest that even if the coefficients of production were fixed, a determinate wage rate and allocation of resources would result. W. Vleugels has been perhaps the most uncritical follower of Wieser.[3]

Several criticisms may be made against the use of the method of fixed production coefficients to determine the distribution of the product: [4]

First, implicit in such an analysis is the assumption that the prices of the final products are given, and that their demand functions are infinitely elastic at the given prices. Taylor saw this clearly; [5] the other writers (except Hicks) ignored the point. It is obvious that if the elasticity of demand for any product is less than infinite, price becomes a function of output, and total sales value no longer equals a constant (*e.g.*, 100 in equation [1])

[1] *Principles of Economics* (8th ed., New York, 1923), Chap. xxx. Only one difference in treatment is noteworthy: Taylor believed that there might be more than one possible combination of the productive agents to make the same product, and the choice of methods would depend upon the relative prices of the agents used. This concession really gives away the whole case for fixity of proportions, for, *a priori*, if two combinations are possible, why should there not be intervening combinations which could also produce the same product? As a matter of fact, Taylor's discussion strongly implies continuous variability of proportions.

[2] "Marginal Productivity and the Principle of Variation," *Economica*, XII (1932), 79–89; *The Theory of Wages* (London, 1932), pp. 11–19.

[3] To emphasize "Die Brauchbarheit und Bedeutung der Wieserchen Formeln," Vleugels expands Wieser's system to 6 equations with 8 unknowns! "Die Lösung des Wirtschaftlichen Zurechnungsproblems bei Böhm-Bawerk und Wieser," *Schriften des Königsberger Gelehrten Gesellschaft* (1930), pp. 241–77.

[4] Edgeworth made an unfair criticism, in his review of *Natural Value*. By postulating increasing returns he points out the absurdity of Wieser's approach; but the marginal productivity theory would yield similarly absurd conclusions with this assumption. Cf. *Collected Papers Relating to Political Economy* (London, 1925), III, 53.

[5] *Op. cit.*, pp. 389–90.

times output. The assumption of infinite elasticity may be valid for the single entrepreneur, but it is absurd if applied to the total demand for any product. In this latter case—and it is the one with which these writers deal—it would be impossible to secure a determinate solution of the distribution problem without recourse to another set of equations, those of the demand for the final products. This is done by Walras,[1] who is followed by Cassel and Hicks.

Secondly, in order to measure productive contributions by a system of simultaneous equations, it is necessary that there be as many unique sets of coefficients of production (equations) as there are productive agents (unknowns). Wieser recognizes this, but his answer to the problem is naive and unsatisfactory. He points out the unquestionable fact that there are an indefinite number of different productive agents but asserts that there are an even greater number of equations (sets of technical coefficients), since the same agents can be used to produce many different commodities (p. 89 n.).[2] This would make the system overdeterminate, and stable equilibrium would be impossible. Such a conclusion is distasteful, and we may well follow in this case Cournot's happy practice of refusing to accept indeterminate solutions as correct. *A fortiori* the system must be determinate, because the experiment with Wieser's equations indicates that his system may be viewed as a restatement of the conventional marginal productivity theory for a given point of static equilibrium.

The primary criticism has just been suggested. A

[1] Cf., *infra*, Chap. IX.

[2] The suggestion is made (pp. 89, 101) that changes in the supply of an agent would necessitate recalculation of only those equations into which it entered. This is of course untrue; an entirely new equilibrium would have to be determined.

point of static equilibrium reached by the marginal productivity principle can be restated in terms of fixed coefficients of production. But this restatement adds nothing, and it does sacrifice both applicability to economic life and the important principle of diminishing returns (the marginal productivities of Wieser's agents are constants). As a matter of fact, Wieser's equations are homogeneous and of the first degree, and therefore fulfill the requirements of Euler's theorem. They are consequently open to all of the criticisms which can be levied against the economic validity of such equations (criticisms which will be examined subsequently), and yet do not serve nearly so well for economic analysis as certain other equations of the same general type.[1]

The Specific Shares

Supplementary to this general theory of distribution, Wieser analyzes the separate returns of the "holy trinity"—land, labor, and capital.[2] The first two, land and labor, will be presented in very summary form, since they contribute nothing to the advance of economic thought. The treatment of capital is the most penetrating by far, and, accordingly, attention will be concentrated on that subject. He gives virtually no attention to the problem of pure profit.[3]

[1] Cf., *infra*, Chap. XII.

[2] Wieser attaches no value other than that of convenience to this classification of productive agents, it need scarcely be said. Cf. pp. 89 n., 94; *Social Economics*, p. 11; *Ursprung*, p. 171.

[3] In the *Ursprung* a theory of profits is suggested: "So lange die Production neu ist, ist dieser Process des Aufsaugens erst im Gange. Befor die neue Productionsweise bekannt war, hatte das Productivgut gar keinen oder nur einen geringen Wert. Die Kentniss des neuen Verfahrens bewirkt ein Eindringen oder doch ein Anschwellen des Wertes, ein Wertsteigerung, die oft ausserordentlich gross ist. Dies ist die Quelle der oft erstaunlich grossen Productionsgewinne" (p. 145). This is clearly a "dynamic" approach to profit, and it is of no analytical value; in actual practice the decrease of the product's price is usually much more important than the rise in factor prices.

The Theory of Rent

Any critical analysis of Wieser's presentation of rent theory must be as negative as is Wieser's own treatment of Ricardo (cf. Bk. III, Part II, Natural Land Rent, and also Bk. V, Chap. xii, Land Rent as an Element in Cost). Certain basic errors were alleged to be incorporated in Ricardo's statement, but these "errors" are in fact the result of Wieser's hypercritical but confused exposition of the classical theory.[1]

One aspect of Wieser's theory of rent does deserve detailed consideration, however. He was one of the first of the well-known writers to suggest that conventional rent theory could also be used to explain the return to productive agents other than land. The applicability of the doctrine to all factors is suggested: "The more fertile land, the land which lies nearer to the sphere of demand, the more skilled labourer, the more capable machine, are not only more highly paid, but have imputed to them as well, on account of their better quality, a comparatively greater share in the return,—which, indeed, is the cause of their being more highly paid" (p. 113; cf. also Bk. III, Chap. xiii, and pp. 119 n., 122 n.). Wieser in fact raises the Ricardian theory to a "universal law of differential imputation," and applies it especially to the return from concrete capital (p. 128). This implicit recognition that classical rent theory was not contradictory to generalized explanations of all returns is a contribution of Wieser's, although he failed to explain thoroughly the method of reconciling these two approaches.[2]

[1] For example, it is implied (pp. 119–20) that Ricardo was unaware that his doctrine requires that the amounts of the best land and of capital and labor be limited; it is asserted (pp. 120 ff.) that the theory is applicable only when there is no-rent land; etc.

[2] For such a detailed reconciliation of the Ricardian rent and the marginal productivity theories, cf. Wicksteed, *infra*, Chap. XII.

Theory of Wages

Wieser, like Menger, is a severe critic of the labor theory of value (Bk. III, Chap. iii; Bk. IV, Chap. iv, etc.). After literally every important (and usually every unimportant) point of theory, he points out the relevance of the analysis in question to a communistic state. The following quotation suffices to indicate his views: "The labor theory alone attempted it [the explanation of costs], but it has thereby—as we shall go on to show—introduced into theoretic political economy the greatest errors that have ever been perpetrated within its sphere" (p. 185).[1]

Wieser treats labor services exactly as he treated the services of every other agent in distribution. The sole difference between labor and other agents is that the value of the free laborer is not discussed, since future earnings cannot be capitalized (p. 161). An interesting aspect of his theory is the refutation of the rigid form of the subsistence theory of wages (Bk. V, Chap. vii). Two not too-convincing grounds are found for rejecting the doctrine. First, only certain classes of laborers are at a minimum, yet is not the sexual instinct equally operative in all classes? Second, when certain economists concede that a customary standard of living may be the minimum which workers successfully endeavor to retain, a stability of wages is implied which is empirically false.

The Theory of Capital and Interest

Preliminary to a presentation of Wieser's theory of capital, it is necessary to give explicit statement to the postulates of his theory:

[1] The following statement with regard to the effort of certain socialists to reduce circulating capital to labor deserves quotation: "Was aber die Schlussfolgerung anbelangt, so scheint mir mit derselben die äusserste noch erreichbare Grenze des Misverständnisses der Aufgabe und des Verfahrens der Wirtschaftslehre erreicht zu sein" (*Ursprung*, p. 113).

i. Capital consists of perishable goods (but not the means of subsistence of laborers), and is completely used up in the productive process.[1]

ii. The capital reproduces a gross product whose value exceeds that of the capital which is consumed in the process.[2]

iii. Throughout the discussion, the total supply of capital is implicitly assumed to be fixed.

The first two of these postulates are examined, the second immediately, the first as a second approximation.[3] The analysis of the productivity of capital—a term which Wieser rightly limits to the net return above replacement (p. 126)—is primarily a refutation of the labor theory of value, but there does emerge the essential point that the wide use of capital is pragmatic proof of its productivity. With regard to durable capital, Wieser suggests that the interest rate, already determined in connection with perishable capital, is used to discount the future returns of fixed capital, and thus the value of income sources is determined. Fixed capital *per se* is "of no importance to the principle of valuation of capital" (p. 152).

Returning to Wieser's capital theory, with the three conditions given, the determination of the interest rate is relatively simple. The total imputed return of capital is composed of two parts: reproduction of capital and net return (reproduction and maintenance coincide, since the

[1] "I understand by the term capital the perishable or the movable means of production" (p. 124 n.). "I do not include the means of subsistence which must be held ready at hand for the labourers. These are conditions of production, but not its causes" (p. 125 n.; also p. 190). This last point shows clearly the danger of grouping the subjective value theorists together as the "Austrian school"; the means of subsistence of the laborer are the only form of capital, according to Jevons and Böhm-Bawerk.

[2] "In the gross return must be found newly produced all the consumed capital, and beyond this there must be a certain surplus" (p. 125). It is clear that Wieser assumes that capital goods are completely worn out in the production process. His capital category consists of machines, etc.

[3] The problem of durable capital is taken up in Bk. IV, Chap. vi.

capital goods are completely worn out). Capital cannot claim this net return: "If, from the value of 105, 5 are set aside as fruits which may be consumed without preventing the full replacement of the capital, only the remainder of 100 can be reckoned as capital value" (p. 141).[1] This net return, in answer to Böhm's criticisms of Thünen, can never be assimilated into the capital value so long as there is net physical productivity of capital.[2] Interest is determined by the ratio of net return to capital value; "Interest represents a net increment to or fruit of capital" (p. 144; also Bk. IV, Chap. iii, *passim*).[3] When the percentage of increments to capital "obtains in a large number of connected cases" it becomes the rate of interest. The equalization of the rates of interest between employments is of course attributed to competition.

In the case of the interest rate on consumption loans Wieser comes close to Fisher's later "income stream" concept (Bk. IV, Chap. viii). "Accidental and personal circumstances" determine whether an individual wishes greater income now or in the future, and preference for the latter need not be irrational. It is implied that preferences vary between individuals so that the net effect is for them to cancel. Since lenders can always secure the productive rate of interest, however, it is also suggested

[1] Wieser seems to have the crude notion that the product comes at the end of the production process, *i.e.*, the life of the capital goods, all at once.

[2] Wieser admits (p. 126) that "The task of our theory is, in the last resort, to prove the value productivity of capital," but the value aspect is never treated separately. This practice is internally consistent with his distribution theory, for if (1) there is no diminishing return from increased use of capital, and (2) final product prices are constant, physical and value productivity will always be proportional. As a matter of fact only the second assumption is needed to establish this conclusion for the individual entrepreneur. Böhm-Bawerk makes the same assumption.

[3] Cf. *Social Economics*, p. 138: "The rate of interest is nothing more or less than an expression of the marginal productivity of capital."

that the rate on consumption loans must be equal to that on productive loans (p. 153; Bk. IV, Chap. ii).

One further aspect of Wieser's capital theory deserves mention. His heaviest barrage against the socialists (though *Natural Value* was filled with such attacks) centers on their attempt to reduce capital to labor, an effort caustically described as a kind of "theoretical infatuation" (Bk. V, Chap. x). Two general methods used to substantiate the socialists' thesis are criticized. First, although frequently capital does supplant labor, as they asserted, often (as in the case of raw material) it does not, and sometimes the converse is true.[1] The second line of argument goes back to the origin of capital, which, the socialists say, is ultimately obtained by labor. The refutation is emphatic, though irrelevant:

> Let the reader judge! First, the economic valuation of labour is explained by the peculiar nature of labour—that its employment necessitates personal sacrifice. Then capital, after being recognized as materialized labour, and so labour that has become impersonal, is subjected to the same valuation:—a proceeding for which there is no possible justification (pp. 200–1).

Wieser's theory of capital is of a peculiar hybrid nature. It is related to the Jevonian concept by the unrealistic assumption of complete disinvestment of capital, yet it contains no element of the period of production. The assumption of fixity of supply of capital in net effect reduces the theory to a pure productivity explanation of interest. It cannot be said to be a marginal productivity theory, however, because of the fallacious concept of imputation upon which it is based.[2] The failure to consider

[1] The concept of variation of the proportion of productive factors conveniently emerges at this point in the argument (p. 200).

[2] This dependence is recognized (p. 127). This point is really an internal criticism; the net product may also be secured properly by marginal productivity analysis, without affecting Wieser's capital theory.

interest on capital during the period of investment is a further defect.[1] Finally, the assumption of constant product prices which underlies Wieser's distribution theory automatically eliminates the problem of the relation of physical to value productivity, and consequently ignores also the problem of effects of variations of factor supplies on their relative shares of the product.

But, turning to the other side, it is no exaggeration to say that Wieser presented one of the best theories of capital which had emerged up to that time, and perhaps this questionable praise is too light. His assertion that capital is essentially permanent, since net productivity is measured only after full maintenance of capital has been provided (p. 133),[2] is not detracted from by his postulate of complete liquidation. The latter assumption is an analytical device for purposes of simplification, and it does not touch the core of fundamental insight. The emphasis which Wieser lays on the demand for capital—in contrast with the supply of new savings—was, furthermore, a real advance. The fact is, empirically, that annual new savings form such a small part of existing capital that their effect on the interest rate is negligible even in "moderately long" periods of time. And, finally, Wieser's opposition (which is shared by Jevons) to the thesis that people are by nature prone to overestimate the present in comparison with the future is well taken.[3] The detailed treatment of this aspect of capital theory will be deferred, however, to the next chapter, which deals with Böhm-Bawerk.

[1] Wieser's treatment assumes investment to be instantaneous, except, of course, for the growth of the investment itself through time.

[2] *Social Economics*, p. 65.

[3] *Ibid.*, p. 38: "One may thusly say that it is a sound maxim among all peoples of normal development to appraise alike the present and the future." Cf. also *Natural Value*, p. 19 n.; Bk. IV, Chap. xi.

Mathematical Note

From equations (1.1), (2.1), and (3.1)[1] the total value product (*T. V. P.*) can be written:

$$\text{(I)}\quad T.\ V.\ P. = 100A + 290B + 590C.$$

Equations (4), (5), and (6) can be written as follows:

$$\text{(II)}\quad A + 2B = X$$
$$\text{(III)}\quad A + 4C = Y$$
$$\text{(IV)}\quad 3B + 5C = Z,$$

where X, Y, and Z are the total supplies of the factors of production. If these equations are solved for A, B, and C in terms of X, Y, and Z, the following values are secured:

$$A = \tfrac{6}{11}X + \tfrac{5}{11}Y - \tfrac{4}{11}Z$$
$$B = \tfrac{5}{22}X - \tfrac{5}{22}Y + \tfrac{2}{11}Z$$
$$C = \tfrac{1}{11}Z - \tfrac{3}{22}X + \tfrac{3}{22}Y.$$

If these values are substituted into equation (I), the result can be simplified to

$$\text{(II)}\quad T.\ V.\ P. = 40X + 60Y + 70Z.$$

Then if the stock of any productive agent is reduced by one unit (or any other number of units, since this is a linear equation), the product will decrease by exactly the amount of its "productive contribution."

[1] *Supra*, p. 167.

Chapter VIII

EUGEN VON BÖHM-BAWERK

EUGEN VON BÖHM-BAWERK is the best known and most influential of the founders of the "Austrian" school.[1] He, like Wieser, proceeds from the foundations of Menger's theory of subjective value, and extends this body of doctrine into the fields of production and distribution. But these two foremost intellectual disciples of Menger differ greatly both in their interpretation and in their developments of the theory presented in the *Grundsätze.*

Böhm-Bawerk's pre-eminent position is explicable on several grounds. In the later years of the *Methodenstreit* when a German economic theorist could assume, as Schumpeter has phrased it, only "the propensity for often fantastic aberrations" on the part of his readers,[2] Böhm-Bawerk battled valiantly in behalf of the rights of theory. For although he did not engage to any important extent in that largely barren controversy over methodology, his own theoretical contributions, supported by an energetic participation in the polemical literature of the day, were offered with a confidence and a finality which were much

[1] For a description of Böhm-Bawerk's environmental influences, consult Joseph Schumpeter, "Das Wissenschaftliche Lebenswerk Eugen von Böhm-Bawerk," *Zeitschrift für Volkswirtschaft, Sozialpolitik, und Verwaltung,* XXIII (1914), 454–528. Schumpeter's analysis of Böhm-Bawerk's doctrines is useful for a general view, but the interpretation is, in my opinion, unduly generous throughout. The introduction by F. X. Weisz to the *Gesammelte Schriften* (Vienna, 1924), pp. iii–xv, is also of interest.

[2] *Op. cit.*, p. 459: ". . . die Disposition zu oft abendteuerlichen Verirrungen. . . ."

more effective in breaking down the prejudice against theoretical analysis than a more tempered and self-critical approach, say that of Marshall, could have been. In foreign countries, especially England and America, moreover, Böhm-Bawerk has had a much wider audience than either Menger or Wieser. The early translation of his leading works was important in this respect,[1] as were also his sorties, chiefly against J. B. Clark and Edgeworth, in the English and American economic journals. Finally, of course, Böhm-Bawerk offered a broad generalization of the subjective value theory approach, a thing for which English-speaking countries had perhaps been prepared by Jevons but of which they lacked an indigenous supply before Clark (in America) and Wicksteed (in England).

Böhm-Bawerk's theoretical work centers about the problem of capital and interest. Yet it would be superficial to treat only this part of his analysis, for in fact, in the course of the development of his views, Böhm-Bawerk not only treats price and distribution theory but also, in effect, offers a conception of general economic structure via the medium of his capital theory. But these two parts, price theory and capitalistic production theory, are largely independent of each other. Böhm-Bawerk's production theory, under which he treats distribution, is an alternative cost doctrine taken over from Wieser. His capital theory and production and motivation theories are, on the contrary, based primarily on a study of the role of *time* in economic life. The following treatment will therefore follow this general dichotomy.

A final introductory word may be added with regard

[1] Menger's *Grundsätze* was never translated and had become rare long before it was reprinted in the London School Series (1934); the translation of Wieser's *Natürliche Wert* (1893) followed two years after that of Böhm-Bawerk's *Kapital und Kapitalzins.*

to Böhm-Bawerk's methodological conceptions. These are not highly consistent: Böhm-Bawerk feels no reluctance in making extremely heroic general assumptions, but in matters of relatively minor importance he frequently introduces numerous qualifications to suit empirical observation. This may be illustrated from his utility theory, where it is asserted that utility magnitudes are measurable even in a *cardinal* sense, and that they are comparable as between individuals; yet the postulate of continuity of utility and demand functions (which is unrealistic only to a minor degree, and essential to analytic treatment) is never granted. A more important weakness is Böhm-Bawerk's failure to understand some of the most essential elements of modern economic theory, the concepts of mutual determination and equilibrium (developed by use of the theory of simultaneous equations).[1] Mutual determination (*gegenseitige Interdependenz*) is spurned for the older concept of cause and effect,[2] although unconsciously he makes frequent use of the modern approach. This methodological misconception is perhaps most clearly revealed in the course of a criticism of Fisher's interest theory:

> . . . where causal relationships exist, the mathematical solution, which always goes from knowns to unknowns, can proceed equally well from effects to causes as from causes to effects. . . . Unique determination is neutral in relation to the problem of causation; it has nothing to do with causation.
>
> And therefore the "unique determination" of a "problem" by no means signifies the possession of a correct causal solution of the problem in hand, and especially it does not sig-

[1] Böhm-Bawerk was not trained in mathematics. Cf. *Positive Theory of Capital* (London, 1891), p. 396 n.; *Positive Theorie des Kapitals* (4th ed., Jena, 1921), I, 426 n.

[2] Cf. *Positive Theorie des Kapitals* (4th ed.), II, 173–74 n.

nify a guarantee for the freedom from circular explanation. One can reason in a circle even about a mathematically determinate problem.[1]

The Short-Run Theory

THE ALLOCATION OF RESOURCES [2]

In essential aspects Böhm-Bawerk's statement of the solution of the problem of the allocation of resources is similar to, and based upon, that of Wieser, although Wieser's exposition is considerably more lucid. Accordingly, only the outlines of Böhm-Bawerk's theory will be sketched.

Subjective value is the sole ultimate determinant of economic value. All productive factors (goods of second or higher rank) derive their value from that of their final products.[3] Nevertheless the "law of costs" does find a partial, secondary role in value determination. The utility of the marginal product of a given stock of resources (of a type which is used in producing several different commodities) determines the price that any in-

[1] *Ibid.*, p. 315.

[2] This discussion is found in Books III and IV of the *Positive Theory of Capital*. These sections are a slightly condensed reproduction of his articles, "Grundzüge der Theorie des Wirtschaftlichen Güterwerts," *Conrad's Jahrbücher für Nationalökonomie und Statistik*, XIII (1886), 1–66, 477–541, which have been reprinted under the same title as No. 11 of the London School Reprints. The *Positive Theory* is only slightly altered in the second and third editions (the fourth edition, which is used here, is a posthumous reprint of the third edition). "The Ultimate Standard of Value," *Annals of the American Academy*, V (1894–95), 149–208, should also be consulted. I am indebted to The Macmillan Company for permission to quote from the *Positive Theory*.

[3] ". . . it must be self-evident that a productive good, like any other good, can only obtain value for us through our recognition that on its possession or non-possession depends our gain or loss of some one utility, of some one satisfaction of want" (*Positive Theory*, p. 180; also pp. 180 ff.). In this connection Böhm-Bawerk notes the difference due to the presence of interest, but he defers consideration of this margin between the value of productive factors and the value of their products to the sections containing his theory of interest.

dustry must bid for a unit of that resource.[1] All products whose values are too low to permit payment of this marginal product value will be excluded from the use of the resource in question. All industries whose product values permit payment of a higher price for the resource will expand under the inducement of unusual profits, until an equilibrium point is reached at which the marginal utility added by a unit of the resource is the same in all employments.[2]

This general framework of resource allocation is identical with that of Wieser, but Böhm-Bawerk's detailed exposition differs in one important respect. The usual Austrian assumption of complete fixity of the quantity of productive resources (or, more properly, of the flow of productive services) is an explicit part of his analysis.[3] Yet Böhm-Bawerk deviates at two points from this assumption. The first exception is with respect to capital, the variations in the supply of which are discussed at great length; this point will be considered subsequently.

The second exception, to which Böhm-Bawerk denies any quantitative importance, is that the disutility of labor indirectly affects the value of goods by limiting the

[1] "The value of the productive unit adjusts itself to the marginal utility and value of that unit which possesses the least marginal utility among all the products for whose production the unit might, economically, have been employed (*ibid.*, p. 186).

[2] If a man had a stock of resources which could be devoted to producing several commodities, "the amounts produced (of each commodity) would be so regulated that, in each kind, wants of something like the same importance would depend on the last sample of the kind, and the marginal utility of every sample would therefore be approximately equal" (p. 185; also p. 228). This statement is laboriously qualified for the case (typical in Böhm-Bawerk) of discontinuous utility and demand curves. The assumption of discontinuity is defended—quite unsuccessfully, in my opinion—against the acute criticisms of Schumpeter, *Positive Theorie des Kapitals* (4th ed.), II, 163–70.

[3] *Positive Theory*, p. 229.

supply of labor.[1] The laborer will—*when he may*—vary his hours or intensity of labor until the marginal disutility of the labor expended equals the marginal utility of the product secured from that labor. This is identical with Jevons' theory, and "no criticisms are to be raised against its validity." [2]

A complete acceptance of the Jevonian theory, it is clear, effectively undermines the doctrine (which Böhm-Bawerk has done more than anyone else to disseminate) that utility of product is the sole ultimate determinant of value (unless one considers the utility of leisure and the relative disutilities of different kinds of work), and that a unit of resource is valued solely on the basis of its marginal product value. Böhm-Bawerk finds several reasons, however, for retaining this theory.

The first reason lies in the characteristic impossibility for the individual workman to vary the amount (daily duration) of his labor, since large industrial organizations are not adapted or adaptable to his special circumstances.[3] This point is sound (although, as will be seen, irrelevant) and recognizes a difficulty which was overlooked by Jevons, Wicksteed, and indeed most of the economists who have applied the alternative cost doctrine to the determination of an individual's supply of

[1] This exception is presented in his "Grundzüge" (London School Reprint), pp.42–45. It is omitted in the *Positive Theory*, but is subsequently restored as Bk. III, I. Abschnitt, Chap. viii, "Wert und Arbeitsleid" of the fourth edition of the *Positive Theorie des Kapitals*. Exkurs IX, "betreffend die Stellung des 'Arbeitsleids' ('disutility') im System der Werttheorie" (*ibid.*, Vol. II), and the long discussion in "The Ultimate Standard of Value," *op. cit.*, pp. 166–80, should also be consulted.

[2] *Positive Theorie des Kapitals* (4th ed.), II, 194.

[3] "Allein die abstrakte Möglichkeit einer so gearteten Verkettung [as the equating of marginal utility and marginal disutility] wird unter den herrschenden Einrichtungen unseres arbeitsteiligen Produktionsprozesses wohl nur selten zur konreten Wirklichkeit" (*ibid.* [4th ed.], I, 225–26). Böhm does not consider variations in labor brought about through "absenteeism."

labor (and other resources). Disutility can affect the relative supplies and prices of commodities only by affecting the quantities of productive services performed by given resources or by influencing the allocation of these services between occupations. Böhm-Bawerk denies the empirical significance of the former alternative; his denial of the latter alternative will be considered below.

The quantitative importance of the limitations on varying working hours is, of course, debatable. Edgeworth minimizes it, claiming that piece work, choice of occupation, the cost of rearing children, the actual flexibility of working hours are factors which endow the Jevonian theory with general applicability.[1] Böhm-Bawerk, contrariwise, considers the limitation to be very important, so that disutility plays only, say, one of twenty parts in the ultimate determination of value, and utility the remainder.[2] This suggestion is difficult to interpret. Either disutility operates in one of the two ways mentioned above, in which case utility is not a "sole" determinant, or it does not have any influence on relative values.[3]

[1] *Collected Papers Relating to Political Economy* (London, 1925), III, 59–64.

[2] "Ultimate Standard of Value," p. 200.

[3] Marshall also combated Böhm's views: "If a man is free to cease his work when he likes, he does so when the advantages to be reaped by continuing seem no longer to over-balance the disadvantages. If he has to work with others, the length of his day's work is often fixed for him; and in some trades the number of days' work which he does in the year is practically fixed for him. But there are scarcely any trades in which the amount of exertion which he puts into his work is rigidly fixed. If he be not able or willing to work up to the minimum standard that prevails where he is, he can generally find employment in another locality where the standard is lower; while the standard in each place is set by the general balancing of advantages and disadvantages of various intensities of work by the industrial populations settled there. The cases, therefore, in which a man's individual volition has no part in determining the amount of work he does in a year, are as exceptional as the cases in which a man has to live in a house

Two other reasons are advanced in behalf of utility's "ultimacy." Skilled labor is used in the production of almost every article, yet "skilled labor . . . is not more painful than that of the common miner. . . ."[1] But skilled labor is paid for at a higher rate, therefore pain or disutility cannot determine value. This constitutes a rejection of the second possible manner in which disutility may affect relative values, *i.e.*, by influencing the allocation of productive services between various occupations or uses. The failure of laborers to equalize money incomes of alternative occupations does impair the disutility theory. But in order to show that disutility has no influence on the relative values of products, Böhm-Bawerk would have to go farther and demonstrate that, for example, the distribution of skilled laborers between the occupations making up this category is not affected by the relative disutilities of these occupations—a possibility he fails to consider.

But finally, even waiving the limitations on disutility discussed above, Böhm-Bawerk thinks it still proper to assert that marginal utility is the final basis of value.[2] This conclusion, so paradoxical in the light of Marshall's mutual determination conclusions on the basis of the same assumptions, rests on Böhm-Bawerk's obsolete view of causation, already noted. Even when marginal utility must equal marginal disutility, it is sufficient to *know* the former to determine value, he argues. This may be freely granted, but since the determination of the supply of an individual's labor service (and hence of commod-

of a size widely different from that which he prefers, because there is none other available. . . . There seems therefore to be no good foundation for the suggestion made by v. Böhm-Bawerk . . ." (*Principles of Economics* [8th ed., London, 1920], p. 527 n.).

[1] "Ultimate Standard of Value," p. 176.

[2] *Positive Theorie des Kapitals* (4th ed.), II, 196–97.

ities) depends on the intersection (*Schnittpunkt*) of the curves of marginal utility and marginal disutility, the determination of marginal utility is itself dependent upon disutility. Böhm-Bawerk completely overlooks this dependence.

The fundamental irrelevance of all such discussion to the question of the "ultimate" determination of value is, however, quite patent. If production functions enter into value determination, if the relative number of units of two products produced by a given resource (more properly, by a given set of resources) is fixed functionally by technical conditions—and Böhm-Bawerk concedes all this—then cost is also an independent determinant of value.[1] If "ultimate" does not mean "independent," the entire discussion is meaningless.[2]

The Theory of Distribution

Böhm-Bawerk's theory of imputation is his only important contribution to Austrian price theory. Ostensibly it builds on Menger's theory,[3] but the principle of

[1] Edgeworth therefore grants too much when he says, "I admit that, upon what may be called the general Ricardian assumption of a fixed quantity of labour . . . the explanation given by Professor Böhm-Bawerk would be correct—utility, without disutility, would be the ultimate standard" (*Collected Papers, op. cit.*, III, 62).

[2] Since the foregoing was written, a possible alternative interpretation of Böhm-Bawerk's position has been suggested to me. This alternative view is based on two facts: (1) Böhm-Bawerk assumes that the supplies of resources and the productivity functions do not change; and (2) he assumes utility schedules may vary. It would follow then, from his peculiar idea of causation, that marginal utility is the "cause" or ultimate determinant of value. This interpretation is very plausible, but Böhm-Bawerk's own discussion seems to me to suggest rather the interpretation in the text. The point is of course unimportant, for the problem reduces to whether he is wrong or whether he is "defending" a very barren tautology.

[3] Böhm-Bawerk speaks of his distribution theory as "auf gewissen von Karl Menger gelegten Grundlagen weiterbauend . . ." (*Positive Theorie des Kapitals* [4th ed.], II, 132). Hans Mayer is typical of the practice of confusing the theories of the two men; cf. "Zurechnung," *Handwörterbuch der Staatswissenschaften* (4th ed., 1928), VIII, 1212.

variability in the proportions in which productive agents are joined, so important to Menger's theory, is completely absent from Böhm-Bawerk's doctrine. The theory is presented in connection with complementary goods of either first or higher ranks, *i.e.*, either consumption or production goods.[1] Four cases are distinguished, as follows.

If none of the factors of a combination can be used without the cooperation of the other combination members, and if none is replaceable, "then one single member has the full value of the group, and the other members are entirely valueless." [2] The last member factor needed to complete a combination (the *Schlussstück*) receives the full value of the product of the combination.

Since this first case is in fact the cornerstone of Böhm-Bawerk's theory,[3] it may be considered at once. The theory is bad. Böhm-Bawerk is not dealing with an economic problem; in the case of rigidly fixed proportions between member-factors (and he illustrates this case with a pair of gloves), the totality of the members is *one* commodity, and the individual member-goods apart from one another have no economic significance. In the case of production goods, specifically, no imputation would be possible under his conditions. The owner of each member could and obviously would demand the full

[1] *Positive Theory*, Bk. III, Chap. ix. The treatment in the fourth edition is virtually identical, and in the discussion of criticisms (*ibid.*, Vol. II, Exkurs VII, "Theorie der Zurechnung"), Böhm-Bawerk makes no concessions or alterations. See esp. pp. 151 ff. of the last cited work.

[2] *Ibid.*, p. 171. It is interesting to note that this case is identical with the distribution theory presented by Gossen. Gossen assumed fixed coefficients of production, as does Böhm-Bawerk, and came to the substantially identical conclusion that a factor's share ". . . hängt von den vorhandenen Umständen ab." Cf. *Entwicklung der Gesetze des menschlichen Verkehrs* (Berlin, 1927), pp. 25–27.

[3] As, indeed, he admits. Cf. *Positive Theorie des Kapitals* (4th ed.), II, 156.

product of the factor-group, and there is no economic principle by which this dispute could be settled. To determine the distribution by appeal to the irrelevant circumstance of order of acquisition of member-factors (*i.e.*, the *Schlussstück* secures the full value of the product) is completely unsatisfactory. In actual economic life, which Böhm-Bawerk purports to describe, chaos would result if "circumstances" dictated a variable reward for a factor—most obviously almost all economic activity would be devoted to altering the "circumstances."

The second case differs from the first in one respect: the member-agents (which are still irreplaceable) have less profitable employments open outside the combination. This lower "isolated" value [1] of the agent forms its minimum compensation; its maximum value is equal to the total product minus the sum of the minimum or isolated values of the cooperating members. Assume members *A*, *B*, and *C* to have isolated values of *10*, *20*, and *30*, respectively, and a joint product valued at *100*. The maximum value of *A* is *100* minus *20*-plus-*30*, or *50;* its minimum value is assumed to be *10*. The total of the maximum values is *180;* here again there is overdistribution, to be overcome by "circumstances."

The third case, and, it is claimed, the most common by far, differs from the second in that some (not all) of the factors are replaceable. These replaceable values (in Böhm-Bawerk's terminology, substitution values), determined by "the value conferred by the utility in those branches of employment from which the replacing goods are obtained," [2] (and, due to competition, only these

[1] Determined, clearly, by application of the first case.

[2] *Positive Theory*, p. 173. Again, quite obviously, such values must be secured by application of the first or second cases, in Böhm-Bawerk's theory.

values) are paid to the factors in the joint use. The values of these replaceable agents go to the agents in question and the remainder of the joint product is divided by the irreplaceable agents, according to the principle of the second or first case. These irreplaceable members are assumed to be identical with "land" in actual life, an assumption which in general is clearly false.[1]

In the final case all members are freely replaceable. The joint value will then equal the sum of the replacement or substitution costs. It may be noted that Böhm-Bawerk erroneously suggests that the marginal utility of the joint product may be greater than the sum of the replacement costs, which will then have no effect on its price.[2]

A fundamental weakness in Böhm-Bawerk's general approach to the problem of imputation has been expressed well by Hans Mayer:

> . . . [Böhm-Bawerk] assumes at the start that the complete general organization of the productive system is given, and accordingly that the marginal combinations are already completely known for the individual productive agents, and with these combinations he attempts to ascertain *ex post* the values of the productive agents. Yet these values are formed at the same time that the structure of production is determined, and this structure of production [*i.e.*, allocation of resources] could not be carried out rationally without knowledge of the utilities dependent upon the individual productive agents.[3]

To restate the criticism, values of services of productive agents depend upon the values of their products, and the range of economically profitable uses in turn depends upon the values of the services of the productive agents.

[1] *Ibid.*, p. 176.
[2] *Positive Theory*, pp. 170–71.
[3] "Zurechnung," *op. cit.*, p. 1218.

Neither factor alone is sufficient to solve the problem of allocation of resources; mutual determination, which Böhm-Bawerk refuses to apply to economic phenomena, is the only conceptual method by which circular reasoning can be avoided.

Böhm-Bawerk expressly denies the necessity for equality between the value of a product and the sum of the maximum values of its productive factors,[1] a total which he calls "an empty, purely arithmetic sum of numbers."[2] He distinguishes between the "imputation" (*Zurechnung*) of a share to a factor and the share actually "distributed" (*Verteilung*) to it.[3] The actual share is based primarily on the imputed share, but only "under completely free and atomistic competition does there appear *a tendency toward approximate* identity of the imputed and actually distributed shares." [4] A second factor typically enters to differentiate the imputed and distributed shares. "That particular set of circumstances (*Lebenssituation*) which leads to a concrete act of evaluation of a productive agent, firmly establishes the set of facts for which the valuation is to serve, and for this set of facts my formula gives a precise, unique solution." [5] Wieser's preconception that all factors should have determinate shares imputed and (what is the same thing) distributed to them, shares not directly affected by any *Lebenssituation*, is held to be neither possible nor necessary.[6]

Böhm-Bawerk could never solve the problem of dis-

[1] *Positive Theorie des Kapitals* (4th ed.), II, 132–38, esp. p. 138. The essence of the argument is that the *Schlussstück's* value is *alternative*, *i.e.*, any one factor may have this value, but only one factor at a time can be the completing member and thus secure its maximum remuneration.

[2] *Ibid.*, p. 136.

[3] *Ibid.*, pp. 146–48.

[4] *Ibid.*, p. 147 n. (his italics).

[5] *Ibid.*, p. 150.

[6] *Ibid.*, p. 156.

tribution of a product among its cooperating productive agents by his type of analysis. It is possible to solve the distributive problem by analysis of the industry, if one assumes variability in the proportions of the factors of production; this approach leads to the marginal productivity theory. One may also assume fixed coefficients of production, but then for the individual industry there is no solution; there are several unknowns and but one equation. In this latter case of fixed coefficients, one must view the economy as a whole, as Walras and Wieser do, the latter unconsciously. Their solution is not logically wrong; it merely rests on assumptions of a character contrary to those which make the problem solvable in real life. Böhm-Bawerk, using neither approach, simply cannot solve the problem of distribution, or, for that matter, of complementarity in consumption.[1]

The Factors of Production

Of the Austrian economists considered in this study, only Böhm-Bawerk attaches any real significance to the classical tripartite division of the factors of production

[1] In his last work, "Control or Economic Law" (Eng. trans. by J. R. Mez [Eugene, Oregon, 1931], mimeographed; *Gesammelte Schriften*, pp. 230–300), Böhm-Bawerk occasionally gives verbal allegiance to the marginal productivity theory of wages (thus pp. 18 ff., 36 ff. of translation; pp. 251 ff., 272 ff. in *Gesammelte Schriften*). Nevertheless his own theory is reaffirmed (translation, pp. 27 ff.; *Gesammelte Schriften*, pp. 261 ff.), and technical errors reveal a lack of understanding of marginal productivity theory. The following is typical: "The last worker employed at a given time adds the 'marginal product'; each one previously hired adds a little more to the produce. . . . Now, if wages increase above the marginal product, the entrepreneur will suffer a loss from the employment of the last worker, or workers. This may, however, be offset to some extent by the gain from the workers employed previously" (translation, p. 51; cf. also p. 46; *Gesammelte Schriften*, p. 289, cf. also p. 283). A similar profession of acceptance of Clark's specific productivity theory is made in "Capital and Interest Once More; II. A Relapse to the Productivity Theory," *Quarterly Journal of Economics*, V. XXI (1906–7), 248–49, 272. Böhm reveals no real understanding of variable proportions.

into land, labor, and capital. His acceptance of the classification is complete and his defense unoriginal.[1]

Land is differentiated from capital on the economic grounds of fixity of supply (which is true of all factors under his static approach), immobility, costlessness, and differences in the nature of its income. Certain non-economic differences are also alleged: land has a certain peculiar role in production; the landowner's social and economic conditions are different from those of the capitalist.[2] These distinctions need not be considered here; they are cited only to show how classical and naive Böhm-Bawerk's position is.[3]

In connection with Böhm-Bawerk's cost theory it was pointed out above that he assumes "land" to be the irreplaceable factor, that is, the factor not transferable between industries. This point hardly requires refutation; even the strictly classical J. S. Mill had pointed out forty years before that various uses might compete for the same piece of land.

Böhm-Bawerk is scarcely more successful in distinguishing between capital and labor. Labor could be included with capital only "if the labourers were to be looked upon, not as members of the civil society in whose

[1] The classical division is to be found in almost every one of Böhm-Bawerk's writings. Perhaps the clearest statement is that given in the *Positive Theory*, Bk. I, Chap. v, "Competing Conceptions of Capital."

[2] *Positive Theory*, p. 55.

[3] When Menger ("Zur Theorie des Kapitals") points out the inconsistency involved in calling all land "land," no matter how much capital and labor have been expended upon it, while other natural products—fruit, wild trees, etc.—are reckoned as capital as soon as labor has been expended upon them, Böhm-Bawerk admits the logical weakness present. But the inconsistency is "unavoidable and healthy," and although "in strictest consistency there is hardly a purely natural factor today," the general distinction between capital and land is too important to abandon. Cf. *Positive Theorie des Kapitals* (4th ed.), I, 66 n. Böhm-Bawerk in fact excludes capital permanently invested in land from his capital category (*ibid.*, p. 65).

interest industry and commerce are carried on, but as material machines of labour." [1] Here the cost of maintenance (and replacement) of labor is the center of the discussion, and while it is true that such costs are not, in fact, primarily economic in nature, this is not the important distinction. The more significant difference lies on the side of salability; free laborers cannot capitalize their earnings effectively under existing legal institutions.

The Role of Time in Economic Theory: The Theory of Capital

Böhm-Bawerk's theory of capital and interest, upon which his fame rests, includes also a general theory of production and fragments of a theory of wages. At the very outset a fundamental dualism in his approach to the central problem must be noted. The theory of interest is given two separate and unrelated treatments in connection with explanation of interest.[2] One statement

[1] *Positive Theory*, p. 68.

[2] The introductory paragraphs of the last article written by Böhm-Bawerk's ablest follower in capital theory, Knut Wicksell, are so illuminating with respect to this dualism that they deserve at least footnote quotation:

"The first and only time that I was permitted to meet Böhm-Bawerk personally—it was in Vienna in the fall of 1911—I asked why it was that his *Positive Theory* gave the impression, to me at least, of flowing not from *one* mould, but much rather coming from several parallel-running lines of thought. . . .

"I thought, however, most of all of the similarly varied treatment of—what basically is one and the same problem—the emergence of interest on productive capital, at one point from the much-debated 'third ground,' which is anything but easily comprehended, and then in the chapter on 'The Interest Rate in Market Exchange,' with whose ingenious structure and convincing power only a very few critics have found anything with which to disagree.

"My question did not appear to surprise him, but his answer surprised me greatly indeed. He said quite simply, that because of external circumstances he had to hurry so in the publication of the first edition of his book, that the first half of the manuscript already found itself at the printing office before he had completed the writing of the second half. In this latter section he had in fact been confronted by difficulties of a theoretical nature emphasizes the discounting of future goods, and this section is an important source of the "impatience" and "time preference" theories of interest, such as those of Fisher and Fetter. The other statement offers an explanation of interest based on the marginal productivity of the lengthening of the period of production. This latter variant has obvious classical origins, was anticipated in most respects by Jevons and in some by Ricardo, and received its clearest exposition from Böhm's self-acknowledged disciple, Wicksell.

It is not convenient to separate completely Böhm-Bawerk's development of these two approaches to the interest problem. Instead the treatment will be divided into four sections: income and capital; productive organization; discount of the future; and the determination of the rate of interest.[1]

in the last hours of its writing. For example, in the well-known tables in the above-mentioned chapter, 'The Interest Rate in Market Exchange,' the figures wanted to be twice as high as he had a feeling they should be, until eventually the fortunate idea of the so-called 'staggering' [*Staffelung*] of production brought everything into order.

"If I have correctly comprehended and repeated this statement of his, it may explain a great deal, since by such a method of work it is clearly unavoidable that discrepancies will slip in here and there, against the will of the author. Everything points, however, toward the view that even from the first Böhm-Bawerk did not consider the original edition of the book to be definitive; even in the short foreword to the second (unaltered) edition he spoke of the future 'resumption' of his plan 'to submit the Positive Theory to a thorough-going revision in connection with its "shaping up" [*Ausgestaltung*],' a plan on which he declared he would persist.

"But nothing came of this. For many years he was generally prevented from laying hand to the work—it is well known that the second edition is an unchanged reprint of the first—by political duties, and when finally near the end of his life he proceeded to the development of the definitive text, his book had already stood so long in the real center of scientific discussion that it was a matter of honor, I suppose, to change nothing or only what was most urgently deficient in it, otherwise the book is left to stand in good and bad, as has once been said."

"Zur Zinstheorie," *Die Wirtschaftstheorie der Gegenwart* (Vienna, 1928), III, 199–200.

[1] The *Geschichte und Kritik der Kapitalzins-Theorien* (Innsbruck, 1884),

INCOME AND CAPITAL

Böhm-Bawerk's definition of income, which is essentially the definition of wealth given by the classical economists, restricts the concept to material goods, excluding all intangible services:

> A dwelling-house, a hired horse, a circulating library bear interest to their respective owners without having anything to do with the production of new wealth . . . this alone is sufficient to show that the bearing of interest cannot by itself be an indication of the productive power of capital.[1]

The narrowness of this concept—in contrast to Menger's proper emphasis on usefulness rather than materiality as the primary aspect of income[2]—leads to a major omission in Böhm-Bawerk's capital concept, the exclusion of durable consumption goods.[3]

The formal definition of capital is also strongly orthodox:

> Capital in general we shall call a group of Products which serve as means to the Acquisition of Goods. Under this general conception we shall put that of Social Capital as a narrower conception. Social Capital we shall call . . . a group of products destined to serve towards further production; or, briefly, a group of Intermediate Products. . . .

translated by Smart as *Capital and Interest* (London, 1890), is an exhibition of dialectics unique in the history of economics. It suffers heavily from two defects: the misinterpretation of previous writers (*e.g.*, Senior, Menger), and the strafing of dead horses. It has little that is positive to contribute and will receive scant attention in the present work.

[1] *Positive Theory*, p. 2; also pp. 10, 346.

[2] In the fourth edition of the *Positive Theorie*, Böhm-Bawerk criticizes at length Fisher's vastly superior income and capital concepts. Böhm-Bawerk asserts, essentially, that capital need not yield income, and that income need not come from capital (cf. *ibid.*, I, 54–59, 72–73). Marshall is specifically arraigned for the inclusion of durable consumption goods in his capital concept (*ibid.*, pp. 72–74).

[3] *Positive Theory*, pp. 65–66.

> Social Capital again, . . . may be well and concisely called Productive Capital.[1]

Acquisitive or private capital is the broader concept, defined to include not only all productive goods but also durable consumption goods and means of subsistence advanced by entrepreneurs to their laborers.[2] Consumption goods owned by dealers are capital in both senses; if they are owned and leased out by consumers they are only private capital.[3] Böhm-Bawerk considers the concept of social capital appropriate to the theory of production, private capital appropriate to the theory of distribution. In practice he ignores these fine-spun distinctions, as we shall presently see.[4]

The distinction between productive goods and private capital would not be necessary if Böhm-Bawerk did not limit his income concept to material goods. The definition also recommits the classical error which Jevons had criticized, in making ownership a criterion of capital, when in fact this aspect is completely irrelevant. Böhm-Bawerk draws from his definition the conclusion, or perhaps more accurately, so forms his definition, that the productivity theory of interest is defective. Interest is not due to the productivity of capital, since durable consumption goods, which are not productive—in his sense—nevertheless yield interest.[5]

In connection with his concept of capital, Böhm-

[1] *Ibid.*, p. 38; also Bk. I, Chaps. iii–vi, *passim.*

[2] *Ibid.*, p. 71.

[3] *Ibid.*, p. 66.

[4] Böhm-Bawerk also accepts the classical distinction between fixed and circulating capital, the criterion being the difficulty of liquidating the capital good in question within a given period of time. This classification is not utilized, however, and need not be examined here. Cf. "Kapital," *Handwörterbuch der Staatswissenschaften* (3d ed.), V, 780–81, reprinted in *Kleinere Abhandlungen* (Vienna, 1926), pp. 9–11.

[5] *Positive Theory*, pp. 2, 346.

Bawerk develops the peculiar doctrine of "original factors of production." Land and labor are original or primary factors, capital is a secondary or intermediate factor:

> We put forth our labour in all kinds of wise combinations with natural processes. Thus all that we get in production is the result of two, and only two, elementary productive powers—Nature and Labour. This is one of the most certain ideas in the theory of production. . . . There is no place for any third primary source.[1]

This egregious distinction springs from two defects in Böhm-Bawerk's general methodology: the utter confusion of technical with economic considerations; and the practice of moving too swiftly from an abstract Crusoe economy to an enterprise economy. It is sufficient here to summarize the defects in the "original factors" notion.[2] Historically the distinction is false—we know of no society, however primitive, which does not possess capital goods, and it would be difficult even to conceive of such a society. And at the present time there are immense capital investments in the two "original" factors, labor and land. But such historical considerations are totally irrelevant to economic theory; they have no influence on

[1] *Ibid.*, p. 79.

[2] Walker was one of the first to criticize this point: "Whether capital, as an element of production, be derivative and secondary or original and independent, does not affect the inquiry how interest on capital is generated. . . . Each factor of production will claim and receive a share of the product. And for none of the purposes of that partition does it matter a pin whether one of these powers was, in its source, different from the others." Cf. "Dr. Böhm-Bawerk's Theory of Interest," *Quarterly Journal of Economics*, VI (1891–92), 406, 408. Compare also Menger, "Zur Theorie des Kapitals," *op. cit., passim;* F. H. Knight, *Risk, Uncertainty and Profit* (Cambridge, 1921), pp. 123 ff. Fairly complete bibliographies of the recent literature on the nature of capital are given by F. Machlup, "Professor Knight and the 'Period of Production,'" *Journal of Political Economy*, XLIII (1935), 577 n., and N. Kaldor, "The Recent Controversy on the Theory of Capital," *Econometrica*, V (1937), 201 n.

rational economic behavior. The commodity of today has an economic history which dates back to the dawn of civilization, but in theoretical economics it must be considered as the immediate product of certain productive agents of *correlative* importance. There is no place for the antiquarian in the theory of production.

This doctrine of original factors is designed in part as another attack on the productivity theories of interest.[1] If capital is merely a combination of two primary productive powers, how can it be said to yield a separate type of income (interest) from an independent source? Böhm-Bawerk's attack, however, does not prevent him from attributing interest to the productivity of capitalistic methods of production, as we shall see presently. Another role of the concept of "original factors," in connection with the period of production, will also be discussed below.

We may very briefly sketch Böhm-Bawerk's orthodox theory of the formation of capital goods.[2] Two steps are essential. First, there must be saving: ". . . before capital can actually be formed, the productive powers necessary to its making must be saved by encroaching on the moment's enjoyment." The second stage is investment: ". . . the negative element of saving must have added to it the positive element of devoting the saved goods to production, as intermediate products." To maintain consistency with his doctrine of original factors, Böhm-Bawerk adds that saving is "not among the *means* of production, but among the *motives* of production, . . ."[3]—which is, to say the least, ambiguous. The nature, in contrast to the form, of saving will be con-

[1] Cf. *Positive Theory*, pp. 94–99; *Capital and Interest*, p. 423.
[2] *Positive Theory*, Bk. II, Chap. iv, *passim*.
[3] *Ibid.*, p. 123.

sidered in connection with the section on discount of the future.

One final part of Böhm-Bawerk's capital theory, important in his treatment of interest, remains yet to be stated. It is, in essence, the proposition that "capital" is (*i.e.*, productive goods are), economically, future consumable commodities.[1] The reasoning is simple: machines, factories, tools, and the like cannot be consumed directly; they can be consumed only after they have been transformed into finished commodites, a process requiring time. Closely related to this view is his assertion that all "wealth" is subsistence: "In any economical community the supply of subsistence, available for advances of subsistence, is—with one trifling exception—represented by the total sum of its wealth (exclusive of land)."[2] All wealth is therefore made up of present or future subsistence available for advances to labor, since landowners and capitalists are eliminated for the sake of simplicity.[3] Here "wealth," which is not defined, is substantially identical with "capital" for purposes of interest theory, and all of the finer distinctions within the last category are also ignored.[4]

Böhm-Bawerk raises and answers, in this connection, the objection that much capital exists as goods which are not adaptable to immediate consumption. This is admittedly true, but laborers do not want *all* of their wage advances at once; they wish their advances to be distributed evenly through time, as the goods are needed.[5]

[1] *Ibid.*, Bk. VI, Chaps., ii, v.

[2] *Ibid.*, p. 319. The "trifling exception" consists of "that portion which the owners themselves consume" (*ibid.*, p. 321).

[3] *Ibid.*, p. 320 n.

[4] Cf. *ibid.*, Bks. VI and VII, *passim.*

[5] This argument is sharply inconsistent with Böhm-Bawerk's general views on discount of future goods. Moreover, the argument does not meet

This discussion leads directly to the concept of the period of production, to which we now turn.

THE ROLE OF CAPITAL IN PRODUCTION

The essential role of capital in production is to permit the following of roundabout methods, which are more productive than direct or non-capitalistic methods. "That roundabout methods lead to greater results than direct methods is one of the most important and fundamental propositions in the whole theory of production." [1] Why? "It must be emphatically stated that the only basis of this proposition is the experience of practical life. Economic theory does not and cannot show a priori that it must be so; but the unanimous experience of all the technique of production says that it is so." [2] Böhm-Bawerk leaves this basic assumption of the greater productivity of roundabout methods with this defense, and indeed it is methodologically adequate, although the proposition it proves is misleading or false. As is implied here and at other points, the pragmatic proof lies in the fact that such methods would not be used if they were not more productive.[3]

But this is not enough for his theory. Böhm-Bawerk adds the further crucial assumptions: (i) that every intelligently selected extension of the period of production (and increase of the durability of the product) increases the product secured from a given amount of resources other than capital; (ii) that every such extension requires more capital; and (iii) that increased amounts of

the problem of durable wealth which does not completely "ripen" into consumption goods in the near future. On this aspect, compare Wicksell, *infra*, pp. 273 ff.

[1] *Positive Theory*, p. 20.

[2] *Ibid.*

[3] Cf. also *ibid.*, pp. 99, 355; *Positive Theorie des Kapitals* (4th ed.), II, 22.

capital can be used only to extend the period of production (and to increase the durability of the product). These basic assumptions must be examined in detail.

First, every wisely chosen extension of the period of production increases the total product. "On the whole it may be said that not only are the first steps [in the roundabout process] more productive, but that every lengthening of the roundabout process is accompanied by a further increase in the technical result; as the process, however, is lengthened the amount of product, as a rule, increases in a smaller proportion." [1] This proposition, again, is based "on experience, and only on experience." The proof in the first edition of the *Positive Theory* consists only of plausible, hypothetical examples [2] and it is admitted that "in an exceptional case" the roundabout method may be speedier.[3] Two theoretical arguments in support of the proposition are added in the fourth edition of the *Positive Theory*.[4]

The first proof is essentially syllogistic: [5]

[1] *Positive Theory*, p. 84. The emphasis on "wisely chosen" extensions appears in the fourth edition (it is largely implicit in the first edition) in reply to critics (notably Irving Fisher, *The Rate of Interest* [New York, 1907], pp. 353–54). *Positive Theorie des Kapitals* (4th ed.), I, 16, 115, 123 n.; II, 2–3, 9–10, 76–77, etc.

[2] Thus, *Positive Theory*, Bk. I, Chap. ii, *passim*. The following argument is adduced in support, although it is only explanatory: ". . . every roundabout way means the enlisting in our service of a power of nature which is stronger or more cunning than the human hand; every extension of the roundabout way means an addition to the powers which enter into the service of man, and the shifting of some portion of the burden of production from the scarce and costly labour of human beings to the prodigal powers of nature" (*ibid.*, p. 22; also p. 82).

[3] *Ibid.*, p. 83.

[4] The former of these is first presented in "Einige strittige Fragen der Kapitalstheorie" (1899), reprinted in *Kleinere Abhandlungen*, pp. 144–48. Both arguments rest on a concept of an average period of production for an economy, a concept to which objection will be offered below. Wicksell appears to have been the first to suggest these proofs, in his *Finanztheoretische Untersuchungen* (Jena, 1896).

[5] *Positive Theorie des Kapitals* (4th ed.), II, 29–32, Exkurs V.

i. Capital is previously applied labor (*vorgetane Arbeit*); the more capital there is at any time—other things being equal—the farther back in time, on the average, the labor which constitutes it must have been applied.[1]

ii. The more capital a laborer is supplied with, the greater his product.

iii. Therefore, increases in capital per laborer are equivalent to a longer production period, at the same time insuring a larger product.

Increases in capital per laborer, to summarize, involve increases of product, but increases of capital per laborer also necessarily imply that the initial labor was expended farther back in the past, *i.e.*, that the period of production is longer and more productive.

This argument is inconclusive; it is essentially question-begging. Capital is not *vorgetane Arbeit* even in Böhm-Bawerk's theory; services of natural resources (land) also enter into capital. And so the qualification must be added that previously applied labor forms the same or a larger proportion of capital, as its size increases.[2] But much more important, by what right may it be assumed that larger amounts of capital imply that the labor comprising them must have been expended farther back in the past? For, essentially, this *premise*, which contains the conclusion it seeks to establish, that more capital can be expended (given the labor supply) only in lengthening the production period, is Böhm-Bawerk's third proposition concerning production, which in turn is based on the first proposition which it "proves."

[1] Specifically, if annual wages are $300, $50 capital per laborer was expended at most two months ago as subsistence, $300 per laborer at most a year ago.

[2] Böhm-Bawerk dismisses this point (which had been raised by Fetter) as irrelevant (*Positive Theorie des Kapitals* [4th ed.], II, 95). This first proof, it may be noted, rests on the assumption that, in neo-Austrian terminology, the "labor-dimension" of capital is constant; cf. V. Edelberg, "The Ricardian Theory of Profits," *Economics*, XIII (1933), 51–74.

The final proof of the first proposition is again essentially *a priori:*

i. Increased capital per laborer can be employed only with diminished effectiveness, *i.e.*, to yield a lower interest rate, in the absence of new inventions.
ii. The employment of more capital by given labor is possible only through changes in productive processes (since new commodities are excluded as unimportant), and such changes *must* be extensions of the production period, since shorter processes are already profitable before the interest rate falls.
iii. Therefore increases in capital, with concomitant increases in productivity per laborer, can take place only through extensions of the period of production.[1]

This argument is closely related to the foregoing "proof": the previous analysis looks back into the history of capital increases; the present argument looks forward to their application. And again there are two internal defects in the argument. The exclusion of new products is not a legitimate empirical assumption, certainly not without some defense. But more important, the minor premise is unsound, since it overlooks the possibility of developing shorter period investments because their costs are also reduced by a fall in the interest rate. If the period of production concept has validity—and this will be denied—it has an intensive as well as an extensive margin, as Böhm-Bawerk himself realizes in other connections.[2]

There is, however, a still more fundamental criticism to be levied at Böhm-Bawerk's formulation of the production period. These proofs are based on the "original factors" doctrine, and go even further, for the sake of simplicity, in explicitly excluding land! If capital equipment is considered in its real sense as a cooperating factor

[1] *Positive Theorie des Kapitals* (4th ed.), II, 33–39.

[2] *Positive Theory*, pp. 403–6.

of production, the production period disappears as an economic concept, as we shall now see.

The period of production, the length of the roundabout process, first requires definition: ". . . the production period of a consumption good is, strictly speaking, to be reckoned from the moment on which the first hand was laid to the making of its first intermediate product, right down to the completion of the good itself." [1] But, as Böhm-Bawerk admits, "in any strict calculation" the production period, thus defined, of "almost any consumption good" began in early centuries—the schoolboy's pen knife may contain iron from a mine opened in the time of Caesar.[2]

This is obvious nonsense, so Böhm-Bawerk resorts to the conception of an *average* period of production, wherein such early expenditures of effort will form only an "infinitesimal fraction—not worth the calculation even if that were possible." [3] This average—in his numerical examples the weighted arithmetic mean is used—is thus offered merely as a device for overcoming the difficulty of dating the beginning of the production process of a commodity. In that it clearly fails, for aside from the fact that "early century" investments are weighted by time and therefore greatly influence the average,[4] this statistical concept has absolutely no economic significance.[5]

[1] *Ibid.*, p. 88.

[2] When Clark said, "Production periods begin with civilization and never end. *It is not possible to lengthen them* . . . ," Böhm-Bawerk replied, "One may have reference to the 'absolute period.' . . . Of the production period in *this* sense everything holds that Professor Clark has said. . . ." ("The Origin of Interest," *Quarterly Journal of Economics*, IX [1894–95], 383–84); also compare *Kleinere Abhandlungen*, p. 135.

[3] *Positive Theory*, p. 88; also p. 89.

[4] The "original factors" doctrine is important in this self-deception; if all capital can be traced back to labor and land expended recently in the past, the early expenditures can be ignored.

[5] Böhm-Bawerk devotes many pages to Fisher's question (*The Rate of*

This last charge is equally apropos of the total production period. It is, first of all, a technical phenomenon, that is freely conceded.[1] And, more important, it is a nonexistent technical phenomenon, unless one wishes to date the beginning of all production periods back to the dawn of human history.

Clark was one of the first economists to point out that from an *economic* viewpoint production and consumption are "synchronous." Production and consumption are carried on simultaneously; only idle curiosity could prompt one to investigate the time of emergence of a physical unit of product from an industrial process, even if that were possible. Böhm-Bawerk virtually concedes this:

> . . . in a static economy everything runs smoothly because of the harmonious interlocking of the production-periods of the concrete capital goods existing in various stages of completion. . . . In any interval of time the concrete production-periods closed are just as many as the new ones opened. So it comes about that at any time just so many finished products are turned out as enable each producer to exchange his own raw product immediately for the finished product of another's labor. One may therefore, if he will, with theoretical inaccuracy but practically with impunity, imagine that, through some mystical quality of true capital, production-periods have been quite done away with in the world. . . .[2]

But he finds shelter in a dynamic economy, ". . . where concrete capital goods are, as it were, changing their

Interest, op. cit., pp. 56–57, 351–53), "why the particular method of averaging which Böhm-Bawerk employs is assumed to be the correct one." The reply by Böhm-Bawerk (*Positive Theorie des Kapitals* [4th ed.], II, Exkurs III) is indefensibly sophistical and evasive; it is merely an attack on Fisher's *manner of asking* the question. No rationale of the weighted arithmetic mean is ever presented.

[1] *Positive Theory*, pp. 79, 82.

[2] "The Positive Theory of Capital and Its Critics," *Quarterly Journal of Economics*, IX (1894–95), 127.

stratification, and production-periods no longer interlock in a perfect circle, here it might be demonstrated whether or not true capital has the power ascribed to it, the power to do away with production-periods."[1] Here Böhm-Bawerk is shifting ground, for his is a static theory of interest,[2] where production periods are admittedly of only academic interest. Certainly his theory is not, and does not purport to be, a description of dynamic change. The problem in a dynamic economy is not one of production periods, but of the *time* necessary for *readjustments*—which is entirely different from the concept of the production period.

The lengthening of the production period increases the product, but "in a lesser ratio" than the relative increase in the production period.[3] Diminishing returns is necessary, if the production period is not to be extended indefinitely in the original "investment." Böhm-Bawerk refers to proportional or ratio decreasing returns; this is an improper criterion for resource allocation.[4]

[1] *Ibid.*

[2] In the very same volume Böhm-Bawerk says, in "The Origin of Interest," "I fully agree with Professor Clark that interest is a 'static income,' and that it owes its origins to 'static causes'; also that creating new capital is not a part of the process by which interest is secured" (*op. cit.*, p. 383).

[3] Cf. *Positive Theory*, pp. 84–85, 91, 377 ff. At one point (*ibid.*, pp. 307–8), Böhm-Bawerk uses an arithmetical example in which increasing returns is assumed, but this seems clearly to be a slip. The distinction between ratio and incremental forms of the law of diminishing returns is never seen. Compare *Gesammelte Schriften*, pp. 194 ff.

[4] Böhm-Bawerk denies that diminishing returns from the extension of the period of production is the same thing as diminishing returns from the more intensive use of the elements (land and labor) involved. Cf. "The Positive Theory of Capital and Its Critics," *Quarterly Journal of Economics*, X (1895–96), pp. 148 ff.

The classical doctrine of diminishing returns to "land" is supported by an interesting mathematical proof in one of Böhm-Bawerk's last essays, "Einige nicht neue Bemerkungen über eine alte Frage," reprinted in *Gesammelte Schriften*, pp. 188–204. Letting H (*Hektar*) represent one unit of land, K (*Kosten*) one unit of capital-and-labor, and P, product, and assuming $1H + 100K = 100P$, then under his formulation of the law,

In the first edition of the *Positive Theory*, Böhm-Bawerk discusses only the period of *construction*, presumably assuming that utilization of the final product is instantaneous. In the (third and) fourth edition an "important parallel phenomenon," that of increasing the durability of consumption goods, is recognized:[1] ". . . very often through a more solid and durable construction of enduring consumption goods, the durability and with it the total sum of utilities drawn from the good in question increase in a greater proportion than the expense of production."[2] This element of production theory, which was first given elaborate consideration by Rae, is not an invariable "law," but it is held to operate in "an exceedingly large number of cases." This new element, moreover, is similar to the original concept of production, for increases in durability *ipso facto* lengthen the "waiting period" (*Wartezeit*) before an investment can be realized.[3] But the construction and utilization periods are independent, and either can be lengthened without lengthen-

$1H + 200K < 200P$. Since $1H + 200K < 200P$, then $2(\frac{1}{2}H + 100K) < 200P$ or $\frac{1}{2}H + 100K < 100P$. Therefore the internal implication of the "law" is that more can be produced by one unit of land plus 100 units of capital and labor than by half a unit of land plus 100 units of capital and labor, and this law is held to be "a self-evident truth bordering on a truism." The conclusion is true, of course, but the "proof" depends on the assumption of diminishing returns. T. N. Carver had previously used a similar proof.

[1] *Positive Theorie des Kapitals* (4th ed.), I, Bk. II, Chap. ii, "An Important Parallel Phenomenon of Capitalistic, Roundabout Production." Cf. also *ibid.*, II, 12–13. In view of Böhm-Bawerk's definition of income, which excludes services of durable consumption goods, durability of such goods is irrelevant to production, as he recognizes (*ibid.*, I, 126). The possibility of increasing durability was first recognized in the *Strittige Fragen* (1899), reprinted in *Kleinere Abhandlungen*, pp. 163–64.

[2] *Positive Theorie* (4th ed.), I, 121.

[3] The *Wartezeit*, or "degree of capitalism," is "the average period which lies between the successive expenditure in labor and uses of land and the obtaining of the final good." (*Positive Theory*, p. 90.) In the case of uniform investment it is equal to half the period of production, ignoring interest on early outlays. Compare also *Kleinere Abhandlungen*, p. 137 n.

ing the other. The two concepts cannot be merged, but in his discussion of the technical superiority of present over future goods, their substantial identity for purposes of interest theory is asserted.[1] And in the discussion of the interest rate, changes in durability are considered only in a footnote, as involving no new principles.[2]

This new element of durability has an immediate economic significance which the construction-period does not possess. Durability is not a merely technical consideration, since increased durability implies reduced maintenance and replacement costs for a capital good. But it is not so easy to introduce completely durable income sources into Böhm-Bawerk's theory of interest as he assumes; this problem will be noted in connection with Wicksell. Böhm-Bawerk never develops a theory of interest applicable to durable consumption goods—or durable production goods; he uses the interest rate secured from his general theory of the construction period to discount all durable income sources.[3]

The second proposition [4] on production asserts that every extension of the period of production requires an increase in the capital investment, and the third (and closely related) proposition maintains that more capital can be used only in extending the period of production:

> . . . the current productive powers will and must, on the average, be directed to remote productive purposes (or, in other words, invested in longer production periods), in

[1] *Positive Theorie* (4th ed.), I, 352–54.

[2] "The increase in productivity through lengthening the actual production period is in effect completely identical with the increase of utility services bound up with a lengthening of the average waiting period. . . . I . . . believe that this general reference to the following discussion [of the construction period and the interest rate] . . . ought to be satisfactory" (*ibid.*, p. 444 n.).

[3] Cf. *Positive Theory*, Bk. VI, Chaps. vii, viii.

[4] See, *supra*, p. 201.

> proportion to the length of time for which the existing stock of wealth is able to provide. . . . The average period of production in a community is in exact correspondence with the amount of its stock of wealth, and is entirely conditioned by it.[1]

The second proposition is simple and, if the production period concept had any significance, it would be valid. It asserts, essentially, that the average amount of investment (capital multiplied by time) increases with the period (time) for which a given amount of capital is invested. For example, shifting from an annual to a biennial crop will require double the advances to labor. This conclusion is presented for the special case of uniform rate of investment throughout the production period,[2] by numerous arithmetical examples.[3] Since the argument is quite simple,[4] only the conclusion need be presented: "The stock of wealth must be sufficient for half the production period, plus half the usual stage period." [5] But the converse, that increases in capital necessarily lead to extensions of the average period of production, is not supported by argument; it is a bald assertion.[6] The view

[1] *Positive Theory*, p. 325.

[2] Böhm-Bawerk again ignores interest on earlier outlays.

[3] *Positive Theory*, pp. 327 ff., 425–26.

[4] If there are N stages of equal length and C capital is invested in each stage (where a stage is one technical process—usually a year in Böhm-Bawerk's theory), then

in stage x_1, C is invested for N stages,
in stage x_2, C is invested for $N - 1$ stages,
etc., until in stage x_n, C is invested for 1 stage.

Then for the total period of production (Σx), NC, total capital, is invested for total number of stages equal to $\frac{N^2 + N}{2}$, and C, the average period investment, is invested for $\frac{N+1}{2}$ periods, the conclusion given in the text.

[5] *Positive Theory*, p. 327.

[6] Cf. *ibid.*, p. 319. In the fourth edition of the *Positive Theorie* (II, 4; also *Kleinere Abhandlungen*, pp. 185–87), Böhm-Bawerk asserts categorically

obviously derives from the exclusive attention which Böhm-Bawerk devotes to the time aspect of the production process. Yet this is but one of an infinite number of technical conditions governing the manner in which an increase of capital will be absorbed by an economy, and its relative importance is unknown. Certainly there is no reason to believe that it is the dominant consideration.[1]

A final word may be added regarding the "social period of production," *i.e.*, the average of the average periods of production in an economy.[2] This concept is never defined, and the problem of definition is avoided in the discussion of interest by assuming all industries to have the same productivity function. The concept itself is even more dubious, if possible, than that of the period of production, since it requires an interest rate before the relative importance of industries can be weighted.

that his theory does not claim that increases in productivity of capital come *only* through lengthening the production period; it is enough if this is the method in a majority of cases. Yet unless the lengthening of the period is the sole method of employing more capital, his theory is incomplete in that it examines only *one* of the margins of profitable investment opportunities. And in this latter case his theory becomes indistinguishable from most of the productivity theories of interest he so vigorously attacks. If capital could be treated as labor times the average period of production (see the reference to the "labor dimension" in note 2, p. 203), then, of course, the conclusion in the text would be truistical: an increase in capital, with a constant labor dimension, would require a lengthening of the period of production.

[1] An argument purporting to support this last proposition is offered at one point (*Positive Theory*, pp. 324–25). Increases in capital, says Böhm-Bawerk, will not be used in the current year's production because (i) direct methods are less productive, and (ii) the market for present goods is already stocked. But these reasons either beg the question (why are present methods of production and markets inferior to future markets, in equilibrium?) or offer merely a restatement of the assumption.

[2] *Ibid.*, Bk. VI, Chap. v, esp. pp. 315, 325. All of Böhm-Bawerk's discussion of the influence of inventions on the period of production (*Positive Theorie des Kapitals* [4th ed.], II, esp. Exkurse I and II) clearly premises a social average.

THE PREFERENCE FOR PRESENT OVER FUTURE GOODS [1]

Böhm-Bawerk finds the basic explanation of interest to lie in the preference of people for present rather than future goods of like quantity and quality. The analysis of production which has just been presented is an important datum in this interest theory, but it operates—at this point—only through its effect on subjective valuations of present and future goods. This time preference is based on three independent factors: different circumstances of want and provision; and irrational impatience; and the technical superiority of present goods. These will be considered in turn.

"The first great cause of difference in value between present and future goods consists in the different circumstances of want and provision in present and future." [2] Two typical cases are cited in support: "cases of immediate distress and necessity"; and cases of people "who have reason to look forward to economical circumstances of increasing comfort." One may immediately object that these are individual cases and that in a static society they will be offset more or less exactly by converse situations. Böhm-Bawerk attempts to answer this criticism by a peculiar argument:

i. All people who will be relatively better off in the future will put a premium on present goods.
ii. All those persons who will not be so well off in the future as at present will store durable goods (*e.g.*, money) rather than put a premium on future over present goods.[3]

The net effect for society as a whole, therefore, is to value present goods higher than future goods of like quantity and quality.

[1] *Positive Theory*, Bk. V, *passim.*
[2] *Ibid.*, p. 249.
[3] *Ibid.*, pp. 250 ff.

Böhm-Bawerk's reply to the possibility of offsetting individual conditions is not convincing. People with a future preference cannot *store* the goods they desire in most cases, *e.g.*, food and clothing, except at a cost. When Bortkiewicz raises this objection,[1] Böhm-Bawerk restricts this first ground to *money* economies,[2] but even money cannot be stored without cost. It would lead us into monetary theory (which Böhm-Bawerk does not discuss) to analyze the general effects of monetary savings which are not invested (*i.e.*, hoarded); here it may merely be noted that such hoarding would not necessarily accomplish its aim. In general, why should not people with high future needs lend to those with high present needs (in the present case of consumption loans), without involving a pure interest charge at all? [3]

The second ground for valuing present goods more highly is that " . . . to goods which are destined to meet the wants of the future, we ascribe a value which is really less than the true intensity of their future marginal utility." [4] This is a failure of perspective, an irrationality in human behavior—the only irrationality, it may be noted, that Böhm-Bawerk introduces into his "economic man." Three reasons are offered for this "fact," of which "there is no doubt." [5] Men have defective imaginations, hence they underestimate future needs (but not future provision). Men, moreover, have limited will power; they cannot resist present extravagances even when they are aware of great future needs. And, finally, life itself is short and uncertain. This factor operates only for rela-

[1] "Der Kardinalfehler der Böhm-Bawerkschen Zinstheorie," *Jahrbuch für Gesetzgebung, Verwaltung, und Volkswirtschaft,* XXX (1906), 946–47.

[2] *Positive Theorie des Kapitals* (4th ed.), I, 331 n.

[3] Risk and management expenses are abstracted, of course.

[4] *Positive Theory,* p. 253.

[5] *Ibid.*, p. 254.

tively remote future goods, but arbitrage makes the discount on future goods immediate and continuous with time.[1] The discount on future goods due to weakness of perspective, it may be noted, is *added* to the discount arising out of differences in circumstances of want and provision.[2]

This element of irrationality is blandly assumed, and its support lies chiefly in plausible and irrelevant examples of human frailty. That this irrational preference for present goods exists in many people is certain; that it is more than offset by a largely irrational (non-economic) preference for future over present goods by those people who can and do save also seems fairly probable. Social approval of saving is an important characteristic of modern western civilization; the wealthy save from necessity and for prestige, and everyone tries to save because "it's the thing to do." Certainly, again, Böhm-Bawerk's hunger examples are complete nonsense; no one wishes three meals at breakfast, rather than breakfast, lunch, and dinner, and similarly for longer periods. Böhm-Bawerk's basic error is in assuming the choice to be between *all now* or *all later*, when in fact the basis is a uniform distribution through time.[3]

A very considerable and highly critical literature has grown up about Böhm-Bawerk's third ground for human preference for present goods, the technical superiority of

[1] It is the weakest of the three factors, in Böhm-Bawerk's opinion, and it is further weakened by people's desire to care for heirs.

[2] *Positive Theory*, pp. 258–59.

[3] Little attention will be devoted to this ground, since it has been criticized so effectively elsewhere. Cf. Knight, *Risk, Uncertainty, and Profit*, *op. cit.*, pp. 130 ff. Bortkiewicz points out (*op. cit.*, pp. 948–49) a certain inconsistency: the first ground is applicable only in a money economy; the second ground cannot be considered proved unless it is observed in an economy in which interest does not exist, for otherwise the "overdiscount" may be due merely to the realization that present investments will yield interest.

present over future goods.[1] While the first two factors may be—and to the writer seem clearly—fallacious, they are relevant. But the question of the relevance of the third independent element, technical superiority, to the interest problem has been questioned at length.[2]

As one increases the average period of production, the total product increases indefinitely, but in an ever decreasing proportion.[3] On this postulate, drawn from his theory of production, Böhm-Bawerk bases the "technical superiority" of present over future goods, independent of the factors of provision and perspective.[4] The argument is illustrated by the example given in Table 4. Present productive goods are more valuable than those coming into possession in the future, because for any given year (present or future) we may secure a greater product from given productive goods immediately at our disposal than from productive goods accruing to us at a later date. This is the third independent factor leading to undervaluation of future goods.

Neither Böhm-Bawerk's elaboration of this point nor the criticisms which have been directed at it need be considered in detail, since the question of the independence of the "third ground" is unimportant, despite Böhm-Bawerk's belief that it is the important and original part

[1] A possible "fourth ground," or, alternatively, the most important part of the third ground, is suggested by Böhm-Bawerk in the fourth edition of the *Positive Theorie:* the increases of durability of consumption goods. It is not discussed at any length, however. Cf. *ibid.*, I, 352–54; II, 25 n.; *supra*, pp. 208 f.

[2] The most important literature is as follows: Fisher, *The Rate of Interest*, *op. cit.*, Chap. iv and Appendix; Bortkiewicz, "Der Kardinalfehler," *op. cit.*, pp. 942–72; Wicksell, "Zur Zinstheorie," *op. cit.*, III, 199–209. Böhm-Bawerk's lengthy reply to the first two of these critics is found in the *Positive Theorie des Kapitals* (4th ed.), II, Exkurs XII. A general treatment, sympathetic to Böhm-Bawerk, is Erik von Sivers' *Die Zinstheorie Eugen v. Böhm-Bawerk's im Lichte der deutschen Kritik* (Jena, 1924).

[3] Cf. *Positive Theory*, pp. 260–61, 262 n., 269–70, etc.

[4] *Ibid.*, Bk. V, Chap. iv, *passim.*

of his theory of interest.[1] The increase in the productivity of capital arising out of the employment of longer periods of production is a (non-existent) technical datum; it can have no *direct* effect on human valuations, any more than can such other technical details as hardness or flexibility. The possibility of using goods more productively if they are not consumed in the present can act on

TABLE 4

BÖHM-BAWERK'S DATA FOR DEMONSTRATING THE TECHNOLOGICAL SUPERIORITY OF PRESENT OVER FUTURE GOODS

WILL YIELD A PRODUCT IN	A MONTH'S LABOR INVESTED IN			
	1888	1889	1890	1891
1888 of	100	...	...	...
1889 of	200	100	...	...
1890 of	280	200	100	...
1891 of	350	280	200	100
1892 of	400	350	280	200
Etc.				

the relative value of present and future goods only through the first ground, the difference in "circumstances of want and provision in present and future." The real question, as Böhm-Bawerk admits in the course of his long and confused polemic against Fisher and Bortkiewicz, is ". . . whether the addition of my third ground to an otherwise given situation . . . does or does not exercise another influence on the degree of superiority of the value of present goods." [2] For the rest the long argument, presumably a matter of *Ehrgeiz* and polemical spirit, rests on a confusion between *independent* and *implicit* variables, in the language of mathematics.[3]

[1] *Ibid.*, p. 277 n.

[2] *Positive Theorie des Kapitals* (4th ed.), II, 283.

[3] Professor Haberler, in his review of Fisher's *Theory of Interest,* finds an escape from the charge of circular reasoning by use of the concept of a

The incorporation of the third ground within the first is quite simple.[1] The increased productivity (subject to diminishing returns) of more roundabout production processes makes it possible to supply, with the same resources, more goods in the future than at present. This factor is then an element, or rather *the* element, in the first ground of discount of the future, by increasing provision in the future relative to the present.

Superficially this procedure may seem to offer no real escape. In a truly stationary economy, it may be asserted, capitalistic methods are fixed. Therefore, while such methods increase the product secured from given resources, this increase is received at *all* times. Specifically, let us assume a three-year process (Table 4) which yields a product of 280, in contrast with a product of 100 by a one-year process. Then in 1890 we may expect a return of 280 in 1892, but in 1890 we are already receiving 280 from the investment of 100 in 1888. No matter where we cut into a stationary economy, the flow of provision is constant. This line of thought is important in Schumpeter's theory, to which Böhm-Bawerk is strongly opposed.[2]

This latter line of refutation of the third ground is clearly unsound. Even if the supply of capital is absolutely fixed, interest will emerge unless no more capital

"finite economic period," which does yield a preference for present over future goods on the third ground. The writer, however, sees no possible definition of such a period without the use of an interest rate, and this rate must come either from the first two grounds, or from the third ground—and then circular reasoning is involved. Cf. "Irving Fisher's 'Theory of Interest,' " *Quarterly Journal of Economics*, XLV (1931), 509–12.

[1] Wicksell first made this suggestion, *Über Wert, Kapital und Rente* (Jena, 1893), p. 84.

[2] Cf. "Eine 'dynamische' Theorie des Kapitalzinses," *Zeitschrift für Volkswirtschaft, Sozialpolitik, und Verwaltung*, XXII (1913). For Böhm-Bawerk's view compare *ibid.*, pp. 1–62, 640–56; Schumpeter's reply, *ibid.*, pp. 599–639.

can be used productively by an economy. This state will be arrived at only when all goods are free goods, *i.e.*, when it is no longer possible to substitute capital for other factors. In the absence of this situation interest is a price necessary to secure an economic allocation of capital, and, conversely, only through such a price mechanism may supply of and demand for capital be equated (in the absence of rationing).

The truly astonishing aspect of Böhm-Bawerk's labored discussion of the future is that it is virtually ignored in his own theory! In his sections on the determination of the interest rate, Böhm-Bawerk assumes that the supply of capital is owned by those who do not undervalue the future,[1] and that the demand for capital comes primarily from entrepreneurs. The technical superiority of present goods becomes the direct determinant of interest, and the circuitous treatment indicated above is completely forgotten.

It is perhaps most appropriate to consider here the implication of Böhm-Bawerk's analysis of discount of the future for the problem of saving. The entire analysis is conducted in terms of the exchange between present and future *goods*, the present commodity in comparison with an identical commodity at some time in the future.[2]

Two fundamental weaknesses are present in such a comparison. The concrete articles are rarely desired equally (in terms of, say, a given money income) at various points in time; the individual's utility surface shifts through time, and comparisons between dates are

[1] *Positive Theory*, pp. 315–16, 330, 382.

[2] "Economists are today completely agreed, I think, that the 'abstinence' connected with saving is no true abstinence, that is, no final renunciation of pleasure affording goods . . ." ("The Function of Saving," *Annals of the American Academy*, XVII [1901], 460).

difficult if not impossible. Similarly with respect to the *time* of comparison: what date or period in the future should be compared with the present? Here, as Wicksell says, "the difficulty clearly arises that both the *supply* of future goods and the *period of consumption* are quite indeterminate." [1] The escape from these difficulties lies in the adoption of a more appropriate conception of saving, such as the exchange of present incomes of given size for larger future perpetual incomes, thus recognizing that saving involves true abstinence.

THE DETERMINATION OF THE RATE OF INTEREST

The foundations of Böhm-Bawerk's theory of interest have been presented; we may now pass on to the final development, the determination of the rate of interest. Before presenting this subject it may be well to collect the threads of the previous analysis in the form of propositions:

- i. Virtually all wealth (or capital) consists, according to Böhm-Bawerk, of material means of subsistence of laborers, and to a relatively unimportant extent of landowners and capitalists, available not all at once but practically at will through future time.
- ii. The product secured from a given amount of labor increases with the extension of the period of production, but in a decreasing proportion.
- iii. All capital increases must be utilized in extending the period of production, assuming the amount of labor to remain fixed, and, conversely, all increases in the length of the period of production require increases of capital.

These propositions bear a marked resemblance to those of the classical wages fund doctrine. The important difference lies in the variability of the period of produc-

[1] *Lectures on Political Economy* (New York, 1934), p. 169.

tion. Virtually all of the wealth—or capital—of an economy is a subsistence fund available for the employment of labor in time-consuming processes; this is the first postulate.[1] Entrepreneurs, the employers of labor, will, on the other side, demand these means of subsistence in order to be able to follow more remunerative production methods.[2] And the productivity of the extension of the period of production provides a quantitative basis for valuing the use of the subsistence. "In the production loan . . . the important thing is the difference in productiveness between the methods open to him who gets the loan, and those open to him who has to do without it." [3] This productive demand is practically infinite, if the interest rate is low enough: ". . . it continues at least so long as the return to production goes on increasing with the extension of the production process, and that is a limit which, even in the richest nation, lies far beyond the amount of wealth possessed at the moment." [4] Therefore interest *must* appear, or otherwise very long processes, which require more capital than exists, would be pursued.[5] The function of interest, from this viewpoint, is to insure that the length of the production period will be properly adjusted throughout the investment field to the amount of subsistence available. The productivity function of each industry will determine the amount of capital for which it will be able to compete successfully.

There remains only the determination of the specific equilibrium rate of interest.[6] Assuming, as Böhm-

[1] Cf. also *Positive Theory*, pp. 322, 330.

[2] *Ibid.*, pp. 332–33.

[3] *Ibid.*, p. 376.

[4] *Ibid.*, p. 332.

[5] *Ibid.*, pp. 333–35. The wage rate determination is ignored for the moment.

[6] *Ibid.*, Bk. VII, *passim.*

Bawerk does,[1] the amount of capital to be fixed, the determination is clear. "The rate of interest—on the assumptions already made—is limited and determined by the productiveness of the last extension of process economically permissible, and of the further extension economically not permissible." [2] An arithmetical example (condensed in Table 5) illustrates the application of the theory. Four assumptions underlie this table: labor is the only productive factor used;[3] the labor is invested evenly throughout the period in question, so that the total capital is invested for only half of the production period; [4] "all branches of production show the same productiveness"; [5] and, finally, physical and value productivity are proportional.[6] We must also know the total amount of capital and labor available; Böhm-Bawerk selects $15,000,000 and 10,000 laborers.

The equilibrium point, at which the interest rate is determined, will be such that the supply of labor exactly equals the demand for labor (*i.e.*, wages offered, or the total subsistence); the establishment of equilibrium is insured by competition.[7] With a one-year period the laborer can (and because of competition will) be paid $350 less interest on the wage advance; with a ten-year process, $700 less interest—in each case his discounted

[1] *Ibid.*, Bk. VII, Chap. ii.

[2] *Ibid.*, p. 393. The last clause is added to meet the problem of discontinuities in the extension of the period of production, *i.e.*, the "marginal pair" of periods determine the rate. The word "permissible" should be replaced by "permissible under competition."

[3] *Ibid.*, p. 381.

[4] *Ibid.*, p. 379 n.

[5] *Ibid.*, p. 382.

[6] *Positive Theorie des Kapitals* (4th ed.), I, 344 n., 441 n. This permissible methodological step is strongly attacked in the *Geschichte* as one of the fundamental weaknesses of the productivity theories; cf. *Capital and Interest*, Bk. II, Chap. ii.

[7] *Positive Theory*, pp. 384 ff.

TABLE 5

Hypothetical Data for the Determination of the Wage Rate and the Rate of Interest

Production Period (Years)	Annual Product per Laborer	Annual Wages $300			Annual Wages $600			Annual Wages $500		
		Profit per Laborer	Number of Laborers	Total Profit	Profit per Laborer	Number of Laborers	Total Profit	Profit per Laborer	Number of Laborers	Total Profit
1	$350	$ 50	66.6	$3333	−$250	33.3	Loss	−$150	40	Loss
2	450	150	33.3	5000	− 150	16.6	Loss	− 50	40	Loss
3	530	230	22.2	5111	− 70	11.1	Loss	30	13.3	$ 400
4	580	280	16.6	4666	− 20	8.3	Loss	80	10	800
5	620	320	13.3	4266	20	6.6	$133	120	8	960
6	650	350	11.1	3888	50	5.5	277	150	6.6	1000
7	670	370	9.5	3522	70	4.7	333	170	5.7	970
8	685	385	8.3	3208	85	4.1	354	185	5	925
9	695	395	7.4	2925	95	3.7	351	195	4.4	866
10	700	400	6.6	2666	100	3.3	333	200	4	800

product.[1] The ultimate wage paid and the interest rate set are therefore mutually dependent.

Assume the annual wage rate to be $300. Then an entrepreneur with $10,000 capital can hire 66.6 laborers for one year, 33.3 laborers for two years, etc.[2] His choice among these alternatives will be that period which yields him a maximum net return. As the table indicates, this will be a three-year process, from which a net return of $5111 or 51 per cent is secured. With a $600 wage the maximum return ($354 or 3.5 per cent) will be secured in the eight-year process; with a $500 wage it will be six years (yielding $1000 or 10 per cent).

Most of these combinations of wage rates and interest rates (of which there are an infinite number) will not employ all of the capital or all of the labor. With a $300 wage, for instance, $10,000 will employ 22.2 workers, and the total capital ($15,000,000) will employ 33⅓ thousand workers. There are only 10,000 laborers, however, so all the capital could not be employed and wages would be forced up by the competitive bidding of capitalists. At $600 wages, 4.16 workers are employed by $10,000, and thus the total capital could employ only 6¼ thousand workers, and competition for employment would force wages down. At $500 wages, however, 6.66 laborers will be employed by $10,000, hence the total capital will employ the total number of laborers. It is the unique equilibrium point.

[1] Obviously this is not a marginal productivity theory of wages, for labor is the only material productive resource. It may be termed a discounted productivity theory.

[2] The following simple formula gives the number of laborers that can be employed by $10,000 at given wage rates and for given periods of time:

$$N = \frac{2 \times 10{,}000}{t \times w},$$

where N is number of workers, t is number of years, and w is the annual wage rate.

It should be pointed out, although Böhm-Bawerk fails to do so, that $500 is not the only wage rate which will simultaneously employ all capital and labor. Given any wage rate, there is a production period such that $10,000 will hire 6.66 workers, and therefore all labor and capital will be employed. For example, at a $300 wage a ten-year process will employ an appropriate number of laborers; at a $600 wage the period is five years. But these are not stable points of equilibrium under competition. Taking the former case, any entrepreneur may secure a higher rate of return on a given investment by shortening his production period and increasing his labor force, if initially he used a ten-year process. But the withdrawal of these laborers will leave other capitalists without sufficient labor to pursue the ten-year process. The latter capitalists, moreover, must bid so high a price to secure the return of these laborers that they will not have sufficient capital to employ all of them for ten years. By such competition, therefore, wages will be increased and the interest rate lowered until the unique equilibrium point is reached.[1]

The determination of the rate of interest may be put in another way. The extension of the period of production requires $250 per worker per year, if the annual wage is $500. A one-year extension beyond a previous five-year period yields an additional product of $30, or 12 per cent on $250. A second one-year extension would yield $20, or 8 per cent. Since the market rate of interest is 10 per

[1] Compare the contrary conclusion of Jak. Kr. Lindberg, "Die Kapitalzinstheorie Böhm-Bawerks," *Zeitschrift für Nationalökonomie*, IV (1932–33), 501–14, esp. 504–5. Lindberg argues that all of the points of full employment of resources are stable. Two errors contribute to this view:

i. He assumes that wages and interest need not be uniform throughout the market, and
ii. He fails to see that at any wage above $300 the given capital is insufficient to employ all laborers for a ten-year period.

cent, this last extension will not be made, and in general it is unprofitable for any producer to extend his period of production beyond that period just permitted by the supply of capital. It follows, then, that "The rate [of interest] is determined by the surplus return of the last permissible extension of production." [1] This formula holds true as a *description* of the equilibrium point (assuming continuity in the possible lengths of the production period), but it is not true, as Wicksell has pointed out, in the sense that additional capital increments will secure a return determined in such a manner. For increases in capital will also increase the wage rate, thus decreasing the actual extension of the production period under the extension possible without a wage increase. This ratio of additional product to additional capital investment is therefore always lower than the interest rate.[2]

The data which determine the rate of interest are, in summary, three: ". . . interest will be high in proportion as the national subsistence fund is low, as the number of labourers employed by the same is great, and as the surplus returns connected with any further extension of the production period continue high." [3]

Of the innumerable qualifications and casuistical details which Böhm-Bawerk adds to the theory, one is the recognition that the production functions of various commodities are not identical.[4] Here the sole change in

[1] *Positive Theory*, p. 394.

[2] Compare Wicksell, *Über Wert, Kapital und Rente*, *op. cit.*, pp. 108–13, for a mathematical demonstration of this point. Böhm-Bawerk retains this form of statement, however, refusing to accept the, to me, irrefutable analysis of Wicksell. Cf. *Positive Theorie des Kapitals* (4th ed.), I, 455 n. In another connection the influence on wage rates is admitted, *ibid.*, II, 36 n.

[3] *Positive Theory*, p. 401.

[4] *Ibid.*, pp. 305–11, 404–6.

the theory is that all production periods will not be the same length; the total amount of capital will be so distributed that the surplus (marginal) returns will be the same in all industries.

The second qualification concerns non-productive demands for capital, the demands for consumption and for the maintenance of landlords and capitalists.[1] Consumption credit demands are merely a part of the total demand for capital, hence they serve to decrease slightly the amount of capital available for production and thus to raise the rate of interest. Landowners' demands have the same effect if rents are *advanced;* they have no effect if the landowner lives by his labor and is paid *after* the production period is ended.[2] The capitalist's advances, finally, are again like consumption loans in their effect on the interest rate, except that first an interest rate must exist before they can draw interest.[3]

Although Böhm-Bawerk fills many pages with criticisms of the productivity theories of interest, this analysis is clearly such a theory, as indeed he admits.[4] This last

[1] *Ibid.*, pp. 407–10; also p. 373.

[2] There is clearly a complete confusion here between stationary conditions and those of capital accumulation. If landowners *advance* the use of their lands, they are clearly acting as capitalists and have therefore previously increased the amount of capital. Wicksell's criticism is essentially the same: ". . . the portion of capital paid out as ground rent together with the capital actually applied in production secure interest from the net profit [*Reingewinn*] of production" (*Über Wert, Kapital und Rente, op. cit.*, p. 124 n.). Böhm-Bawerk refuses to concede the validity of this criticism, however; cf. *Positive Theorie des Kapitals* (4th ed.), I, 470 n.

[3] Here again there is an ambiguity regarding the conditions of the problem, *i.e.*, is the economy stationary or progressive? If capitalists consume their incomes—that is, do not accumulate capital—the interest rate will not be affected.

[4] When Wicksell and Pierson point out that his theory is essentially a productivity theory of interest, Böhm-Bawerk replies, "I would not object greatly to this [charge], except perhaps that according to my view the 'productivity of capital' is never the direct and moreover not the only ground for the emergence of interest." Yet consumption demands for capital—

section on the determination of the interest rate is his very best economic theorizing. It is much more lucid, consistent, and penetrating than the analyses of distribution, production, and discount of the future. But its premises, which lie in the first two of these fields, are completely fallacious. Therefore, although it is interesting as a display of great ingenuity and of considerable (if unconscious) insight into the problem of general equilibrium, its substantive contributions must be rejected.[1]

the other ground for loans—have relatively small influence, as he admits, and the question of "directness" is of no moment. Cf. *Kleinere Abhandlungen*, pp. 37 n., 39; *Geschichte und Kritik* (3d ed., Innsbruck, 1914), p. 705 n.

[1] The production period for a single investment is never considered by Böhm-Bawerk, and accordingly need not be discussed here. Cf. K. Boulding, "Time and Investment," *Economica*, N.S. III (1936), 196–220.

Chapter IX

LEON WALRAS

LEON WALRAS is best known as one of the discoverers of the theory of subjective value.[1] In Anglo-Saxon countries, however, even this reputation is based largely on hearsay; there is no general history of economic thought in English which devotes more than passing reference to his work. On the continent he has been more cordially treated. Most of the Italian economists—Pantaleoni, Barone, and Pareto, for instance—acknowledge their indebtedness to him, as does Wicksell of Sweden and Antonelli of France. But in America and England, Walras (like Gossen and Thünen) is often referred to and seldom quoted.

This sort of empty fame in English-speaking countries is of course attributable in large part to Walras' use of his mother tongue, French, and his depressing array of mathematical formulas. Walras was a better mathematician than Jevons, but his developments were clumsy and prolix. Walras devotes more than 150 pages to outlining the general system of exchange equilibrium in the consumer's market; Wicksell performs the task in about 20 pages and Edgeworth does it in a footnote! The work of a discoverer is not expected to be so elegant as that of

[1] For his biography and correspondence consult W. Jaffé, "Unpublished Papers and Letters of Leon Walras," *Journal of Political Economy*, XLIII (1935), 187–207. Cf. also J. R. Hicks, "Leon Walras," *Econometrica*, II (1934), 338–48. E. Antonelli, *Principles d'économie pure* (Paris, 1914), contains a convenient semi-mathematical summary of Walras' *Eléments d'économie politique pure* (Lausanne, 1926) and some facts on his life.

successors, but Walras was singularly obstinate in retaining unnecessarily involved mathematics.

Walras' reputation as an economist, moreover, rests almost exclusively on his theoretical studies. Jevons achieved much of his fame from his works on the coal question, monetary problems, and index numbers. Menger soon acquired a group of vigorous disciples, and he was a leading figure in the *Methodenstreit*. But Walras consistently maintained a very high level of abstraction at a time when pure theory was not flourishing in his *Sprachgebiet*. We may note also that Walras' fundamental contribution, the concept of general equilibrium, is stated more clearly and simply by his followers, so only the historical student goes back to the *Eléments*. But it must be emphasized that these are explanations, and not justifications, of his neglect; the writer, for one, would place his contributions above those of Pareto.

The present chapter will follow in the main Walras' emphasis on the general equilibrium theory. Some implications of his doctrine for the theory of costs and returns are assembled below, but such "specific" doctrines play little part in his thinking.[1]

Costs and Returns

Walras devotes very little attention to the problem of the nature of costs. His preoccupation with the problems of general equilibrium leads him to ignore almost all economic problems other than that of mutual determination.[2] In the *Eléments*, however, there is a rather clear

[1] The 1926 edition of the *Eléments* is the chief source, and all references are to it unless otherwise noted. The first edition (1874) and the third edition (1896) were read but not collated; Prof. William Jaffé's forthcoming variorum translation makes a detailed textual exegesis unnecessary. I am indebted to F. Rouge et c[ie] of Lausanne for permission to quote from the *Eléments*.

[2] This statement is not so true of his utility analysis, but it describes his treatment of production without important exception.

application of the alternative cost theory to the problem of the allocation of resources. "Under this regime of free competition, if the selling price of commodities exceeds their cost of production in certain businesses, so that there is a *profit,* the entrepreneurs expand or develop their production, which increases the quantity of product and forces down the price and reduces the spread; and if in certain businesses, the cost of production of products exceeds their selling prices, so there is a *loss,* the entrepreneurs divert or restrict their production, which decreases the quantity of product and raises the price and again reduces the spread" (p. 194; also p. 394). The same process of equalizing the return from alternative uses of resources holds true of all unspecialized resources. Labor in particular is unspecialized. "What do the majority of men consult at the time of choosing a profession? Precisely the rate of wages that is paid there, that is to say, the value of the productive services in that profession" (p. 396). In the case of specialized resources, their prices are determined solely by the value of the products (p. 396).

An alternative cost theory, moreover, is implicit in the general demand equations of the individual.[1] The fundamental equations expressing the condition for maximum satisfaction state that such a quantity of each resource will be retained by its owner as to equate its marginal utility for direct consumption with the marginal utility of income received from the use of the remainder in production. This "equation of exchange" is applied to all types of land, labor, and capital.

These equations, however, may be interpreted as con-

[1] Cf., *infra*, pp. 237–239. Rigidity in the hours of labor is recognized elsewhere, but this problem is not faced. Cf. *Etudes d'économie politique appliquée* (Paris, 1936), p. 275.

taining either an alternative cost theory or a real cost theory. They are stated in terms of utility, but they emphasize the marginal equality of leisure alternatives and particular industrial employments of productive services. The double problem of allocating productive services, to recall, consists of: (1) determining the allocation of the services of a given productive resource between leisure and monetary uses; and (2) determining the allocation of these services between various monetary uses. Concerning this first problem (on which Walras' discussion centers), it may not be amiss to note here that a correctly stated real cost theory differs primarily in terminology from the alternative cost theory. One may say either that the labor supply, for instance, is limited by psychological costs or that it is limited by alternative leisure uses. Formally, the result is the same. But the alternative cost approach nevertheless possesses certain advantages. It contains no invitation to delve into psychological grab-bags and emerge with such anomalous commodities as "producer's surplus." The alternative cost theory, furthermore, properly emphasizes the fact that anything which competes with industry for the use of a resource decreases its supply, whereas the real cost theory begins with psychological considerations (*e.g.*, irksomeness) which in themselves are irrelevant. The second problem in allocating productive services (between various monetary uses) is given inadequate analysis by Walras; reference may be made to the difficulties in the real cost theory when division of labor is present.[1]

[1] On this point cf. F. H. Knight, " 'The Common Sense of Political Economy' (Wicksteed Reprinted)," *Journal of Political Economy*, XLII (1934), 660–73. Edgeworth, in his review of the second edition of the *Eléments*, "Mathematical Theory of Political Economy," *Nature*, XL (1889), 435, implied that Walras had ignored all considerations of disutility. L. von Bortkiewicz, in what was ostensibly a review of the same work but really a defense of Walras and criticism of Edgeworth, pointed out the im-

It may be noted that Walras follows the contemporary practice of defining diminishing returns in terms of proportions (pp. 405, 408–9).[1]

The Factors and Services of Production

Walras' discussion of the productive factors and services is one of his most valuable—and least appreciated—contributions to the theory of production. He is the first to build on the fundamental dichotomy between resources and their services. The resources or service-sources are called capital: ". . . *fixed capital* or *capital* is in general all durable goods, all forms of social wealth which are not consumed or which are consumed only in the long run, all utility limited in quantity which survives its first use,—in a word, which serves more than once . . ." (p. 177). Analytically distinct from such resources are the services which they yield. These services, or revenues, include "all forms of social wealth which are consumed immediately, everything rare which does not exist after the first use it renders, in short, which is used only once . . ." (p. 177). If a house is capital, the protection from the elements which it affords in any given period of time is its service or revenue. A given resource may be either capital or service, depending on the use to which it is put. Thus a fruit tree is capital, but if it is cut down and used as fuel, a revenue emerges. Either a capital good or its revenue may be immaterial, but there is one fundamental relationship between them: "It is of the essence of capital to give birth to revenue; and it is of the

plicit theory of cost in Walras' equations. Cf. Bortkiewicz, *Revue d'Economie Politique*, IV (1890), 83–84. Edgeworth replied somewhat ambiguously on this point in the article, "La Théorie Mathématique de L'Offre," *ibid.*, V (1891), 10–28, but in his *Papers Relating to Political Economy* (London, 1925), II, 311–12, the criticism was completely withdrawn.

[1] His discussion of the production function is so general as to constitute no exception. Cf. p. 374; also, *infra*, p. 258.

essence of revenue to originate directly or indirectly in capital" (p. 178). Capital, that is to say, yields successive uses, and each of these is a revenue or service.

The distinction between a resource and its service is fundamental to production theory, for entrepreneurs require only services, *i.e.*, the temporary use of resources. But Walras' criterion, the number of economic uses of a given good, is not completely satisfactory. The number of services is incidental from an economic point of view; the fundamental difference relates to the time period over which the services of a capital good are spread. If this period is short, the consumption of the capital good and its service merge. If the period is considerable, and the test is whether the discounted value of the services differs significantly from their total value, services must then be treated separately. Services are always the fundamental concept; capital values are derivative. Even if Walras' ground for differentiating capital and services may be slightly misleading, the distinction is of paramount importance.[1]

Capital goods and services are each classified into three groups: land, labor, and capital proper (pp. 179–81). This distinction rests on received doctrine; Walras' justification for the classification is very superficial. "Land" (*capitaux fonciers*) includes only the unimproved terrain, the feature of extension (p. 184). It cannot, with comparatively few exceptions,[2] be produced or destroyed

[1] "It is, in my opinion, the key to all pure economic theory. If one neglects the distinction between capital goods and revenues, and especially if one refuses to admit the immaterial services of capital to social wealth, alongside of material revenues, one inhibits every scientific theory of the determination of price" (p. xi). Jaffé, *op. cit.*, pp. 190–91, suggests that the distinction between capital goods and revenues was taken over by Walras from the works of his father, Auguste Walras.

[2] The exceptions are physical in character: land is created by drainage of swamps; it is destroyed by earthquakes and floods (p. 182).

(pp. 182, 246). Personal capital is natural but destructible by either use or accident.[1] Artificial capital goods, or capital goods proper, are produced and destructible (p. 183). These hoary distinctions are indefensible in the form Walras proposes them, and do not deserve further attention.[2]

On the basis of these three types of capital goods, a rather elaborate classification of goods and services is erected. The general content of the classification may be summarized:

1. Landed capital used in consumption, *e.g.*, a park or residential plot.
2. Personal capital used in consumption, *e.g.*, domestic servants, public officials.
3. Capital proper used in consumption, *e.g.*, houses, furniture, and clothing.
4. Landed capital used in production, *e.g.*, agricultural lands.
5. Personal capital used in production, *e.g.*, laborers.
6. Capital proper used in production, *e.g.*, buildings, factories, and machines (pp. 185–87).

Among the numerous other categories suggested, two classes of services deserve mention at this point. The first, *objets de consommation*, consists of the perishable consumable goods in the hands of consumers: bread, meat, wine, etc. (pp. 178, 181, 186). The second class of

[1] He recognizes "that principle of social morality which is more and more generally accepted," that persons cannot be purchased or sold, nor are they produced on economic considerations, as with domestic animals. He includes personal capital, however, since personal services are in the market, and there is thus a basis for valuing personal capital (p. 183). This is unconvincing, as is also Walras' subsequent excuse, that economics is a science which abstracts from the element of interest or realism as well as from the element of justice. Personal capital plays only a formal role in his theory, however.

[2] He seems also (and not too consistently) to accept, in connection with his favorite scheme of nationalization of land, the doctrine of "original factors." Cf. *Economie politique appliquée*, p. 470.

revenues contains the perishable raw materials used in production: fuel, seed, and the like (pp. 181, 186). This extensive classification (which is here reproduced only in part) is a vestige of previous economic thought, and it plays virtually no part in Walras' analysis of production.

The General Scheme of Production

One of Walras' great contributions to economic theory is the clear portrayal of the nature of production in a competitive economy. Before summarizing this portrayal it is necessary to follow him in separating out the functions of the entrepreneur. The entrepreneur is one who hires the services of various kinds of capital goods from their owners. Analytically this function of coordination may and must be divorced completely from the ownership of resources, although "in real life" the entrepreneur is certain to own some resources and perhaps to perform some service in labor of management (p. 191).

There are two general markets in an enterprise economy. The first is the market for services (pp. 191–92). In this market the various owners of the capital goods (including laborers) appear as sellers of capital services, and the entrepreneurs appear as purchasers. It is important to note that the sale of capital services does not necessarily involve the sale of capital goods. Walras properly emphasizes a corollary of the separation of goods from their services:

> Services, by the very fact that they no longer exist after the first service they render, can only be sold or given away. . . . Capital goods, on the contrary, by the very fact that they survive the first use which is made of them, may be *hired*, whether at burdensome rates or gratuitously. . . . *The hiring out of a capital good is the alienation of the service of that capital* (p. 190).

The price of each capital good's service will at equilibrium be such as to equate the supply of and demand for it. These prices are called rents, for land services; wages, for personal services; and interest, for the services of capital proper.

The second market is for finished products (pp. 192–93). In this market the entrepreneurs appear as sellers and the resource owners as buyers, so the circulation of goods within the economy is complete. Here again equilibrium prices will equate supply and demand.

The two markets are related in two respects. The resource owners "with the money they have received in the first market for their productive services, . . . go to the second market to buy products, and it is with the money that they have received in the second market from their products that the entrepreneurs go to the first to buy productive services" (p. 193). The second relationship between resource and product markets is summarized in the now celebrated words, "*les entrepreneurs ne font ni bénéfice ni perte*" (p. 195). The absence of profit or loss, the equality of price and cost, is admittedly "an ideal, not a real, state" (p. 194). But it is the condition which competition tends to bring about, for profits lead to expansion of output and lowering of prices, and vice versa in the case of losses.

From this general sketch of production, Walras proceeds to the mathematical theory of the relations involved. The following section is devoted to Walras' first explicit theory, which was based on the assumption that the technological coefficients of production are fixed. The theory of production based on variable production coefficients, which was first developed explicitly in the famous appendix to the third edition of the *Eléments* (1896), will be treated in Chapter XII.

The Theory of Production

The following set of symbols is employed by Walras in his general equations of production (pp. 208 ff.):

1. The finished products, m in number:

   $A, B, C, \cdots$—goods consumed within a given period of time.

2. The productive services, n in number:

   $T, T', T'', \cdots$—services of land per unit of time;
   $P, P', P'', \cdots$—services of labor per unit of time;
   $K, K', K'', \cdots$—services of capital per unit of time.

3. The utility functions:

   $r = \phi(q)$—the marginal utility function of the individual for any good.

Here we may pause to note that the individual has a utility function for productive services as well as for consumption goods. This doctrine, frequently ascribed to Wicksteed, is clearly stated in the *Eléments*.[1]

4. The prices (given to the individual):

   $p_t, p_{t'}, \cdots$
   $p_p, p_{p'}, \cdots$ } prices of productive services;
   $p_k, p_{k'}, \cdots$
   $p_b, p_c, \cdots$ prices of consumption goods.[2]

5. The individual possesses given initial quantities:

   $q_t, q_k, q_p, \cdots$ of the productive services.

6. The quantities demanded and supplied:

   $o_t, o_p, o_k, \cdots$ of the services offered (if positive) or demanded (if negative);
   $d_a, d_b, d_c, \cdots$ of the finished goods demanded at equilibrium prices.

[1] "The services themselves have a direct utility for each person. And not only may one wish either to hire or to keep for himself all or part of the services of land, of his personal faculties, and of his capital, but in addition one may acquire, if so wishing, the services of land, labor, or capital, not in the role of entrepreneur to transform them into products but in the role of consumer to use them directly, that is to say, not as productive services but as consumable services" (p. 209).

[2] All prices are defined in terms of the *numéraire*, commodity A, so $p_a = 1$. Cf. pp. 48 *et seq.*, 150 *et seq.*

7. The technical coefficients of production:

$$\left.\begin{matrix} a_t, a_k, a_p, \cdots \\ \\ b_t, b_k, b_p, \cdots \end{matrix}\right\}$$

—the technical "*coefficients de fabrication*," *i.e.*, the quantities of the various factors (T, P, K, $\cdots$) which enter into the production of one unit of each of the products A, B, C, $\cdots$

In the first three editions of the *Eléments* these coefficients are assumed to be determined by technical facts, although it is admitted that they are in fact variable. In the third edition,[1] for instance, Walras says:

> It would be easy to express this condition [*i.e.*, the selection of coefficients in order to minimize the cost of production] by a system of as many equations as there are coefficients of production to determine. We will make abstraction, for the sake of simplicity, in supposing that the above coefficients figure among the givens and not among the unknowns of the problem [p. 232].

Only in the fourth (1900) edition, and in the revised (1926) edition, is the promise made to determine subsequently these production coefficients.[2]

The general equilibrium conditions for the individual are now easily established (pp. 210–11). At this point the problems of amortization and maintenance of capital goods and of new savings are abstracted (p. 209); they are treated subsequently in the theory of capital. The individual is, first of all, subject to the budget equation:

$$o_t p_t + o_p p_p + o_k p_k + \cdots = d_a + d_b p_b + \cdots, \quad (1)$$

which is to say, his expenditures must equal his receipts. The general condition of "*satisfaction maxima*" requires, moreover, that the marginal utilities of the various goods

[1] The identical passage occurs on page 249 of the first edition.

[2] Cf., *infra*, Chap. XII.

and services be proportional to their prices.[1] This leads to $n + m - 1$ equations of the type:[2]

$$\begin{aligned} \phi_t(q_t - o_t) &= p_t\phi_a(d_a) \\ \phi_p(q_p - o_p) &= p_p\phi_a(d_a) \\ &\cdots\cdots \\ \phi_b(d_b) &= p_b\phi_a(d_a) \\ \phi_c(d_c) &= p_c\phi_a(d_a) \\ &\cdots\cdots \end{aligned} \qquad (2)$$

There are thus a total of $m + n$ equations to solve for the $m + n$ unknowns $o_t,\ o_p,\ o_k, \cdots d_a,\ d_b,\ d_c, \cdots$. These unknowns may be expressed in terms of the prices, which are fixed and known to the individual. The individual's supply or demand functions for the productive services are then secured:

$$\begin{aligned} o_t &= f_t(p_t, p_p, p_k, \cdots, p_b, p_c, p_d, \cdots) \\ o_p &= f_p(p_t, p_p, p_k, \cdots, p_b, p_c, p_d, \cdots) \\ &\cdots\cdots \end{aligned}$$

and the demand functions for the various commodities follow:

$$\begin{aligned} d_b &= f_b(p_t, p_p, p_k, \cdots, p_b, p_c, p_d, \cdots) \\ d_c &= f_c(p_t, p_p, p_k, \cdots, p_b, p_c, p_d, \cdots) \\ &\cdots\cdots \end{aligned}$$

The demand for A is readily secured from equation (1).

In the case of the general equilibrium of the market, three additional sets of symbols are employed:

$$O_t = \Sigma o_t;\ D_a = \Sigma d_a;\ F_t = \Sigma f_t,$$

where O_t, for instance, is the total market supply of T.

[1] Cf. pp. 81 ff., or Jevons, *Theory of Political Economy* (4th ed., London, 1911), pp. 95 ff.

[2] There is no equation for commodity A, the *numéraire*.

The general market equilibrium is then defined by four sets of equations (pp. 211–12):

i. The quantities of the productive services supplied are functions of the prices:

$$
\begin{aligned}
O_t &= F_t(p_t, p_p, p_k, \cdots, p_b, p_c, p_d, \cdots) \\
O_p &= F_p(p_t, p_p, p_k, \cdots, p_b, p_c, p_d, \cdots) \qquad (3) \\
&\cdots\cdots\cdots\cdots\cdots\cdots\cdots\cdots\cdots\cdots
\end{aligned}
$$

a total of n equations.

ii. The quantities of the finished goods demanded are functions of the prices:

$$
\begin{aligned}
D_b &= F_b(p_t, p_p, p_k, \cdots, p_b, p_c, p_d, \cdots) \\
D_c &= F_c(p_t, p_p, p_k, \cdots, p_b, p_c, p_d, \cdots) \qquad (4) \\
&\cdots\cdots\cdots\cdots\cdots\cdots\cdots\cdots\cdots\cdots
\end{aligned}
$$

and

$$D_a = O_t p_t + O_p p_p + \cdots - (D_b p_b + D_c p_c + \cdots)$$

a total of m equations.

iii. The quantity of services employed must equal the quantity offered:

$$
\begin{aligned}
a_t D_a + b_t D_b + c_t D_c + \cdots &= O_t \\
a_p D_a + b_p D_b + c_p D_c + \cdots &= O_p \qquad (5) \\
\cdots\cdots\cdots\cdots\cdots\cdots\cdots\cdots\cdots\cdots&
\end{aligned}
$$

a total of n equations.

iv. Costs of production must equal prices:

$$
\begin{aligned}
a_t p_t + a_p p_p + a_k p_k + \cdots &= 1 \\
b_t p_t + b_p p_p + b_k p_k + \cdots &= p_b \qquad (6) \\
\cdots\cdots\cdots\cdots\cdots\cdots\cdots\cdots\cdots\cdots&
\end{aligned}
$$

a total of m equations.

No discussion is offered regarding the cost conditions of the individual entrepreneur.[1]

[1] The following confused and superficial comment dismisses the subject: "Since we assume the entrepreneurs make neither profit or loss, we may

There are a total of $2m + 2n$ equations in this system. One of these equations, however, is not independent, and may readily be eliminated. If the equations in system (5) are multiplied respectively by $p_t, p_p, p_k, \cdots$, and the equations in system (6) are multiplied respectively by $D_a, D_b, D_c, \cdots$, and each set is added separately, the left members of the two equations will be identical, and they lead to the last equation in system (4).[1] Only $2m + 2n - 1$ independent equations remain.

They are, however, exactly equal in number to the unknowns:

Unknowns	*Number*
i. Quantities of productive services offered $(O_t, O_p, \cdots)$.	n
ii. Quantities of finished goods demanded $(D_a, D_b, \cdots)$.	m
iii. Prices of the productive services $(p_t, p_p, p_k, \cdots)$.	n
iv. Prices of the finished goods $(p_b, p_c, p_d, \cdots)$.	$m - 1$
	$2m + 2n - 1$

This is the theory of general equilibrium.

The general equilibrium theory is an impressive achievement. Walras was the first economist to show that under perfect competition, full employment of re-

well assume that they produce equal quantities of goods, in which case all expenses of every kind may be considered as proportional" (p. 213). Walras does not tell us to what they are proportional.

[1] This may be illustrated for the case of two commodities and two productive services. System (5), multiplied respectively by p_t and p_p, becomes

$$a_t p_t D_a + b_t p_t D_b = O_t p_t$$
$$a_p p_p D_a + b_p p_p D_b = O_p p_p.$$

System (6) similarly becomes

$$a_t p_t D_a + a_p p_p D_a = D_a$$
$$b_t p_t D_b + b_p p_p D_b = D_b p_b.$$

The two left members are obviously identical, so

$$O_t p_t + O_p p_p = D_a + D_b p_b,$$

which is the last equation in system (4).

sources is compatible with the desire of each individual to maximize the return from his resources. The demonstration is scarcely rigorous, but that fundamental concept of economic analysis, the universal interdependence of economic quantities, is propounded with a lucidity impossible without the use of algebraic notation. The writer has no sympathy with those modern economists who spend their time establishing and counting systems of equations, always discovering with elation that their systems may be determinate. Indeed the general equilibrium theory has contributed little to economic analysis beyond an emphasis on mutual dependence of economic phenomena; the problems are far too complicated to be grasped *in toto*. Yet this particular theory describing the nature of general equilibrium was essential; such an idea had to appear before rigorous study could proceed. It was Walras' greatest contribution—one of the few times in the history of post-Smithian economics that a fundamentally new idea has emerged.

The actual demonstration is of course defective in several respects. The fundamental weakness lies in the inadequate conception and treatment of production. The assumption of fixed technological coefficients of production eliminates most of the interesting and important questions in this field. The no-profit entrepreneur is an hypothesis rather than an analytical theorem. The subtle and complicated relations between costs and prices are ruled out: the two are equal by definition.

In addition the system is open to certain objections more significant to a mathematician than to an economist. Free goods are not considered in the system of equations; yet only relative to demand can it be discovered whether a given productive service is free or not. A simple modification of the Walrasian system has been suggested by Schlesinger, to allow for this oversight.[1] In system (5) the first equation should be written

$$a_t D_a + b_t D_b + c_t D_c + \cdots + U_t = O_t,$$

and similarly for the other equations in this set. U_t, the unused portion of T, will be zero if the resource is not free. There are then n additional unknowns. The system retains determinacy, however, since there are n additional equations of the type,

$$\text{when } U_t > O, \qquad \text{then } p_t = O.$$

This minor omission is therefore easily remedied.

The second and more impressive criticism is that the equality of the number of equations and unknowns is no assurance that there is a unique, positive solution—which is the sensible economic solution.[2] Wald, a Viennese mathematician, has demonstrated that such a solution to the Walrasian system does exist, using the following assumptions, which are certainly implicit in Walras' theory:[3]

i. The supplies of the productive resources are positive.
ii. All technological coefficients of production are zero or positive.
iii. At least one productive service enters into the production of each commodity.
iv. The demand function, $f_i\ (d_i)$, is defined for every positive quantity of commodity I, and is always positive, continuous, and monotonically decreasing.[4]

[1] K. Schlesinger, "Über die Produktionsgleichungen der ökonomischen Wertlehre," *Ergebnisse eines Mathematischen Kolloquiums* (Karl Menger, Vienna), VI (1933–34), 10–11.

[2] As a matter of fact, there may be an acceptable solution with fewer or more equations than unknowns.

[3] A. Wald, "Über die eindeutige positive Losbarkeit der neuen Produktionsgleichungen," *Ergebnisse eines Mathematischen Kolloquiums*, VI (1933–34), 12–18.

[4] Cf. also A. Wald, "Über einige Gleichungssysteme der mathematischen Ökonomie," *Zeitschrift für Nationalökonomie*, VII (1936), 637–70, and the references there cited.

The powerful analysis necessary to prove a unique and positive solution was of course well beyond Walras' limited mathematical equipment. It is an interesting commentary on the general equilibrium "school" that such a solution was not questioned or proved until sixty years after the theory was first enunciated. The uncritical acceptance was not undesirable, however, since the central idea of general equilibrium is correct and important. But the experience suggests that in the future it might be desirable to leave equation-counting to professional mathematicians.

Walras is not content to formulate merely the general theory of production. "There still remains to be shown . . . that this problem of which we have given the theoretical solution is also that which is in practice solved in the market by the mechanism of free competition" (p. 214). In the theory of production, as in the theory of exchange,[1] the celebrated notion of *tâtonnements* (approximations) is employed. The theory of approximations purports to describe in general fashion how the economic system moves from any position of disequilibrium to the position of final equilibrium. This is a problem in economic dynamics proper, as the term dynamics is used in mechanics; *i.e.*, the path of movement to equilibrium within a fixed system of data. Walras is the only economist in the history of economics to propose a general solution for it. Despite the fact that he presents an elaborate discussion of the method, only its central notion need be presented here.

The theory of *tâtonnements*, stripped of its rather "luxurious algebraic foilage," may be stated very simply. Two conditions must be fulfilled at equilibrium: the quantity of the productive services demanded must

[1] As also in the case of capital theory (*Elêments*, Lecture 25).

equal their supplies; and the cost of production of a good must equal its selling price. If the first condition is not fulfilled, there will be an increase in the prices of those services whose demands exceed their supplies, and a decrease of price in the opposite case. Changes in quantities produced (increases if prices exceed costs, and decreases if costs exceed prices) will similarly lead to the equality of price and cost of production.

The fundamental objection to the theory of approximations has been stated well by Edgeworth:

> He [Walras] diffuses over some thirty-five pages an idea which might have been adequately presented in a few paragraphs. For it is, after all, not a very good idea. What the author professes to demonstrate is the course which the higgling of the market takes—the path, as it were, by which the economic system works down to equilibrium. Now, as Jevons points out, the equations of exchange are of a statical, not a dynamical, character. They define a position of equilibrium, but they afford no information as to the path by which that point is reached. Prof. Walras's laboured lessons indicate *a* way, not *the* way, of descent to equilibrium.[1]

Walras' demonstration indicates the possibility of returning to equilibrium from a position of disequilibrium. It fails to prove that equilibrium will ever be reached or that the movement toward equilibrium does not affect the final position. These crucial matters, indeed, are taken for granted. The difficulties are perhaps insoluble; certainly the only satisfactory analytic method of reaching general equilibrium so far evolved is Edgeworth's process of "recontracting." [2]

[1] "Mathematical Theory of Political Economy," *op. cit.*, p. 435. Consult also the other references in note 1, p. 231. Walras makes a very ineffectual reply (pp. 472–73).

[2] On this problem consult the interesting essay by N. Kaldor, "A Classificatory Note on the Determinateness of Equilibrium," *Review of Economic Studies*, I (1934), 122–36.

A second aberration in Walras' theory of general equilibrium is the tedious and erroneous proof that free competition leads to maximum satisfaction (Lectures 8, 22, 26, 27). This ethical conclusion requires, as Wicksell has shown,[1] the further assumption that all persons have identical utility functions and equal incomes. The detailed nature of Walras' demonstration of the doctrine of maximum satisfaction had best be ignored—a happy practice which most subsequent economists have followed.

The Theory of Capital

Walras' theory of capital is another significant contribution to economics. He possesses one great advantage over almost all other economists, at the outset: a clear and consistently-held distinction between capital goods and their services (*capitaux* and *revenus*). This correct analytic approach eliminates most of the problems in a correct definition of capital, and it places proper emphasis on the central element of the interest problem, *i.e.*, perpetual net income.

Capital goods are desired for the (consumption) income they yield (p. 242). This is true even of durable consumption goods (*e.g.*, houses), and Walras suggests that "a man who buys a home to live in may be disassociated into two individuals, one of whom makes an investment and the other consumes directly the service of his capital" (p. 242).

Two deductions from gross revenue are necessary before the net revenue of a capital good can be determined.[2] The first deduction is for depreciation, the sec-

[1] *Lectures on Political Economy* (New York, 1934), I, 79 ff.

[2] Revenue is henceforth used in the sense of annual service consumed (in physical units) times price, where previously it has referred only to the service (p. 242).

ond for insurance against the chance of loss (*e.g.*, fire). The deduction for depreciation is easily made: one need merely deduct from the annual gross revenue an amortization premium (*prime d'amortissement*), which is "proportional to the price of the capital good" (p. 243).[1] For risks of loss a similar deduction (*prime d'assurance*) must be made, and it is also proportional to the price of the capital good (p. 243).[2]

The argument so far may be stated in simple algebra. Let P be the price of a capital good and p the gross value of its annual services. Then some fraction, μP, must be deducted for amortization, and a further fraction, νP, must be deducted for insurance. The net revenue, π, is then defined (p. 243):

$$\pi = p - (\mu + \nu) \cdot P.$$

All capital values are "rigorously proportional" to net revenues, at a given interest rate. The interest rate, indeed, is defined as the ratio of the perpetual net income to the capital value (which is still undetermined), *i.e.*,

$$i = \frac{p - (\mu + \nu)P}{P}$$

or

$$P = \frac{p}{i + \mu + \nu}.$$

The foregoing equation is insufficient to determine the two unknowns, capital values (P) and the interest rate (i). In a stationary economy, where there is no net saving or dissaving, however, the problem of determinacy does not arise because there are no capital values. "Under such circumstances, there could be no purchase or sale of capital goods, for these goods could only be

[1] Presumably this premium also varies inversely with the life of the capital.

[2] Neither deduction is necessary in the case of land, which, as has already been noted, Walras believes to be perpetual (p. 246).

exchanged for each other in the proportion that their net revenues bore to each other, and this operation, which theoretically would have no reason for existence, would not furnish any price in *numéraire*" (p. 244). This is uneven analysis: it is excellent in emphasizing the important feature of the capital market that the central exchange is between perpetual net incomes; it is erroneous in implying that it is possible intelligently to provide for maintenance and replacement without knowing the interest rate.

The subsequent analysis is restricted to the case of a progressive economy—one in which there is net saving (pp. 249, 252). In such an economy, new capital goods will be constructed with the net savings, and it is possible to secure the net rate of interest on such investments. Old capital goods can be valued by capitalizing their net revenues at the rate of interest established in the new capital goods market.[1]

The fundamental condition placed on new capital goods is that their costs of production equal their prices. Again assuming the coefficients of production for new capital goods to be known and fixed (pp. 247, 256–57),[2] this condition may be written:

$$
\begin{aligned}
k_t p_t + \cdots + k_p p_p + \cdots + k_k p_k + \cdots &= P_k \\
k_t' p_t + \cdots + k_p' p_t + \cdots + k_k' p_k + \cdots &= P_{k'} \qquad (7) \\
\cdots\cdots\cdots\cdots\cdots\cdots\cdots\cdots\cdots\cdots
\end{aligned}
$$

If there are h types of new capital goods, there will be h such equations. There will be h further equations (for each individual) defining capital values as capitalized net incomes.

[1] This is expressly stated for land and labor (p. 246) and for existing capital goods (pp. xiv, 290–93). Cf. also *Etudes d'économie sociale* (Paris, 1936), pp. 278 ff.

[2] For interest during construction, see *infra*, note 2, p. 251.

$$P_k = \frac{\pi_k}{i} = \frac{p_k}{i + \mu_k + \nu_k},$$

$$P_{k'} = \frac{\pi_{k'}}{i} = \frac{p_{k'}}{i + \mu_{k'} + \nu_{k'}}, \qquad (8)$$

. . . .

Walras distinguishes between the excess of an individual's income over his total expenditure on consumption goods (*i.e.*, gross savings) [1] and the individual's net savings (pp. 248–50). Net savings are ascertained only after full allowance has been made for depreciation and insurance on existing capital goods. A detailed argument is given for using gross rather than net savings in the subsequent equations, but the practice amounts only to adding replacement demand to the net demand for new capital goods.

Walras introduces at this point the useful concept of a good called perpetual net revenue (E), whose price is the reciprocal of the interest rate. The demand for perpetual net income is merely another way of looking at the demand for new investment goods. It follows that d_e, the quantity of E demanded, times its price (p_e), will equal gross savings at equilibrium.[2] The utility of E is assumed to be a function of its quantity, so the condition of maximum satisfaction requires that the weighted marginal utility of E be equal to those of other commodities.[3] In symbols,

$$\phi_e(q_e + d_e) = p_e\phi_a(d_a).$$

[1] If e is the excess of income over consumption expenditures, and r is income, then

$$e = r - [(q_t - o_t)p_t + \ldots + (q_k - o_k)p_k + \ldots d_a + d_bp_b + \ldots]$$

[2] *I.e.*, $e = d_ep_e$, or $i \cdot e = d_e$.

[3] It is worth noting that perpetual net income was not introduced as a commodity in the first edition of the *Eléments*. In that edition, moreover, the supply of savings is treated as an empirical function of prices (pp. 283–84), and not based on utility analysis.

By use of this equation and system (2) above, it is possible to express d_e as a function of all the prices, *i.e.*,[1]

$$d_e = f_e(p_t \cdots p_p \cdots p_k, p_{k'} \cdots p_b, p_c, \cdots p_e), \qquad (9)$$

and for the economy as a whole, $D_e = F_e = \Sigma f_e$.

The formulation of general market equilibrium is easily extended to include new capital goods (pp. 254 ff.). To system (6), which asserts the equality of selling prices and costs of production, the h equations of system (7) are added. System (8), "expressing the equality of the net rate of interest on all capital goods" (p. 258), with h additional equations, is now another part of the general system. The equality at equilibrium of the quantity supplied and demanded of new capital goods is expressed by equation (10):[2]

$$D_k P_k + D_{k'} P_{k'} + \cdots = E, \qquad (10)$$

where D_k, $D_{k'}$, $\cdots$ are the respective quantities of K, K', $\cdots$ manufactured. Finally, the total supply of gross savings is a function of all the prices:

$$E = D_e p_e = F_e(p_t \cdots p_p \cdots p_k, p_{k'}, \cdots p_b, p_c, \cdots p_e)p_e. \qquad (9.1)$$

These $2h + 2$ new equations equal in number the $2h + 2$ new unknowns: h prices of new capital goods; h quantities of new capital goods; the interest rate $\left(i = \frac{1}{p_e}\right)$; and supply of gross savings (E).

The foregoing theory of capital treats only of durable capital goods. Walras extends his analysis to circulating capital, which is introduced along with the theory of money—in contrast with *numéraire* (Lecture 29, pp.

[1] Cf., *supra*, p. 239.

[2] Where E is $F_e p_e = D_e p_e$, or the total excess of incomes over expenditures on consumption.

297 ff). Since these two elements are inseparably interwoven in his theory,[1] the formal algebraic statement will be omitted but the theory of circulating capital will be presented in summary form.

Four types of circulating capital are recognized (cf. esp. p. 299; also p. xiv). There are two classes of circulating capital held by consumers: stocks of consumers' goods; and a cash balance ("*monnaie de circulation et d'épargne*"). The entrepreneur holds two similar types of circulating capital: stocks of raw materials and of finished goods; and cash balances, which "he must have in order to restore these stocks and to buy productive services while waiting for (*en attendant*) collection on the products he has sold" (pp. 300–1; also p. 304).[2]

Stocks of various goods and cash balances are accordingly introduced into the general equilibrium equations. The quantities of inventories demanded and supplied are derived as functions of all prices,[3] where the price of holding the product A', for instance, is $p_{a'} = ip_a$. Interest on inventories, in other words, is introduced as a cost of production. Cash-balance equations are similarly derived for money.[4] The usual conditions of equality of quantities supplied and demanded and equality of cost of production and selling price are developed, and a more general equilibrium is established.

[1] They are interwoven, not out of necessity, but because Walras chooses to introduce both elements into his system simultaneously.

[2] This is as close as Walras comes to considering working capital as an advance to resource owners. He does not explicitly consider interest on construction outlays, but it seems more or less implicit in this quotation.

[3] Raw materials are held to be fixed in supply, since they have no direct utility (p. 304).

[4] On the monetary aspects cf. A. W. Marget, "Leon Walras and the 'Cash-Balance Approach' to the Problem of the Value of Money," *Journal of Political Economy*, XXXIX (1931), 569–600; and Oskar Lange, "The Rate of Interest and the Optimum Propensity to Consume," *Economica*, N.S. V (1938), 12–32.

Before appraising Walras' theory of capital, Wicksell's criticisms may be considered. He is the only economist to devote much attention to Walras' theory. In his earliest work, Wicksell is very critical: "I have been able to convince myself that his theory of production suffers from a fundamental error, which is related to his obsolete and one-sided view of the capital concept, and which could be removed only through a fundamental recasting of his presentation." [1] The essential reason why Wicksell rejects Walras' theory is that it disregards the period of production, but the entire criticism is worth quoting:

> Walras characterizes and treats as capital only the durable goods, not, however, the raw materials and unfinished products, not the means of subsistence of the laborer, thus in general *not those* advances which the possessor of circulating capital makes to the laborers, the landlords, etc. Consequently, it is implicitly assumed by Walras that the laborer and other producers maintain *themselves* during production, and only after the end of the production do they draw the compensation for their productive services out of the proceeds of the product in question. This is obviously wrong; this approach completely overlooks the true role of capital. As a necessary result there appears here the peculiarity, that his equations of production and exchange *cannot give any information on the rate of interest.* If one views only durable goods as capital, then indeed a definite rent is determined by the above-mentioned equations for each of these goods, but the *capital value* of these goods is not determined, and as a result, neither is the rate of interest, "*le taux du revenu net.*" Walras explicitly admits this; he asserts, however, that to be able to determine the interest rate one must pass from the consideration of a stationary economy to a progressive economy, one where *new* interest-bearing capital goods are produced, whose values can be determined by the costs of production. That is certainly

[1] *Über Wert, Kapital und Rente* (London School Reprint [London, 1933]), p. viii.

> wrong. Also in the stationary economy, and even if the total productive resources are taken as fixed, an interest rate on circulating capital would undoubtedly be established just on the ground, that longer production methods prove to be more productive (pp. 142–43).

The substance of this argument is repeated in the *Lectures*,[1] and in the review of Pareto's *Manuel*. The last criticism, that Walras' theory presupposes a progressive economy, is withdrawn in a later essay.[2]

Barone, in his review of *Über Wert*, defends Walras' theory against these charges.[3] With regard to the alleged omission of circulating capital from Walras' production equations, this charge is held to be due to a misunderstanding on Wicksell's part:

> In Walras' equations of production, account is taken of this, since Walras clearly says that the entrepreneur requires not only services of land, or labor, of capital (meaning goods of durable productivity) but also the *use of a certain quantity of numéraire*. And it is precisely the price of the use of the quantity of *numéraire* required by the entrepreneur, that constitutes that interest of which Wicksell has believed that abstraction is made in Walras' theory (pp. 136–37).

Barone illustrates the argument by developing somewhat more explicitly than Walras the equation for working capital (pp. 137–38).

Wicksell's second argument, that in Walras' theory the interest rate is not determinable if there is no new saving, is also opposed by Barone. He emphasizes the necessity for replacing even durable goods, so the interest rate is determined in the market for reinvestment of deprecia-

[1] *Lectures on Political Economy*, *op. cit.*, I, 171.

[2] "Professor Cassel's System of Economics," reprinted in the *Lectures*, *op. cit.*, I, 226 n.

[3] "Sopra un Libro del Wicksell," *Giornale degli Economisti*, XI (1895), 524–39, reprinted in *Le Opere economiche* (Bologna, 1936), I, 117–43, to which reference is here made.

tion funds (pp. 141–42).[1] This additional element is not very clear in Walras' exposition.[2]

If we extend the concept of a stationary economy to mean that all capital goods have perpetual existence, then, as Walras rightly says, all, if any, dealings would be in perpetual net income. In the stationary economy where capital goods wear out, the reinvestment of depreciation funds would serve to determine the interest rate and therefore capital values (as is indeed explicit in Walras' exposition, since he uses gross savings in his system). But perpetual net income would still be the fundamental concept, and to discern and emphasize this concept is an important merit of Walras' exposition.

So far as it goes, in fact, Walras' capital theory is superior to that of any of his contemporaries. Real criticism can center on only two points. The nature of supply of and demand for capital is not analyzed in sufficient detail. With respect to supply, the hypothesis that capital goods are instantaneously constructed (for that is what his explicit treatment amounts to) should be replaced by the view that during a construction period a net income stream is invested. The demand for capital, on the other hand, should be brought under the marginal productivity theory. The second point is that a progressive economy (*i.e.*, one with net savings) should not have been introduced, at least not so superficially. Walras attempts a theoretical analysis of an historical development without that indispensable prerequisite, a theory of economic growth. The effects of capital accu-

[1] The same suggestion is made by Hicks, *op. cit.*, p. 346.

[2] As indeed Barone implies: "Certainly we should not dare assert that in Walras' book that distinction is always clearly made between capital and savings and between *free savings* and *invested savings*, which to us appears necessary to the clear exposition of the phenomenon of interest, nor should we be able to affirm that Walras' treatment could not give rise to some equivocation . . ." (*op. cit.*, p. 142).

mulation on other resources and on technology, the economic role of uncertainty arising out of historical change, and a multitude of such problems are ignored. The very determination in his theory of the amount of new savings is objectionable; savings are doubtless functionally related to prices, but there are so many more important variables that his assumption is not even a good first approximation. Such problems must be solved before any satisfactory theory of capital accumulation can be evolved.

The Theory of Rent

There is some value in analyzing in detail Walras' restatement of the classical rent theory. He accused Wicksteed of plagiarism of the marginal productivity theory, on the basis of certain alleged identities between Walras' equations on rent and Wicksteed's equations in his *Co-ordination.*[1] Wicksell seems to have accepted Walras' claim to priority,[2] and the writer has not discovered anyone who denied it. Since Wicksteed had read the *Eléments* as early as 1882,[3] it is important to discover when Walras first advanced the marginal productivity theory.[4]

Walras first restates the Ricardian theory in mathematical form.[5] The following notation is employed:

[1] The details of the charge are considered in Chap. XII, *infra.*

[2] *Infra,* Chap. XII.

[3] Robbins remarks that a much-marked copy of the second (first?) edition of the *Eléments,* purchased in 1882, was in Wicksteed's library. Cf. Introduction to *Commonsense* (London, 1933), p. vii.

[4] In this section the third edition (1896) of the *Eléments* will be used. The discussion is presumably the same as that in the second (1889) edition, since the third edition is virtually a reprint (except for the appendix on Wicksteed's *Co-ordination*). Cf. 3d ed., p. v note. The first edition is also virtually the same as the third on this point.

[5] The relevant passages are all in Lecture 31, "Exposition and Refutation of the English Theory of Rent" (pp. 344–58).

$h_1, h_2, h_3 \cdots$ = net products (in physical units) after payment of wages, on lands 1, 2, 3 $\cdots$;

$x_1, x_2, x_3 \cdots$ = capital (in *numéraire*) employed on lands 1, 2, 3, $\cdots$;

t = the rate of interest (in physical units);

$r_1, r_2, r_3 \cdots$ = rents (in physical units) of lands 1, 2, 3, $\cdots$.

We may note that Walras does not understand the true nature of the English dose of capital-and-labor. He subtracts labor costs from the product, whereas in the classical theory the composite dose of capital-and-labor was treated as a unit (and fundamentally, as a dose of *capital*).

The first set of equations defines rent:

$$\begin{aligned} r_1 &= h_1 - x_1 t, \\ r_2 &= h_2 - x_2 t, \\ &\cdots\cdots\cdots\cdots \end{aligned} \tag{1}$$

System (1) merely restates the fact that rent is a residual after deducting the return to capital from the product (from which wages have already been deducted). The product, h, is a function of the amount of capital applied to a given piece of land, so we secure the second set of equations:

$$\begin{aligned} h_1 &= F_1(x_1), \\ h_2 &= F_2(x_2), \\ &\cdots\cdots\cdots \end{aligned} \tag{2}$$

Since capital is rewarded according to its marginal productivity,

$$t = F_1'(x_1) = F_2'(x_2) = \cdots \tag{3}$$

One final equation is yet to be introduced—the employment of all available capital:

$$x_1 + x_2 + x_3 + x_4 + \cdots = X. \tag{4}$$

This is Walras' restatement of the Ricardian theory; we turn now to his reformulation of the theory.

In order to find the relationship between his general equilibrium theory and the Ricardian theory, Walras modifies the notation slightly. The product of a given piece of land (T) is B, with price p_b. Further,

H = total product (in physical units) per hectare of land;

$b_t = \frac{1}{H}$ = technical coefficient of production for land;

p_t = rent per hectare (in *numéraire*);

i = interest rate (in *numéraire*).

Hence,

$$\frac{p_t}{p_b} = r; \qquad \frac{i}{p_b} = t.$$

Equation (1) may be rewritten, therefore, as

$$\frac{p_t}{p_b} = h - x\frac{i}{p_b}.$$[1]

The total produce less wages (h) may also be rewritten:[2]

$$h = H - \frac{H}{p_b}(b_p p_p + b_{p'} p_{p'} + \cdots),$$

or, if amortization and insurance are ignored for the sake of simplicity,

$$h = H - \frac{Hi}{p_b}(b_p P_p + b_{p'} P_{p'} + \cdots).$$

[1] This is not a marginal productivity theory of interest, since wages are also a residual. In order to relate this to Ricardo's theory one must understand x to be capital-and-labor.

[2] Cf., *supra*, p. 237, for symbols previously defined.

The capital (x) per unit of land is readily defined:

$$x = H(b_k P_k + b_{k'} P_{k'} + \cdots),$$
$$= \frac{H}{i}(b_k p_k + b_{k'} p_{k'} + \cdots).$$

Since the ratio of wages to the capital value of a laborer is in Walras' theory identical with the rate of interest (p. 383), he "departs" from Ricardo's theory by including capitalized labor with other capital in a new dose of capital-and-labor (x'):[1]

$$x' = H(b_p P_p + b_{p'} P_{p'} + \cdots + b_k P_k + \cdots)$$
$$= \frac{H}{i}(b_p p_p + b_{p'} p_{p'} + \cdots + b_k p_k + \cdots).$$

One question remains: Is H a function which "does not increase proportionally" with x'? Walras answers in the affirmative:

> It is certainly a fact of experience that in applying increasing quantities of personal and capital services to land, one does not obtain proportionally increasing quantities of product; otherwise one could obtain an unlimited quantity of product by applying an unlimited quantity of personal and capital services on a single hectare of land, or on an even smaller space. Thus, in precise terms, one may say, as we have done (§ 274) that b_p, $b_{p'}$, $b_{p''}$, $\cdots$ b_k, $b_{k'}$, $b_{k''}$, $\cdots$ are not constants, but decreasing functions of b_t,—that is to say, increasing functions of H.[2]

Variable production coefficients.—Walras considers variable production coefficients in the third edition (and also in the earlier editions) of the *Eléments* only in paragraph 274.[3] Its importance for the problem at hand justifies rather full quotation:

[1] He is, of course, really returning to the Ricardian theory.

[2] He censures the classical economists for stating the law in money rather than physical terms (pp. 354–55). This is both erroneous and irrelevant.

[3] This is paragraph 325 in the 1926 edition; paragraph 307 in the first edition.

. . . in the production of a commodity one may employ more or less of certain productive services, for example, more or less land services, on the condition of employing less or more of other productive services. That is to say, the coefficients b_t, b_p, b_k, $\cdots$ are variable and are related by an equation

$$\phi(b_t, b_p, b_k, \cdots) = 0,$$

such that, if the coefficient b_t decreases, the other coefficients b_p and b_k increase. Thus the respective quantities of each of the productive services which enter into a unit of each of the products are determined only after the prices of the productive services have been determined, by the condition that the cost of production be a minimum. In other words, the above implicit equation is solved for each of its variables, or placed successively in each of the explicit forms

$$b_t = \theta(b_p, b_k, \cdots),$$
$$b_p = \psi(b_t, b_k, \cdots).$$

The unknowns, b_t, b_p, b_k, $\cdots$ are determined by the condition that

$$p_b = \theta(b_p, b_k, \cdots)p_t + \psi(b_t, b_k, \cdots)p_p + \cdots$$

be a minimum (3d ed., pp. 320–21).[1]

So far so well—but here the analysis stops. The remainder of the paragraph is devoted to the thesis that variable production coefficients are usefully applied in the study of a progressive economy![2] There is not the remotest suggestion of an explicit marginal productivity theory.

[1] The sentence stating the erroneous doctrine that the production coefficients are determined *after* the prices of the services have been determined is changed in the 1926 edition to simultaneous determination of prices and coefficients.

[2] " . . . we state only that in fact every time the production function has changed, it is due to technical progress introduced by science . . ." (p. 321); and he permits changes in the production coefficients if the relative supplies of productive services change. The brief discussion of this last point is unfortunately restricted to the growth of capital relative to land (very much as in the Ricardian theory), so Walras is not led to the marginal productivity theory.

We may briefly summarize the remainder of Walras' discussion of rent. Rent may be represented in physical units:

$$\frac{p_t}{p_b} = H - \frac{H}{p_b}(b_p p_p + b_{p'} p_{p'} + \cdots + b_k p_k + \cdots),$$

or in *numéraire:*

$$p_t = H p_b - H(b_p p_p + b_{p'} p_{p'} + \cdots + b_k p_k + \cdots).$$

Finally, H may be replaced by $\frac{1}{b_t}$:

$$p_t b_t = p_b - (b_p p_p + b_k p_k + \cdots),$$

or

$$p_b = b_t p_t + \cdots + b_p p_p + \cdots.$$

The last equation is one identical with the second equation in system (6). Walras erroneously concludes that the Ricardian theory is a special case of his own general system; it is in fact a special case only when variable production coefficients are tacitly introduced.

Such is Walras' rent theory in 1896. In his celebrated appendix on Wicksteed, Walras identifies the above equations with Wicksteed's marginal productivity equations. The detailed claims will be considered in Chapter XII, but here it may be stated in conclusion that there is not even a pointed suggestion (to say nothing of a clearly formulated theory) of marginal productivity in the *Eléments* before 1896.

Chapter X

KNUT WICKSELL

FEW economists of our period are more difficult to appraise or to classify as to antecedents than Knut Wicksell.[1] In part this difficulty arises from his own catholicity. He read widely and with a singularly open mind the works of the English classical and neo-classical economists, and of the Austrian and Walrasian schools. He absorbed much of the best analyses produced by each of these three sources, and synthesized them into a brilliant theoretical whole. But it must be added immediately that Wicksell's work extends beyond synthesis. In certain fields (*e.g.*, the marginal productivity theory) he must be considered a true discoverer, and frequently his restatements of received doctrines are so refined as to be virtually independent analyses.

The closest antecedents of Wicksell's work seem to be Austrian, lying particularly in Böhm-Bawerk's theory of capital. In price theory, Walrasian analysis is generally followed, both in method and in content. In production and distribution theory, however, Austrian influence is dominant, although certain English economists, notably Wicksteed, are also influential.

A brief sketch of Wicksell's major writings on economics is essential, since certain parts of his theory

[1] For a general appraisal consult Emil Sommarin, "Das Lebenswerk von Knut Wicksell," *Zeitschrift für Nationalökonomie*, II (1930–31), 221–67; L. Robbins, Introduction to the English edition of the *Lectures on Political Economy* (London, 1934), I, vii–xxiii.

changed substantially in the thirty-seven years which elapsed between his entrance into and departure from the arena of economic discussion (1892 to 1928). His first major work, *Über Wert, Kapital und Rente* (Jena, 1893), is a genuinely brilliant exposition of price and capital theory. In it are to be found most of the doctrines presented in the later *Lectures.* The prominence of the use of mathematics in the *Über Wert*, and the antagonism it aroused among certain "schools" of economics, earned Wicksell a very cool reception—a gross injustice to the high caliber of the analysis the book contains.[1]

Wicksell's doctoral dissertation, *Finanztheorische Untersuchungen* (1896), contains minor changes in his capital theory. With the appearance in 1900 of his long article, "On Marginal Productivity as the Basis for Economic Distribution," [2] Wicksell's theoretical structure was substantially completed, although this is not to say that valuable bits of analysis did not come from his pen in the next quarter century. The *Lectures on Political Economy*, volume one of which concerns us, first appeared in Swedish in 1901. Here the first German edition (1913) and the English translation (1934) of the third Swedish edition will be used. The *Lectures* systematize his previous writings; they add little that is new.[3]

[1] Enrico Barone, "Sopra un Libro del Wicksell," *Giornale degli Economisti*, XI (1895), 524–39, gives an able review but denounces very harshly Wicksell's attitude toward Walras' theory of capital; A. W. Flux's review, *Economic Journal*, IV (1894), 305–8, is inaccurate and unduly critical; W. Lexis' review, *Schmoller's Jahrbuch für Gesetzgebung, Verwaltung und Volkwirtschaft*, XIX (1895), 332–37, is more an attack on Böhm-Bawerk than a review of Wicksell's book.

[2] *Ekonomisk Tidskrift*, II (1900), 305–37.

[3] The writer regrets that linguistic handicaps prevent him from taking full cognizance of Wicksell's numerous articles in the *Ekonomisk Tidskrift.* Several of the more important of these articles, especially those bearing on distribution theory, are considered, on the basis of translations made for the writer.

A final word may be added with regard to the arrangement to be followed in presenting Wicksell's theory. Production theory and capital and interest theory will be treated first, and his general theory of distribution will be taken up last, since it is built upon the Böhm-Bawerkian theory of capital.

The Quantity and Allocation of Resources

Wicksell's discussion of the quantity of resources existing in an economy is of very uneven quality. He emphasizes at many points the importance for his theory of the assumption of a stationary state,[1] and he is cautious in his use of this assumption (or, more properly, this set of assumptions). But he does not explicitly analyze the implications or detailed nature of a stationary economy. As an illustration of his cursory treatment, he asserts that in a static state there can be no net profits, since such profits would be increases in capital;[2] yet he offers no analysis of why this should be so.

Wicksell adopts the doctrine that leisure is an alternative which competes with productive employments for resources. At first he admits the leisure alternative only for labor,[3] but later non-economic alternatives are conceded for all productive resources.[4] Yet the non-economic alternatives are considered to be relatively unimportant in the case of many material resources, such as valuable urban land, technical capital, and the like.[5] This is a realistic conclusion, but this difference between labor

[1] Compare *Über Wert*, pp. 77, 87–88, 95–96, 101, 139 ff. At the last point he suggests the possibility of a theory of moving equilibrium, if the rates of increase of the various productive factors are known. Compare also the *Lectures*, Part II, *passim*. I am indebted to the London School of Economics for permission to quote from *Über Wert*, and to The Macmillan Company for permission to quote from the *Lectures*.

[2] *Über Wert*, pp. 95–96.

[3] *Ibid.*, p. 139.

[4] *Lectures*, pp. 98, 103.

[5] *Ibid.*, pp. 103–4.

and material resources does not affect Wicksell's development since he assumes all resources in productive use to be given in amount.[1]

The theory of the allocation of resources is brief but correct. The essential point is that the return from a given resource will be equalized in all its occupations (assuming perfect fluidity), which at the same time maximizes the total product:

> If an economy embraces the production, distribution and consumption of only two goods, the exchange ratio between them will be such that
>
> i. the wages, rent, and interest rate are the same in the production of each commodity,
>
> ii. at the position which the wages and rent have attained, interest (and in general at the given values of two of these three quantities, the third) is a maximum, . . .[2]

The share of the product which goes to each of the cooperating productive agents is regulated by the marginal productivity of that agent. Wicksell devotes little attention to the allocation of resources between industries because his analysis is almost always based upon the individual plant or, what is equivalent, the one-commodity economy (with identical plants).

Variability of Proportions, Diminishing Returns, and Costs

In the *Über Wert* Wicksell does not devote explicit attention to the problem of variability of the coefficients of production. An acceptance of complete variability is nevertheless deeply imbedded in his theory of distribution. Variations in the length of the production period, *i.e.*, in his theory, the amount of capital cooperating with given land and labor resources, are fundamental to his interest theory. Variability in the amount of labor

[1] *Ibid.*, p. 104.

[2] *Über Wert*, p. 135.

per unit of land, or, conversely, the amount of land per unit of labor, is also indispensable to his general theory of distribution.

In the course of his later writings the concept of variability of proportions becomes progressively clearer. Thus, in the *Finanztheorische Untersuchungen;*

> The relative increase of *one* of these quantities [wages and rent] will above all influence the *proportion* in which labor and land will be used in production, and in such a manner that if wages rise relative to rent, relatively more land and less labor (an extensive economy) . . . will be used. . . .
>
> Conversely, wages and rent are dependent on the proportion in which land and labor are used, as well as on the investment periods of the two parts of capital. . . .[1]

In the *Lectures*, the acceptance is complete: "one factor of production can always, to some extent, be substituted for another." [2]

In the presentation of Wicksell's theory of distribution it will be shown later that he has a clear and correct mathematical statement of the law of diminishing returns for all factors of production. In the discussion of diminishing returns, however, he is apparently unaware of the distinction between marginal and average returns, and, as a rule, improperly deals with the latter variety.[3] This confusion is revealed in his proof of the law of diminishing returns from productive services applied to land, presented in the course of a controversy with Waterstradt, who believed that by a statistical investigation he had upset this famous postulate of economic theory.[4]

[1] (Jena, 1896), pp. 46, 47.

[2] Page 99 (italicized by Wicksell); cf. also pp. 100, 113 ff., 124 ff., 284 ff.; also "Zur Verteidigung der Grenznutzenlehre," *Zeitschrift für die gesammte Staatswissenschaft,* LVI (1900), 590–91.

[3] Cf. *Lectures*, pp. 111, 122 ff.; *Finanztheorische Untersuchungen*, p. 53.

[4] "Über einige Fehlerquellen bei Verifikation des Bodengesetzes," "Noch einiges über die Verifikation des Bodengesetzes," *Thünen Archiv,* II (1909),

Wicksell's attack is directed at the validity of *constant* average returns, but it is even more effective when levied against *increasing* average returns. If one is discussing an economy in which all land is cultivated with equal intensiveness,

> . . . then the validity of the law of return from land [*Bodengesetz*] in general does not require any experimental proof, but rather appears more as a logical postulate or corollary. If it were shown that on a given piece of land twice as much labor and capital would also secure twice as much product, then an even more impressive result *per unit of labor and capital* could be secured, if one concentrated the already existing labor and capital forces on *half* of the previously used area. . . .[1]

The law of diminishing returns is therefore not an empirical rule, it is "a theorem of mathematical necessity."[2] The criticisms to be levied at this "proof" are that it is concerned with *average* returns, when in fact economic allocation of resources is guided by *marginal* returns, and that, of course, the proof is by no means conclusive—the

347–55, 568–77; in part repeated in the *Lectures*, pp. 122–24. The acute criticisms levied at Waterstradt's methodology are not considered here. Substantially the same reply was made to Rohtlieb, who repeated Waterstradt's error, in "Den 'kritiska punkten' i lagen för jordbrukets aftagande produktivetet," *Ekonomisk Tidskrift*, XVIII (1916), 285–92.

[1] *Thünen Archiv*, pp. 354–55. A similar proof is also given algebraically (*ibid.*, p. 569). Apply A labor to B land, securing P product. Then $\frac{A}{2}$ plus $\frac{B}{2}$ will yield $\frac{P}{2}+\frac{p}{2}$, where $\frac{p}{2}$ is the natural product of the now uncultivated half of the land. Then

$$\frac{P}{A}\bigg/\frac{\frac{P}{2}+\frac{p}{2}}{\frac{A}{2}} = \frac{P}{P+p} < 1.$$

If $p > 0$, then average productivity must be declining, *i.e.*, the ratio of the product other than natural products to the amount of labor must decrease as the amount of labor increases, since p is a constant.

[2] *Ibid.*, p. 569.

assumptions are not rigorous enough to insure diminishing returns.[1]

Certain general considerations on costs and returns will be taken up in connection with Wicksell's discussion of the Euler-Wicksteed problem in distribution theory. Wicksell's treatment of cost and supply is very fragmentary. In general he assumes that there is atomistic competition, free transferability of resources, and identical production functions for every producer of one (and only one) commodity, so that problems of costs are largely avoided. One exception to this statement is his early elaboration of the important doctrine that competition and decreasing costs are incompatible:

> Pareto makes the correct observation that in industries which follow the Marshallian so-called law of "increasing returns" . . . with constant selling prices a real equilibrium is impossible. . . . It would be even more correct to say that with such assumptions economic equilibrium in general cannot exist under free competition. For the entrepreneur who *first* expanded his production would be able to force all of his competitors out of the field, until eventually everything ended up as a monopoly or a monopolistic combination. If, on the contrary, one assumes—as frequently would correspond closer to actuality—that unit costs are subject to the law of *decreasing* returns, . . . there appears (as moreover Pareto himself suggests at another point) sooner or later a definite optimum scale for every individual firm. If these firms are still sufficiently numerous to offer each other effective competition, each of them can be conceived as a productive unit, and the entire industry then stands—as is approximately true in agriculture—under the law of "constant return." [2]

Wicksell also approves, although tacitly rather than ex-

[1] Compare the articles by Karl Menger, cited above, p. 49, n. 2.

[2] "Vilfredo Paretos Manuel d'economie politique," *Zeitschrift für Volkswirtschaft, Sozialpolitik, und Verwaltung*, XXII (1913), 140; also *Lectures*, p. 131.

plicitly, of Marshall's theory of external economies and diseconomies.[1]

Factors of Production; Original Factors

Although Wicksell generally conducts his analysis in terms of the three productive factors, land, labor, and capital, his acceptance of the classical trichotomy is not complete. Two differences are noteworthy. The classification is admittedly only for convenience of exposition; in actual life there are numerous kinds of labor and land.[2] No real economic distinction exists between these two groups of factors; there is "a practically complete parallelism" with regard to their returns.[3] The second distinction lies in the practice of subsuming all durable income-yielding goods, be they natural or created by man, under "land"; discussion of this point may be deferred.

Wicksell adopts without question, however, Böhm-Bawerk's doctrine of original factors: "We have already pointed out that capital itself is almost always a product, a fruit of the co-operation of the two original factors: labour and land." [4] The "original factors" doctrine plays as crucial a role in Wicksell's theory as in that of Böhm-Bawerk. Wicksell, as we shall see, uses the concept of an investment period rather than a production period, although the two are closely related. Nevertheless his treatment of interest theory, particularly for the case of durable consumption goods, is open to the same criticism

[1] Cf. *Lectures*, pp. 123–24, 133; also *Thünen Archiv*, p. 355; *Ekonomisk Tidskrift*, 1902, pp. 288 ff.

[2] *Über Wert*, pp. 136–38; *Lectures*, pp. 107, 113, 123–24. He also approves (*ibid.*, p. 101) of the statements of the theory of production given by Walras and Barone, both of which are based on *n* factors.

[3] *Lectures*, p. 132; also "No special theory of rent is necessary, but every acre of land may be treated in just the same way as a labourer. . . ."

[4] *Ibid.*, p. 149; also pp. 99, 145, 150, 165, 172; *Über Wert*, p. 85.

that was levied above at Böhm-Bawerk. Wicksell's subsequent analysis is based on this untenable view; he also uses the doctrine in reproducing Böhm-Bawerk's criticism of productivity theories.[1]

The Theory of Capital

Wicksell is the great follower of Böhm-Bawerk's theory of capital and interest. His restatement of the doctrine amounts almost to an original contribution, for he removes many of the simpler objections to which Böhm-Bawerk's presentation is so vulnerable. Wicksell's statement is a model of conciseness and internal consistency, and it is much more general in scope. This restatement of the period of production concept is, even today, one of the best presentations of the Böhm-Bawerkian theory available. The presentation which follows is based primarily on the *Über Wert*, although later changes or new elements in his thought are noted.[2]

WICKSELL ON BÖHM-BAWERK

It would be grossly unfair to Wicksell to give the impression that he is merely a systematizer of Böhm-Bawerk's doctrine. Wicksell is largely independent in his critical evaluation of the Austrian's presentation, and scarcely any portion of the latter's analysis is not changed in some respect. The range and depth of his criticisms, furthermore, increase through time. A brief review of

[1] *Lectures*, pp. 146–47. Wicksell alters his stand in the *Lectures* from his previous view in the *Über Wert*, where he says that Böhm-Bawerk's theory also fails to show why capital goods should secure a return greater than their value, but that this problem disappears in a stationary economy (*Über Wert*, p. 87).

[2] The presentation in the *Lectures*, Part II, sec. 2, differs little in substance although considerably in form.

Wicksell's more general criticisms is therefore desirable; minor points have already been dealt with in the chapter on Böhm-Bawerk or will be treated in connection with Wicksell's positive statement.

In the *Über Wert* there is a general appraisal of two parts of Böhm-Bawerk's theory: the "three grounds" for discount of the future, and the criticisms of the productivity theories.[1] The criticisms of the "three grounds" have already been referred to, and may be summarized.[2] The first ground is questioned for substantially the same reasons as those advanced by the present writer: In a stationary economy individual differences in want and provision in the future relative to the present will cancel out, and the ability of people with future preferences to store goods without cost is very limited. The second ground, lack of perspective, is accepted. It is "without doubt of the very greatest importance." [3] The third ground, technical superiority of present over future goods, is also accepted and indeed it forms the cornerstone of Wicksell's theory; but it is accepted as a direct, *productivity* explanation of interest.

Wicksell in fact sees no difference between Böhm-Bawerk's theory and that of, say, Thünen, except that the former's statement is much more generalized and penetrating (in the recognition of the role of time).[4] A major criticism leveled by Böhm-Bawerk against previous productivity theories is the failure to distinguish between value productivity and physical productivity. Yet, as Wicksell points out, when Böhm-Bawerk compares (as he must) present and future goods of the *same*

[1] A considerable portion of the material on interest theory had already appeared in "Kapitalzins und Arbeitslohn," *Jahrbücher für Nationalökonomie und Statistik, LIX* (1892), 852–74, and was virtually reprinted in the *Über Wert.*

[2] *Über Wert,* pp. 83–85. [3] *Ibid.*, p. 84. [4] *Ibid.*, pp. 85–90; also pp. viii-lx.

kind, he is in fact ignoring value productivity. A further criticism raised by Böhm-Bawerk is the failure of the productivity theorists to show why the capital goods do not absorb the whole value of the product (as imputation theory would suggest), leaving no margin for interest. Wicksell asserts that Böhm's theory, which is also a productivity theory of interest, does not solve this problem either. All such criticisms rest on the related failure clearly to postulate a stationary economy; once this is done "his objections against Thünen's theory dissolve themselves." [1] The precise basis for this view is not clear; there is a faint suggestion that in a rapidly progressing economy the interest rate will disappear.

In later writings the sphere of criticism is broadened still more. The first two grounds, provision and perspective, are important only in determining the accumulation of capital, not its return in a stationary economy.[2] The doctrine that interest is an agio arising out of the exchange of present for future goods contains the error, noted previously, that the future consumption period and supply with which the present is compared are completely indeterminate.[3] The third ground is "equally unsatisfactory": "Böhm-Bawerk's real error—his cardinal error, as Bortkiewicz calls it—is that at this point in his exposition he seeks to solve the problem of the *existence* of interest—as distinct from its actual rate—without referring to the market for capital and labour." [4] In his final work Wicksell attempts to rehabilitate the third ground, but he succeeds only in restating it as a productivity explanation of interest, not as an independent

[1] *Ibid.*, p. 87.

[2] *Lectures*, pp. 154–55. Wicksell seems here implicitly to define a stationary economy as one with a fixed amount of capital.

[3] *Ibid.*, p. 169.

[4] *Ibid.*, p. 171.

third "ground" for the preference of present over "future" goods.[1]

WICKSELL'S CAPITAL CONCEPT

Wicksell begins his thorough restatement of Böhm-Bawerk's theory with a vastly improved capital concept.[2] One general feature of superiority may be noted at the outset. A complex and artificial classification of types of capital is absent. A single capital concept is offered, and that concept is used in his theory of interest.

The alleged distinction between "social" capital and "private" capital is denied. "But I hold as unjustified the attempt to set up definite categories of goods, some of which are also capital from the social viewpoint, others of which are capital *only* from the private viewpoint." [3] For although it is true that durable consumption goods yield services without additional applications of labor (an unnecessary concession on Wicksell's part), this is also largely true of such things as meadows, forests, and game preserves, which cannot be denied the name of capital (and, indeed, of "social" capital).[4] As long as a durable good yields economic services, it must be considered either as a capital good or as a durable income-yielding good (*Rentengut*).

A second departure from Böhm-Bawerk's position is the inclusion of means of subsistence of laborers, even when these means are owned by entrepreneurs. Such prospective advances to labor are excluded from social

[1] "Zur Zinstheorie," *Die Wirtschaftstheorie der Gegenwart* (Vienna, 1928), III, 199–209.

[2] Cf. *Lectures*, pp. 144–47, 185 ff. The present discussion is based on the *Über Wert*.

[3] *Über Wert*, p. 74; also p. 75: "The view that durable goods are no longer capital so soon as they are being consumed by their owners and accordingly yield no money income, is, as A. Marshall observes, really nothing but a vestige of the prejudices of the old mercantile system."

[4] *Ibid.*, pp. 74–75.

capital by Böhm-Bawerk, yet he includes money in social capital. This is inconsistent: if the entrepreneur pays his wage bill in money, he expends social capital; if he buys means of subsistence and pays wages in kind, only private capital is expended on wages! Wicksell avoids this paradox by excluding all subsistence goods from his capital concept when they are owned by the laborer, because a productive equivalent has been rendered for them; if they are in the entrepreneur's possession (whether as goods or as money) they are capital.[1] The test of ownership is here definitive with respect to capital goods.[2]

Turning now to Wicksell's positive formulation of the capital concept, it may be summarized as essentially stored-up wealth (*aufgespeicherte Reichtum*), or, more accurately, as stored-up subsistence.[3] The distinction between capital goods and durable income-yielding goods (*Rentengüter*), such as land, offers difficulty in this regard. Yet a distinction is found. "The most important economic difference between land and produced material goods appears to lie in the fact that the former yields its successive utilities only in a previously determined and unalterable temporal order, which however is also endless, while on the contrary the produced goods yield only a finite number of utilities, these however in almost any desired order. . . ." [4] Even this criterion is not complete; it is "clearly only empirical." [5] A mine may be exploited at varying rates of speed; a house, contrari-

[1] *Ibid.*, p. 77; also *Lectures*, p. 187.

[2] *Über Wert*, p. 79 n.

[3] *Ibid.*, p. 72; also *Untersuchungen*, p. 28: "It [capital] will be considered, so to speak, virtually as a single sum of finished consumption goods." Cf. also *Lectures*, pp. 147 ff. This definition is substantially the same as that used by Böhm-Bawerk in the latter sections of the *Positive Theory*.

[4] *Über Wert*, pp. 72–73.

[5] *Ibid.*, p. 138.

wise, may last perhaps centuries and is therefore very similar to land. Nevertheless the distinction is basic: "One can say that the more readily a productive tool can be used up at will, the more of a capitalistic character (in the narrow sense) it secures." [1]

The definition of capital thus turns on the economic life of the good in question. All goods which must be replaced within a relatively short period of time are capital; those which need not be are *Rentengüter*. Permanent capital investments in land are *Rentengüter*, not capital.[2]

Wicksell's capital concept emerges in a considerably more sophisticated form than his predecessor's statement, but it is equally unrealistic. The definition centers in the belief that new capital goods are created (only by "original" factors) during a certain period of time and then wear out during another given period of time, as in Jevons' more candid theory. Here is a confusion between the technical and the economic life of a capital good, and because of this confusion Wicksell is led far astray. There is no valid economic distinction between *Rentengüter* and capital; the rate at which capital goods can be changed from one form to another is influenced less by technical considerations, which are all he discusses, than by economic factors. Mobility of specific capital goods between industries, and the rate of liquidation of capital goods, are both functions of *prices*. Only in the case of unanticipated readjustments of production (to changed data, technical or economic) do they take on significance, and practically nothing can be said *a priori* regarding their "liquidity" under such circumstances.

Rentengüter, it may be noticed, are not produced in a stationary economy; they are only maintained.[3] This premise, on the basis of which Wicksell raises criticisms

[1] *Ibid.*, p. 73. [2] *Ibid.* [3] *Ibid.*, pp. 137, 142.

of Walras' capital theory which are later retracted,[1] is somewhat qualified. "The replacement of goods of this sort [*Rentengüter*] which are completely used up, by new specimens, need not, of course, be excluded, but can perhaps be conceived as the repair of a larger complex of goods." [2] *Rentengüter* secure returns which are exactly comparable to the rent of land.[3]

From the content of capital we may turn briefly to its role in production. Since capital consists of stored-up subsistence owned by capitalists, it permits advances to laborers, landowners, and capitalists.[4] The subsistence of capitalists, Wicksell implies, may be viewed as having its source in interest (in a static state).[5] Wicksell's definition differs from Jevons' only in the inclusion of advances to landowners and capitalists as well as to laborers.[6] The role of capital sheds light on its definition: we may consider as *Rentengüter* those commodities whose quantity is independent of the period of production.[7]

[1] *Supra*, pp. 252 f.

[2] *Über Wert*, p. 137 n.

[3] *Ibid.*, pp. 137–38.

[4] It is in this time element, the advancing of wages to laborers, that Wicksell finds justification for Mill's famous dictum: "Demand for commodities is not a demand for labour." (Cf. *Lectures*, pp. 100, 191). While this interpretation is not conclusive, it appears to be substantially correct. When Mill says (*Principles*, Bk. I, Chap. v, § 9), "What supports and employs productive labour, is the capital expended in setting it to work, and not the demand of purchasers for the produce of the labour when completed. . . . This theorem, that to purchase produce is not to employ labour; that the demand for labour is constituted by the wages which precede the production, and not by the demand which may exist for the commodities resulting from the production. . . ." the time element is very strongly implied. If Mill's statement is divested of its erroneous conceptions of productivity and saving, and, above all else, restricted to a single investment, it is very close to the Böhm-Bawerkian theory of capital.

[5] *Über Wert*, p. 78.

[6] Compare the review of Einar Einerson's *Begrebet Kapital i Oekonomien*, *Zeitschrift für Volkswirtschaft, Sozialpolitik und Verwaltung*, VI (1897), 321–22; also *Untersuchungen*, pp. 43–45, esp. p. 45: "Jeder Hektar des Bodens ist in der Tat ein Arbeiter. . . ." Cf. also *Lectures*, pp. 150–51, 154, 185, 191.

[7] *Über Wert*, p. 137 n.

THE PRODUCTION CONCEPT

In the field of production theory, Wicksell's acceptance of Böhm-Bawerk's theory is virtually complete.[1] The fundamental role of capital is to make possible a time interval between the beginning and the end of the period of production. The more free capital (or sum of means of subsistence) there is available, the longer the production period may be, and accordingly the greater the product which will be secured from the productive resources, land and labor.[2] The capital must be invested for a period equal to about half of the production period (with a linear rate of investment). "The greater . . . [the period of production] and accordingly the invested capital, the smaller in every case is the proportion of laborers employed on the final stage of production, but this small number produces a larger quantity of finished goods than a larger number would by a shorter production period. . . ." [3] This is the great contribution of Böhm-Bawerk, the discovery of a functional relationship between the length of the production period and the productivity of labor. The annual product of a laborer will grow with the length of the production period for which he is employed, but it will grow less rapidly than this period. Extensions of the period are subject to diminishing returns, "the scale of additional products [*Mehrerträgnisse*] is a decreasing one." [4] Wicksell adds the further assumption that the length of the period of production is continuously variable.[5]

Even in the *Über Wert* Wicksell recognizes certain

[1] *Ibid.*, p. 90; also *Lectures*, pp. 150 ff.

[2] The longer the period of production (given the supply of labor), the greater also is the amount of capital, according to Wicksell's definition. It is therefore necessary to treat the amount of capital as a function of time even in a static economy, which he fails to do.

[3] *Über Wert*, p. 91. [4] *Ibid.*, p. 92. [5] *Ibid.*, p. 92.

difficulties in the period of production concept. It is not possible conceptually to combine all the various industries which produce a commodity under division of labor.[1] A factory may produce machines used in the manufacture of a dozen products. Here a possible compromise is to group similar commodities.

Durable productive goods offer further difficulty.[2] If the machine lasts only a few years, it is possible to take the average life of the machine as the average length of that portion of the production period.[3] But this method is not applicable to more permanent capital goods, those lasting perhaps fifty or a hundred years. Such capital goods are too important to be disposed of as negligible, through some averaging device. The original construction costs of such goods have "absolutely no more effect" on their present earnings or value, and similarly, the value of present capital goods is not materially affected by their incomes in the distant future. As a result, once such durable goods are built, they must be considered exactly like land.[4]

Within three years Wicksell feels himself forced to abandon the period of production concept: "On the whole the concept of the 'period of production' is somewhat indistinct, in no case capable of exact definition." [5] Instead, the closely related concept of the period of investment is substituted. In the simple case of a linear rate of investment of resources in a project, the relationship between the two concepts is obvious; the average investment period is half of the production period.[6] A formal

[1] *Ibid.*, pp. 92–93.

[2] *Ibid.*, pp. 93–94.

[3] Wicksell forgets that the life of the machine is itself affected by the interest rate.

[4] *Über Wert*, p. 94.

[5] *Untersuchungen*, p. 30 n.

[6] A more complicated case is also examined, *ibid.*, pp. 29–30.

definition of the new concept is presented. "The time which elapses between the investment of a unit of capital through purchase (paying off) of labor and its replacement through the sale of finished objects of consumption (goods of first order) is called the circulation or investment period of the unit of capital in question." [1] The period of investment receives no further formal definition, but is used throughout his later writings.[2]

The new concept is just as vulnerable as the old one—since they stand in fixed relationship to one another. The period of investment, like the period of production, cannot be defined unless one assumes that capital goods can be separated from other "factors" (land and labor), and unless the latter work separately in capital creation. Wicksell never defends this crucial and, the writer is convinced, erroneous postulate of his system. As a result, the technical analysis to which we now turn deserves high praise on the score of elegance, but it becomes primarily a display of technique.

THE RESTATEMENT OF BÖHM-BAWERK'S THEORY OF INTEREST

A major portion of the second half of the *Über Wert* is devoted to a mathematical restatement of Böhm-Bawerk's theory of interest.[3] Wicksell explicitly states the Austrian's assumptions: [4]

i. Land is a free good.
ii. The production of a single commodity, or, what is the same thing, that all productivity functions are identical.
iii. Only simple interest is used.
iv. There is no net profit in a stationary economy.

[1] *Ibid.*, p. 29.
[2] Cf. *Lectures*, pp. 147 ff., 274 ff.
[3] *Über Wert*, pp. 95 ff.; also *Lectures*, pp. 144 ff.
[4] *Über Wert*, pp. 94–96.

We may postulate a given number of workers who may borrow any required sum of capital at a given rate of interest. They produce all necessary tools and equipment and use these up completely in the production period. These laborers seek to maximize their annual wages, which with interest equal the annual product, since in a static state there will be no profits and land is a free good.

A table of symbols is required before we turn to Wicksell's very elegant exposition of Böhm-Bawerk's theory:

s = value of the final product (either in physical units or a *numéraire*).
w = annual wage of one laborer.
t = length of the production period, measured in years and fractions of years.
z = the interest rate.
$\frac{s}{t} = p$ = annual product of one laborer.

The total wages paid each laborer during the production period will be $t \cdot w$. If all capital were borrowed at the beginning of the period, the simple interest payment would be $t \cdot w \cdot z \cdot t$, or $t^2 \cdot wz$. But it would be more economical to borrow capital only as it was needed to pay wages. It is assumed that the labor is expended uniformly, so the total capital will be invested for only half the period.[1] The first equation becomes

$$s = t \cdot w \cdot \left(1 + \frac{zt}{2}\right), \tag{1}$$

which asserts that the total product will be equal to wages plus interest on borrowed capital. $\frac{t}{2}$ is the "average length of capital investment." [2] Dividing both sides

[1] Consumption is presumably instantaneous, though this is not stated.

[2] As a more general formula than $\frac{t}{2}$, the expression, $\epsilon \cdot t$, where ϵ is a proper

of equation (1) by t, we secure

$$p = w \cdot \left(1 + \frac{zt}{2}\right), \tag{2}$$

or the annual product of a laborer is equal to his annual wage plus the interest thereon.

The problem is to secure a maximum annual wage (w). This is a simple problem in calculus, for we know the annual product (p) is a function of time (t); z is a known constant. A maximum for w is secured when

$$\frac{dp}{dt} = \frac{wz}{2}. \tag{3}$$

Solving this equation simultaneously with (2), we secure the value of t for which w is a maximum.[1] The same solution is secured when the annual wage rate (w) is assumed to be given and the interest rate is maximized.[2]

fraction, may be used. ϵ is a variable, for the distribution of labor within the production period may be altered (*Über Wert*, pp. 100–1). In the *Untersuchungen* t is defined as the average period of investment; for the present equations this involves only the substitution of t for $\frac{t}{2}$.

[1] Wicksell uses the following method of maximization: since $dw = 0$ at the maximum, he differentiates with respect to t as if w were a constant. The same result is secured by the more familiar method:

Rewrite equation (2) $$w = \frac{p}{1 + \frac{zt}{2}}.$$

Then $$\frac{dw}{dt} = \frac{\left(1 + \frac{zt}{2}\right) \cdot \frac{dp}{dt} - p \cdot \frac{z}{2}}{\left(1 + \frac{zt}{2}\right)^2} = 0.$$

Multiply out the denominator, and substitute $\frac{p}{w}$ for $\left(1 + \frac{zt}{2}\right)$ in the numerator,

$$\frac{p}{w} \cdot \frac{dp}{dt} - \frac{pz}{2} = 0.$$

Divide out the p's, and transpose,

$$\frac{dp}{dt} = \frac{wz}{2}.$$

[2] *Über Wert*, pp. 98–99, 102–3.

The graphical presentation is equally lucid: [1]

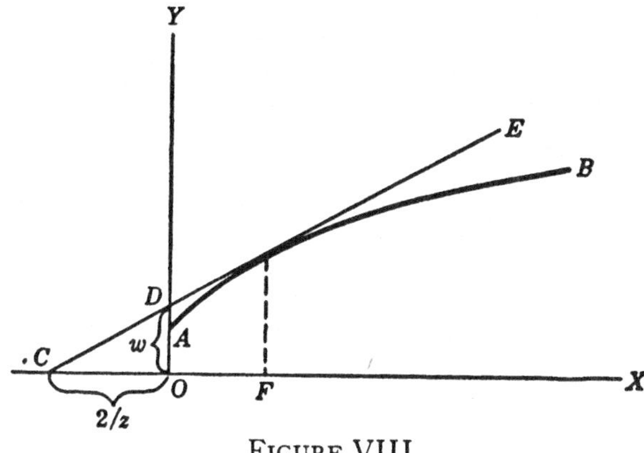

FIGURE VIII

Measure time along the X axis, product (in either physical or monetary units) along the Y axis. The line CDE intersects the X axis to form an angle whose tangent is equal to $\frac{wz}{2}\left(=\frac{dp}{dt}\right)$.[2] This line represents the interest charge on a laborer's wage per year, as a function of the number of years for which the wage is advanced. At the point where this line is tangent to AB, the produce curve, the optimum production period is fixed. At this point the increment in the length of the production period yields an additional annual product per laborer which is exactly equal to the increase in the interest on his annual wage advance. To the left of F the laborer can still produce more value product through a lengthening of the produc-

[1] *Ibid.*, p. 97. In the *Untersuchungen* (p. 40) the productivity curve (AB) begins at the origin, since Wicksell now believes that laborers could produce nothing without some capital (land being excluded).

[2] The tangent $\frac{dp}{dt}$ is equal to $\frac{w}{\frac{2}{z}}$ by equation (3), and this in turn is equal to $\frac{OD}{CO}$. It is shown (*Über Wert*, p. 98 n.) that the same solution is secured as a first approximation in the case of compound interest.

tion period than such a lengthening would cost in interest on wage advances; to the right the reverse is true.

The fact that this is a single investment means that the capital must find employment outside the business half of the time. This difficulty may be overcome by assuming that production is "staggered," so that there is an equal amount of labor invested in every stage of production.[1]

The general relations between wages, interest, and the period of production are not all that can be ascertained. If the number of laborers (A), the total capital (K) of an economy, and the production function are known, the actual rates of wages and interest and the period of production can be determined. Since each laborer requires $\frac{tw}{2}$ of capital, and all capital must be employed under competition,[2]

$$K = \frac{A \cdot w \cdot t}{2}. \tag{4}$$

This equation, in combination with the equations (2) and (3), will determine the three unknowns, t, w, and z. Or, more simply, z can be eliminated between equations (2) and (3), so

[1] *Ibid.*, pp. 99–100.

[2] Wicksell sees clearly the importance of the assumption of competition for his theory (*ibid.*, pp. 104–5). Should the capitalists combine, still seeking to employ capital fully, they will seek a period of production for which interest is maximized, but no longer subject to the condition that wages are fixed, so equation (3) becomes

$$\frac{dp}{dt} = \frac{-w}{t}.$$

Since w and t are positive, the marginal productivity of the extension of the period of production must be negative at the point of the maximum interest rate; the stage of negative returns must be reached! Since this point does not exist in practice, there is no maximum point, and non-economic considerations would have to limit the extent to which wages were depressed.

$$p = w + t \cdot \frac{dp}{dt}. \qquad (5)^1$$

The value of w secured from equation (5) may be substituted in equation (4), giving

$$K = \frac{A \cdot t}{2}\left(p - t \cdot \frac{dp}{dt}\right),$$

which has only one unknown, since p and $\frac{dp}{dt}$ are known functions of t.

The similarity of this theory to the wages fund doctrine is emphasized by Wicksell. The classical theory of wages can be stated as

$$w = \frac{K}{A}.$$

Capital divided by number of laborers gives the average wage. But K, the amount of capital available for advances to labor, is unknown; it depends at equilibrium on the length of the period of production. Hence we have two unknowns but only one equation. Böhm-Bawerk restates this postulate (adding the investment period concept),

$$w = \frac{2K}{tA}. \qquad (4)$$

And since the new unknown, t, is introduced, he adds the further equation (5), the equivalent of a production function based on time.[2]

[1] This expression reveals clearly that capital as a time-prolongation device is remunerated according to its marginal productivity, and wages are essentially a residual, in Böhm-Bawerk's theory.

[2] A previously noted criticism may be repeated at this juncture. K is also a variable, since the amount of subsistence means is a function of time, in Wicksell's theory. Hence an additional equation, $K = f(t)$, is necessary.

Wicksell recognizes clearly the antecedents of Böhm-Bawerk's theory in the classical wages fund doctrine, and, in fact, attributes the essence of that theory to Ricardo.[1] The fundamental criticism of the classical theory is its failure to see that only part of productive capital—and *a priori* an undetermined part—is included in the wages fund. The classicists base their theory on the division of capital between fixed and circulating capital, a matter of *technology*. As a matter of fact the distinction lies in *time*. Therefore the Ricardians were faced by a dilemma: with a given total productive capital, the wage rate depends on the division between fixed and circulating capital, but this division in turn depends on the wage rate!

One must therefore investigate the effect of wage increases on capitalistic production. This was done by Ricardo. Machines will become more profitable when wages rise, Ricardo argued, for although the labor cost of machines also rises, the interest rate falls.

> If one pursues more precisely the line of thought which Ricardo has explained only by a numerical example, it is clear that the kernel of this thought lies in the fact that the introduction of the machine in question lengthens the total process of production, and indeed in Ricardo's example from one to two years. . . . As a result the same quantity of labor creates a greater quantity of final products, but on the other hand the capital used to maintain the labor is invested for a longer time, for about two years rather than for one, and therefore eventually must be paid off with interest for two years rather than for one year. This necessarily means, as we will soon show, that the longer capital investment (the introduction of machines) first "becomes economic" with a very definite wage rate.[2]

[1] *Untersuchungen*, pp. 23–27; cf. also *Lectures*, pp. 193–95.
[2] *Untersuchungen*, p. 27.

This is unquestionably a brilliant interpretation of Ricardo's theory of the influence of varying durability of capital goods on relative values of commodities.[1] Wicksell nevertheless imputes more to Ricardo than a careful reading of the latter's text would support. In Ricardo there is no statement of the greater productivity of longer construction periods (although this assumption may well be implicit in his argument). The superiority of durable capital goods is due to the decline of the interest rate, and this decline is not related to the productivity of capital. Ricardo, moreover, discussed variations in the construction period between different commodities, not variations in the production of a given commodity. Wage and interest variations affect the scale on which different commodities will be produced, not the method of producing any given commodity. Ricardo assumes, indeed, that all capital in agriculture is circulating capital.

RELATIVE AND ABSOLUTE SHARES OF DISTRIBUTION

An allied topic, the division of the total product between capital and labor, also receives attention from Wicksell:

> Wages rise and the interest rate declines when there is an increase in the total capital of an economy. As a rule this circumstance is interpreted that with increasingly capitalistic production the *share* of the laborer in the total product always becomes larger, that of capital on the contrary always smaller. However this is not absolutely true.[2]

The problem may be stated and solved mathematically. Does $\frac{w}{p}$, the share of the product paid to the laborer,

[1] Cf. Ricardo's *Principles of Political Economy and Taxation* (Gonner ed., London, 1932), Chap. i, secs. iv and v. The lengthening of the construction period referred to by Wicksell is found on p. 29 of the *Principles*.

[2] *Über Wert*, pp. 113–14.

grow or decrease as the production period is lengthened? The differential of this expression is

$$p \cdot \frac{dw}{dt} - w \cdot \frac{dp}{dt}.$$

Substituting for $\frac{dw}{dt}$ and for w,[1] we secure

$$-pt \cdot \frac{d^2p}{dt^2} + t \cdot \left(\frac{dp}{dt}\right)^2 - p \cdot \frac{dp}{dt}.$$

Since $\frac{d^2p}{dt^2}$ is less than zero, the first two terms are positive, the third negative. Therefore it cannot be said *a priori* whether the laborer's share rises or falls; the nature of the production function ($p = f[t]$) is all-decisive.

The influence of increases in capital on the total amount of the earnings of capital is also considered.[2] In this case the annual interest secured from the wage advance to a laborer is $(p - w)$, which in differential form is

$$d(p - w) = \frac{dp}{dt} \cdot dt - dw.$$

Substituting for dw,[3] we secure

$$d(p - w) = \left(\frac{dp}{dt} + t \cdot \frac{d^2p}{dt^2}\right) dt.$$

Since the signs of the two members are opposite, here again the sign of the changes in capital's absolute return cannot be told *a priori*. But if $\frac{d^2p}{dt^2}$ is very small, that is, if the marginal productivity of the extension of the period

[1] From equation (5) $w = p - t \cdot \frac{dp}{dt}$, therefore

$$\frac{dw}{dt} = \frac{dp}{dt} - t \cdot \frac{d^2p}{dt^2} - \frac{dp}{dt} = -t \cdot \frac{d^2p}{dt^2}.$$

[2] *Über Wert*, pp. 114–16.

[3] See note 1, *supra*.

of production is almost constant, the total expression is positive; the total share of the capitalists increases.[1]

THE ALTERNATIVE APPROACH

In his *Lectures*, Wicksell offers an alternative solution of the problem of interest which, while not essentially different from his restatement of Böhm-Bawerk's theory, is capable of further technical applications than the previous approach.[2] Because its fundamental theory does not differ, the alternative treatment will only be summarized.

Aging wine is taken as the example, "a copybook example rightly favoured by economists." The value of a unit of wine (W) is assumed to be a function only of the original value and the age of the unit of grapejuice which comprises it. The present value of a unit of grapejuice is V. The entrepreneur seeks to maximize the present value of his product, which may be represented as

$$W(t)(1 + i)^{-t} = W(t) \cdot e^{-\rho t} \tag{i}$$

where, at equilibrium, $W = Ve^{\rho t}$. (i.i)

Maximizing this expression, we secure

$$\frac{d[W(t)e^{-\rho t}]}{dt} = W' \cdot e^{-\rho t} - \rho W_e^{-\rho t} = 0$$

or

$$\rho = \frac{W'}{W}, \tag{ii}$$

which is Jevons' formula for the instantaneous rate of interest.

Assuming a given capital, sufficient to support the aging wine for t years, and all the capital to be employed,

[1] If the productivity function is of the nature, $p = \alpha + \beta \log_e t$, then the total share of the capitalists remains constant.

[2] *Lectures*, pp. 172–84.

with continuous production the total capital of the economy will be

$$K = V\int_{0} e^{\rho x}dx = \frac{W - V}{\rho}. \qquad \text{(iii)}$$

This is the equilibrium position if social capital (equal to the whole of stored-up wine) exactly equals K.

It is interesting to examine the new equilibrium if there is an increase in social capital. By logarithmic differentiation of equation (i.i.), and using equation (ii), we obtain

$$\frac{\delta V}{V} = -t\delta\rho = -\frac{\begin{vmatrix} W & W' \\ W' & W'' \end{vmatrix}}{W^2}t\delta t. \qquad \text{(iv)}$$

Since the determinant in the last expression is negative,[1] we secure the following changes from an increase in social capital:

i. Both the value of grapejuice and the period of production will increase (δV and $\delta t > 0$).
ii. The instantaneous rate of interest will decline ($\delta\rho < 0$).

It may readily be shown that increases in capital (K) lead to increases in the period for which wine is held (t). Differentiate equation (iii), and use equation (iv), securing

$$\delta K = \frac{\rho W' - \rho'[W - V(1 + \rho t)]}{\rho^2}\delta t.$$

Since ρ' is negative, and $W = Ve^{\rho t} > V(1 + \rho t)$, δt must be positive. Similarly, we obtain

$$\frac{dW}{dK} = \rho + K\frac{d\rho}{dK} + \frac{dV}{dK} = \rho + (K - Vt)\frac{d\rho}{dK}.$$

[1] This follows from the condition, $\frac{d^2[W(t)e^{-\rho t}]}{dt^2} < 0$.

Since $\frac{d\rho}{dK} < 0$, and $K > Vt$,[1] therefore $\frac{dW}{dK} < \rho$. Thus the assertion of von Thünen and Böhm-Bawerk is untrue; the rate of interest is not equal to the increment of product divided by the increment of capital. This ratio is lower than the interest rate. The explanation lies in the fact that part of an increase in capital is absorbed by wage increases (here V) and thus the period of production cannot be extended so far—subject to diminishing returns—as would be possible if wages (and rents) remained constant. For the entrepreneur their theory is correct, for his capital investments do not affect the prices of resources.

Wicksell's treatment of the problem of durable capital will only be mentioned, although it contains an unusual performance in purely theoretical analysis (written at the age of 72).[2] The solution appears to the writer to be less valuable than elegant, because of the peculiar assumptions on which it rests.[3] It would be impossible, however, to restate his argument within reasonable space, and its proper evaluation would involve a consideration of most of the issues in contemporary capital theory.

The General Theory of Distribution

The earliest statement of Wicksell's general theory of distribution is an extension of Böhm-Bawerk's theory of interest to the case in which land and labor are productive factors.[4] The latter's theory is so generalized that all shares, rent, wages, and interest, receive remunerations per unit equal to their marginal products.

[1] From (iii), since the integrand is always > 1 if $\rho > 0$.

[2] "Real Capital and Interest," *Lectures*, 258–99.

[3] The assumptions include: there are only two resources, labor and axes; additional labor can be invested only in increasing the durability of axes; etc.

[4] *Über Wert*, pp. 121–27.

Certain simplifying assumptions are made at the outset.[1] All laborers are equally productive, and are paid at the same rate. All units of land, similarly, are of equal productivity and receive the same rent. Each worker is supplied with the same amount of land. All industries have the same productivity function, or, what amounts to much the same, only one product is made.[2]

The same symbols are used as in the presentation of Böhm-Bawerk's interest theory, with three additional ones:

r = the annual rent of a unit of land.

h = the number of units of land with which each laborer is supplied.

B = the total number of units of land in the economy.

The product of a given laborer is now dependent on two factors, the length of the period of production and the amount of land he uses. Diminishing returns hold with respect to the use of each of these factors.[3] The total amount of capital required for each laborer, since advances are also made to landowners, is $\frac{t}{2}(w + h \cdot r)$. The fundamental equation becomes

$$p = (w + h \cdot r) \cdot \left(1 + \frac{zt}{2}\right), \tag{6}$$

which reduces to equation (1) if r is set equal to zero.

The problem for the entrepreneur consists in maximizing the rate of interest when wage and rent rates are

[1] *Ibid.*, pp. 121–22.

[2] It is also implied that the average investment periods of labor and rent advances are equal. In the *Untersuchungen* this assumption is dropped (pp. 46, 51 ff.), with only formal changes in the results.

[3] If $p = f(t,h)$, then $\frac{\partial p}{\partial t} > 0$; $\frac{\partial p}{\partial h} > 0$; $\frac{\partial^2 p}{\partial t^2} < 0$; $\frac{\partial^2 p}{\partial h^2} < 0$.

given. Differentiating equation (6) partially with respect to t and h, we secure the conditions for a maximum:

$$\frac{\partial p}{\partial t} = (w + h \cdot r)\frac{z}{2} \tag{7}$$

$$\frac{\partial p}{\partial h} = r\left(1 + \frac{tz}{2}\right). \tag{8}$$

With these three equations we may determine the three unknowns, t, h, and z.

But this is a solution only for the individual entrepreneur. For an economy as a whole the wage rate and the rent charge are also unknown. By adding the conditions that all land and all capital be employed, we secure the necessary additional equations:

$$K = \frac{t}{2} \cdot A \cdot (w + h \cdot r) \tag{9}$$

$$h = \frac{B}{A}. \tag{10}$$

The Ricardian rent theory can be shown to be a special case of these equations.[1] Assume that the interest rate is constant, and, for convenience, that it is zero (or that it is included in wages and rent), and that the period of production is of fixed length. Equation (7) disappears and equations (6) and (8) become

$$p = w + h \cdot r \tag{6.1}$$

$$\frac{dp}{dh} = r. \tag{8.1}$$

The former equation states that the annual product of a laborer must equal his wage plus the rent on the land he uses. The second equation informs us that " . . . production is most advantageously organized when every

[1] *Über Wert*, pp. 125–26.

laborer utilizes just so many units of land that the addition of a further unit would increase his product merely by the amount of the rent of this unit. . . ." [1]

It can readily be shown that these equations, like any other system expressing a marginal productivity theory, contain the conventional theory of rent.[2] Let us take a larger unit of land, on which many laborers are employed. The former h is now a proper fraction, equal to $\frac{1}{n}$, where n is the number of laborers per larger unit of land. If all the labor on such a unit produces q per year, $p = \frac{q}{n}$. Differentiating this last expression we secure

$$\frac{dp}{dh} = \frac{d\left(\frac{q}{n}\right)}{d\left(\frac{1}{n}\right)} = q - n \cdot \frac{dq}{dn}.$$

We may substitute to secure

$$q = n \cdot w + r \tag{6.2}$$

and

$$q - n \cdot \frac{dq}{dn} = r$$

or

$$\frac{dq}{dn} = w. \tag{8.2}$$

The first equation, (6.2), expresses the equality between the product of a large tract of land and the wages and rent expended upon it. The last equation, (8.2), states that " . . . the most profitable method of production exists when just so many laborers are applied to each [large] unit of land that the use of another laborer will bring in *only his annual wage* and no more. . . ." [3]

[1] *Ibid.*, p. 125. [2] *Ibid.* [3] *Ibid.*, p. 126.

Wicksell's mode of presentation in the *Über Wert* unfortunately obscures the fact that he is presenting the first complete mathematical formulation of the marginal productivity theory of distribution. He first assumes that there is *one* laborer and a variable number of units of land, then that there is *one* (larger) unit of land and a variable number of laborers. In the former case, the variable agent (land) is rewarded in accordance with its discounted marginal productivity, for

$$\frac{\partial p}{\partial h}\left(1 + \frac{tz}{2}\right)^{-1} = r. \tag{8}$$

But the single laborer is clearly a residual claimant. In the latter case the variable agent (labor) is paid its discounted marginal product,[1] for

$$\frac{\partial q}{\partial n}\left(1 + \frac{tz}{2}\right)^{-1} = w \tag{8.3}$$

and the (large) unit of land is a residual claimant. Capital, finally, also receives its marginal product, for

$$\frac{\partial p}{\partial t} = (w + h \cdot r) \cdot \frac{z}{2} \tag{7}$$

where the capital is invested for half the period of production.

A slight modification of this approach leads directly to the general marginal productivity theory of distribution. Equation (6) may be rewritten,

$$p = w + h \cdot r + \frac{wzt}{2} + \frac{hrzt}{2}. \tag{6}$$

And substituting from equation (8),

$$p = w + h\frac{\partial p}{\partial h}\left(1 + \frac{zt}{2}\right)^{-1} + \frac{wzt}{2} + \frac{hrzt}{2}. \tag{6.3}$$

[1] This equation differs from (8.2) only in that interest is included; it is given in *Über Wert*, p. 126 n.

Multiplying by n and substituting from equation (8.3) [1]

$$np = q = n\cdot\frac{\partial q}{\partial n}\left(1+\frac{tz}{2}\right)^{-1} + n\cdot h\cdot\frac{\partial p}{\partial h}\left(1+\frac{tz}{2}\right)^{-1} + \frac{nwzt}{2} + \frac{rzt}{2}. \quad (6.4)$$

If, now, we assume with Wicksell that the production function is homogeneous,[2] so $n\frac{\partial p}{\partial h} = \frac{\partial q}{\partial h}$, and substitute for the last two terms of (6.4),[3] then

$$q = n\frac{\partial q}{\partial n}\left(1+\frac{tz}{2}\right)^{-1} + h\frac{\partial q}{\partial h}\left(1+\frac{tz}{2}\right)^{-1} + t\frac{\partial q}{\partial t}. \quad (6.5)$$

The discounts on the marginal products of land and labor are equal to the share of capital $\left(t\frac{\partial q}{\partial t}\right)$, for

$$n\cdot\frac{\partial q}{\partial n}\cdot\frac{tz}{2} + h\cdot\frac{\partial q}{\partial h}\frac{tz}{2} = t\frac{\partial q}{\partial t}.$$

If time is eliminated, or the interest rate is set equal to zero, equation (6.5) becomes

$$q = n\frac{\partial q}{\partial n} + h\frac{\partial q}{\partial h}. \quad (6.6)$$

Wicksell must be acknowledged as one of the founders of the general marginal productivity theory of distribution. His own development contains all the essentials of this theory, and he suggests, even though he does not

[1] Remembering that $n = \frac{1}{h}$.

[2] This condition of homogeneity is implicit in Wicksell's equation, $q = n\cdot p$, from which it follows that

$$\frac{\partial q}{\partial h} = n\frac{\partial p}{\partial h}.$$

[3] Wicksell gives the equation (*ibid.*, p. 126 n.):

$$\frac{\partial q}{\partial t} = \frac{nwz}{2} + \frac{rz}{2}.$$

give explicit mathematical statement of, the general theorem:

> If one considers the total yield from production as an actual (and continuous) function of the cooperating productive factors, . . . economic behavior obviously requires that every factor should be used to just such an extent that the loss of a small portion of it would decrease the result of production exactly as much as the share of product received by this quantity. . . .
>
> Mathematically expressed, this means that the shares of product of the various productive factors must be proportional to the partial derivatives of the above-mentioned production function with respect to the factor in question as variable. . . . (pp. xii–xiii).

In the *Untersuchungen* this subject receives little further attention. Wicksell gives explicit statement to a general approximation of the production function of the individual laborer, however:

$$p = c \cdot h^m t^k b^v,$$

where p is product, m, k, and v are proper fractions, c is a constant, h is units of land, and t and b are the lengths of the investment periods of labor and land respectively.[1] The production function does not receive detailed consideration, however. Discussion of Wicksell's further work in distribution theory is deferred to the chapter on the history of Euler's theorem in distribution theory.

[1] *Op. cit.*, p. 53.

Chapter XI

JOHN BATES CLARK

UNTIL at least the turn of the century, most American economists were concerned more with empirical studies and social reforms than with theoretical price analysis—a situation due in no small part to the influence in this country of the German Historical School. The increasing participation in economic theorizing during this period can be characterized more accurately as vigorous than as profound. The naissance—there could be no renaissance—was led by John Bates Clark in the field of distribution theory,[1] and it is to him that the present chapter is devoted.[2]

Clark independently discovered both the marginal utility and the marginal productivity theories.[3] He is

[1] A biographical sketch and some discussion of Clark's work are available in *John Bates Clark, A Memorial* (privately printed, 1938). A few details are given by Alvin Johnson, "John Bates Clark, 1847–1938," *American Economic Review*, XXVIII (1938), 427–29; and a general appraisal is offered by P. Homan, *Contemporary Economic Thought* (New York, 1928), Chap. i. A good, although unduly critical, review of the *Distribution of Wealth* by Knut Wicksell should also be consulted; cf. "Neue Beiträge zur Theorie der Verteilung," *Jahrbücher für Nationalökonomie und Statistik*, III Folge, XXVI (1903), 817–24, which was called to my attention by Professor A. W. Marget.

[2] A more complete survey of the marginal productivity theory would be forced to include the original and suggestive work of Stuart Wood, in addition to the well-known studies of T. N. Carver and F. W. Taussig.

[3] Judged with reference to elegance of analysis, Clark's formulation of the utility theory was inferior to that of Jevons or Walras. But this must be due at least in part to the fact that Clark saw and appreciated difficulties in the utility theory that were overlooked by the earlier discoverers of the theory. Cf. *The Distribution of Wealth* (New York, 1899), Chaps. xiv, xv. Clark's statement of independence in the discovery of the utility theory is given in the *Distribution*, p. vii.

best known, of course, for his exposition of the marginal productivity theory; it is indicative that, even at present, many continental economists consider Clark's theory to be *the* marginal productivity theory. His chief task, indeed, was that of popularization—a task that was fulfilled with appropriate detail, emphasis, and lucidity.

On the other hand, Clark performed one function for which economics has less cause for gratitude. In all of his major works, although perhaps to a decreasing extent through time, he introduced what has been called a "naive productivity ethics"—his marginal productivity theory contained a prescription as well as an analysis.[1] The dubious merits of this ethical system need not concern us, but it is a cause for regret that Clark's exposition, more than that of any other eminent contemporary economist, afforded some grounds for the popular and superficial allegation that neo-classical economics was essentially an apologetic for the existing economic order. Clark was a made-to-order foil for the diatribes of a Veblen.

It may be desirable to summarize Clark's earlier writings, since for the main discussion chief reliance will be placed on his *Distribution of Wealth*. His early essays (1877 to 1882) in the *New Englander* were republished as *The Philosophy of Wealth* in 1885. This work reveals a strong antipathy towards the classical economics, in which "the better elements of human nature were a forgotten factor," [2] and, indeed, the discussion manifests some of the idealism and mysticism of the Christian Socialist movement.

From the viewpoint of distribution theory the book is

[1] Cf. *The Philosophy of Wealth* (Boston, 1885), esp. pp. 135, 169; *The Distribution of Wealth*, Preface; also pp. 3, 4, 6, 7, 9, 49 n., 323–24 n., etc.

[2] *Philosophy of Wealth*, p. iii.

unimportant. Clark's purpose is primarily to answer scientifically the question of equity in the distributive process.[1] Competition, which is clearly dying out,[2] is very ineffective in establishing a fair wage.[3] The source of both wages and interest is the product,[4] but there is no suggestion of a marginal productivity theory. The Ricardian rent theory is held to be unsatisfactory,[5] for the very good reasons that it does not take cognizance of increases in the supply of land due to transportation improvements, and because capital and labor may be invested in improving land.[6]

After the *Philosophy of Wealth*, Clark's fundamental ideas on production and distribution theory appeared as monographs and articles within a half-dozen years. The almost definitive statement of his capital theory was made in 1888,[7] and the next year the marginal productivity theory was given a detailed formulation.[8] Subsequent essays develop the theory that the Ricardian rent analysis can be applied to any productive service, and the notion of a stationary economy (in the modern sense).[9] The *Distribution* is a synthesis of these and other works; the *Essentials of Economic Theory* adds little.[10]

[1] *Ibid.*, pp. 108 *et seq.*, 131–35.

[2] *Ibid.*, pp. 147–48.

[3] *Ibid.*, p. 169: "A few men without employment, and a few employers without souls, are the conditions of a general reduction of wages below the point to which more legitimate causes would reduce them."

[4] *Ibid.*, pp. 126, 127, 130.

[5] *Ibid.*, p. 125 n.

[6] *Ibid.*, pp. 98 ff.

[7] "Capital and Its Earnings," *Publications of the American Economic Association*, III (1888), No. 2.

[8] "Possibility of a Scientific Law of Wages," *ibid.*, IV (1889), No. 1.

[9] Both contained in "Distribution as Determined by a Law of Rent," *Quarterly Journal of Economics*, V (1890–91), 289–318.

[10] New York, 1907. This last-mentioned book was promised as a study in dynamic economics, but it does not develop any dynamic (historical) theories. Clark relies almost exclusively on what is now known as the

Costs and Returns

Clark makes no contribution to the theory of costs. With regard to the ultimate nature of costs, he adheres to the "real" cost approach. His statements on the subject are thoroughly hedonistic:

> . . . a full statement of the theory of value would take us into a psychological region whenever we speak of cost, as it does whenever we speak of utility. Cost is, in the last analysis, pain inflicted, just as utility is pleasure conferred (p. 221 n.).

The two fundamental pain costs are labor and abstinence (Chap. xxiv *passim;* pp. 126 ff., 381), both of which will be considered in detail later.

It is recognized that laborers do not have complete freedom to vary their hours of labor in order to equalize pain cost and utility of wages: " . . . gangs of men are tied to the steam whistle" (p. 383). Clark also recognizes the difficulty in changing occupations, but he finds that mobility is essentially achieved by the appearance of new generations of laborers who choose occupations so as to equalize their returns (pp. 278–79, 398). This latter problem is in fact, of course, not so easily solved, and Clark never redeems his promise to solve the former problem, fixity of hours.

In the theory of the allocation of given productive services (which are not distinguished from productive resources) between industries, a simon-pure alternative cost theory is followed. Equilibrium is reached, under pure competition, when every productive service is securing its maximum return, *i.e.*, when all alternative

method of comparative statics, *i.e.*, he compares different stationary equilibria. Subsequent references are to the *Distribution of Wealth* unless otherwise indicated. I am indebted to The Macmillan Company for permission to quote from this work.

uses of the service yield equal returns.[1] Complete mobility is characteristic also of land, and the returns from the alternative uses of a given type of land are also equalized (pp. 298–99). Either "friction" or "dynamic" changes in the economy will disturb this equilibrium, the former temporarily, the latter perpetually.[2]

The law of diminishing returns is accorded the status almost of an axiom: it is a "universal" law of economic phenomena (pp. 48–50). A possible early state of increasing incremental returns is not recognized in Clark's earlier writings.[3] When Walker criticizes the obvious error of failure to qualify for this possible stage,[4] Clark replies to the charge by the following use of the concept of a stationary economy:

> The combination and division of labor to which the increased returns are attributable constitute a dynamic influence that is not recognized in the supposed case. It is expressly excluded from the conditions of the ideal society that we create. The transition from a state in which one man works alone to a state in which two work together and exchange services or products means a more radical change in the constitution of society than can ever be made at a later date. It falls under number three [organization] in the list of dynamic influences that are specified and that are supposed, for the time being, not to operate.[5]

[1] Pp. 62 ff., Chap. xix *passim; e.g.*, "There is a general rate of wages; and employers in this group can have laborers for what it costs to get them out of the other groups, in which their productive power is smaller. . . . The movements of capital are brought about in the same way, by the action of *entrepreneurs*. Competition does it all . . ." (p. 290).

[2] Pp. 81–82. Clark considers all defects of competition, including monopoly, as "friction" (p. 76 n.)!

[3] *E.g.*, "Distribution as Determined by a Law of Rent," *op. cit.*, p. 304: "Put one man only on a square mile of prairie, and he will get a rich return. Two laborers on the same ground will get less per man; and, if you enlarge the force to ten, the last man will perhaps get wages only."

[4] "The Doctrine of Rent, and the Residual Claimant Theory of Wages," *Quarterly Journal of Economics*, V (1890–91), 433–34.

[5] "The Statics and Dynamics of Distribution," *Quarterly Journal of Economics*, VI (1891–92), 115–16; cf. also *Distribution*, pp. 164, 166 n.

This argument surely rests on a misconception of a stationary economy. One may and must hold technology constant, in the sense that no new inventions are developed. A fixed technology, however, is a set of known possible ways of producing commodities, and the specific methods chosen depend on the quantities and prices of the productive services and of the finished product. Clark's argument involves a denial of diminishing returns, in that it must ultimately reduce (under stationary conditions) to a single possible method of combining resources.[1]

The law of diminishing return is explained as due to the "crowding" of the resources held constant in quantity, particularly in the case of land (p. 164). The law is not defined carefully; sometimes it is expressed in incremental form (pp. 48, 50, 189, 374), and at other times in terms of averages (pp. 165, 192, 208, 280, 300–1). The problem of the determination of the scale of plant is not faced.[2]

[1] In his review, "Marshall's Principles of Economics," *Political Science Quarterly*, VI (1891), 146 ff., Clark describes Marshall's principle of substitution as a dynamic law (which it is not, in the sense in which Clark uses "dynamic")—another manifestation of the same obscurity in Clark's thought. He denies, in fact, the possibility of diminishing returns to "pure" capital: "Now one thing that is certainly true of the general fund of productive wealth is that it cannot be subject to the law of substitution" (*ibid.*, p. 149).

In "Distribution by a Law of Rent," *Publications of the American Economic Association*, Series 3, IV (1903), 154–65, Macfarlane uses the same misconception, that diminishing returns is a dynamic theory, to "refute" portions of Clark's marginal productivity theory.

[2] In his earlier work, "Possibility of a Scientific Law of Wages," *op. cit.*, p. 52, Clark says that the relative marginal productivities of capital (including land) and labor would not be affected if capital and labor increased in equal proportion; this implies a homogeneous, first-degree production function. Compare the next chapter.

Two years earlier, however, in "Profits under Modern Conditions," *Political Science Quarterly*, II (1887), 611, the following passage occurs: "Double the labor and capital expended on an acre of ground and you do not double the crop; double the labor and capital entrusted to an efficient manager and you more than double the product."

The Marginal Productivity Theory

Clark's very extensive exposition of the marginal productivity theory may be summarized very briefly, since its essential theses are so well known.[1] The return to each productive service is at equilibrium equal to the marginal product of a unit of that productive service, under "pure" competition. The marginal product of a service is measured, of course, by the effect on the total product of the addition or withdrawal of a unit of the productive service in question, the amounts of the other productive services in the combination being held constant. Competition among entrepreneurs will insure that the value of the marginal product will be paid to the owner of the service, and competition among the owners of the services will insure that the remuneration does not exceed the marginal product (which would entail unemployment). We may pass directly to certain aspects of Clark's elaboration of the theory.

Henry George had asserted that the marginal product of labor could be separated from that of land only at the no-rent margin, where the wage rate was "set." This crude form of marginal analysis suggested the marginal productivity theory to Clark (p. viii).[2] He concedes an element of truth to George's argument, but refuses to accept a "theory of 'squatter sovereignty' over the labor market" (p. 89). The theory is extended to the case where laborers use no-rent machines of any variety (pp. 92 ff.). But there is a still more general method of

[1] It would be pedantic to document the statements in this summary paragraph; the doctrine is stated in almost every chapter of the *Distribution*, but especially Chaps. vii, viii, xii. It was advanced with varying detail in at least a dozen articles during the 1890's.

[2] The subsequent argument was first presented in "Possibility of a Scientific Law of Wages," *op. cit.*, although the first suggestion of a marginal productivity theory appeared the preceding year. Cf., *infra*, pp. 315 f.

measuring the marginal product of an agent: there is an intensive margin in the utilization of all resources other than the one being measured, and the last unit of the variable agent, which adds nothing to the cost of these complementary resources, will secure the value of the amount of product it adds to the total product (pp. 98 ff.), which will also (due to the "law of indifference") be paid to all units of the variable agent.

There is a problem, however, arising out of the readaptation of a given amount of other resources to an increased amount of the agent whose marginal product is being determined.

> A given machine often requires one man to run it, and no more. It is not, then, at every point in a great establishment that the working force can be enlarged or reduced without any change in the character of the outfit of capital goods (p. 101).

From this difficulty two escapes are found. In the first place, there is some flexibility in the amount of one productive service that can be combined with a certain quota of other resources, as in agriculture (pp. 100 ff., 113 ff.). The more important solution, however, which is available only in the long run, lies in the possibility of rearrangement of the services held fixed in quantity so that they are best adapted to the changed quantity of the variable service. A given amount of capital, in Clark's terminology, can employ a widely variable quantity of labor, whereas a fixed amount of capital goods can employ only a relatively fixed amount of labor.[1] Reciprocally, given time for a new generation of men to appear, the occupational distribution of labor can be altered to adjust itself to a changed quantity of capital.[2]

[1] Pp. 112–15, 170, 175–76, 183 ff., 186, 247 ff.

[2] Pp. 159–60, 187. It is held, however, that changes in labor are primarily quantitative (p. 267).

Clark properly speaks as if there is, in the long run, virtually no limit to the possible rearrangement of given quantities of resources.[1]

A second aspect of Clark's presentation is the denial that the marginal productivity theory is an exploitative wage theory. If the product of the last unit of labor determines the wage rate, and laborers work subject to diminishing returns, it would appear that the "intramarginal" laborers (in his words) are getting less than their product. Thünen is accused of entertaining this belief, and with some justification (p. 321 n.), and Böhm-Bawerk certainly held the view.

There are two steps in Clark's reply to this criticism of the theory. In the first place, all of the laborers of a given type are homogeneous (Clark says "average"), so that if one is withdrawn, the entrepreneur will rearrange the duties of the remaining laborers, hence "the work that is left undone in consequence of one man's departure is always of the marginal kind" (p. 103; also pp. 103–6, 161). Secondly, an increase in the number of laborers using a given amount of capital goods means that each laborer has poorer equipment than previously; the marginal product of the new (increased) number of laborers has been reduced (pp. 322 ff.). The greater marginal product of the fewer laborers must therefore be attributed to the productivity of capital (pp. 195, 202, 323 n., 325). This argument, which is of course conclusive, may be restated graphically. In Figure IX let *AD* represent units of labor applied to a given amount of capital, and *BC* the marginal product of these laborers. Then *DC* will be the wage rate, *ADCE* the wage bill, and *ECB*, the "surplus," is really the product of the cooperating capital.

[1] Pp. 173–76. The notion of qualitative changes in productive factors, as their proportions are varied, was first made explicit in "Distribution as Determined by a Law of Rent," *op. cit.*, pp. 302–3.

This argument leads us directly to the last feature of Clark's exposition. Can it be shown that *ECB*, the "residual" return to capital, is identical with the return determined by the marginal productivity of capital? Clark answers the question in the affirmative (p. 201). His conclusion is primarily a matter of definition. Under pure competition, each hired productive service will be paid according to its marginal productivity, and the residual goes to the hiring factor, entrepreneurship. But

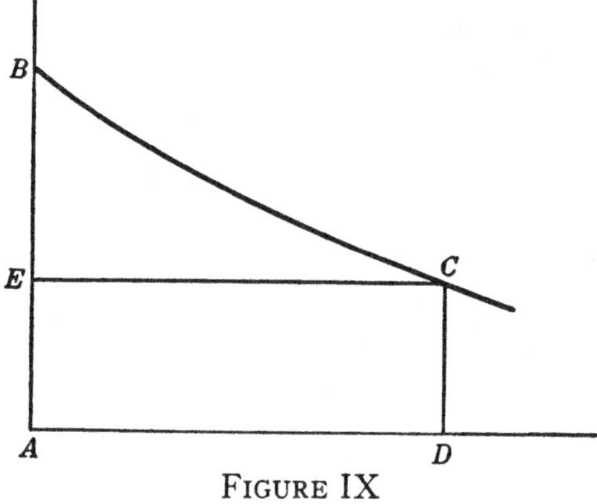

FIGURE IX

this residual ("profit") is by definition zero under pure competition: "Static conditions, however, exclude such a profit by making these two areas [*i.e.*, rent or interest as a residual and as a marginal product] equal." [1] This formal demonstration is supplemented by a more cogent argument:

> May not all *entrepreneurs* be making the same rate of net profits, and making them at the same time? May there not be a condition of equal and universal profit? Clearly not: for this would be a universal invitation to capitalists to become *entrepreneurs* and, as such, to bid against each other for labor and capital till the profit should everywhere

[1] P. 203. Also p. 331: "The static hypothesis prevents the entire figure *ABCD* from containing more than wages and interest."

> vanish, by being made over to laborers and capitalists in the shape of additions to wages and interest (p. 291 n.).

This point is slightly more convincing, but far from conclusive: Clark does not examine the specific conditions under which it is possible for remuneration of the productive services according to their marginal productivities exactly to exhaust the product, nor does he examine the stability of competition under these conditions.

Attention may now be turned to certain errors in Clark's presentation of the marginal productivity theory. He does not specify explicitly the size of the unit added or withdrawn to measure the marginal product of a productive service (cf. pp. 93, 320). R. S. Padan, in a rather confused polemic against Clark's theory,[1] points out that when large units are used, the product will be less than the distributive shares. In a reply, Clark acknowledges the necessity of taking small units:

> If the mathematical study had been carried farther, it would have shown that the amount of the excess of apparent wages and interest over total products varies directly with the size of the increments of labor and capital used in making the tests. If we made them equal to the whole amounts of labor and capital, we should attribute the entire product first to labor and then to capital, and the sum of the two incomes would be twice the product. As the increments are made smaller, the excess of the two incomes over products becomes smaller, and it practically vanishes when minute increments are used.
>
> . . . The truth to which Mr. Padan's reasoning would, if it were completed, lead is that in any application of the general principle on which the theory of value and the theory of

[1] "J. B. Clark's Formulae of Wages and Interest," *Journal of Political Economy*, IX (1900–1), 161–90. Substantially the same point is raised by A. Aftalion, "Les trois notions de la productivité et les revenus," *Revue d'Economie Politique*, XXV (1911), 145–84.

distribution rest, which may be called the Law of Final Economic Efficiency, minute increments of the agent whose efficiency is testing [sic] need to be used.[1]

The most fundamental defect in Clark's theory, however, is its reliance on two "factors" of production: social labor and social capital. Units of productive services must be defined, of course, in order that one may talk about quantitative variations. Units of services cannot be classified on the basis of productivity without all the services losing their identities, for on this basis they all become homogeneous, as indeed Clark sees.[2] The modern practice is to define productive services in their own physical units, *i.e.*, an hour of common day labor, or acre years of a certain type of agricultural land.

But Clark resorts to a third definition of units of services, by which he seeks to reduce all labor to social labor, all capital goods (including land) to social capital, and, indeed, all productive services (and all of their products) to one comparable basis not directly involving productivity.[3] The rationale of this approach is not clear; mere relative values will not suffice, says Clark, because they do not enable us to compute the interest rate of "the wealth of a nation" (pp. 374–75). "For these purposes,—and for more than it is now necessary to enumerate,—" (p. 375), marginal utility is used as the unit to measure all economic quantities. Since, by Jevonian

[1] "Wages and Interest as Determined by Marginal Productivity," *Journal of Political Economy*, X (1901–2), 108.

[2] Thus, p. 374 n.: "It is clear that the product of capital cannot, in such connections as these, be the basis of the measurement of capital. If we say that whatever produces a unit of consumers' wealth is a unit of capital, we assert nothing by adding that, at any one time, all units of capital are equally productive. On the other hand, when we say that a series of units of capital show diminishing returns, while still measuring the units by their products, we assert what is a self-contradiction."

[3] Most of the relevant discussion is in Chap. xxiv; cf. also pp. 63, 190, 207, 298.

analysis, marginal utility is equal to marginal disutility of labor at equilibrium, the latter, as measured by society, is actually chosen (pp. 378 ff.). It would require many pages to explore the assumptions underlying this procedure, such as the measurability and comparability of utilities and disutilities,[1] the incidence on the doctrine of the division of labor,[2] and similar conditions. The palpable unrealism of this peculiar combination of Smith's labor theory and extreme nineteenth-century hedonism is enough, however, to justify passing on without further comment.

The Theory of Capital and the Interest Rate

Although Clark is famous primarily for his exposition of the marginal productivity theory, a strong case can be made for the proposition that he plays a more important role in the history of capital theory. The marginal productivity theory, that is to say, was already established in the 1890's; Clark's capital theory contains some excellent points generally minimized or ignored by Anglo-Saxon economists. As far as the writers in the present study are concerned, his views are most closely affiliated with those of Walras; Clark's analysis is definitely superior in certain respects.

The fundamental thesis is well known: "capital" is the name of two fundamentally different things. It may refer to the concrete capital goods, *e.g.*, machinery, equipment, raw materials, and land,[3] or it may refer to "social" or "pure" capital, meaning the (permanent)

[1] Clark asserts that utilities are measurable only ordinally (p. 380); yet he speaks of consumers' surplus and allied notions (pp. 383 ff.).

[2] Which he says does not affect the principles involved (p. 379).

[3] Clark peremptorily excludes labor from this group, on emphatic but not very cogent grounds (pp. 116–17). The distinction between concrete and abstract capital was first advanced in "Capital and Its Earnings," *op. cit.*, pp. 9–18.

value of transitory concrete goods. The concrete capital goods include all material aids to production, excluding labor (p. 116). This criterion of materiality is an unreasonable one; it may perhaps be explained by Clark's peculiar definition of a stationary economy, which excludes such things as patents (p. 76 n.).

The essential distinction between concrete capital goods and capital as a "quantum of wealth" is expressed as follows:

> The most distinctive single fact about what we have termed capital is the fact of permanence. It lasts; and it must last, if industry is to be successful. Trench upon it—destroy any of it, and you have suffered a disaster. Destroy all that you have of it, and you must begin empty-handed to earn a living, as best you can, by labor alone. Yet you must destroy capital-goods in order not to fail. Try to preserve capital goods from destruction, and you bring on yourself the same disaster that you suffer when you allow a bit of capital to be destroyed. Stop the machines in your mill that they may not wear out, wrap and box them in order that they may not rust out, and the productive action of your capital stops. What is more, the capital itself will also ultimately perish; for your machines will, in time, become so antiquated that it will be impracticable to use them.
>
> Capital-goods, then, not only *may* go to destruction, but *must* be destroyed . . . (p. 117).[1]

Capital, on the other hand, is "an abstract quantum of productive wealth, a permanent fund— . . . an abstraction" (p. 119).

Both of Clark's concepts are expressed poorly, and as a result they have frequently given rise to an intrinsically unwarranted charge of mysticism. If the superficial paradox regarding the permanence of capital and the de-

[1] The penultimate sentence is of course inapplicable in Clark's stationary state; no machine would ever become "antiquated."

structibility of capital goods is abandoned, the fundamental and important argument may be restated as follows. Concrete capital goods may wear out rapidly or slowly or not at all,—the last case is improperly attributed to land (pp. 118, 121–22). Whether and how fast concrete goods wear out, however, is fundamentally a matter of minor importance; it is a technical datum. From the economic point of view, the important fact is that the product of such capital goods contains adequate provision for maintenance or replacement or both, and this provision is made (currently or via reserves) before the net yield is computed.

This eminently sensible statement is really what Clark's position amounts to. There are many passages in the *Distribution* to the effect that the permanence of "pure" capital is really brought about by a policy of maintenance or replacement of concrete goods: [1]

> The fact that a mill wears out, and has to be reconstructed or altogether replaced, does not, of itself, contribute to production. It is not a welcome fact in the experience of the owner of the mill, and he permits it to occur only so far as it is unavoidable (p. 148).
>
> Only where an endless succession of instruments does more than to maintain itself—only where such a series of capital-goods creates a net surplus for its owner—is capital, as such, productive (p. 271).

This fact of the ability of a concrete capital good to produce a net return is a "literal and concrete fact" (p. 272). The only real objection to be offered against Clark's formulation of the capital concept is that it is based on material wealth, rather than on the discounting of the values of a series of income rights. In spite of this unfortunate classical bias, he inconsistently excludes durable consumers' goods from capital (pp. 154, 273 n.).

[1] Cf. also pp. 250 ff., 262–64, 268 ff., 272–73, 278, 335, 341–42.

The relation of abstinence to the growth of capital deserves brief mention. Abstinence means the exchanging of present consumption goods for "wealth-creating goods" (p. 126), *i.e.*, for perpetual future income.

> Abstinence is the relinquishment, once for all, of a certain pleasure from consumption and the acquisition of a wholly new increment of capital. The particular enjoyment that the man might have had, if he had spent his money for consumers' goods, he will never have if he saves it. He has abandoned it forever; and, as an offset for it, he will get interest (p. 134; also p. 139).

Abstinence therefore leads to new capital goods, and no additional abstinence is required for the maintenance of the existing capital stock (pp. 127, 133, 134). The notion of saving and dissaving (*i.e.*, the notion of a "single investment," liquidated in consumption) is properly rejected because it is not descriptive of actual behavior (pp. 130–31).[1]

Although Clark is emphatic in asserting that the amount of capital is fixed in a stationary economy, he rests this fact not on the definition of a stationary economy, but on the following argument: "In the static state there is no abstinence or creation of new capital; because, with the capital now on hand, men would lose more by foregoing pleasure and making their fund larger than they would gain by doing so" (p. 136). This is not at all compatible with his general thesis that the stationary state is an abstraction; it is much more the classical view, that an economy becomes stationary because the forces making for growth have been exhausted.

The interest rate is determined by the marginal productivity of capital (pp. 82 ff.). This doctrine is expanded in certain respects. First, it is the marginal productivity

[1] Cf. also "The Genesis of Capital," *Yale Review*, II (1893–94), 302–15.

of capital, not of capital goods, that determines the interest rate. This point is important, Clark holds, because the increment of capital usually manifests itself in a qualitative change in the existing capital goods, not in the addition of identical capital instruments (pp. 246 ff., 266 ff.). A single unit of a concrete good could not be withdrawn without deranging the entire plant.

> It is clear that this final increment of the capital of this industry [railroads] is not one that can be physically taken out of it, as it could be if it consisted of a few locomotives or a few cars that could be sold to another company. It is in the plant to remain. It runs through the whole tissue of the complex instrumentality that engineers, trainmen, superintendents, etc., make use of in the carrying of goods and persons. If we wish to make a good test of the productive power of this particular bit of capital, we should have to invoke a magic that would at once shrink the whole plant into inferiority (p. 251).

Depreciation of the existing capital goods gradually permits the readaptation of forms, however, and the increment of capital is finally utilized so as to yield a maximum possible product.

Interest is defined as the percentage return on capital and rent is defined as the yield of a concrete capital good, so the two are really different names for the same return (pp. 123 ff.). Clark does not face the difficult problem, however, of how the quantity of capital is to be measured,[1] although he seems to imply that capital value is determined by the cost of production of concrete goods (pp. 125, 140 n.). It is apparent that he is aware of interest during construction (p. 140 n.), but this element plays no significant role in his theory.

[1] Except, of course, in terms of the marginal disutility of labor, already referred to in the previous section.

A final aspect of Clark's capital theory which merits attention is his attack on Böhm-Bawerk's theory.[1] Clark combats the view that, in a stationary economy, capital consists of "advances" to laborers.[2] His first ground is essentially that parity of reasoning would require that advances also be made to the capitalists in the early stages of production (pp. 154–56). This disputable point is supplemented by a much more important argument against the concept of a period of production.

Concrete capital goods do have periods of production (pp. 127–28). One can speak of the lapse of time between the construction and the complete utilization of a machine. But this is a technical irrelevance; capital, in contrast with concrete goods, is perpetual, and has for its role the synchronization of production and consumption. Suppose a certain type of tree requires fifty years to mature; then in a stationary economy there will be fifty rows of trees, of all possible ages between one and fifty years. We can say that any one row takes fifty years to mature, but since there is a constant rate of output of timber forever, there is simply no point in saying it (pp. 131–33).

[1] Compare, *supra*, Chap. VIII. Clark's criticisms were presented first in "The Genesis of Capital," *op. cit.*, and "The Origin of Interest," *Quarterly Journal of Economics*, IX (1894–95), 257–78.

[2] Periodicities of production, as with agricultural products, are ruled out, since the notion of "advances" is applicable to uniform production, if at all (pp. 150–52). Clark's opposition to the notion of capital as "advances" antedates the appearance of Böhm-Bawerk's theory. Thus, in "Capital and Its Earnings" (1888), two errors are pointed out. The first is that wages represent product already in the hands of the entrepreneur (*op. cit.*, p. 20). This objection is partially retracted, for it is admitted that during the payroll interval the laborers have been capitalists (*ibid.*, p. 27 n.). The second objection, from the viewpoint of concrete capital goods, is that, although consumption goods must be available for the worker, they form an "exchanging stock" (in which wages may be invested) which bears no fixed relation to the possible wage rate (*ibid.*, pp. 21–23). Clark had not yet arrived at his crucial thesis, the simultaneity of production and consumption.

From the viewpoint of capital, therefore, the fact of maintenance and replacement means that capital *per se* is invested forever.

> If the first hatchet was made by labor, without any capital created still earlier, then the life of the unit of productive wealth has a beginning; but it has no end. Its existence is bounded on one side, but not on the other. When we create a bit of new capital, we start another endless period: we do not lengthen any period that has already begun (p. 137).
>
> It is, in short, possible to add to the units of capital that are to exist through the ages; but it is not possible to add to the ages through which capital exists (p. 138).

The only correct way to view the production process is as the synchronization of production and consumption (pp. 305 ff.). In a stationary economy there is a uniform flow of consumers' goods (abstracting from periodicities) and a uniform flow of productive services calculated to maintain the output of consumers' goods.

One cannot escape this objection by turning to the concrete capital goods, granted that these do have definite production periods. An increase of capital may not involve a lengthening of the period of production of capital goods (pp. 138–39). We may substitute a dozen ferry-boats for a bridge, and thereby shorten the production period—although either alternative requires the same amount of capital. This latter criticism is less penetrating; it grants too much to Böhm-Bawerk.[1]

Clark's theory of capital is fundamentally sound, in the writer's opinion. The treatment is not complete; in particular, the important questions relating to the construction of capital goods (the investment process) are scarcely

[1] Clark goes so far as to say that the production period of concrete goods is usually lengthened when capital increases, because the goods are made more durable (p. 140 n.).

recognized, let alone solved. On the other hand, his emphasis on capital as having considerable mobility (over longer periods of time), and yielding a perpetual income, is an important insight.

The Theory of Rent

The most extensive analysis of the Ricardian rent theory, particularly with regard to its historical pretensions, was presented in "Capital and Its Earnings." [1] The indestructibility of the soil is denied, except for its spatial aspect, and this is so large in supply that it is a free good.[2] Fertility is controllable, as is also the general economic location of land.[3] There remains a "residual utility" in being located near a market, by which Clark seems to mean that as long as it costs anything to transport goods, land in the immediate vicinity of a market will have some rent of location.[4] Except for this last element, which is of decreasing importance, land has a definite supply price based on cost of production.[5]

From this argument, Clark goes on to interpret the Ricardian theory as an explanation of the return to all concrete goods in the short run, and not as a "normal" return. Since the fundamental passage contains the first approach to a marginal productivity theory in Clark's writings, it merits full quotation:

> Here is a piece of land; let us test by the rule the rent that may be had from it.
>
> We take its product as a minuend, and, for a subtrahend, let the eye range downward through the list of similar instruments till it falls on a field that yields just enough to pay

[1] *Op. cit.*, pp. 32 ff.
[2] *Ibid.*, pp. 33–34.
[3] *Ibid.*, pp. 34, 36. Transportation improvements "may be said to manufacture place utility in land" (*ibid.*, p. 34).
[4] *Ibid.*, pp. 35–36.
[5] *Ibid.*, pp. 40, 46–47, 54.

> wages on the amount of labor spent on the field that we are testing, and interest on the auxiliary capital used in connection with it. This, we can prove, is the poorest field that it will pay to cultivate, and we call it the poorest in actual cultivation. If worse ones are, in fact, in use, we throw them out of account. The income from our test farm then obeys the rule,—rent equals product minus such other product as ought to be, and probably is, equal to wages and interest on auxiliary capital. The rent of any instrument is gauged by its capacity to enlarge the product of industry. Let x units of labor and y units of capital command in the general field of industry a product expressed by z. Give to their owners an instrument of production to aid them in some process; and if the product is now $z + 1$ the rent of the instrument is 1. This is all that can be mathematically gotten out of the Ricardian formulae; but such as it is, the rule is of universal application.[1]

He reaffirms that this marginal analysis is universal in application, but it is apparent that he does not yet see the full significance of the approach.[2]

Land is not, to Clark, a separate factor of production; it is merely a special type of concrete capital goods (pp. 189, 190 n.). The two distinguishing characteristics of land, from the classical viewpoint, are held to be invalid. The first characteristic, fixity of the supply of land, is true of all productive services in the stationary state (pp. 338 ff.). This is of course true, but hardly relevant. The classical economists thought that the supply of land was fixed; Clark *defines* the supplies of all productive services to be fixed. He seems actually to concede the historical fixity of the supply of land (pp. 189, 256).

[1] *Ibid.*, pp. 41–42.

[2] *Ibid.*, p. 44: "The law becomes, indeed, a circuitous statement of the simple truth stated by Adam Smith when he said, in effect, that the rent of land is its product less what a tenant must reserve for wages and interest."

The corollary of Clark's position is much more significant. The supply of land in any one industry is completely variable, exactly as is true of the supply of "artificial" capital (pp. 340 ff.). Not all land is equally adaptable to numerous uses, but enough is on the margin of transference to insure that the rate of return on land in different occupations will be equalized—exactly as with capital.[1]

The second characteristic of land, in the classical theory, which is the differential nature of its return, is held to be equally true of all distributive shares. This generalization of the rent concept was first advanced by Clark in 1891,[2] simultaneously with J. A. Hobson.[3] This point is too familiar at present to require more than a brief summary.[4] In the Ricardian theory, the amount of land is held constant and the amount of capital-and-labor is varied. The capital-and-labor is paid at the rate of its marginal productivity, and the surplus or residual is rent. By parallel reasoning, one may hold the amount of capital-and-labor constant and vary the amount of land, thus determining interest-and-wages as a residual and rent as a marginal product.[5]

Although the general tenor of Clark's discussion is critical toward the Ricardian theory, he vacillates on many issues and makes several unnecessary concessions.[6] Thus he admits, unnecessarily, that a remission of rents will not affect prices, although this is held to be true also

[1] Pp. 342–44. There is one difference, according to Clark: capital can, in the long run, become completely mobile; special aptitudes in land remain forever—which nullifies the position in the text.

[2] "Distribution as Determined by a Law of Rent," *op. cit.*

[3] "The Law of the Three Rents," *ibid.*, 263–88.

[4] Compare, *infra*, Chap. XII.

[5] Pp. 192–200, 299–300, 330 ff., 345 ff., 361 ff.

[6] As a matter of fact, in one passage (p. 372) the Ricardian theory is accepted as a "dynamic" law, with only trivial reservations.

of the other distributive shares.[1] Rent is held to be a cost of production on two erroneous grounds: because land affects the quantities of goods produced (p. 357), and because rent is determined by the marginal productivity theory (p. 358). He now also concedes that land has no cost of production (p. 339), and in a later work goes so far as to assert that land is indestructible if it is properly cultivated.[2]

Wages and Profits

Besides a marginal productivity theory of wages, Clark offers a pain cost explanation of the supply of labor. His analysis is virtually identical with that of Jevons: the duration of labor per day is set at the point where the marginal utility of the laborer's product equals the marginal disutility of his labor.[3] Clark recognizes that "gangs of men are tied to the steam whistle" (p. 383), but he fails to redeem his promise to solve this difficulty.

The relationship of risks to profits is developed in an early essay arising out of the contemporary discussion of the so-called "risk" theory of profits.[4] Certain risks would be present even in a stationary economy, *e.g.*, fire. The assumption of such risks is paid for, not according to the objective actuarial values of the risks, but according to their subjective (utility) actuarial values, *i.e.*, the

[1] Pp. 358 ff. Much is made of this argument when it is first presented, in "Possibility of a Scientific Law of Wages," *op. cit.*, pp. 64 ff.

[2] *Essentials of Economic Theory*, p. 180.

[3] Pp. 382 ff. He differs from Jevons only in holding that the disutility of labor increases continuously from the first hour of labor (pp. 383 ff.). This doctrine was first elaborated in "The Ultimate Standard of Value," *Yale Review*, I (1892–93), 258–74. In "Patten's Dynamic Economics," *Annals of the American Academy*, III (1892–93), 30–34, the foregoing of leisure is added to the "weariness" of labor as the second component of the disutility of labor.

[4] "Insurance and Business Profit," *Quarterly Journal of Economics*, VII (1892–93), 40–45.

various objective probabilities of losses of various amounts, multiplied by the appropriate marginal utilities.[1] We may pass over this hedonistic refinement to consider the role of the entrepreneur and the theory of "pure" profits.

The entrepreneur is presumably a type of laborer, in Clark's theory. The entrepreneurial function is that of coordinating the other productive factors, labor and capital (pp. 3, 289–90). Dynamic changes suddenly bring these coordinators into existence, but they disappear as soon as the dynamic changes have ended.[2] Under stationary conditions, the entrepreneur becomes a superintendent, presumably just one type of laborer (p. 111). It is not necessary to reproduce here Professor Knight's criticism of Clark's theory; [3] the essential point is that it is the uncertainty which comes from historical change (*i.e.*, not subject to "laws," including laws of probability, and hence not always correctly anticipated), and not the change itself, that gives rise to pure profits.

[1] *Ibid.*, esp. pp. 43 ff. In symbols, let a_j be the probability of losing j dollars per year, and let v_j be the marginal utility of the jth dollar. Then the premium for static risks must be

$$\sum_{j=1}^{k} a_j v_j$$

where k is the total amount risked.

[2] Pp. 78–81, 179, 290–91. It is suggested that the entrepreneur's return under dynamic conditions is equal to his marginal product.

[3] *Risk, Uncertainty and Profit* (Cambridge, 1921), Chap. ii.

Chapter XII

EULER'S THEOREM AND THE MARGINAL PRODUCTIVITY THEORY

THE completion of the marginal productivity theory of distribution was achieved only with the development of the proof that if all productive agents are rewarded in accord with their marginal products, then the total product will be exactly exhausted. This exhaustion-of-product problem is of course unique to the general marginal productivity theory. In this respect previous distribution theories fall into one of two categories. The residual theories form the first group. Distribution theories of this type always premised at least one residual share; in the classical system, rent was accorded this position in a first dichotomy, "profit" in a second. Clearly no problem of the exhaustion of the product can arise when there is a residual claimant. The second general category includes all distribution theories in which the exhaustion of the product by distributive shares is made an explicit *assumption*. In this class fall the doctrines based on fixed coefficients of production which were advanced by Walras and Wieser, and their more recent followers. Only the marginal productivity theory has determined separately the share of each productive factor.[1] Only the marginal productivity theory, consequently, has been confronted by the question, does this method exactly exhaust the total product?

[1] But, as we shall see, frequently the exhaustion-of-product was assumed even by marginal productivity theorists.

It has been shown that Wicksell had already answered this question in the affirmative in 1893, and that Edgeworth's discussion in 1889 strongly implied the same answer. But it was Philip Wicksteed who first raised the question explicitly, in his magnificent *Co-ordination of the Laws of Distribution* in 1894. Thereafter almost every important European economist of our period offered contributions to a discussion which did not lack either personalities or arguments.[1] Wicksell was Wicksteed's leading contemporary defender; Edgeworth, Pareto, Barone, and Walras led in the attack on the theory (and sometimes on the man). It is this controversy which the present chapter seeks to summarize and evaluate. Valuable though incomplete references to the literature of the controversy have been made by Schultz,[2] Hicks,[3] Robbins,[4] Douglas,[5] and Joan Robinson,[6] but these writers have neither treated in detail nor evaluated the positions of the various participants in the controversy.

Arthur Berry

Before turning to Wicksteed, it may be in order to note one of the earliest mathematical formulations of the marginal productivity theory, that of Arthur Berry.[7] The theory was presented in a paper, "The Pure Theory of Distribution," which was read before Section F of the

[1] The controversy was mathematical, and this eliminated the contemporary American economists except Fisher, who did not participate in the discussion.

[2] "Marginal Productivity and the General Pricing Process," *Journal of Political Economy*, XXXVII (1929), 505–51.

[3] *The Theory of Wages* (London, 1932), Appendix i.

[4] Introduction to the reprint of the *Commonsense of Political Economy* (London, 1933), I, ix–xi.

[5] *The Theory of Wages* (New York, 1934), Chap. ii.

[6] "Euler's Theorem and the Problem of Distribution," *Economic Journal*, XLIV (1934), 398–414.

[7] The writer's attention was directed to Berry by Professor Viner.

British Association in 1890.[1] The writer has not been able to find a single reference to this paper in the literature, although Marshall and Edgeworth attended the session and delivered papers. Marshall, moreover, acknowledged assistance from Berry on the mathematical appendix to the first three editions of the *Principles.*[2]

Berry's analysis deals with the individual entrepreneur. He assumes the prices of the productive services and of the product to be fixed, and further assumes that the entrepreneurial labor does not change with small changes in output. The following symbols are employed:

$g_1, g_2, g_3, \cdots =$ yards of land of qualities 1, 2, 3, $\cdots$;
$l_1, l_2, l_3, \cdots =$ hours of labor of qualities 1, 2, 3, $\cdots$;
$c =$ capital (in pounds sterling);
$\rho_k =$ rent per yard of land of k quality;
$w_j =$ wages per hour of labor of j quality;
$i =$ interest rate per annum;
$p_1 =$ price of the product of entrepreneur 1.

A production function is defined: $f_1(g_1, g_2, g_3, \cdots l_1, l_2, \cdots, c)$, where "the form of f depends on the entrepreneur's skill, 'opportunity,' etc." [3] The "equations of marginal productivity" are then

$$p_1 \frac{\partial f_1}{\partial g_k} = \rho_k; \cdots$$

$$p_1 \frac{\partial f_1}{\partial l_j} = w_j; \cdots$$

and

$$p_1 \frac{\partial f_1}{\partial c} = i.$$

The return to the entrepreneur is a residual, *i.e.*, $p_1 \cdot f - \Sigma g\rho - \Sigma lw - ci$.

[1] A summary of the paper is printed in the *Report of the British Association for the Advancement of Science* (1890), pp. 923–24.

[2] Compare the respective prefaces of the *Principles.*

[3] "The Pure Theory of Distribution," *op. cit.*, p. 924.

For the economy as a whole, there are the additional equations that express the full utilization of land, labor, and capital. Allowance for the consumption demand for resources may be added to the demand by entrepreneurs. The supply of labor is determined by the disutility function, *i.e.*,

$$w_j = \frac{dx(\Sigma l_j)}{dl_j}$$

where x is the "average" disutility function for laborers of j quality.

Since Berry's theory still contains a residual ("profits"), he avoids the exhaustion-of-product problem. The older English conception of the entrepreneur inhibits the application of marginal productivity analysis in Berry's case as in Edgeworth's. Berry deserves passing credit, however, for his early anticipation of the marginal productivity theory.

Philip H. Wicksteed

Philip H. Wicksteed's *Co-ordination of the Laws of Distribution* (1894)[1] is enough alone to insure for him a place of lasting importance in the history of economic thought.

[1] In the present study the London School Reprint, No. 12 (London, 1932), is used. The *Co-ordination* contained numerous misprints, which were corrected in an unbound reprint also dated 1894. Certain of these slips were corrected by Wicksteed in the original, bound edition; others may have been pointed out by W. S. Johnson, in whose copy they are entered. Johnson's copy contains no important comments. The London School Reprint still contains several misprints:

Page 31, line 1	For $F(c) - cF(c)$ substitute $F(c) - cF'(c)$.
Page 36, line 3	It seems clear that $f(x)$ is price, so the text should read $xf(x)$, as it did in the original edition.
Page 44, line 16	For $\int f_c(x)$ substitute $\int f_c(x)dx$.

I am indebted to Professor Viner for both calling my attention to and permitting me to use the various copies of the *Co-ordination* referred to in this note. I am also indebted to the London School of Economics for permission to quote from the reprint.

The *Co-ordination* is a small brochure, a mere fifty-three pages in length, yet its daring and its originality command the highest respect.

The title of the brochure expresses well its major theme: the reduction of all distributive shares to one, and therefore a comparable, basis. Wicksteed's criticism of received distribution theory is so succinct as to deserve full quotation:

> In investigating the laws of distribution it has been usual to take each of the great factors of production such as Land, Capital and Labour, severally, to enquire into the special circumstances under which that factor co-operates in production, the special considerations which act upon the persons that have control of it, and the special nature of the service that it renders, and from all these considerations to deduce a special law regulating the share of the product that will fall in distribution to that particular factor.
>
> Now as long as this method is pursued it seems impossible to co-ordinate the laws of distribution and ascertain whether or not the shares which the theory assigns to the several factors cover the product and are covered by it. For in order that this may be possible it seems essential that all the laws should be expressed in common terms. As long as the law of rent, for example, is based on the objective standard of fertility of land, while the law of interest is based on the subjective standard of estimate of the future as compared with the present, it is difficult even to conceive any calculus by which the share of land and the share of capital could be added together and an investigation then instituted as to whether the residual share will coincide with what the theory assigns as the share of wages.[1]

The basis selected for coordinating the factors is *service rendered*, a parallel explicitly drawn from the marginal utility theory of value. Just as the marginal utility of a commodity determines its value, so the marginal efficiency of a productive factor will determine its value.

[1] *Ibid.*, p. 7.

The marginal efficiency of a factor is determined by "the effect upon the product of a small increment of that factor, all the others remaining constant." [1] If P is product and K is capital, then $\frac{\partial P}{\partial K}$ is the marginal efficiency of capital, and $\frac{\partial P}{\partial K} \cdot K$ is the share of capital in the total product. It is held "self-evident," even a "truism," that each factor is paid at a rate equal to the product added by a unit of that resource.[2] Everyone knows that units of a factor will be hired up to the point where the added product just covers the added cost. The sensible employer will "take on more men as long as the last one earns at least as much as his wage, but no longer." [3]

The crucial problem in the coordination of the laws of distribution, Wicksteed believes, is to show that the sum of the payments to each factor, at the rate of its marginal productivity, exactly exhausts the total product. If $P = F(A,B,C, \cdots)$, where P is product and $A,B,C, \cdots$ are the various factors of production, it must be shown that

$$P = \frac{\partial P}{\partial A} \cdot A + \frac{\partial P}{\partial B} \cdot B + \frac{\partial P}{\partial C} \cdot C + \cdots.$$

This theorem can be deduced from numerous points of view, the simplest of which is to assume outright that the production function is homogeneous and linear. That is, if $\lambda P = F(\lambda A, \lambda B, \lambda C, \cdots)$, then the desired conclusion follows almost immediately.[4] Wicksteed does not utilize

[1] *Ibid.*, pp. 8–9 (italicized by Wicksteed). The question of whether physical efficiency or value product is intended will be examined below.

[2] *Ibid.*, pp. 9–10.

[3] *Ibid.*, p. 12.

[4] For the proof, cf. W. F. Osgood, *Advanced Calculus* (New York, 1935), pp. 121–22; or E. B. Wilson, *Advanced Calculus* (Boston, 1912), pp. 107–8,

directly this well-known property, the so-called Euler theorem,[1] although he explicitly states the assumption of homogeneity and linearity at numerous points.[2] The explanation probably lies in the uneven nature of Wicksteed's mathematical training; in this field he was self-taught.[3]

Whatever the reason, Wicksteed chooses instead to prove the exhaustiveness of the distribution by the marginal productivity method by reconciling this theory

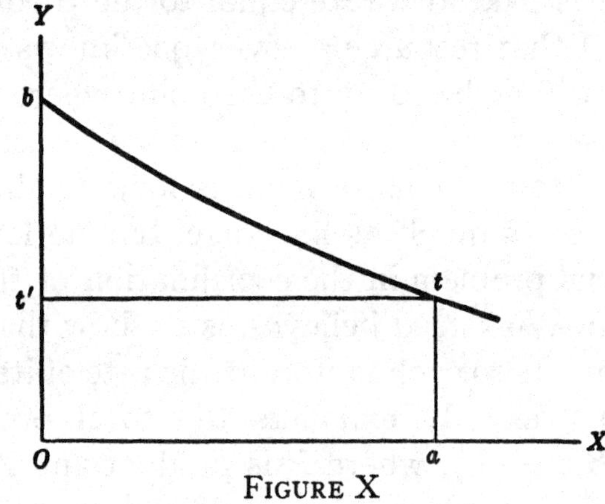

FIGURE X

with the classical theory of rent. Because he says perhaps as many judicious things about the Ricardian theory as one man has ever said, this portion of his analysis deserves detailed presentation. Wicksteed follows the conventional graphic analysis shown above. Let *OX* represent units of capital-and-labor, per unit of land, and *OY* product; then *bt* represents the marginal produc-

[1] Wicksteed did not mention that this was in fact Euler's theorem; A. W. Flux was the first to associate the theorem with Euler, in his review of Wicksteed, *Economic Journal*, IV (1894), 311.

[2] *Co-ordination*, pp. 4, 15, 24.

[3] In a letter to Walras, dated October 10, 1884, Wicksteed wrote that he found the first edition of the *Eléments* difficult to read, because "my knowledge of mathematics is so limited." Again, in the preface to the *Alphabet of Economic Science* (London, 1888), Wicksteed apologizes for his "want of systematic mathematical training" (p. xiii).

tivity of capital-and-labor, under the usual assumptions regarding returns.[1] Interest-and-wages are *Oatt'*; rent is the residual, *btt'*.

Three important theorems are deduced from the classical theory. First, the Ricardian theory deals exclusively with proportions; *OX* represents the *ratio* of capital-and-labor to land, *bt* the marginal product of capital-and-labor, *at* is the return *per unit* of capital-and-labor,[2] and *btt'* is the return *per unit* of land.[3] It follows that the theory does not depend upon absolute magnitudes. Secondly, the procedure is obviously reversible. When we move to the right on *OX*, we increase the amount of capital-and-labor per unit of land; when we move to the left we increase the amount of land relative to capital-and-labor.[4] And thirdly, as a corollary of the second observation, rent may be shown to be the marginal productivity of land and interest-and-wages the residual. Graphically the sole difference is that *OX* now represents land per unit of capital-and-labor, *OY* the product per unit of land. This reversing of the rent theory is not original to Wicksteed, as we have seen,[5] but certainly there is no clearer statement in the earlier literature.

The next step is to show the compatibility of the classical theory with the marginal productivity theory. Under the classical theory, a marginal productivity theory is offered for that "idealised amalgam," capital-and-labor, for *at* is clearly $\frac{dp}{dc}$, where p is product and c is capital-and-labor per unit of land. The total share of

[1] Wicksteed defines the condition of diminishing returns correctly, still a rare feat in 1894. That is, if $F(x)$ is product where x is capital-and-labor, $F''(x) < 0$ (*Co-ordination*, pp. 13–14).

[2] This coordinate is introduced primarily for symmetry. Compare the acute discussion of dimensions (*ibid.*, pp. 15, 19 n.).

[3] *Ibid.*, pp. 14–15. [4] *Ibid.*, pp. 15–23, *passim*. [5] Cf., *supra*, Chap. xi.

capital-and-labor is therefore *Oa* times *at* or $\frac{dp}{dc} \cdot c$. Similarly, under the reversal (where land is now applied to capital-and-labor), the share of land is $\frac{dp}{dl} \cdot l$. The two marginal productivities are complementary, not inconsistent, for an increase in the capital-and-labor per unit of land is also a decrease of land per unit of capital-and-labor. Both points of view lead to increasing rent per unit of land and decreasing interest-and-wages per unit of capital-and-labor.

But to show that rent as a marginal product is not inconsistent with rent as a residual is not to show that the two rents are identical. This is the last stage in the argument. In its development Wicksteed employs a very complex set of symbols and six pages of clumsy and involved mathematics.[1] We shall use here the greatly simplified condensation given by Flux in his review of the *Co-ordination*.[2] The following symbols will be employed:

C = capital-and-labor
L = land
$x = C/L$
$z = 1/x = L/C$
$F(x)$ = product per unit of land, when x units of C are applied to one unit of L
$\Phi(z)$ = product per unit of capital-and-labor, when z units of L are applied to one unit of C

Under the classical theory the rate of return to capital-and-labor is its marginal productivity, or $F'(x)$. The total share of the factor will be $xF'(x)$, so the residual rent will be

$$F(x) - xF'(x). \tag{1}$$

[1] *Co-ordination*, pp. 23–31.

[2] *Op. cit.*, pp. 308–13.

Since $F(x)$ is the total product of capital-and-labor per unit of land, $\frac{F(x)}{x}$ is the product per unit of capital-and-labor. This may be written

$$\Phi(z) = \frac{F(x)}{x} = zF(x). \tag{2}$$

Since $\frac{dx}{dz} = -\frac{1}{z^2}$, it follows that

$$\begin{aligned} \Phi'(z) &= F(x) + zF'(x)\frac{dx}{dz}, \\ &= F(x) - xF'(x). \end{aligned} \tag{3}$$

The total product is equal to the product per unit of capital-and-labor times the number of units of capital-and-labor, so we may write [1]

$$\begin{aligned} P &= C\Phi(z), \\ \partial P &= C\partial\Phi(z). \end{aligned} \tag{4}$$

We have defined $L = C \cdot z$, so if C is held constant, then

$$\partial L = C\partial z. \tag{5}$$

Divide now equation (4) by equation (5), to secure

$$\begin{aligned} \frac{\partial P}{\partial L} &= \frac{C\partial\Phi(z)}{C\partial z} = \frac{\partial\Phi(z)}{\partial z} \\ &= \Phi'(z). \end{aligned} \tag{6}$$

Substituting now from (6) into (3), and writing $\frac{\partial P}{\partial C}$ for $F'(x)$,

$$\frac{\partial P}{\partial L} = F(x) - \frac{C}{L} \cdot \frac{\partial P}{\partial C}$$

or

$$L \cdot \frac{\partial P}{\partial L} + C \cdot \frac{\partial P}{\partial C} = L \cdot F(x) = P. \tag{7}$$

[1] This is of course equivalent to the assumption that the production function is homogeneous and linear. This assumption is the basis of equation (4), which may be rewritten, $P = C\Phi\left(\frac{L}{C}\right)$, or, if $C = \frac{1}{\lambda}$, $\lambda P = \Phi(\lambda L)$.

The last equation is our desired result; the sum of the distributive shares, when each factor is remunerated at the rate of its marginal productivity, exactly exhausts the total product. Rent as a residual is equal to rent as a marginal product.

This development forms the basis of most of the controversy in the subsequent literature, yet Wicksteed does not leave the theory in this form. He considers, first, the limitation to two factors of production, land and capital-and-labor. The nature of the product (P), whether physical, commercial, or social, is then debated, and finally the role of competition in the theory is analyzed. We shall consider these points in turn.

Wicksteed is fully cognizant of the difficulty in grouping all factors except land into that catch-all, capital-and-labor. This hopper contains only an "idealised amalgam"; capital-and-labor is a "very vague factor" which includes "we know not what." [1] His proof in terms of only two factors seems rather clearly to be dictated by the limitations of plane geometry. Two methods (which really reduce to one) are proposed, however, for overcoming the difficulty. The first, which receives chief preference in the *Co-ordination*, is that of extending the theorem to an indefinite number of factors, say n:

> The formula is quite general. The unit of the particular kind of labour may be an hour of attention (of a given quality) to the management and direction of a business. . . . It may be land of given capacities . . . or tools. . . . Each factor is expressed in its own unit and treated as having its independent influence, at the margin, on the increment or decrement of the product.[2]

[1] *Co-ordination*, p. 20.

[2] *Ibid.*, pp. 12–13; also pp. 33–34, 47. Even risk-taking is mentioned as a factor of production (p. 42).

The second approach, which is implicit in the foregoing, assumes that all factors can be reduced to equivalence on the basis of their effect upon the product. The statement in the *Co-ordination* is not very clear or satisfactory on this point,[1] but in the later *Commonsense of Political Economy* (1910), the substitutability of factors is expressed with all desirable generality and precision.[2]

The consideration of the nature of the productivity function is in effect a defense of the assumption that the function is homogeneous and linear. If the product is interpreted in the sense of physical product, then "it is of course obvious that a proportional increase of all the factors of production will secure a proportional increase of the product." [3] This conclusion is based upon an implicit acceptance of the possibility of varying all of the factors of production while the product remains constant; [4] but Wicksteed offers no explicit defense.

As an alternative, the product may be the social utility. Since marginal utility decreases, the theorem then holds only if consumers are included among the factors of production.[5] This result is of no practical significance; let us pass to the third and important concept.

The fundamental concept of product for purposes of distribution theory is "commercial product," or the "amount of industrial vantage that command of that product confers on its possessor." [6] Euler's theorem holds rigorously only if the price of the commodity remains constant. Is this a permissible assumption? Strictly speaking, Wicksteed says, fixity of price will follow only if there is a corresponding increase in the

[1] Cf. pp. 39–40.
[2] Cf., *supra*, p. 48.
[3] *Co-ordination*, p. 33.
[4] Cf. *ibid.*, p. 37 n.
[5] *Ibid.*, pp. 34–35.
[6] *Ibid.*, p. 33.

"area of operations," *i.e.*, the market.[1] Yet "to assume this is obviously unwarrantable." [2]

Two escapes are found from this apparent dilemma. We may assume perfect competition, so that the effect of a single firm's output on price will be negligible.[3] Or, on the other hand, we may assume the demand to be highly elastic, so that, in modern terminology, marginal revenue differs little from price.[4] These two cases are, of course, analytically identical, but this refinement need not concern us. We emerge from the *Co-ordination* not with a universal law of distribution, but one which is appropriate to the usual assumptions of economic theory, under perfect competition.

Wicksteed's later contributions to our history may be summarized very briefly. In his review of Pareto's *Manuale* in 1906,[5] Wicksteed acknowledged the validity of the criticisms that Pareto had levied at the use of Euler's theorem.[6] The cogency of Edgeworth's "implicit application" of the same criticisms was acknowledged at the same time.[7] In the *Commonsense* the recantation was repeated, and the central argument was formally withdrawn.[8]

Whether these or other, unacknowledged, critics have really undermined Wicksteed's general marginal productivity theory we shall attempt to decide later. Here it is necessary to emphasize that his retraction was merely verbal; he continued to retain the fundamental assump-

[1] *Ibid.*, p. 34.

[2] *Ibid.*

[3] *Ibid.*, p. 36.

[4] *Ibid.*, pp. 36, 37. Wicksteed's statement is rigorously identical with that in the text. He writes $f(x)$ for price, where x is output, so total revenue is $xf(x)$ and the increment of revenue from a small increase of output is $f(x) + x \cdot f'(x)$. Wicksteed's condition is that $f'(x)$ be "insensible."

[5] Reprinted in the *Commonsense of Political Economy*, *op. cit.*, II, 814–18.

[6] Cf. Pareto, *infra*. [7] Cf. Edgeworth, *infra*. [8] *Op. cit.*, I, 373 n.

tion, that the production function is homogeneous and linear. Several grounds may be adduced for this assertion.[1] In the chapter on the *Commonsense* devoted to distribution theory,[2] Wicksteed elaborates the central doctrine that all factors of production can be substituted for one another:

> Within limits, the most apparently unlike of these factors of production can be substituted for each other at the margins, and so brought to a common measure of marginal serviceableness-in-production. Thus, though no amount of intelligence or industry can make bricks without straw, yet intelligence may economize straw, and one man with more intelligence and less straw may produce as good bricks as another with more straw and less intelligence.[3]

The doctrine is stated in all generality; even "managing ability may, at the margin, be a substitute for skill and intelligence in the hands, and vice versa." [4] From this substitutability "within limits" at the margin, it follows that all resources can be reduced to a common measure, that of performance. The solution of the distributive problem then follows easily. "We can now express the contributions made to the result by all the different factors in one and the same unit, and if we divide the proceeds by the sum of these units we shall determine the share to be claimed on account of each." [5] If the price of any factor does not equal its marginal product (in all

[1] Cf. Robbins, Introduction to the *Commonsense,* I, x–xi. Robbins also points out that Wicksteed used the explicit mathematical formula of the *Co-ordination* in his classes in 1905, after the criticisms had appeared (*Commonsense,* II, 849, 852). But this was one year before his first public retraction, so the point is inconclusive. And even the subsequent use of the theorem in classes would not mean much; recall Mill's reason for retaining the wages-fund doctrine in the seventh edition of his *Principles of Political Economy,* after admitting the validity of Thornton's criticisms (Ashley ed., New York, 1929, p. xxxi).

[2] Bk. I, Chap. ix.

[3] *Commonsense,* p. 361.

[4] *Ibid.,* p. 363; but also pp. 361–73, *passim.*

[5] *Ibid.,* p. 369.

employments), the quantity of that factor will be reduced or increased until this equality is secured; whatever the entrepreneur's resources, "he must so balance their application that the marginal significance of a pound is identical whether expended in wages, rent, interest, or however else." [1] This very satisfactory explanation of the general marginal productivity theory does not depend upon the assumption that the production function is homogeneous and linear, although it is open to another objection.[2] Elsewhere in the *Commonsense*, however, the homogeneity and linearity of the production function is still retained, as will now be shown.

The strongest proof that Wicksteed retained his earlier views, despite verbal changes, is contained in his chapter on rent in the *Commonsense*.[3] The entire argument of this chapter is based on the assumption that

> The scale of
>
> 1260 quarts per 80 land-units under 60 hours' cultivation is the scale of
>
> 630 quarts per 40 land-units under 30 hours' cultivation, . . . [4]

This is as explicit a statement that the production function is linear and homogeneous as could well be demanded. There seems to be doubt that Wicksteed retained his original theory; the sole question is why he ever made even a verbal abandonment of the thesis of the *Co-ordination*.

[1] *Ibid.*, p. 371.

[2] Cf., *infra*, pp. 386 f.

[3] Bk. II, Chap. vi.

[4] *Ibid.*, p. 555. Cf. "Scope and Method of Political Economy," reprinted in *Commonsense*, II, esp. p. 792: "But three pounds sterling applied to one acre is the same thing as a third of an acre coming under one pound's worth of culture, and five pounds per acre is a fifth of an acre per pound."

His abandonment of the general marginal productivity theory apparently was not due to the cogency of his critics' views. A small part of the explanation may lie in the sheer weight of the prestige of Edgeworth and Pareto. However, the real answer, the writer submits, is the widespread confusion in Wicksteed's theory of the laws of return. The chapter in the *Commonsense* on increasing and diminishing returns [1] is probably the least satisfactory section in that very able work. The fundamental weakness of his presentation, which is of crucial importance in the present connection, is his failure ever to subject the *firm* to analysis. He was therefore unable to develop fully the implicit assumptions on which his argument rests.

Flux, Chapman, Edgeworth

We may now turn to three English economists who directly or indirectly passed upon Wicksteed's theory in the period up to the World War. Flux reviewed the *Co-ordination* for the *Economic Journal* soon after its publication; two years later Chapman offered the first simple diagrammatic exposition; and Edgeworth criticized both Wicksteed and Chapman. This presentation, it should be noted, will not be strictly chronological.

A. W. Flux's review of the *Co-ordination* is in some respects a genuine improvement over Wicksteed's original statement.[2] Thus his proof, which was adopted above, that rent as a residual is equal to rent as a marginal product, is much more elegant than Wicksteed's development. Flux emphasizes, moreover, the fact that the linear and homogeneous production function can easily be extended to an indefinite number of factors of production, to avoid the unreal two-factor analysis. This

[1] Bk. II, Chap. v; cf., *supra*, Chap. III.

[2] *Op. cit.*

emphasis should not lead to the unfair inference, however, that Wicksteed is not aware of this property.

Flux's reaction to the thesis of the *Co-ordination* is favorable but not enthusiastic. His chief objection is against the dismissal of the idea of rent as a residual:

> [Wicksteed is] . . . far from weakening the position of those who regard rent as a surplus. . . . To show that the payment for land may be expressed in the form of the marginal productivity of land does not destroy the value of the conception of it as a surplus. The essential feature which distinguishes the treatment of land and some other agents, and makes it useful to regard their earnings as a surplus, is that, even if the circumstances of society be such as to render their marginal usefulness very great indeed, either a considerable period must elapse before a changed supply of these agents modifies the excessive demands made on the existing supply, or else the supply is practically incapable of any change.[1]

This objection does not require comment, since it concedes Wicksteed's central thesis, the exhaustion of the product when the distributive shares are determined by the marginal productivity principle. Nevertheless, it may be asserted that even if one accepts the classical theory of rent, this theory loses little, and gains much in accuracy and clarity, if stated in terms of the marginal productivity theory. It may be noted that Flux in his later *Economic Principles* [2] is slightly more favorable to Wicksteed.

[1] *Ibid.*, p. 312. Cited approvingly by Edgeworth, *Collected Papers* (London, 1925), III, 272; and Marshall, *Principles* (4th ed., London, 1905), p. 609 n.

[2] London, 1904. In that work he says (p. 314), "A striking proposition is that expressed by Mr. Wicksteed in his discussion of the problem of distribution," and restates the Euler theorem. Flux also points out the fact that the theorem may hold in actual life for small though not for large values of the multiplier *m* (our λ, *supra*, p. 325): "If *m* be not far from unity, this proposition may be true for kinds of production for which it is not true for all values of *m*."

Sidney J. Chapman plays a relatively unimportant part in the controversy over the use of Euler's theorem. Yet his article, "The Remuneration of Employers," [1] deserves attention on three counts. He presents a most elegant diagrammatic proof that the residual share is equal to the marginal product of the factor receiving the residual. He introduces explicitly, although he does not solve, the problem of external economies; and finally, his analysis is necessary to an understanding of Edgeworth's objections to the general marginal productivity theory.

The diagrammatic exposition follows the orthodox practice of assuming only two factors, in this case entrepreneurs and laborers, each of which is homogeneous. The argument proves that entrepreneurs receive their marginal product, but by a parallel argument it can easily be shown to be true of land. Let the marginal productivity of successive units of labor hired by one entrepreneur (of which there are Z, in the given economy) be represented by DD' in the following graph.

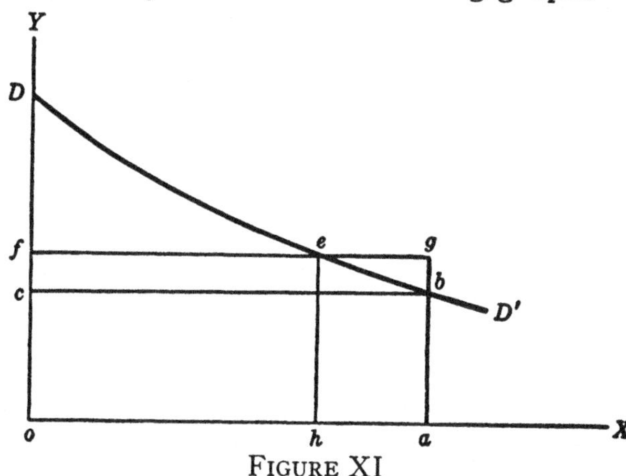

FIGURE XI

OX represents units of labor, OY the marginal product, as is customary. The total product of one entrepreneur

[1] *Economic Journal*, XVI (1906), 523–28.

is *OabD*, as there is *Oa* labor per entrepreneur. The wage rate is then *ab*, the wage bill *Oabc*, and profits of the employer *Dbc*. The total product of the economy is $Z \times OabD$.

Add, now, a similar employer to the economy. Each employer will then manage *Oh* laborers, if labor remains constant in supply, *ha* laborers going from each employer to the $(Z+1)$th entrepreneur. The new product per tract will be *OheD*,[1] of which *Ohef* is wages and *Def* profit. The total product of the economy will be

$$\begin{aligned}(Z+1)(OheD) &= Z \times OheD + OheD \\ &= Z \times OheD + Ohef + Def.\end{aligned}$$

It is necessary to show that $Ohef = Z \times hage$. This equality implies only that the new wage bill and the profits are equal for all employers. For *ha* is the total number of laborers yielded up by each of the *Z* employers of land to the $(Z+1)$th employer, and therefore $Z \times ha$ is the amount of labor hired by the $(Z+1)$th employer. By hypothesis this is equal to *Oh*.[2] Since all employers are equally productive, the marginal productivity of labor will be *he* for every employer. To continue:

$$\begin{aligned}(Z+1)(OheD) &= Z \times OheD + Def + Ohef \\ &= Z \times OheD + Def + Z \times hage \\ &= Z \times OheD + Def + Z \times heba + Z \\ &\quad \times egb.\end{aligned}$$

[1] Assuming that the *DD′* curve (*i.e.*, the productivity function) is not altered by the rearrangement of resources, *i.e.*, that the productivity function is homogeneous and linear, and that there are no external economies.

[2] Algebraically, the proof is as follows: $Z \times Oa = k =$ total labor in economy, before the $(Z+1)$th employer was added. $(Z+1) \times Oh = k$ = same amount of labor, after the addition of an employer. Therefore, $Z \times Oa = (Z+1) \times Oh = Z \times Oh + Oh$. But since $Oa = Oh + ha$, therefore, $Z \times Oa = Z \times Oh + Z \times ha = Z \times Oh + Oh$, so $Z \times ha = Oh$.

But the product before adding the $(Z + 1)$th employer was

$$Z \times OabD = Z \times OheD + Z \times heba.$$

Subtracting the old from the new product, we secure the additional product due to the $(Z + 1)$th employer, which is $Def + Z \times egb$. As Z becomes very great, however, ha, and with it $Z \times egb$, approach zero, and can be neglected. The residual *Def* is therefore identical with the marginal product *Def*.

The curve DD' will remain unchanged only if the number of employers does not affect the marginal productivity of labor in any given firm, *i.e.*, if there are no external economies. If external economies arise, the case may be called increasing returns; the curve DD' will rise as new entrepreneurs are added. This case is "highly probable," for an increased number of entrepreneurs will permit "intenser specialism of businesses." [1] It is sufficient to quote Chapman's conclusion for the case of increasing returns:

> When the number of employers is large, and returns are "increasing" as above explained, profits ultimately equal the marginal worth of employers less the effect wrought by the marginal employer on the product of each firm multiplied by the number of firms. As the increasing returns would be slow in revealing themselves, profits and the marginal worth of employers would for an appreciable time be indistinguishable amounts.[2]

The case of decreasing returns, due to external diseconomies, would be represented by a shift downward of the DD' curve. In this latter case, profits will exceed the marginal worth of employers.[3] The argument can readily

[1] "The Remuneration of Employers," *op. cit.*, p. 524.
[2] *Ibid.*, p. 525.
[3] *Ibid.*, p. 526.

be extended from entrepreneurs to other factors of production.[1]

Since Chapman is the only economist included in this study who has explicitly introduced external economies and diseconomies into the analysis of the marginal productivity theory, the problem may be disposed of at this point. Chapman states the production function as $f(x,z)$, where x is the amount of labor and z the number of entrepreneurs.[2] This approach implies that the number of

[1] The argument of this paragraph may be stated more precisely in mathematical form. Chapman's notation (*ibid.*, p. 526 n.) is slightly modified. Let

$$x = \text{laborers in one firm}$$
$$z = \text{employers}$$
$$P = f(x,z) = \text{product of one firm.}$$

Then
$$\frac{dP}{dz} = \frac{\partial P}{\partial x}\frac{dx}{dz} + \frac{\partial P}{\partial z}. \tag{1}$$

Since labor is held constant, $xz = c = \text{constant}$,

and
$$\frac{dx}{dz} = -\frac{x}{z},$$

Therefore,
$$\left(\frac{dP}{dz}\right)_c = \frac{\partial P}{\partial x}\left(-\frac{x}{z}\right) + \frac{\partial P}{\partial z} \tag{1.1}$$

and
$$\left(\frac{d[zP]}{dz}\right)_c = P + z\left(\frac{dP}{dz}\right)_c. \tag{2}$$

Substituting in (2) from (1.1),

$$\left(\frac{d[zP]}{dz}\right)_c = P + z\left[\frac{\partial P}{\partial x}\left(-\frac{x}{z}\right) + \frac{\partial P}{\partial z}\right] \tag{2.1}$$

or
$$P = \left(\frac{d[zP]}{dz}\right)_c + x\frac{\partial P}{\partial x} - z\frac{\partial P}{\partial z}.$$

Since $\frac{\partial P}{\partial x}$ is the wage rate, and $x\frac{\partial P}{\partial x}$ the wage bill, the residual of the product is equal to the marginal product of the employer, $\left(\frac{d[zP]}{dz}\right)_c$, plus or minus the effect of the number of firms on the output of each firm times the number of firms, or $z\frac{\partial P}{\partial z}$. If there are no external economies or diseconomies, $\frac{\partial P}{\partial z} = 0$.

[2] Since the *number* of firms is of only incidental importance in the theory of external economies, Pigou's notation (based on the size of the industry)

firms will be a function only of the number of entrepreneurs, and that is not true. Since entrepreneurs can become laborers, the size of the firm (and hence the number of firms) will be established at the point where its average costs are minimized,[1] given the demand conditions, technology, and supply conditions of the factors of production. Once this equilibrium position is reached, then $\frac{\partial f}{\partial z} = 0$. The number of firms never enters explicitly into the distribution problem, because it is not a variable in the individual firms' production function.[2] Chapman introduces z because his production function is that of the industry as a whole. The production function of the industry, however, simply has no significance to individual entrepreneurs in a competitive industry; only in "welfare" economics need such a function be posited.

Edgeworth's role in the controversy is neither important nor praiseworthy. Some of his arguments are nothing more than ridicule; the remainder are based upon rather obvious misapprehensions. His more vehement comment is well known:

> This [*i.e.*, the linear and homogeneous production function] is certainly a remarkable discovery; for the relation between product and factors is to be considered to hold good irrespectively of the play of the market: "An analytical and synthetical law of composition and resolution of industrial factors and products which would hold equally in Robinson

is preferable. Starting with total costs, rather than returns, he writes the function of the *rth* firm as $f_r(x_r,y)$, where x_r is the output of the firm, y the output of the industry. Cf. *The Economies of Welfare* (4th ed., London, 1932), Pt. II, Chaps. ii, xi; Appendix III.

[1] The conditions under which the (long-run) average cost curve has one minimum point are examined in the conclusion to this chapter. Cf. also A. C. Pigou, *The Economics of Stationary States* (London, 1935), Chap. xxiv.

[2] External economies are, of course, an implicit variable of the total cost function of the firm, acting on the prices and quantities of the productive services and the nature of the production function.

> Crusoe's island, in an American religious commune, in an Indian village ruled by custom, and in the competitive centres of the typical modern industries." There is a magnificence in this generalization which recalls the youth of philosophy. Justice is a perfect cube, said the ancient sage; and rational conduct is a homogeneous function, adds the modern savant.[1]

This passage is highly misrepresentative of Wicksteed's position. Wicksteed does indeed talk of Crusoe's island and the like, but only in connection with physical returns, which is unduly eloquent but not absurd in his context. In the very paragraph from which Edgeworth quotes, Wicksteed says that in "practical form the law asserts that, in a freely competing community," no factor will accept less than its marginal product.[2] Elsewhere Edgeworth surmises that the "preposterous" theory is due to the exigency of explaining away the profits of the entrepreneur.[3]

In the course of his able paper on the laws of return (1911), Edgeworth offers a criticism of the assumption that the production function is homogeneous and linear:

> It may well be that, by comparing increments corresponding to points on some line not passing through the origin, the surface may be shown to be *convex* in the neighborhood of (x_1, y_1), though by the test of the "secondary" sort it

[1] *Collected Papers, op. cit.*, I, 31. This passage was first published in 1904 in the *Quarterly Journal of Economics.*

[2] *Co-ordination*, p. 42.

[3] "It was perhaps the exigency of the theory in question that profits equal zero in a competitive state which led a distinguished economist to maintain that the product was a *homogeneous function* of the factors of production, and has led other theorists to make by implication statements about the function which are only less preposterous because less distinct" (*Collected Papers*, II, 469 n.). It may also be noted that in an ambiguous passage Edgeworth seems to deny that the sum of the marginal products times the factors will exhaust the total produce (*ibid.*, II, 305). The first passage first appeared in 1915 in the *Economic Journal;* the second passage appeared in 1889 in an address before the British Association.

> appeared concave. Accordingly, I do not hold with the writers who attach a mighty importance to the question whether, if all the factors of production are increased in a certain proportion, say $\alpha : 1$ (where α is greater than 1), the product is, or is not, increased in that proportion. The matter has little to do with that character of the function z with which the entrepreneur is, and the economist should be, especially concerned, the fulfillment of the condition of a maximum.[1]

This is a most ambiguous passage. If it is read literally (the context suggests this), Edgeworth seems to be saying that a linear, homogeneous production function violates the correct diminishing returns concept—and that is simply not true.[2] But it may also refer to the instability of competition under the condition of constant returns to scale of plant.[3]

Edgeworth's other participation in the controversy relates to Chapman's restatement.[4] Edgeworth does not attack the general marginal productivity theory on its superficially vulnerable side, the presence of external economies or diseconomies. Such economies, he says, are "not negligible in general," but in ignorance of whether there are economies or diseconomies, one may postulate their absence or equality as "the most *probable* general statement"—a favorite use of his *a priori* or unverified probabilities.[5] But instead of proceeding to acknowledge the theory as at least a first approximation, he introduces a totally irrelevant consideration. In Figure XI, wages are shown to rise by bg, and on this rise centers Edgeworth's criticism: "The reasoning appears to presuppose

[1] *Ibid.*, I, 75–76.

[2] The second partial derivatives of the production function, $P = X^{\alpha}Y^{\beta}$, where $\alpha + \beta = 1$, for example, are obviously negative.

[3] Cf., *infra*, Conclusion.

[4] *Collected Papers*, II, 331–39 (*Economic Journal*, 1907).

[5] *Ibid.*, II, 332, 333.

that not only the total number of workmen, but also the total quantity of work done, is constant. But in general this is not to be supposed. The raised offer on one side of the market is apt to be attended with an increased offer on the other side." [1] Edgeworth then concedes that the theorem would be "accurately true" if instead of labor some fixed resource such as land were used. Yet he continues, "But what of it? Where is the consolation to the cottiers whose complaint is that their share of the product is so small, that 'this principle of remuneration is in itself an injustice.' " [2]

The first criticism, that other factors will not remain fixed in quantity, is completely beside the point. We may assume—and usually do—that other factors remain fixed, since the theorem relates to "normal," and not to "secular," value. Nor does variation in the supply of the factors of production violate the marginal productivity theory, as Edgeworth is fully aware at other points.[3] The second criticism is absurd: since when are economic theories supposed to be unimpeachable from an ethical viewpoint? In Edgeworth's positive formulation of the theory of distribution, we have seen,[4] he virtually accepts the marginal productivity theory.

Alfred Marshall

Before turning to the continental economists, we may consider Marshall's views. In the early *Economics of Industry* (1881), Marshall advanced the marginal productivity theory in England for probably the first time since Longfield and Butt wrote. The doctrine is, of

[1] *Ibid.*, II, 337.
[2] *Ibid.*, II, 338.
[3] Thus in his reply to Böhm-Bawerk, *ibid.*, III, 61–62; also I, 35–36.
[4] *Supra*, Chap. V.

course, treated much more extensively in the *Principles*, so a few quotations will suffice to reveal his early position:

> Thus the Demand for the loan of capital obeys a law similar to that which holds for the sale of commodities. Just as there is a certain amount of a commodity which can find purchasers at any given price, and when the price rises the amount that can be sold diminishes, so it is with regard to the use of capital. In any given state of the arts of production in a country, there is a certain amount of capital which it would be worth while for the various trades to employ in industry if they have to allow capital's share of the year's Earnings-and-interest Fund to be 7 per cent. on the capital. . . . If they have to pay 6 per cent. for its use, it will be worth their while to employ a larger amount. . . . The current rate of interest measures the Final Utility to each borrower; that is, the advantage to him of that capital which he is only just induced to employ.[1]
>
> Thus the Earnings of Management of a manufacturer represent the value of the addition which his work makes to the total produce of capital and industry: they correspond to the effective demand that there is for the aid of his labour in production, just as the wages of a hired labourer correspond to the effective demand for his labour. . . . So it is with regard to skilled labour of any kind; every increase in the supply of it tends to diminish the Final value in use of the work it does, and therefore to lower its wages.[2]

The difficulty in isolating the net product of a productive service, which, we shall see, plays a crucial role in the *Principles*, is already suggested,[3] and we are even reminded, in a footnote to a statement bordering on the marginal productivity theory of wages, that "a statement of this kind has been mistaken by some writers for a

[1] *Economics of Industry* (2d ed., London, 1881), pp. 123–24. The first (1879) edition has not been available; the preface of the second and last edition does not suggest, however, that the relevant sections have been altered.

[2] *Ibid.*, pp. 142–43.

[3] *Ibid.*, p. 133.

theory of wages. But really it is only the Law:—'Value tends to equal Expenses of production'—written in a new form." [1]

Passing now to the *Principles*, it may be observed at the outset that in the eighth edition Marshall's position is at least as far from an open or complete acceptance of the marginal productivity theory as it had been thirty years before—although the first (1890) edition contains the essence of the theory. The development of his thought on this subject is worth detailed consideration.

The analysis of the demand for the factors of production is brief in all editions of the *Principles;* in the first edition it occupies less than a dozen pages. The fundamental basis of his analysis, the law of substitution, received a thoroughly Marshallian definition:

> It is to be taken for granted that as far as the knowledge and business enterprise of the producers reaches, they will in each case choose those factors of production which are best for their purpose. The sum of the supply prices of those factors which are used is, as a rule, less than the sum of the supply prices of any other set of factors which could be substituted for them.[2]

Marshall never considers explicitly the scope of possible substitution between productive services, but the impression is that the law is in practice widely applicable: ". . . the undertaker is ceaselessly striving so to modify his arrangements as to obtain greater results with a given expenditure or equal results with a less expenditure." [3]

From the doctrine of substitution Marshall moves directly to the demand for the productive factors:

[1] *Ibid.*, p. 133 n.

[2] *Principles of Economics* (1st ed., London, 1890), p. 401; also pp. 517, 543 ff.

[3] *Ibid.*, p. 517.

> The efficiency of each factor at the outer limit of its use for each several purpose, or in other words its marginal efficiency in production, will be directly proportionate to the price which has to be paid for it. . . .
>
> . . . the wages of skilled and unskilled labour will bear to one another the same ratio that their efficiencies do at the margin of indifference.[1]

Although Marshall thus states the *proportionality* of marginal productivities to prices of productive services, he hesitates at the final tenet of the theory, that the distributive share of a service is *equal to* or *determined by* its marginal product. His reluctance seems in part due to an unwillingness to ascribe much importance to the demand factor.

> When we inquire what it is that determines the marginal efficiency of a factor of production, whether it be any kind of labour or material capital, we find that the solution requires a knowledge of the available supply of that factor, and, going a step further, of the causes that determine that supply. The nominal value of everything, whether it be a particular kind of labour or capital or anything else, rests, like the keystone of an arch, balanced in equilibrium between the contending pressures of its two opposing sides. The forces of demand press on the one side, those of supply on the other; and the older economists seem to have been rightly guided by their intuitions when they silently determined that the forces of supply were those the study of which was the more urgent and involved the greater difficulty.[2]

This argument is of course unconvincing; the marginal productivity theory does not explain everything, and

[1] *Ibid.*, pp. 544–45; also pp. 556–58.

[2] *Ibid.*, pp. 546–47. G. F. Shove, in reviewing J. R. Hicks' *The Theory of Wages*, *op. cit.*, argues that Marshall applies the marginal productivity theory only to the amount of labor employed, not to the amount available (cf. *Economic Journal*, XLIII [1933], 462–63). I have not been able to find clear evidence to support such an interpretation.

that everyone admits. It is, however, the fundamental element in the explanation of distribution in a stationary economy (*i.e.*, in Marshall's case of "long-run normal" value); it is misleading to say "It contains a part, but only a small part, of the Law of Wages." [1]

The fundamental reason Marshall rejects an outright marginal productivity theory seems to be the difficulty of measuring the marginal productivity of a productive service.

> The earnings of many different kinds of industry, one of which is almost always that of Superintendence and Management, enter into the expenses of production, and therefore into the price, of almost everything that is sold; and in order to deduce the earnings of one of these kinds of labour from the price of the product, we must find out not only the interest on the capital employed but also the earnings of the other kinds of industry, and deduct them all from the value of the produce raised. We cannot therefore speak with perfect accuracy of the Discounted value of the work of labour; but we may still speak of the Net product of labour. The Net product of a machine is the value of the work that it does, after deductions have been made for expenses of working it, among which are here included the Earnings of Management. . . . It is true that this statement is not, as some have thought, an independent theory of wages, but only a particular way of wording the familiar doctrine that the value of everything tends to be equal to its expenses of production.[2]

In the special case [3] (*e.g.*, the now-famous marginal shepherd) where no additional cooperating productive services are needed when the amount of labor is increased by one

[1] *Principles of Economics* (1st ed.), p. 546 margin. Marshall's emphasis on supply is doubtless attributable to his unwillingness to accept the abstractions of the stationary economy.

[2] *Ibid.*, pp. 547–48.

[3] Marshall is not clear on the scope of this case; he says, "It cannot be applied practically to all cases" (*ibid.*, p. 548).

unit (*i.e.*, where the variability of production coefficients is obvious), we may say that the wage of the laborer equals his marginal productivity. Marshall concludes, somewhat inconsistently: "And though the form may be different, the substance of the problem is the same in every other industry: the wages of every class of labour tends to be equal to the produce due to the additional labour of the marginal labourer of that class." [1]

We may note finally Mathematical Note XXV, which contains the essence of Note XIV of the second and later editions.[2] Let H represent total satisfaction and V total cost (in terms of effort). V is a function of $a, a', a'', \cdots$, "the several amounts of different kinds of labour," and H is a function of $b, b', b'', \cdots$, "the several amounts of accommodation of different kinds which [the product] would afford." The condition of maximum satisfaction is

$$\frac{dV}{da} = \frac{dH}{db} \cdot \frac{db}{da} = \frac{dH}{db'} \cdot \frac{db'}{da} = \cdots$$
$$\frac{dV}{da'} = \frac{dH}{db} \cdot \frac{db}{da'} = \frac{dH}{db'} \cdot \frac{db'}{da'} = \cdots$$

Since these equations are stated in terms of utility and disutility, they are properly applicable only to the individual, although Marshall does not explicitly make this restriction. They express the theorem that the marginal (utility) product $\frac{dH}{db} \cdot \frac{db}{da}$ of a productive factor a is equal to its marginal cost.

In the second edition of the *Principles* (1891), the treatment is virtually identical. A footnote is added to restrict the scope of the "marginal shepherd" analysis:

[1] *Ibid.*, p. 549; also pp. 563, 564.

[2] *Ibid.*, p. 749. The derivatives in the following equations are partial and not total, of course.

> This method of estimating the Net produce of a man's labour is not easily applicable to industries in which a great deal of capital and effort has to be invested in gradually building up a trade connection, and especially if they are such as obey the Law of Increasing Return. It is hardly worth while to study these difficulties in detail here, for they are technical and intricate.[1]

The other change is the addition to Mathematical Note XIV of an approving reference to Edgeworth's statement of the marginal productivity theory.[2]

In the third edition (1895), however, changes of considerable interest occur. The discussion of the demand for productive factors is expanded and rewritten.[3] The doctrine of net product is stated with slightly less reserve: The entrepreneur "estimates as best he can how much *net* addition to the value of his total product will be caused by a certain extra use of any one agent . . . and he endeavors to employ each to that margin at which its net product would no longer exceed the price he would have to pay for it." [4] Marshall adds a new section containing a similar theory of the demand for capital.[5] A new footnote (that typical Marshallian vehicle for qualifications), however, raises difficulties in measuring the net product of a productive service even when the firm is not subject to increasing returns:

> Further the net product of the shepherd in the exceptional case which we have chosen, plays no greater part in governing the wages of shepherds, than does that of any of the last (marginal) shepherds on farms where they cannot be

[1] *Ibid.* (2d ed., London, 1891), p. 567 n.

[2] *Ibid.*, p. 757; cf., *supra*, pp. 131 ff.

[3] *Ibid.* (3d ed., London, 1895), pp. 576 ff.

[4] *Ibid.*, p. 581. Two consecutive sentences are run together in the quotation.

[5] *Ibid.*, pp. 585 ff. But it is added (p. 585) that such remarks "cannot be made into a theory of interest, any more than into a theory of wages, without reasoning in a circle."

> profitably employed without considerable extra outlay in other directions, as for land, buildings, implements, labour of management, etc. Thus the net product of such shepherds cannot be ascertained simply; but it is a case of derived demand (see Bk. V, Chap. VI), and requires us to take account of the prices which have to be paid for the aid of all these other agents of production.[1]

The reference to the chapter on derived demand is misleading: the assumption of fixed coefficients of production there made estops, not assists, the solution of the problem discussed in this note.

Mathematical Note XIV reaches virtually its definitive form in the third edition.[2] The equations (stated above) are given a much broader interpretation: "the (marginal) demand for carpenters' labour is the (marginal) efficiency of carpenters' labour in increasing the supply of any product, multiplied by the (marginal) demand price for that product." [3] This is equivalent to the statement, says Marshall, that wages equal the value of the net product. "This proposition is very important and contains within itself the kernel of the demand side of the theory of Distribution." [4]

The note is generalized to include other productive services. Let $x_1, x_2, \cdots$ be different classes of labor, $y_1, y_2, \cdots$ various raw materials (including land), z the capital, and u the "labour, worry, anxiety, wear and tear" of the entrepreneur. If V be outlay (in money) and H receipts, then

[1] *Ibid.*, p. 583, n. 2.

[2] *Ibid.*, pp. 798–805. In a letter to Prof. Colson (*circa* 1907), Marshall said that Mathematical Notes XIV to XXI had been formulated about 1870—even before the appearance of Jevons' *Theory*. Cf. A. Marshall, "The Mathematician, as Seen by Himself," *Econometrica*, I (1933), 221–22.

[3] *Principles* (3d ed.), p. 800. It is obvious that this formulation includes also the case of imperfect competition, but that extension is not relevant to the present discussion.

[4] *Ibid.*

$$\frac{dV}{dx_1} = \frac{dH}{db} \cdot \frac{db}{dx_1} = \frac{dH}{db'} \cdot \frac{db'}{dx_1} = \cdots$$

$$\cdots\cdots\cdots\cdots\cdots\cdots\cdots\cdots\cdots$$

$$\frac{dV}{dy_1} = \frac{dH}{db} \cdot \frac{db}{dy_1} = \frac{dH}{db'} \cdot \frac{db'}{dy_1} = \cdots$$

$$\cdots\cdots\cdots\cdots\cdots\cdots\cdots\cdots\cdots$$

$$\frac{dV}{dz} = \frac{dH}{db} \cdot \frac{db}{dz} = \frac{dH}{db'} \cdot \frac{db'}{dz} = \cdots$$

$$\frac{dV}{du} = \frac{dH}{db} \cdot \frac{db}{du} = \frac{dH}{db'} \cdot \frac{db'}{du} = \cdots$$

"That is to say, the marginal outlay which the builder is willing to make for an additional small supply, δx_1, of the first class of labour, viz. $\frac{dV}{dx_1}\delta x_1$, is equal to

$$\frac{dH}{db} \cdot \frac{db}{dx_1}\delta x_1; \ldots\text{''}$$ [1]

A final change in the *Principles* is of great interest in the present connection. Wicksteed's *Co-ordination* had appeared a year before the third edition of the *Principles*, and Marshall refers to Wicksteed's argument several times.[2] Two comments on the *Co-ordination* are relevant. First, Marshall approves of Flux's argument that the fixity of supply of land, not the residual character of its return, is the important feature.[3] The second reference is in connection with the national dividend. In previous editions Marshall said that all distributive shares come from (and exhaust) the national dividend.[4] Now he continues:

> Further it [the product] is distributed among them [the distributive shares], speaking generally, in proportion to the

[1] *Ibid.*, p. 801. Substantially the same point is made in the text (p. 463 n.).

[2] Marshall combats the notion that rent can be negative (*ibid.*, p. 241, n. 2), but this curiosum may be passed over here.

[3] *Ibid.*, p. 604 n.

[4] *Ibid.* (1st ed.), p. 561.

> need which people have for their services—*i.e.*, not the *total* need, but the *marginal* need. By this is meant the need at that point, at which people are indifferent whether they purchase a little more of the services (or the fruits of the services) of one agent, or devote their further resources to purchasing the services (or the fruits of the services) of other agents.
>
> While the national dividend is thus completely absorbed in remunerating the owner of each agent of production at its marginal rate. . . . [1]

In the course of this discussion, page 46 of the *Co-ordination* is referred to, where Wicksteed says:

> As soon as we quite clearly understand that, under conditions usually regarded as normal, the marginal distribution exhausts the product, and that where every factor has taken a share regulated by its marginal efficiency, there is nothing left—then, but not until then, shall we be in a position to attempt a scientific analysis of the ways in which the share of any one factor may be maximized.

The later editions add little of interest on the problem. In the fourth (1905) and subsequent editions the last-quoted reference to Wicksteed is suppressed, but the theory of exhaustion of product by marginal imputation remains.[2] In the fifth edition virtually all limitations on the applicability of the doctrine are withdrawn.

> The supposition that an additional worker can be taken on without a corresponding increase in the supply of capital for plant, raw material, etc., does not alter the substance of the problem of marginal products; but merely simplifies its form a little. In this exceptional case, we have not to dwell upon the need for appropriate adjustment of various agents of production, each being used up to the point at which any

[1] *Ibid.* (3d ed.), p. 605 and note. The last quoted lines are suppressed in later editions.

[2] *Ibid.* (4th ed., *op. cit.*), p. 609.

additional use of it would be less efficient in proportion to its cost than the additional use of some other agent.[1]

This would seem to be an outright capitulation to the marginal productivity theory, but in the text Marshall still denies the "claim that it contains a theory of wages." [2] We may disregard subsequent minor changes and pass directly to an analysis of Marshall's final position.[3]

His reluctance to accept unequivocally the marginal productivity theory is clearly the problem calling for explanation. His desire to emphasize supply considerations (which manifests itself to a decreasing extent in successive editions) is analytically irrelevant to this problem, although it doubtless played an important part in his presentation.

Two possible objections to the marginal productivity analysis are related to Marshall's persistent use of the concept of net product.[4] The first is that the product of an added unit of one resource (*e.g.*, shepherds) is due in part to the more intensive utilization of the other types of resources (*e.g.*, land and capital). This erroneous view has been held by some economists,[5] but Marshall explicitly refutes it.

[1] *Ibid.* (5th ed., London, 1907), p. 517 n. The important last sentence is suppressed in later editions.

[2] *Ibid.*, p. 519.

[3] Henceforth all references are to the eighth edition (London, 1920), unless otherwise noted.

[4] *E.g.*, "The doctrine that the earnings of a worker tend to be equal to the net product of his work, has by itself no real meaning; since in order to estimate net product, we have to take for granted all the expenses of production of the commodity on which he works, other than his own wages" (*Principles*, p. 518). This statement turns on the distinction between short and long run. Marshall seems to consider the long run to be measured in generations. His viewpoint, in other words, is that of the historian.

[5] For example, H. Mayer, "Zurechnung," *Handwörterbuch der Staatswissenschaften* (4th ed., 1928), VIII, 1206–28.

> He [Hobson] argues that if the marginal application of any agent of production be curtailed, that will so disorganize production that every other agent will be working to less effect than before; and that therefore the total resulting loss will include not only the true marginal product of that agent, but also a part of the products due to the other agents: but he appears to have overlooked the following points:—(1) There are forces constantly at work tending so to readjust the distribution of resources between their different uses, that any maladjustment will be arrested before it has gone far: and the argument does not profess to apply to exceptional cases of violent maladjustment (2) when the adjustment is such as to give the best results, a slight change in the proportions in which they are applied diminishes the efficiency of that adjustment by a quantity which is very small relatively to that change—in technical language it is of "the second order of smalls"—; and it may therefore be neglected relatively to that change. (In pure mathematical phrase, efficiency being regarded as a function of the proportions of the agents; when the efficiency is at its maximum, its differential coefficient with regard to any one of these proportions is zero.) A grave error would therefore have been involved, if any allowance had been made for those elements which Mr. Hobson asserts to have been overlooked. (3) In economics, as in physics, changes are generally continuous. . . .[1]

The second point is of course the conclusive one: the change of productivity of the non-variable resources involves only higher order differentials, and must be neglected.

The only other main possible difficulty in measuring a marginal product arises out of failure of the law of substitution. Otherwise there would be no point in selecting the hypothetical shepherd, who "would not require any further expenditure on plant or stock" and who "would save the farmer himself just as much trouble in some

[1] *Principles*, p. 409 n. This note was first introduced in the fifth edition.

ways as he gives in others."[1] It was doubtless this implicit limitation of the operation of the law of substitution, which was inconsistent with his explicit analysis, that contributed most to Marshall's statement.[2]

The writer would suggest, however, that in general Marshall's net and marginal products are identical, and that his distribution theory is, in spite of contrary admonitions, a marginal productivity theory. Since he does not consider explicitly the possibility of fixed coefficients (at this stage in his argument),[3] the following quotation (which is objectionable only in containing a redundancy) should be interpreted as an outright acceptance of the marginal productivity theory: "In each case the income tends to equal the value of the marginal net product."[4] Furthermore, Marshall accepts the exhaustion-of-product argument of Wicksteed, although in the fifth and later editions he ignores its author, and never passes judgment on the use of Euler's theorem.

Barone; Montemartini

Although it should now be clear that English-speaking economists did not completely ignore Wicksteed's theory, nevertheless it is true that the chief attention to the general marginal productivity theory came from the continental economists, in particular Barone, Pareto, Wal-

[1] *Ibid.*, pp. 515–16.

[2] The present interpretation therefore agrees with that of J. R. Hicks, in "Marginal Productivity and the Principle of Variation," *Economica*, XII (1932), 86–88; and D. H. Robertson, in *Economic Fragments* (London, 1931), pp. 47–48.

[3] Discontinuities, indeed, are mentioned only to be dismissed as unimportant, in the earlier editions, *e.g.*, *Principles* (5th ed.), p. 406 n.

[4] *Ibid.* (8th ed.), p. 535. It may be convenient to refer to the more important passages on the marginal productivity theory: *ibid.*, pp. 341, 355 ff., 404–6, 410–11, 447–49, 514 ff., 532, 534–36, 538, 544, 598–600, 601, 667, and Mathematical Notes XIV, XIV bis, and XVI.

ras, and Wicksell. It is to this group of writers that we now turn.

Barone's earliest publication on the marginal productivity theory is his review (in 1895) of Wicksell's *Über Wert, Kapital und Rente.*[1] This early publication is notable only for the introduction of *numerio per anticipare,* or capital of anticipation, into the production function.[2] Capital of anticipation is equivalent to circulating capital —it is required to make advances to laborers, to purchase raw materials, etc., at the beginning of the period of production. The following quotation indicates that Barone recognizes the marginal productivity theory more clearly than had Wicksell, on whom his treatment is based: " . . . the condition of minimum costs for every unit of product requires that every factor be employed up to that point beyond which another increment of the factor yields an increment of product no longer sufficient to remunerate the increment of the factor." [3] Barone's famous work, "*Studi sulla Distribuzione,*" [4] deserves much more detailed attention. A few words may be said in advance concerning these articles. The central doctrine, the general marginal productivity theory, was arrived at by 1894,[5] presumably before Barone was aware of Wicksteed's work. The series of articles did not appear until 1896, and then publication was suspended after the second instalment because Pareto, in a personal

[1] "Sopra un Libro del Wicksell," *Giornale degli Economisti,* XI (1895), 524–39, reprinted in *Le Opere economiche* (Bologna, 1936), I, 117–43.

[2] *Ibid.,* pp. 535 ff. (*Opere,* I, 136 ff.).

[3] *Ibid.,* p. 536 (*Opere,* I, 138–39).

[4] *Giornale degli Economisti,* XII (1896), 107–55, 235–52, reprinted in *Le Opere economiche,* I, 147–228. The second instalment in the series, which deals with capital theory, does not concern us here.

[5] Letter to Walras, Sept. 20, 1894. Barone's ideas were not yet fully developed, however; he offered the absurd objection that a linear and homogeneous production function did not fulfill the law of decreasing marginal productivity for each factor.

letter, convinced Barone that he had committed errors which vitiated his analysis.[1] The precise nature of these "errors" is unknown, but it is safe to assume that they were identical with those of Wicksteed and Walras, whom Pareto did criticize publicly.[2]

Barone's general assumptions may be sketched briefly. His analysis deals only with stationary equilibrium, *i.e.*, the quantity of resources is assumed to be fixed.[3] Material wealth is classified into three categories: land; technical or productive capital (*Capitali tecnici*); and consumption goods (*Beni di consumo*). All these are quoted in terms of *numerio*, equivalent to Walras' *numéraire.* In addition, circulating capital or capital of anticipation is required by the entrepreneur to meet advances to the factors during the period of production. This capital of anticipation is also quoted in *numerio*, and the interest rate is the price of a unit of *numerio* per unit of time. Perfect competition is assumed throughout the essays.

Production is introduced into the general equilibrium theory in a short but comprehensive analysis.[4] We may omit this analysis and pass on directly to the theory of distribution. The fundamental basis is the law of diminishing physical productivity, *i.e.*, the incremental return to the *n*th factor will, after a certain possible region of increasing returns, decline as additional increments of the *n*th factor are added to the other $(n - 1)$ factors which are held constant.[5]

If time is abstracted, the solution of the distribution problem is as "simple as it is elegant."[6] The entre-

[1] Cf. Schultz, *op. cit.*, pp. 508 n., 547.

[2] Cf. Pareto, *infra.*

[3] "*Studi sulla Distribuzione,*" *op. cit.*, pp. 115–16 (*Opere*, I, 158–59).

[4] *Ibid.*, pp. 121–26 (*Opere*, I, 167–77).

[5] *Ibid.*, pp. 127–29 (*Opere*, I, 171 ff.).

[6] *Ibid.*, p. 131 (*Opere*, I, 177).

preneur will minimize costs or maximize returns if each factor is used up to the point where the increment of cost of the factor equals the increment of return to the entrepreneur.

The theory may readily be generalized to include the time consumed in the production process. The amount of circulating capital must equal some fraction of the total advances to the factors in every period of production, following the concept of "staggered" production popularized by Böhm-Bawerk.[1] Thus if total salary payments during a period of production are K, the average advances will be some fraction, $\frac{1}{\epsilon}$, of K, and similarly for the other factors. Since the period of production is technically variable and circulating capital also has a cost, the interest rate, the entrepreneur must maximize his return subject also to the condition that the increment added to the length of the production period yields a product just equal to the cost of that extension. The incremental cost of the extension is of course the interest charge on the additional capital required by the extension.[2] The general equilibrium condition is now that "for every entrepreneur the remuneration in *numerio* of each factor (labor, land, technical capital) be equal to the marginal productivity in *numerio* of the factor, diminished by the interest on the corresponding portion of the capital of anticipation." [3]

The profits of the entrepreneur remain to be explained.[4] The argument, which receives a rather detailed graphic statement, need only be summarized. Postulating perfect competition and full divisibility of the entrepreneur's

[1] *Ibid.*, pp. 133–36 (*Opere*, I, 180 ff.).
[2] *Ibid.*, pp. 137–39 (*Opere*, I, 185 ff.).
[3] *Ibid.*, p. 142 (*Opere*, I, 190).
[4] *Ibid.*, pp. 143–46 (*Opere*, I, 191–94).

time, entrepreneur ability will then be rewarded exactly like any other kind of labor.[1] Edgeworth's fundamental criticism of Barone's theory centers about this assumption that entrepreneurial ability is divisible, it will be recalled.[2]

We may now pass on immediately to the final theorem, that "after having remunerated all the factors according to their marginal productivities, there remains no residual to be distributed." [3] The proof is necessarily mathematical, and we may restate the previous argument in presenting it.[4] If P is product, and $A,B,C, \cdots$ the various factors of production, including entrepreneurship, all expressed in physical units, then the production function may be written

$$P = \Phi(A,B,C, \cdots). \tag{1}$$

If the unit prices of $A,B,C, \cdots$ are p_a, p_b, p_c, $\cdots$, π is the unit price of P, t is the length of the period of production, and $\frac{1}{\epsilon}$ is the average fraction of the period of production for which the capital of anticipation is invested, then we may write this last quantity as

$$F = \frac{1}{\epsilon}(Ap_a + Bp_b + Cp_c + \cdots)t. \tag{2}$$

The condition of minimum cost may be represented by the following equations, equal in number to the factors of production (including time):

[1] And indeed the entrepreneurial role is characterized as "the work of directing and coordinating production" (*ibid.*, p. 142 [*Opere*, I, 189]).

[2] *Supra*, Chap. v.

[3] "*Studi sulla Distribuzione*," *op. cit.*, p. 146 (*Opere*, I, 196); italicized by Barone.

[4] Cf. *ibid.*, pp. 151 ff. (*Opere*, I, 221 ff.). Barone's notation is here simplified slightly.

$$\begin{aligned}
\pi\frac{\partial\Phi}{\partial A} &= p_a\left(1+\frac{zt}{\epsilon}\right),\\
\pi\frac{\partial\Phi}{\partial B} &= p_b\left(1+\frac{zt}{\epsilon}\right),\\
&\cdots\cdots\cdots\cdots\\
&\cdots\cdots\cdots\cdots\\
&\cdots\cdots\cdots\cdots\\
\pi\frac{\partial\Phi}{\partial t} &= \frac{Fz}{t}.
\end{aligned} \tag{3}$$

The total cost of production is then

$$\pi P = Ap_a + Bp_b + Cp_c + \cdots + Fz, \tag{4}$$

where z is the rate of interest. Finally, if we substitute for the p's from system (3) into equation (4), we secure the fundamental equation

$$P = A\frac{\partial\Phi}{\partial A}\left(1+\frac{zt}{\epsilon}\right)^{-1} + B\frac{\partial\Phi}{\partial B}\left(1+\frac{zt}{\epsilon}\right)^{-1} + \cdots + \frac{\partial\Phi}{\partial t}\cdot t. \tag{5}$$

Barone's final result thus differs from Wicksell's discounted marginal productivity theory in three respects: it is a trifle more explicit; the analysis is extended to an indefinite number of factors of production; and, most important, it is not based on Euler's theorem.

The preceding theory was dropped at the behest of Pareto, as has already been mentioned. Yet even before the series had appeared (1896), Barone had written an adverse review of Wicksteed's *Co-ordination* and submitted it to the *Economic Journal.* Edgeworth praised the review but refused to publish it.[1] The rejected review was sent to Walras, from whom it received a more hospitable reception. He adopted the argument for the second half of Appendix III, "Note on the Refutation of the English Theory of Rent by M. Wicksteed," of the

[1] Letter from Barone to Walras, Oct. 26, 1895.

third edition of his *Eléments d'économie politique pure.* Unfortunately Barone's argument is not clearly separated from Walras', so the two will be treated together.[1] Barone's major criticism, adopted from Pareto, seems to be that Wicksteed does not introduce the scale of plant into the production function.[2] But certainly in Barone's articles in the *Giornale*, in the following year, there is no consideration of the scale of plant.

It must be noted, finally, that in later writings Barone withdrew his general solution of the distribution problem, due to Pareto's objections.[3] Barone used, indeed, one of Pareto's examples: "The amount of a certain mineral ore, for instance, which is required in the production of a kilogram of metal" is definitely fixed.[4] The Böhm-Bawerk-Wicksell theory of capital and interest is also rejected in favor of a marginal productivity analysis containing no period of production.

Montemartini deserves passing attention chiefly as the author of an early general exposition of the marginal productivity theory.[5] His presentation is simple and lucid, and it is still a useful introduction to price theory. The work is essentially unoriginal, however; Barone and Pareto in particular are closely followed. Montemartini proposes the marginal productivity theory with all possible generality,[6] but there is a fatal ambiguity on the

[1] Cf. Walras, *infra.*

[2] Cf. Walras, *Eléments* (3d ed., Lausanne, 1896), p. 490.

[3] *Grundzüge der Theoretischen Nationalökonomie* (Berlin, 1927), p. 22; also p. 16. Cf. "The Ministry of Production in the Collectivist State," reprinted in *Collectivist Economic Planning*, ed. F. A. Hayek (London, 1935), p. 251.

[4] *Grundzüge*, p. 22 (*Opere*, II, 18, 25).

[5] Giovanni Montemartini, *La Teorica delle Produttività Marginali* (Pavia, 1899). A summary appeared as "Über die Theorie der Grenzproduktivität," *Zeitschrift für Volkswirtschaft, Sozialpolitik, und Verwaltung*, VIII (1899), 467–503.

[6] Cf. Theorems XII to XVI in particular, *La Teorica*, pp. 75–79.

crucial point of variability of production coefficients, *i.e.*, the principle of substitution. His theorem VI reads: "The factor which exists in smaller quantity than any other, is the one which determines the quantities of the other factors which combine with it, and consequently the quantity of product." [1] This "law of definite proportions" is presumably derived from Pareto, who is cited.[2] Yet Montemartini does not see the point of Pareto's argument, for he continues to speak of marginal productivity, even in the frequent case where "certain factors can not be substituted for others." [3] His confused reconciliation of these two theories may best be relegated to a footnote.[4]

[1] *Ibid.*, p. 45.

[2] *Ibid.*, p. 48.

[3] *Ibid.*, p. 47; also p. 39.

[4] The relevant passage deserves full quotation. "Also in this case [of fixed production coefficients], the entrepreneur will continue to allocate (*spendere e dividere*) his money among the various factors according to their productivities. Let us suppose that in order to produce grain, one unit of the factor land (100 square meters) is combined with 10 units of labor. Here it will clearly be impossible to substitute an additional quantity of labor for the land. We also assume that such a combination of 100 square meters of land and 10 days of labor yields 100 units of product which can be sold for 100 lire. Let this also be the point of equilibrium of the productive process, so the entrepreneur makes neither gain nor loss. If now the entrepreneur wishes to abandon $\frac{1}{10}$ of the land, or 10 square meters, he must simultaneously abandon a day of labor, because we suppose that the physical marginal productivities of the two factors are equal. But the prices are equal for factors which have equal productivities—so $\frac{1}{10}$ of the land is paid the same as one day of labor. If it is assumed that the productivity of a tenth day is 5, then we must give 50 lire to workers and 50 lire to landlords" (*ibid.*, pp. 79–80).

This is of course question-begging throughout. There is no question regarding the possibility or necessity of substituting labor for all the land. It is impossible, moreover, to ascribe a separate marginal productivity to either land or labor under Montemartini's assumptions. Their equality in the present case seems to be a case of halving the total product. Finally, the productivity of 5 for labor must be an average, not a marginal product; there is no scope for diminishing physical returns.

Pareto

Pareto's role in the controversy over the Euler theorem is important but, as in the case of Edgeworth, not always impressive. Pareto's first criticism is well known.

> Some authors assume that if all the factors of production are doubled, the product will also double. This may be approximately true in certain cases, but not rigorously or in general. Some expenses vary with the size of the enterprise. It is certain that if one could suppose a second enterprise in conditions exactly the same as those of the first, one might double all the factors and the product. But this assumption is not, in general admissible. If, for example, one were to engage in the transportation business in Paris, it would be necessary to assume another business and another Paris. But since this other Paris does not exist, it is necessary to consider two enterprises in the same Paris, and then one can no longer assume that if the factors of production are doubled, the product will also double.[1]

This argument is of course utterly unconvincing. A doubling of the transportation facilities of Paris *would* double the physical product, in this case the traffic capacity. The value product would indeed fail to double, but this is true only because Pareto has selected a monopoly. If he had selected a fully competitive industry, his argument would have been self-contradictory.

The second argument leveled against the use of Euler's theorem is intellectually quite respectable, but of questionable importance. It is, in essence, that there is not full substitutionality between factors of production; some factors have a unique functional relationship to output or to certain other factors, regardless of the amount of the remaining factors. Some coefficients of production are variable; others are fixed. As an illustration of the latter category, the relation of iron ore to pig

[1] *Cours d'économie politique*, II (Paris, 1897), § 714.

iron is fixed at any given stage of technology. In addition to all such industries concerned with minerals and chemicals,

> . . . there are other [cases] where one cannot compensate for the increase of one of the capital goods by the diminution of others. For example, in order to produce a given amount of silks, one requires an area of land to erect a factory, but afterwards, even if one doubles this area, without increasing the other capital goods, the product will not be increased at all.[1]

This is fundamentally the same argument that is raised many times in a short review by Pareto of A. Aupetit's *Essai sur la théorie générale de la monnaie*,[2] where Walras' marginal productivity theory has been followed: "Thus, in a chocolate factory, you may increase as much as you wish the labor, the area occupied by the factory, the machines, and yet if you do not increase the quantity of cacao, you will not appreciably increase the chocolate." [3] For a "large number" of factories an increase in the area of land occupied by the factory will not "increase the product at all." Similarly, only one driver can be used with one truck.[4]

Pareto adds nothing new in his other writings on the marginal productivity theory. The argument continues to be that the individual factors of production cannot be treated as independent of each other. Thus, in *L'économie pure* (1901), Pareto says:

> The theory which claims to determine [the coefficients of fabrication] by consideration of marginal productivities is

[1] *Ibid.*, § 717. Cf. J. R. Hicks, "Marginal Productivity and the Principle of Variation," *op. cit.*, p. 86 n.: "this is merely silly."

[2] Paris, 1901. Pareto's review appeared in the *Revue d'Economie Politique*, XVI (1902), 90–93. Aupetit's treatment is virtually the same as that of Walras, but it is much more elegant, as is indeed Aupetit's entire treatment of the general equilibrium theory. Cf. Aupetit, *op. cit.*, pp. 52–74. W. Zawadski, *Les Mathématiques appliquées à l'économie politique* (Paris, 1914), pp. 226–27, repeats Pareto's criticism of Aupetit.

[3] *Revue*, p. 92.

[4] *Ibid.*

> false. In these theories quantities are treated as independent variables, which are not independent, and the equations which are written in order to determine the minimum costs are not admissible. Such are equations (3) of Walras' *Eléments d'économie politique pure*, 4th ed. (1900), p. 375.[1]

Finally, in Pareto's essay, "Applications of Mathematics to Political Economy," in the German edition of the *Encyclopedia of the Mathematical Sciences*, this criticism is repeated in virtually the same words.[2]

Pareto's criticism of the general marginal productivity theory reduces to this: certain specific factors of production may be functionally related either to each other (the case of truck and driver) or to the produce (*e.g.*, cocao and chocolate, iron ore and iron, gold and gold leaf).[3] Two

[1] *Op. cit.*, p. 10 n. The writer has not been able to secure a copy of this work; the quotation is taken from a letter written by Walras to Barone, Dec. 10, 1901. The letter has been printed by Schultz, *op. cit.*, pp. 547–48.

[2] "Anwendungen der Mathematik auf Nationalökonomie," *Encyklopödie der Mathematischen Wissenschaften*, Part II, Vol. I (1903), 1117 n.: "In the marginal productivity theory as it is presented in this work [of Wicksteed's], there is an error which has been pointed out by Pareto, *Cours*, § 714. This error occurs again in Walras, *Economie politique* (edition of 1900), pp. 374–75. The writer treats as independent variables, quantities which are not independent." There is no reference to the theory in the article in the French edition of the *Encyclopedia*. In the *Manuel d'économie politique* (2d ed., Paris, 1927), nothing new is added. At one point (*ibid.*, p. 328), Pareto says: "Except in exceptional cases, there exist no fixed proportions which must be assigned to the coefficients of production. . . ." Elsewhere, however, and this seems to be his intended view, he says (*ibid.*, p. 636), "these coefficients of production are in part constant, or nearly constant, and in part variable."

[3] The argument has been stated mathematically. If P is product (say iron) and $A,B,C, \ldots$ are factors of production other than O, iron ore, it is alleged to be improper to write,

$$P = F(A,B,C, \ldots O, \ldots).$$

Rather, two equations are necessary:

$$P = F_1(A,B,C, \ldots)$$
$$P = F_2(O).$$

From these equations it follows that A, for instance, is an implicit function of O, and Euler's theorem cannot help us. Cf. Pareto, *Cours*, § 714 n.; also Schultz, *op. cit.*, pp. 549–50.

replies may be made to this criticism. If two resources must be used together in some functional relationship, then the pair form a technical datum. As such they must be treated as a single factor of production, and economic theory has neither the power of nor interest in separating their returns.[1] Should the two resources, however, be used in different proportions in different industries (which *a priori* would cast some doubt on their fixity of proportion in any industry), the problem must be solved by simultaneous equations of the type developed by Walras and Wieser.

A more important criticism of Pareto's position may be adduced in connection with both dependent factors and factors functionally related to the product. For practical purposes, it may be asserted, factors are never so related; there is always some variability in their proportions at the margin. Certainly one driver can operate a truck of various sizes, and two drivers can produce more service per unit of time than one driver. There may be obscure cases of factors functionally related to each other, but these unimportant cases are not important enough to justify rejecting the Euler theorem approach. Similarly, there is always some variability in the product that can be secured from any one factor. Relative prices will determine how much iron is taken from the iron ore, and obviously all the iron is never removed from the ore. Even in the extreme case of gold and gold leaf, there is always some waste of gold in making gold leaf, and this

[1] Edgeworth suggests an escape from this problem: "Nor is the case essentially altered when account is taken of the possibility (noticed by Professor Pareto, *Cours*, Art. 718) that the factors are not independent. Suppose that the amount of labour must always be in proportion to, or on any definite function of, the amount of land. Then eliminating one of these quantities, we may treat the other as independent" (*Collected Papers*, *op. cit.*, I, 20 n.). Granted, but what means would there be for separating the returns of land from those to labor?

waste will be reduced or increased as the relative prices of cooperating factors decline or increase.[1]

To the writer, Pareto's objection seems based upon a fundamental misconception of scientific law in general and economic theory in particular. Generalizations cannot fit every case; Pareto offers small apology for assuming indifference and demand curves to be continuous, and yet this certainly does more violence to the "facts" than does the assumption that a variable amount of product can be secured from a given amount of one factor. This last assumption would have ample methodological defense if it fitted the facts only a third of the time; it seems, empirically, to be well-nigh impregnable.

Walras

Walras first dealt with the marginal productivity theory in the third appendix to the third (1896) edition of the *Eléments*.[2] The note was inspired by Wicksteed's *Co-ordination*, and was essentially a claim that Walras first discovered and formulated the general marginal productivity theory in his chapter on the Ricardian rent theory.

The claim is based on an alleged identity between Walras' and Wicksteed's equations. Of Walras' general production equations, one system states the equality of cost of production and price,[3] *i.e.*,

$$b_t p_t + \cdots + b_p p_p + \cdots + b_k p_k + \cdots = p_b$$

or $$D_b b_t p_t + \cdots + D_b b_p p_p + \cdots + D_b b_k p_k + \cdots = D_b p_b.$$

[1] A student has pointed out to me a more convincing case—the yolk and white of an egg—but a colleague assures me that their proportions can be varied.

[2] "Note on the Refutation of the English Theory of Rent by Mr. Wicksteed," *Eléments* (3d ed., *op. cit.*), pp. 485–92. This appendix was printed earlier the same year in a journal of the University of Lausanne.

[3] Cf., *supra*, pp. 237 ff.

The production coefficients, b_t, b_p, b_k, $\cdots$ are related by a production function,

$$\phi(b_t \cdots b_p \cdots b_k \cdots) = 0.$$

Walras therefore asserts that Wicksteed's equation,

$$P = \frac{\partial P}{\partial A} \cdot A + \frac{\partial P}{\partial B} \cdot B + \frac{\partial P}{\partial C} \cdot C + \cdots$$

is identical with the equations in the *Eléments*, for

$$\frac{\partial P}{\partial A} = p_t, \frac{\partial P}{\partial B} = p_p, \cdots$$

$$b_t = \frac{A}{D_b}, b_p = \frac{B}{D_b}, \cdots$$

and $P = D_b p_b$. Walras finds that Wicksteed's "equation differs from mine (if it really differs at all) only by being a more general form." [1] The only criticism levied at Wicksteed's development is that labor and capital are lumped together. Walras concludes, however, "whatever may be the intrinsic value of this combination [of capital-and-labor], it constitutes nothing but a pure difference of form.[2]

Walras cites passages on the relation of rent to price from his *Eléments* similar to those in the *Co-ordination* "which seem . . . to have been translated from the *Eléments* and which the author should have, in all strictness, placed between quotation marks and he should have taken advantage of the occasion to mention my work." [3]

To the writer, Walras' claim to priority in the formulation of the general marginal productivity theory seems completely unfounded. He proves in his discussion of

[1] *Eléments* (3d ed.), p. 486.

[2] *Ibid.*, p. 488.

[3] *Ibid.*; also pp. 489 and 492: "Mr. Wicksteed, who has not succeeded in establishing it [the marginal productivity theory] in its greatest generality, would have been better guided if he had not been obliged to appear ignorant of the works of his predecessors."

rent that the Ricardian theory can be included (formally at least) in his production equations, which are based on the assumption that production coefficients are constants. He also refers to a section where it is stated only that production coefficients are variable and are related by a production function. But the nature of the production function is *not* analyzed, and there is not the remotest suggestion that $\frac{\partial P}{\partial A} = p_t$. Indeed the P function is not introduced in the first three editions of the *Eléments*.

Walras did not have a marginal productivity theory before Wicksteed's brochure appeared.[1] Walras, therefore, could not and did not prove that rent as a residual is equal to rent as a marginal product. We may charitably attribute to self-confusion his belief that he possessed a marginal productivity theory, but his charge of plagiarism (which would of course be improbable in any case in the light of Wicksteed's character) can be characterized only as gross impertinence.

The section of the appendix so far discussed is dated September 1894.[2] The remainder of the appendix, dated October 1895, is introduced as follows: "In a note which has just been communicated to me, M. Enrico Barone has criticized the portion of Mr. Wicksteed's work on which I have reserved judgment, and the following is the result for me of this criticism." [3] There follows a criticism directed at the use of a linear, homogeneous production function which appears to be due wholly to Barone.[4]

[1] Indeed he withholds judgment on Wicksteed's general thesis that each productive factor is paid in accordance with its marginal productivity.

[2] *Eléments*, p. 489.

[3] *Ibid.*

[4] Walras introduces the basic equations, "Mr. Barone . . . demonstrates . . ." (*ibid.*, p. 490). Barone, moreover, had submitted portions of this analysis (including system [3]) in a letter to Walras on September 20, 1894. In this letter no reference is made to Wicksteed.

In this later analysis, Walras' production function,

$$\phi(b_t \cdots b_p \cdots b_k \cdots) = 0,$$

"already modified by M. Pareto through the introduction of D_b" (the scale of output),[1] becomes

$$\phi(b_t \cdots b_p \cdots b_k \cdots D_b) = 0$$

"which Mr. Barone places in the form," [2]

$$D_b = \phi(D_b b_p \cdots D_b b_t \cdots D_b b_k \cdots),$$

or
$$P = \phi(A,B,C, \cdots). \tag{1}$$

This last equation, Wicksteed's, "may be supposed non-homogeneous and non-linear and P is a quantity and not a value of product." [3] Since selling price equals cost at equilibrium,

$$P\pi = Ap_a + Bp_b + Cp_c + \cdots. \tag{2}$$

If equations (1) and (2) are differentiated to minimize the cost of production,[4] we secure

$$\frac{\partial\phi}{\partial A} = \frac{p_a}{\pi}, \frac{\partial\phi}{\partial B} = \frac{p_b}{\pi}, \cdots \tag{3}$$

[1] *Ibid.*, p. 490.

[2] *Ibid.* Schultz, *op. cit.*, has pointed out that equation (1) must be different from $\phi(b_t \cdots b_p \cdots b_k \cdots) = 0$, although Walras uses the same notation (ϕ). Equation (1) is of course the customary method of writing the production function.

[3] *Eléments*, p. 490.

[4] Walras does not detail the method by which system (3) is derived. The simplest method is to maximize net revenue, V, *i.e.*,

$$V = \pi\phi(A,B,C, \cdots) - (Ap_a + Bp_b + Cp_c + \cdots).$$

Hence
$$\frac{\partial V}{\partial A} = \pi\frac{\partial\phi}{\partial A} - p_a = 0$$

. . . .

whence
$$\pi = \frac{p_a}{\frac{\partial\phi}{\partial A}} = \frac{p_b}{\frac{\partial\phi}{\partial B}} = \cdots$$

If we substitute from (3) into (2) for the prices p_a, p_b, p_c, . . . ,

$$P\pi = A\pi\frac{\partial\phi}{\partial A} + B\pi\frac{\partial\phi}{\partial B} + C\pi\frac{\partial\phi}{\partial C} + \cdots$$

or

$$P = A\frac{\partial\phi}{\partial A} + B\frac{\partial\phi}{\partial B} + C\frac{\partial\phi}{\partial C} + \cdots \tag{4}$$

"Therefore," Walras summarizes,

1. Free competition leads to a minimum cost of production;
2. Under this regime, the rate of remuneration of each service is equal to the partial derivative of the production function, or to its marginal productivity, according to equations (3);
3. The total quantity of product is distributed among the productive services, according to equation (4).[1]

The later editions contain only minor changes in the basic argument. The Appendix on Wicksteed was suppressed in later editions, and the marginal productivity theory was transferred to Lecture 36 of the *Eléments.* The insinuations that Wicksteed had been a plagiarist were abandoned at the same time. In the posthumous 1926 edition, equation (4) was suppressed, as was the third part of the summary, stating the exhaustion of product. This change is attributable to the criticisms of Pareto, which have already been discussed. Walras attempts a reply to Pareto's objections:

> M. Pareto having declared in November, 1901 (*L'économie pure*) this theory to be "erroneous" and equations (3) "inadmissible" because "in them one treats as independent variables, quantities which are not independent," and appearing to have converted M. Barone to his opinion, I willingly take responsibility for the theory in question in making the observation that, in my conception of the establishment of economic equilibrium, during the entire course

[1] *Eléments*, p. 490 (italicized by Walras).

of approximations in production, Q, successively equal to Ω_b (§ 208), Ω'_b (§ 211), D'_b (§ 212), D''_b (§ 218), D'''_b (§ 219), · · · is always determined in a special fashion and is, like the prices of services, a *given* and not an *unknown* of the problem of the determination of the coefficients of production; whence it follows, it seems to me, that $T = Qb_t$, $P = Qb_p$, $K = Qb_k$, · · · here are variables as independent as b_t, b_p, b_k, · · ·.[1]

Walras clearly misses the point of Pareto's objection, that there may be more than one function relating the coefficients of production to the product. Of course $T = Qb_t$ is as independent as b_t, but Pareto's claim is that both may be dependent variables. Pareto's objection has absolutely nothing to do with the question of *tâtonnements*.

Wicksell

The last continental economist of this period to play an important part in the discussion of the Euler theorem problem was Knut Wicksell. It was pointed out previously that Wicksell's equations in the *Über Wert, Kapital und Rente* (1893) contained implicitly the general marginal productivity theory.[2] Seven years later he renewed his participation in the controversy with a long article on the subject in the *Ekonomisk Tidskrift.*[3] The following year he expanded this article into his discussion of the Euler theorem problem in Volume I of his *Lectures on Political Economy,*[4] and in two later articles (1902

[1] *Ibid.* (Lausanne, 1926 ed.), p. 376 n. This footnote is dated 1902.

[2] Cf., *supra*, Chap. x.

[3] "Om gränsproduktiviteten sansom grundval för den nationalekonomiska fördelningen," *Ekonomisk Tidskrift*, II (1900), 305–37.

[4] The writer has been unable to secure a copy of the first Swedish edition (1901); the relevant section in the first German edition (1913) is virtually identical with the English translation (1934) of the third Swedish edition. This English translation will be used in the present work.

and 1916) Wicksell elaborated on certain neglected aspects of the general marginal productivity theory.[1]

It is interesting to note, at the outset, that Wicksell "rediscovered" the marginal productivity theory about 1900; he remained unaware that it was thoroughly imbedded in his earlier work, *Über Wert.* In his 1900 article, he says:

> The point of view developed here was first formulated, as far as I know, by Wicksteed in his above mentioned work [the *Co-ordination*]. Still it is differently oriented in so far as his main purpose was that of defending the marginal productivity theory against older conceptions of the problem of distribution. The important conditions are mentioned there only as a matter of course. For my part, I read Wicksteed's book when it first came out without even noticing this detail [2] and without finding anything new; only later and since I myself have arrived at the same conclusion did I find that Wicksteed actually had arrived before me. The reason why economists previously have given so little consideration to his work probably lies in his frequent use of mathematical symbols and the abstract nature of his reasoning.[3]

Wicksell acknowledged Walras' claim to the discovery of the general marginal productivity theory,[4] but he refused at first to concede that Walras' formulation was more general or that it was independent of the assumption that the production function was linear and homogeneous. Thus, Wicksell points out,

> Wicksteed had demonstrated the marginal productivity theory only for the case where the total product is a *homoge-*

[1] "Till fördelningsproblemet," *Ekonomisk Tidskrift*, IV (1902), 424–33; "Den 'kritiska punkten' i lagen för jordbrukets aftagande produktivitet," *ibid.*, XVIII (1916), 265–92.

[2] Wicksell presumably refers to the minimum cost condition, which will be discussed presently.

[3] "Om gränsproduktiviteten," *op. cit.*, p. 313.

[4] *Ibid.*: "Walras points out here [in the appendix to the third edition of the *Eléments*]; and rightfully it seems to me—that the principle of Wicksteed's theory was already included in Walras' own theory of production."

> *neous* and *linear* function of the productive factors (that is, as I have just indicated [*op. cit.*, p. 314], the mathematical expression for the case where large and small scale production are equally profitable) while Walras thinks he has proved the theorem in question without any such limitation. But here he is mistaken. Walras assumes in his explanation that the profit, as long as there is no monopoly, will decline continuously due to the competition of other firms. But this assumption involves, as one can easily see, the condition that the amount of product is proportional to the scale of production. If this is not the case, so that for instance large scale production is relatively more profitable than small scale, then profits cannot disappear or even tend to decline.[1]

Wicksell wrote to Walras, stating in almost identical words this defense of Wicksteed, but Walras evaded the argument by pleading disinterest in this phase of economic theory.[2]

Wicksell repeated the point in his article, "On the Problem of Distribution" (1902), in the *Tidskrift*,[3] with one additional element. Formerly he had considered all industries to obey the laws of increasing, constant, or decreasing returns. Now he considers these three "laws" to be different phases of the usual cost curve of a firm, rather than mutually exclusive alternatives. A firm may

[1] *Ibid.* Wicksell concludes, "Wicksteed's treatment of the problem is thought through very well, and does not deserve Walras' scornful criticism."

[2] Letter dated Oct. 28, 1900. Walras was of the opinion that Wicksell's defense merited a serious examination, but the former's interest had, he said, shifted from the marginal productivity theory. Letter to Wicksell, Nov. 2, 1900. Nevertheless he was quite interested in Pareto's criticisms one year later.

[3] *Op. cit.*, p. 425: "The criticism which Walras, in the third edition of his *Eléments d'économie politique*—after counsel with the Italian economist, Enrico Barone—offers against Wicksteed seems to me unjustified. He assumes that the cost of production must equal price under free competition. . . . This seems to me again to require that large and small scale production be equally profitable. . . ."

be subject first to increasing, then to decreasing returns, and the usual manufacturing enterprise typically experiences both.[1] The general marginal productivity theory enters because at the point where the firm shifts from increasing to decreasing returns, "it can be said to yield constant return for a moment." [2] This theory is developed in more detail in the subsequent *Lectures*, to which we now turn.

In the *Lectures* Wicksell acknowledges the complete validity, even the finality, of Walras' solution of the theory of production and distribution,[3] but nevertheless expresses astonishment at Wicksteed's recantation (in the *Commonsense*) of the thesis of the *Co-ordination*.[4] Wicksell's discussion of the general marginal productivity theory is restricted primarily to non-capitalistic (*i.e.*, timeless) production. It is with this phase of his discussion that we are concerned here; the treatment of capital and time has already been considered.[5]

Along now conventional lines it is argued that wages will be determined by the marginal productivity of labor and rent by the marginal productivity of land.[6] If these two are the only productive factors, as when laborers are also entrepreneurs, we are led to the fundamental question: "will the distribution of the product between landowners and labourers be the same on each of our assumptions?" [7] Will, in other words, rent as a marginal product equal rent as a residual? Or in still another form, does

[1] *Ibid.*, p. 426.

[2] *Ibid.*, p. 427. A few pages later (*ibid.*, p. 432) Wicksell points out the failure of the general marginal productivity theory in the case of imperfect competition.

[3] *Lectures*, p. 101: "Walras in his *Eléments* once and for all correctly formulated the solution to the problems of production, distribution, and exchange as a whole. . . ."

[4] *Ibid.*, p. 101 n.

[5] *Supra*, Chap. x.

[6] *Lectures*, pp. 110–25.

[7] *Ibid.*, p. 125.

remuneration of productive agents according to their marginal productivities exhaust the total product?

Either one of two assumptions is held to be sufficient to insure that the distributive shares exhaust the total product. One must assume "either that large-scale and small-scale operations are equally productive, so that, when all the factors of production are increased in the same proportion, the total product also increases exactly proportionately; *or* at least that all productive enterprises have already reached the limit beyond which a further increase in the scale of production will no longer yield any advantage." [1] In the absence of one of these conditions, free competition cannot survive.[2]

The first condition, essentially that the production function be homogeneous and linear, is sufficient though not necessary.[3] If the production function may be represented by [4]

$$P = af\left(\frac{b}{a}\right),$$

then
$$P = a\frac{\partial P}{\partial a} + b\frac{\partial P}{\partial b}.$$

One explicit solution is $P = A^{\alpha}B^{\beta}$, where $\alpha + \beta = 1$. This condition is commended on a basis of elimination. For if $\alpha + \beta > 1$, then

$$P < a\frac{\partial P}{\partial a} + b\frac{\partial P}{\partial b}.$$

[1] *Ibid.*, p. 126.

[2] *Ibid.*, pp. 125–26.

[3] *Ibid.*, pp. 127–29.

[4] If $\lambda = \frac{1}{a}$, then Wicksell's equation may be written

$$P = af\left(\frac{b}{a}\right) = \frac{1}{\lambda}f(\lambda b),$$

or $\lambda P = f(\lambda b)$, corresponding to the usual statement of the condition of homogeneity and linearity.

In other words, if doubling the factors more than doubles the product, the shares determined by the marginal productivities are greater than the product to be distributed. But this condition is incompatible with perfect competition, since the larger the scale of plant the lower the cost of production. In the converse case, where $\alpha + \beta < 1$, then

$$P > a\frac{\partial P}{\partial a} + b\frac{\partial P}{\partial b},$$

so the aggregate distributive shares are less than the product. But this amounts to saying that small scale enterprises will be more efficient, since a doubling of factors does not double output. Hence only small units will be established.

The applicability of this first approach is very restricted: it is "very seldom realized as a general principle in a given branch of production; the scale on which an enterprise operates nearly always has some influence on its average product." [1] In a later article on the laws of return, however, it is claimed that this type of production function is typical of agriculture.[2]

The second and more general condition is that each firm, after passing through a stage of decreasing costs, reaches a point beyond which costs increase. At this transitional point constant costs, and returns, are experienced.[3] The stage of decreasing costs, by implication, is due to specialization of labor.[4] The later stage of in-

[1] *Lectures*, p. 129.

[2] "Den 'kritiska punkten,'" *op. cit.*, p. 287: "These [Euler] formulas simply express the well-known fact that a small and a large farm, if they produce the same commodities, are equally profitable."

[3] *Lectures*, pp. 129, 131.

[4] This is expressly stated in "Om gränsproduktiviteten," *op. cit.*, p. 320: if all the factors are increased in equal proportion, the product "will also increase in at least the same, and possibly through division of labor in a larger, proportion,"

creasing costs arises because "the advantages of centralization are outweighed by the increasing costs which are encountered when larger areas must be exploited for the provision of raw or auxiliary materials, or else for the marketing of the product." [1] All firms will operate at this minimum cost point, assuming there are sufficient firms to maintain competition. At this point the business men will employ the factors in such quantities that their marginal productivities are proportional to their prices. At equilibrium for the firm, then, there will be the relationship,

$$k = \frac{\frac{\partial P}{\partial a}}{p_a} = \frac{\frac{\partial P}{\partial b}}{p_b} = \cdots$$

where k is some constant greater than unity. With firms at optimum size, if competition still rules there will be an influx of new firms. These new firms will bid up the prices of the resources,[2] or, what Wicksell fails to express explicitly, the price of the product will be forced down. As long as k is greater than unity at equilibrium for the firm, profits will be present, since the marginal productivities of factors exceed their prices. As long as profits of this sort are present, new firms will continue to enter the field. In long-run equilibrium profits will necessarily disappear; the distributive shares determined by marginal productivity will then exhaust the product. Wicksell emphasizes strongly the necessity of there being enough firms in the industry to insure competition.[3]

Wicksell adds the element of time to his theory of distribution in a later section of the *Lectures*.[4] Since this theory is identical with that advanced in his *Über Wert*,

[1] *Lectures*, p. 129.
[2] *Ibid.*, p. 130.
[3] *Ibid.*, pp. 130–32.
[4] Pp. 144 ff.

it may be passed over here. The central thesis remains identical with that in the earlier work: each factor receives its discounted marginal productivity; capital receives a share equal to the marginal productivity of the extension of the period of investment.

There is only one fundamental criticism to be brought against Wicksell's development of the marginal productivity theory. He failed to examine the conditions under which a firm may have a minimum point on its long-run average cost curve, or, in the other case, the compatibility of competition and constant returns to scale of plant. The final section is devoted to these problems.

Conclusion

It is apparent that the marginal productivity theory has received a variety of interpretations and misinterpretations from its early proponents and critics. The subsequent literature is very extensive, but no new points of importance, so far as the writer knows, have been raised in connection with this subject. It is in order, therefore, to evaluate the fundamental points of disagreement, and to discover what problems, if any, still call for solution.

Two fundamental problems at the very threshold of the theory of production will be dismissed with passing comment. The first problem is Pareto's: should the theory of production be based, in part at least, on fixed coefficients of production? A negative answer has already been given, but to summarize: Empirically there seems to be very little scope for the assumption that the proportions in which productive services are combined cannot be varied significantly; and, in any case, the assumption of variability is an extremely convenient first approximation.

The second problem, which may be associated with Wicksell, relates to indivisibility of productive services. If large and continuing indivisibilities are present in the firms of an industry, those firms will have continuously decreasing long-run average costs, and of course competition is unstable. Although there seem to be some cases of this sort, they are certainly relatively few. It seems much more legitimate, again as a first approximation, to assume either absence or limitation of indivisibilities and then the average cost curve will be either a horizontal line or a curve with more or less periodic minima of constant value so far as technological (*i.e.*, non-managerial) considerations are concerned.[1]

There remains, however, a debatable point within the framework of variable production coefficients: the stability of competition. The crucial question, in other words, is whether stable competition is compatible with the conditions under which the product is distributed among the productive services according to their marginal contributions.

If technological processes are fully divisible, Wicksteed's assumption of a linear, homogeneous production function is of course appropriate. If all of the productive services are increased by a given percentage, the product will be increased by that same percentage. If a given type of house can be built on one lot, equal productive services can duplicate the product next door.

This line of reasoning is doubtless correct if there is no entrepreneurial role in production. The *raison d'être* of entrepreneurship will be examined presently, but we may anticipate the conclusion that average costs will probably

[1] Compare N. Kaldor, "The Equilibrium of the Firm," *Economic Journal*, XLIV (1934), 65–66; E. A. G. Robinson, *The Structure of Competitive Industry* (New York, 1932), pp. 31–33.

begin to rise if coordination and decision-making problems must be solved. In their absence, which is assumed for the moment, there seems to be no important objection to the use of a linear and homogeneous production function, and therefore constant costs rule for the firm.

Assuming constant costs, is Wicksteed's solution of the distribution problem valid? His theory requires perfect competition—otherwise no direct transition can be made from physical to value product even in the case of the individual firm. It is accepted doctrine that the condition of constant returns to scale of output in the firm (*i.e.*, Wicksteed's assumption) is incompatible with stable competition.[1] The reasoning goes as follows: if the long-run average cost line is above the price line, the firm will not come into existence; if the cost line is below the price line, the firm will monopolize the industry. Finally, if the cost and price lines coincide, the output of the firm will be indeterminate.

The important case of coincidence of price and cost lines deserves further attention. This case has received little explicit analysis, but the argument seems to point toward instability. The firm will expand output (at constant costs) until it becomes a significant source of supply. Then the firm's marginal revenue curve will fall below its average revenue curve (which will no longer be a horizontal line). If, moreover, the industry uses any specialized productive services, *i.e.*, services subject to increasing cost, the firm will also find the incremental cost of these services rising above their average costs (again no longer a horizontal line). Either one or both of these conditions will eventually stop the expansion of the

[1] Cf. J. Viner, "Cost Curves and Supply Curves," *Zeitschrift für Nationalökonomie*, III (1932), 33–34; Kaldor, *op. cit.*, p. 72; A. L. Bowley, *Mathematical Groundwork of Economics* (Oxford, 1924), pp. 36–37.

firm. But other firms will probably follow the same course of expansion, so price will fall and costs rise. The industry will then be unprofitable (that is, will yield less than the competitive rate of return), so output will be restricted with a consequent rise of price. A continuous cycle of over- and under-production will ensue.

This argument is clearly based on assumptions incompatible with *perfect* competition. With perfect knowledge and economic rationality, it is difficult to see why firms should expand their outputs; there would not be even a temporary gain from increasing their control of supply.[1] With imperfect competition the fluctuations described above may take place, but, to anticipate, imperfect knowledge changes the entire character of the problem. Under the most rigorous assumptions concerning competition, the distribution of output among firms is indeterminate, but it is stable and therefore essentially irrelevant. No firm would expand because its cost line coincided with the price line, simply because ultimately such a procedure would be futile or costly.

In the second case, limited indivisibilities of certain productive services lead to approximately periodic minima of constant value on the long-run average cost curve. A competitive firm must of course operate at one of these minima, so *a priori* the indeterminacy regarding output is greatly reduced (and, under certain conditions, eliminated). Aside from this feature, the foregoing argument is applicable. But Euler's theorem is no longer appropriate; the production function is no longer homogeneous and of the first degree. One must resort to the solution of Barone, Wicksell, and Walras, although it will be argued

[1] No individual firm, that is to say, could ever increase prices or decrease costs. A combination could increase prices temporarily, but unless entry into the industry could be controlled, there would be no permanent gain.

shortly that they had a different situation in mind.[1] It is manifest, however, that at this high level of abstraction Wicksteed's solution is almost as general and informative (from the economic, if not from the mathematical, viewpoint) as that of Barone.

The foregoing analysis supports Wicksteed's argument—if there is no entrepreneurship. The qualification, however, is very important. If there are real problems of coordination or decision-making, the output of a firm may not, and most probably will not, double if all the productive services are doubled. The entrepreneurial duties (including organization costs), in other words, increase more rapidly than the size of the firm, and as a result, the average costs of the firm begin to rise once a certain output is reached.[2]

Granting the partial applicability of Wicksteed's thesis to an entrepreneurless economy, under what conditions does the entrepreneurial role disappear? It disappears, we know,[3] in the completely stationary economy, where the stocks (not the rates of supply) of productive resources, the technology, and the tastes are rigorously fixed. In such an economy the same things are always done in the same way by the same men. Everything is reduced to routine; the captains of industry—and their innumerable adjutants—are in Nirvana.

We might go down a scale of progressively less stationary economies, but a detailed enumeration or investigation is not necessary for present purposes. A second

[1] The same theory has been advanced more recently by Hicks (*The Theory of Wages, op. cit.*, Appendix i); Pigou (*The Economics of Stationary States, op. cit.*, chap. xxvii); and E. Schneider, "Bemerkungen zur Grenzproduktivitätstheorie," *Zeitschrift für Nationalökonomie*, IV (1932–33), 604–24.

[2] Cf. Robinson, *The Structure of Competitive Industry, op. cit.*, pp. 42 ff.

[3] Cf. F. H. Knight, *Risk, Uncertainty and Profit* (Cambridge, 1921), pp. 76 ff., 145 ff.

variant, in which the rates of supply (not the stocks) of productive resources are fixed, would probably lead to results similar to the previous case. The human material of production would be turning over at a constant rate, but the routine nature of production would require little coordination.

More attention is deserved by another type of stationary economy, which seems to be most frequently implicit in the works of modern economists. Professor Knight has indicated its nature:

> We assume a population static in number and composition and without the mania of change and advance which characterizes modern life. Inventions and improvements in technology and organization are to be eliminated, leaving the general situation as we know it today to remain stationary. Similarly in regard to the saving of new capital, development of new natural resources, redistribution of population over the soil or redistribution of ownership of goods, education, etc., among the people. But we shall not assume that men are omniscient and immortal or perfectly rational and free from caprice as individuals. We shall neglect natural catastrophes, epidemics, wars, etc., but take for granted the "usual" uncertainties of the weather and the like, along with the "normal" vicissitudes of mortal life, and uncertainties of human choice.[1]

Even in this society there would be no important place for the entrepreneur, it might be concluded, because uncertainty is virtually nonexistent. The writer is less certain; a case can be made for the proposition that the mere problem of co-ordination, quite aside from the decision-making duties arising out of uncertainty, is enough to require entrepreneurial labor (subject to diminishing returns). Men, unlike machines, have faulty memories, personal likes and dislikes, and, indeed, all the frailties

[1] *Ibid.*, p. 266.

usually lumped together as "human nature." It is not improbable that in any but the mathematically stationary economics, an expanding firm would require more and more co-ordinating ability to overcome the increasing human "frictions."

It is probably this type of economy that Barone and his followers have had in mind in formulating their version of the marginal productivity theory. Their solution must be applied to an economy in which there is no uncertainty, otherwise the solutions are clearly erroneous (see below). On the other hand, these economists all base their solutions on the presence of *one* minimum point on the long-run average cost of the firm. It follows from the preceding argument that such solutions are valid only if entrepreneurship plays a significant role in production even when uncertainty is absent. To the writer this seems probable, but it is apparent, in any case, that Barone and his followers, just as much as Wicksteed, have failed to develop and defend the assumptions implicit in their solutions of the exhaustion-of-product problem.

Once uncertainty is introduced, the theory of distribution is altered greatly. Anticipations rule economic activity, and many of the anticipations must be erroneous because of the very fact of uncertainty. The entrepreneur becomes a residual claimant, and the exhaustion-of-product problem disappears. Anticipated marginal productivity becomes the basis for remunerating all productive services except entrepreneurship.

The Euler theorem controversy, like most disputes in our science, is instructive primarily regarding the pitfalls in and limitations of theoretical analysis. The entire argument rested on differences between the implicit assumptions of the various participants. Wicksteed's solution is the preferable one, in the writer's opinion, because —at the level of analysis to which it is appropriate—it is informative, yet based on simpler assumptions. The Barone approach is formally valid, but its economic significance depends primarily on the extent of the problem of coordination when uncertainty is absent. However, the two approaches—and indeed also that based on fixed production coefficients—are on different planes of abstraction. There is truth in each of these views, and only the failure to state assumptions explicitly led these economists to believe that their various solutions were contradictory or alternative.

Index

CPSIA information can be obtained
at www.ICGtesting.com
Printed in the USA
FSOW03n2009071216
28315FS